WHO'S BETTER,
WHO'S BEST
in
BASEBALL?

WHO'S BETTER, WHO'S BEST (in) BASEBALL?

"Mr. Stats" Sets the Record Straight
on the Top 75 Players of All Time

ELLIOTT KALB

McGraw·Hill

New York   Chicago   San Francisco   Lisbon   London   Madrid   Mexico City
Milan   New Delhi   San Juan   Seoul   Singapore   Sydney   Toronto

Library of Congress Cataloging-in-Publication Data

Kalb, Elliott.
    Who's better, who's best in baseball : Mr. Stats sets the record straight on the top 75 players of all time / Elliott Kalb ; foreword by Bob Costas.
        p.   cm.
    ISBN 0-07-144538-2
    1. Baseball players—Rating of—United States.   2. Baseball players—United States—Biography.
I. Title.

GV865.A1K34   2005
796.357'0973'021—dc22   2004024973

1 2 3 4 5 6 7 8 9 0   FGR/FGR   0 9 8 7 6 5

ISBN 0-07-144538-2

Interior design by Nick Panos

McGraw-Hill books are available at special quantity discounts to use as premiums and sales promotions, or for use in corporate training programs. For more information, please write to the Director of Special Sales, Professional Publishing, McGraw-Hill, Two Penn Plaza, New York, NY 10121-2298. Or contact your local bookstore.

This book is printed on acid-free paper.

In the spring of 1982, I earned college credits by working as an intern for NBC Sports in the Sports Publicity Department. It was staffed by three people, and when one left early in my internship, there were lots of opportunities for an ambitious kid. One of those opportunities afforded me was to accompany a newly signed baseball analyst named Sal Bando around town. First Sal needed to get an earpiece fitted, then he needed to have a publicity photo taken, and finally, he needed to get to a coffee shop, where he and I would meet the play-by-play announcer that he would be working with. When Bando and I arrived at the restaurant, we were met by a very young Bob Costas and his friend from St. Louis, Steve Horn.

I was a big fan of Bando from his playing days. As good a player as he was, he was a better person, a gentleman whom I shall never forget. But I will forever remember that lunch for other reasons.

I've come to work with Costas and Horn all over the world on various events for NBC and now HBO (including Wimbledon tennis and the Olympics), but we always seem to come back to baseball. Like Bob, I was a "Strat-o-Matic" player (a dice baseball game) for most of my youth. Like Bob, I spent a portion of my days growing up in southern California. Like Bob, I've spent a portion of my working life covering baseball, although there have been "Ted Williams–like" gaps in the résumé.

On the eve of the 1998 major-league baseball playoffs, we were in a meeting at Yankee Stadium when news broke that Yankees slugger Darryl Strawberry had been diagnosed with colon cancer. Costas was not going to accept the bare-bones facts that were trickling in. Initially, we were told that Darryl would be back in a few days, that it wasn't a serious or life-threatening condition. Bob then said, "What am I supposed to say, that Strawberry will be out of tonight's lineup with *semi-colon cancer*?"

In all seriousness, that one line typifies so much of what Costas is about. He combined journalistic integrity with a literate punch line! (Strawberry underwent surgery two days later to remove a walnut-sized cancerous tumor. The Yankees dedicated their World Series victory over the Padres to him.)

Bob and I have debated everything, from Mantle versus Mays to the difference between a nook and a cranny.

This book is for people like us who enjoy a good debate. This book is for those people who aren't old enough to remember seeing Mays or Koufax. This book is for people who want an informed opinion on where the great Negro League, Cuban, and Japanese players might rank in relation to the elite major leaguers. This book is to stimulate conversation on how much the steroid issue taints the statistics of modern-day ballplayers.

Costas didn't agree with all my positions from the basketball version of *Who's Better, Who's Best?* and he won't agree with all of my baseball choices. I hope he enjoys the book. I've spent years giving him my opinions on various issues, and he's always taken them seriously. Thanks, Bob, for everything. This book is dedicated to you.

CONTENTS

FOREWORD
Bob Costas

It's July 1998. The All-Star Game at Coors Field in Denver. Players are coming and going at such a dizzying clip that my scorecard looks like a Jackson Pollack painting. Up in the NBC booth, at my side, as ever . . . Elliott Kalb. For each player and situation, Elliott has a note—sometimes multiple notes. They are the product of his intensive preparation, keen eye for detail, and exceptional editorial judgment as situations unfold.

Late in the game, a 13–8 American League win, National League skipper Jim Leyland calls upon Ugueth Urbina, then of the Expos, to pitch in relief. Scanning Urbina's bio, Elliott notices that the right-hander's middle name is Urtain. In a flash, he hands me this note: "They say everybody in sports these days is all about me, me, me. But not this guy. Here's a guy who is u, u, u." Sadly (or not, depending on your taste), the next pitch ended the inning and that priceless observation went, uh, un-uttered.

So where am I going with this? I'm not sure exactly, but try to understand my dilemma. What do you say in a foreword to a book that has (to your surprise) been dedicated to you? Well, for the sake of balance, and to display my unshakable integrity, I could flatly declare that Elliott Kalb has lost his mind. That the omission of former Giants/Angels/Indians outfielder Leon "Daddy Wags" Wagner from the listings that follow both enrages and befuddles me. And don't get me started on Chico Salmon. But really, who's to say? Bill James, a smarter man than me (according to my own rankings, the 11th smartest American just behind Jeopardy king Ken Jennings—and just ahead of the guy Russell Crowe played in *A Beautiful Mind*) once rated Roy White ahead of Jim Rice! Right. And Danny White was better than Jerry Rice. Go figure. The point—and there is one here someplace—is that everyone has an opinion. Some (like Kalb's) are just better informed, reasoned, and researched.

Kalb's first book (*Who's Better, Who's Best in Basketball?*) was so provocative and popular that the people at McGraw-Hill immediately demanded a baseball follow-up. Resisting the urge to include Michael Jordan in both books, Mr. Stats forged ahead. You hold the results in your hands. This fine piece of work should be the source of both edification and argument. Perhaps some big questions will be answered, but just as many will be raised. Here's just one: How is it that Joe DiMaggio—selected in 1969 as "The Greatest Living Ballplayer" and always introduced that way until his death in 1999—now ranks behind seven major-league players who outlived him and whose careers either overlapped his or were ongoing at the time of his passing? Just asking. Like I said, I don't necessarily have the answers. I just enjoy the discussions. And if there's one thing this book will do, it's start discussions. Or debates. Or passionate arguments. Or maybe bar fights. Anyway, I'm ducking for cover. Read on.

ACKNOWLEDGMENTS

Testosterone. I realized that after 20 years in sports television, I have spent my entire career working with athletes, broadcasters, and executives that are mostly male—and mostly guy's guys. It's a tough job, but someone's got to eat those steaks and listen to those jokes.

Thankfully, I have balance from the women in my life.

I start with my mother, Phyllis Kalb; my sister, Randi Edelman; my sister-in-law, Susan Kalb; and my aunt, Bobbi DeNoble. As proud as my mother is of me, I'm prouder of her and her accomplishments. My sister and aunt have always been my biggest fans and sounding boards. Thankfully, they brought into my life Bill Edelman and Jimmy DeNoble, two rabid baseball fans and wonderful family members.

My wife, Amy Kalb, is my inspiration. I couldn't begin to write about her love, devotion, sacrifice, and hard work to make my professional and personal life so rewarding. I wouldn't have the time to read a book, much less write one, without Amy. She brought with her Alissa, who provides someone to share other interests outside sports.

My lifelong friends Alison Geller, Ruth Harmon, and Ellen Davis have been like family to me; and time and distance can't ever change that. My ex-wife, Lisa, shares with me the enormous responsibility of raising our boys, Wyatt and Heath. Sometimes my job brings deadlines that mean additional burdens on her time. For this I thank her.

I'm very lucky that some very special women provided much-needed estrogen to this book, as well. Carol Mann made the deal with McGraw-Hill and Michele Pezzuti was the sharp editor who had the unenviable task of reading the first drafts of the manuscript and making sense of it all. Ellen Vinz made it a great-looking book.

If all my boys learn from me is to love baseball and befriend and listen to smart women, they'll be ahead of the game.

Speaking of which, I can't acknowledge anyone without speaking of my children. There really is nothing to compare with the joy of playing catch with your sons. My son Wyatt put it best when he told me, "I wish I could meet the man who invented baseball and thank him."

I want to thank Wyatt, and Heath, and Jordan as well—because they make life so enjoyable. I mean, after all the women have their say in your life, you have to have someone to watch *Dodgeball* and *Austin Powers* with, and discuss the merits of Shoeless Joe Jackson versus Honus Wagner.

Finally, there are the usual cast of characters that helped me write the book. Barbara and Irv Levinson; Gary Gilbert, Scott Leabman, David Fisher, Marty Appel, David Harmon; everyone at Black Canyon Productions; Jon Miller, Kevin Monaghan, and Gary Quinn at NBC; Russ Gabay at MLB; my brother, David; and my supportive dad (who took me to my first game, and encouraged this lunacy). Thanks to all.

WHO'S BETTER, WHO'S BEST in BASEBALL?

INTRODUCTION

One of the most poignant moments in baseball history took place in a hotel ballroom the night before the 1969 All-Star Game in Washington, D.C. That moment came when Mrs. Babe Ruth slowly walked to the podium to accept an award for the Babe as the greatest player ever. She received the award from a true American hero, Frank Borman, the man who commanded the first Apollo flight around the moon.

Ruth hadn't played in about 35 years when baseball awarded him that honor. I recently brought that up on the phone with Commissioner Bud Selig, who was at that dinner. I told Mr. Selig that it's been 35 years since that night. He remembered it well, also recalling that Joe DiMaggio was named the "Greatest Living Player" on that evening. I asked the commissioner if Ruth was still the all-time best. He answered that it was hard to say, since he personally never saw Ruth play. He did say that Babe Ruth's influence was legendary. He saved the game. But he also told me that players like Aaron and Mays were at a level where they deserve to be mentioned in the same breath as Ruth. And that, for Selig, was as good as you could be.

"Babe Ruth couldn't make a college team in today's world," onetime Yankees pitcher Jim Bouton told me on the phone from his Massachusetts home.

"You don't think he would have adjusted?" I asked.

"Okay, he would have had a few years of minor-league instruction, been given weight and nutritional training, and all the video work would have helped him. Maybe you're right. He would have been a star."

"I went through that with my basketball book. People put down Bob Cousy and other players from his era. But they would have adjusted. This book (and that one) is about players who dominate games, seasons, and eras."

Bouton continued, "In the old days, there was no way to measure talent."

"So, we're to discount the fact that Walter Johnson was a great fastball pitcher because we couldn't measure him, or exclude Josh Gibson because we don't have accurate and complete statistics?"

"I think we'd laugh if we saw Walter Johnson pitch up close. We would say, 'Is this as hard as you can bring it?' He probably didn't throw 90 miles an hour."

The former pitcher turned author then continued his rant about the old-timers. "Yeah, Josh Gibson hit 88 homers in a season. But what was the competition like? I can show you guys who hit .600 in a season. They're Little Leaguers. It's all relative. Generally, the higher the averages and offensive numbers, the lower the quality of play. Guys who bat

.500 in high school and .400 in college and .300 in the majors are normal. When there is a worse talent pool, it's easier for a few to rise above."

"So, if I'm hearing you right, the quality of play in today's major leagues has gone down significantly because there has been an offensive explosion in the last decade?"

Bouton responded that there are other factors at work here, generally the size of ball-parks and steroids.

"Now, Jim, help me out here. In your days, you wrote about players using 'greenies.' Did that help any of the players?"

"I wrote in *Ball Four* almost 35 years ago that if there were a pill we could take that could guarantee a pitcher 20 wins but take five years off his life, we would have taken it. Greenies weren't performance-enhancing, they just helped overcome the previous evening. But players of my day didn't take performance-enhancing drugs because we didn't know of any!"

"Okay, Jim, one last question. Who was the best player you ever saw—either as a team-mate, an opponent, or on television?"

"Mickey Mantle. He had tremendous power from both sides of the plate, and had speed. You don't see that combination."

Seymour Siwoff, of the Elias Sports Bureau, who has been around the game for half a century and is the official statistician for Major League Baseball, didn't need more than a second to respond to my question. He told me Willie Mays was the greatest, that there was nothing he couldn't do. Curt Gowdy, the Red Sox announcer when Ted Williams played, and later the "Game of the Week" announcer for more than a decade, said that Mays was the best player, but Williams the best batter.

Bill White, the former first baseman, announcer, and National League president, told me that Mays was the best player, but Stan Musial was the best hitter he ever saw.

Tony Kubek, who played in the American League before becoming a national voice on "Game of the Week" for years, had a different take: "Ted Williams was the best hit-ter I ever saw. But I'll say that with a caveat. One man—Mickey Mantle batting right-handed—was better even than Williams. As a left-handed batter, Mantle was a low-ball hitter and an upper-cutter."

Among more modern experts, Fox's Joe Buck—the voice of baseball in this genera-tion—told me that Alex Rodriguez is the best player he's ever seen to be able to play shortstop, hit home runs like he does, and handle everything. He went on to tell me that his dad, the late Jack Buck, always maintained that Mays was the best player he ever saw, but Stan Musial was the best person he was ever around.

Joe Buck's partner in the broadcast booth, Tim McCarver, played in four decades ('50s, '60s, '70s, and '80s) and has announced games in three decades ('80s, '90s, '00s).

McCarver said, "When I retired, I was asked the question a lot of who the greatest player I ever saw was. I said Willie Mays, but the more time goes by, the closer it becomes in my mind between Mays and Aaron. When I retired, it was Mays, head and shoulders over Aaron. Mays is still the best. He could beat you in so many ways."

McCarver also said that Barry Bonds is among the top five players in baseball history. Bobby Bonilla and Johnny Bench told me that Bonds is the best.

We're just getting started. This book isn't only about who is ranked number one—I rank the top 75 players. I talked to owners, commissioners, statisticians, announcers, players, and historians. I went through the microfilm and read through way too many newspaper stories. I read hundreds of books.

I went to Yogi Berra, through his friend Dave Kaplan at the wonderful Yogi Berra Museum in Montclair, New Jersey, for thoughts on Johnny Bench. It's not that Yogi doesn't love Johnny—he does—but I was reminded by Yogi that when Berra and Bench were chosen as the two catchers on the 1999 All-Century Team, Berra went out of his way to mention that he saw Josh Gibson in 1940, and that Gibson might have been the best catcher ever. Gibson is ranked that way in this book.

I have followed baseball since I was eight years old and remember the teachers wheeling in a portable television set to the cafeteria so we elementary school kids could watch a few innings of the 1970 World Series games (when the entire Series was still played entirely during the day). Thousands of tabletop baseball games later, this fan grew up and found a dream job—serving as NBC Sports' chief statistician for their "Major League Baseball Game of the Week"—at the time, a sports institution. Beginning in 1987, I assisted the deepest roster of baseball announcing talent ever assembled—including Vin Scully, Joe Garagiola, Tony Kubek, and Bob Costas. Scully had called Dodgers games since 1950, and when I was growing up, his was the last voice I heard nightly going to sleep with my transistor radio at my side. There was no greater education to an inquisitive kid out of college.

I was in the press box when Kirk Gibson hit his dramatic home run in the 1988 World Series, and for countless other Series games, All-Star Games, and divisional and League Championship Series playoff games. During the pregame ceremonies before one of the 1999 World Series games, I was in the press box at Turner Field when colleague Jim Gray persisted in grilling Pete Rose about admitting to gambling on baseball. In my estimation, he should have grilled Rose about being on the field with the other members of the All-Century Team! Fans voted Rose ahead of Musial? Absurd!

Ever since that fall night in Atlanta in '99, I had dreamed of writing a book ranking the greatest players in history. When I was growing up, the biggest question concerned the great outfielders Hank Aaron and Willie Mays making their run at Babe Ruth's home run record. In the late '80s, when I began working for NBC, the baseball debates often centered on the great third basemen like Mike Schmidt and George Brett, and their place in baseball history. Today, there are jewels at the shortstop position, and the hot-stove talk in the winters concerns the place in history of Alex Rodriguez and Derek Jeter.

Over the years, I've had the opportunity to work on these debates. I realized that the summer of 2004 was a great time to finally sit down and write the book for this reason: the pursuit of Aaron's and Ruth's home run marks by Barry Bonds has called into question all the modern statistics. How does one reconcile the modern statistics with those of the past? How does one compare eras and positions and quality of competition?

I asked many of the same questions with *Who's Better, Who's Best in Basketball?* but soon realized that the task of ranking the top baseball players was a little more involved. For one thing, there are four times as many players (rosters are twice as big for twice as long). For another, pitchers and position players basically play a different game. Black players weren't allowed in the majors until 1947. How many players from the Negro Leagues should be ranked? Many stars of a slightly earlier era lost their prime playing years to World War II. Other stars lost time to World War I. Before the early '60s, the stars had fewer games per season to compile numbers. Most Valuable Player and Cy Young awards weren't given out annually from the beginning. I had to account for slight rule changes: should players be penalized for extending their careers by playing at designated hitter, for example? Should any players from the Japanese major leagues be included?

But they don't call me Mr. Stats for nothing.

I knew that Ty Cobb would get plenty of support for the title of top player ever. Others wanted to cling to Ruth and his legendary feats. Many older fans who grew up in the 1950s swore by Willie Mays. A wave of modernists wanted to look at Barry Bonds.

Do I weight the book with players who played post-1947, when the competition was open to everyone? You bet I do. As great as Josh Gibson was, he didn't regularly face the top pitchers like Lefty Grove. As great as Ty Cobb was, he didn't face the top competition, either.

This book takes into account the inequities in the caliber of competition. If Ty Cobb were playing in the modern game, where the pitchers are 230 pounds and fit and have detailed scouting reports on how to pitch each hitter, then would Cobb still average over .360 for his career? We'll take some educated guesses along the way.

Some of you are asking the right questions now. You're wondering what stats I value in coming up with these rankings. The main ones, basically, that we've all grown up with. I value Most Valuable Player awards and Cy Young awards. I value World Series and post-season wins and performances. I value Gold Gloves. I look at batting averages, runs batted in, runs scored, on-base average, and slugging percentage.

Most people consider slugging percentage a better indicator of batting performance than batting average (because doubles, triples, and home runs are given greater weight than mere singles). Well, 27 of the top 29 single-season performances in slugging percentage have happened in two different eras (1920–1932 and 1994–2004).

Only one man, Ted Williams, slugged higher than .719 in a season between 1940 and 1993. Does this mean that the players from the '40s and '50s were less accomplished batters? Were Mays and Aaron not as good as Ruth (from an earlier era) or Bonds (from a later one)?

Most baseball fans have some idea about on-base and slugging averages, as they've really made their way into the everyday lexicon. Slugging average is particularly revealing, as fans understand the simple concept that total bases are more important than total hits.

On a recent "Curb Your Enthusiasm" episode, Larry David is told that his friend's father had two heart surgeries—a quadruple bypass and a triple bypass. Larry quickly computes in his head and laments that the poor man has seven total bases.

For some researchers, those statistics don't do enough justice, so they tinker and come up with formulas that combine slugging and on-base averages. When I occasionally reference someone else's stat (like Bill James's "win shares" or Thomas Boswell's "total average" or OPS—on-base plus slugging), there will be a reason for it and it will be explained.

Okay, but what do we do about understanding pitchers?

Nolan Ryan was a great strikeout artist, as is Roger Clemens. But what if they were to pitch in the 1940s and 1950s, when batters showed a keener eye? The 1951 season saw just one player in the major leagues strike out as many as 100 times. This was the norm. There were two players in 1950, and in 1957 Duke Snider was the only one. In 1968, when pitchers dominated play, there were 18. By 1990, there were 42 players who struck out at least 100 times. In 2001, 69 different players struck out 100 or more times. In 2002, there were 71 players who whiffed that many.

Players who played in asymmetrical, urban neighborhood ballparks or had an unusual home-field advantage or disadvantage will be noted, as well. Postseason performances will be weighed.

But there can't be an absolute formula to any of this, like showing the league batting average against the player's batting average, for instance. And no matter what any of the great baseball researchers attempt, all defensive stats in baseball are flawed, so I'll do my best at giving the students with good defensive abilities "extra credit."

Are my ratings tilted toward modern players? Of course they are, for the following reasons. Players today are bigger, faster, and better conditioned than they were in previous generations. In 1950, there were only about a dozen players who were 200 pounds.

The 1953 American League MVP, Al Rosen, was 5'10" and 170 pounds, and people referred to him as "big and burly." Today, pitchers are 6'5" and 230 pounds.

None of the old-timers employed weight training or even picked up a bat in the off-season. Some of it was practical—they needed to work and earn money in the winter months. As a result, hardly any of the old-timers lasted into their late 30s as ballplayers. They hit 35 years old and were at the end of their careers. Today, players that age are often given long-term contracts.

None of this means that the list of the all-time greats should be unduly loaded up with modern-day players. But 20 percent of the players in my top 100 were active in 2004.

How come many of the old-timers put up such fabulous numbers? There's a wonderful article by the late Stephen Jay Gould published in *Discover* magazine in August 1986, "Entropic Homogeneity Isn't Why No One Hits .400 Anymore," that addresses the question. Gould pointed out that no one has hit .400 in a season since Ted Williams reached .406 in 1941, yet eight players exceeded .410 in the fifty years before then. Gould wondered, "Were the old guys really better?"

Gould was a master at explaining the concept of *decline in variation*. Simply put, this decline produces a decrease in the difference between average and stellar performance. Because of increased competition and higher standards, baseball has eliminated very weak hitters (once tolerated for their superior fielding skills, possibly). There aren't any .400 batters anymore, but all the weak players have been eliminated as well. When the best hitters averaged .400 in a season, there were a lot of players at the other end of that spectrum, since the league batting averages were about the same as they are now. In short, there are no more .400 batters or pitchers with a 1.00 earned run average because we would have to bring back all the lousy pitchers and batters that have been weeded out. That is a sign of improvement, not decline. Batting averages are no longer as high or as low as they used to be.

That might be a long-winded way of saying that if Alex Rodriguez has a career batting average that is exactly the same as a player who played in the 1920s, A-Rod has a big head start in these rankings over that player.

The other thing I try to do is get people to understand these legendary players better by comparing them not only to other players from different eras, but to pop culture figures. Former major-league pitcher Rick Sutcliffe's dad is in the racing hall of fame, and his idol growing up was A. J. Foyt. I asked Sutcliffe who the baseball equivalent of Foyt was, and he told me Reggie Jackson. He also said Cal Ripken Jr. is the Dale Earnhardt of his sport. I love that stuff. I compare Hank Aaron to actor Sidney Poitier. Lou Gehrig is compared to some of the great second bananas, including Art Carney and an actor on

"The Sopranos." Sandy Koufax is compared to author J. D. Salinger. Dave Winfield's analogy is comedian Jay Leno.

I hope you enjoy the debates and analogies posed in this book. I hope you disagree with many. Every time Major League Baseball puts together one of these lists, it is contested almost instantly. In the 1969 list that ranked Babe Ruth as the greatest player ever, Joe Cronin was listed as the greatest living shortstop, ahead of then-active Ernie Banks. The greatest living outfielders were then Joe DiMaggio, Ted Williams, and Willie Mays. They should have selected Hank Aaron. Even at eight years old, I knew something was wrong.

So much of this is subjective, and I appreciate and respect differing opinions.

Now it's time to get to what promises to be the most controversial choice in this book, my selection for number one.

BARRY BONDS

Before we can evaluate Barry Bonds and his place in history, we have to look at his father, Bobby. Barry Bonds began his major-league career in the shadow of his father, Bobby Bonds, and ended it emerging from the shadow of Babe Ruth and Henry Aaron. But it's the tools of superstardom that Bobby shared with his son that enabled Barry to impact baseball and the record books the way he has.

Bobby Bonds was born in 1946, an original baby boomer, in California's Bay Area. When he was an infant, the Dodgers' Branch Rickey broke the color line and signed Jackie Robinson. When Bobby was in third grade, the Dodgers and Giants moved west to California.

At 17, Bobby graduated from high school, married his sweetheart, and was signed by the San Francisco Giants as an amateur free agent in 1964. He also had a son that summer of '64 whom he named Barry. Oh yes, Bobby had the good sense to marry a left-handed girl. That would prove handy down the line.

Bobby Bonds made his major-league debut on June 25, 1968, on Barry's fourth birthday. It was memorable—he hit a grand slam. He had the tools to be a superstar, and lasted in the majors until being released by the Yankees on June 21, 1982, when he was 36 years old. He had some good years, but it turns out he was just holding a place for his son Barry. Bobby Bonds stole 461 bases and hit 332 home runs, which would constitute an excellent career unless you were always compared to onetime teammate Willie Mays. It wasn't exactly like Zeus and other Greek gods challenging young Hercules, but Bobby and Willie (the boy's godfather) pushed young Barry, challenging him.

Despite it being fashionable to condemn Barry Bonds and his career due to hints of steroid use, Bonds is my choice as the greatest baseball player ever. His career should not be judged on the steroids issue. Barry Bonds has been an incredibly talented player for a number of years. Let's rewind to the start of his career.

In 1985, the Pittsburgh Pirates were 57–104, and drug trials were under way with former Pirates Dave Parker, John Milner, Lee Lacy, Dale Berra, and Rod Scurry being mentioned as prominent suspects. Pittsburgh selected Barry Bonds of Arizona State with their first pick in the 1985 draft. Barry started his career with a terrible team that everyone thought was filled with druggies. Bonds led the Pirates to the postseason within a few years, but no more "saved" the Pirates than Ruth "saved" baseball following the gambling scandal of 1919. After just two months in the minor leagues in 1986, Barry was promoted to the Pirates. Despite being just 21 years old, the minors were a waste of time to him, for as Pittsburgh general manager Syd Thrift said at the time, "All the pitchers were doing down there was pitching around him." Bonds struggled at first with the Pirates, but his talent was evident from the beginning.

Rick Sutcliffe: "When Bonds got to the big leagues, I was with the Cubs, and our manager was Don Zimmer. The Pirates were thinking of sending Bonds back to the minors, I remember, and he was taking batting practice before a game one day. Pirates manager Jim Leyland called Zim over to watch. He hit about 7 out of 10 balls out of the park. Zim said that was nothing, anyone could pull the ball. Bonds must have heard. He looked back at Zim and said, 'Watch this.' He hit the next pitch deep to left center. He hit the next pitch out to center field. He was amazing, even then."

A *Sport* magazine article by Bob Klapisch in March 1991 contains some great quotes from Barry about the expectations placed upon him in his 1986 rookie season. "The national media created expectations that were totally unrealistic. People wanted a superstar right from Jump Street. . . . They never got it that my dad was bigger and stronger and didn't have to work at it. He just walked up to the plate and boom. Me, I have to spend the whole winter in the weight room just to build myself up to play all season. . . . But I'm there to also build up who I am; to identify myself as Barry Bonds."

And build himself he did.

With a physical resemblance to his father, and inheriting his father's combination of power and speed, Bonds was put in the leadoff spot by the Pirates. For five years he averaged 21 home runs per season but struggled with his batting average, hitting .223 in 1986, .261 in 1987, .283 in 1988, and .248 in 1989.

You had to look further—beyond his heavy bat—to see the talent emerging. In those first four seasons, Bonds stole 117 bases and had 231 extra-base hits.

When Bonds was still learning how to play, the majors were dominated by pitching. In 1988, the National League average was 3.8 runs per game. The next season, it was still only 3.94 runs per game. By contrast, the majors have averaged over five runs per game in each year since 2000, just as in Ruth's best seasons.

In that context, what Bonds did in 1988—as a 23-year-old kid still developing—was positively marvelous. Barry batted "only" .283—but the league average was .255 that season. Barry slugged "only" .491—but the league average was .363, and Darryl Strawberry led the league at .545. Bonds was ninth in homers, seventh in on-base average, seventh in slugging percentage, and sixth in OPS (on-base plus slugging).

By 1990, Barry had it all figured out. He batted .301, hit 33 home runs, drove in 114, and added 52 stolen bases. Bonds captured the MVP Award (with a near-unanimous vote) at the age of 26.

He came into the following season in the best shape of his life. "He's not Schwarzenegger (not at 6'1", 185) but Bonds spent last winter working out five times a week at Three Rivers Stadium," wrote Bob Klapisch in a 1991 *Sport* magazine preseason article.

He didn't acquire his bat speed when he added muscle to his toned body. In 1990, his bat speed was spoken of in reverent terms. Darryl Strawberry said, "Watch how Bonds goes the opposite way with some of his home runs . . . that's the sign of a good hitter." His bat speed was the reason Bonds was able to belt 33 home runs (fourth in the N.L.) despite weighing under 200 pounds.

If we split up his slugging percentage by six-year increments and compare him with the other N.L. leaders, we can see how Bonds has improved over time.

Barry Bonds Slugging Percentage
1986–91 .485
1992–97 .620
1998–03 .719

N.L. Slugging Percentage Leaders, 1986–1991
1. .520 Darryl Strawberry
2. .518 Kevin Mitchell
3. .512 Will Clark

Even if Barry wasn't the mega-superstar from day one that people expected him to be, no one in the league slugged higher than .520. Bonds slugged .485, not far from the league leaders despite batting leadoff, stealing a ton of bases, and being one of the youngest players in the game.

N.L. Slugging Percentage Leaders, 1992–1997
1. .620 Barry Bonds
2. .580 Larry Walker
3. .576 Mike Piazza

Bonds was the best player in the league, slugging .620 over a six-year run. Our mistake at the time was thinking that this represented the apex of his great career.

N.L. Slugging Percentage Leaders, 1998–2003

1. .719 Barry Bonds
2. .683 Mark McGwire
3. .635 Sammy Sosa

McGwire had two big seasons (1998, 1999), then managed just 535 more at-bats in his career. McGwire, basically the same age as Barry (both were rookies in 1986), was through at 37 years old, and his last big year came at age 35. That's when Bonds began his historic seasons.

My friend Allen Barra wrote in 2002 that "it positively amazes me that everyone now watching Barry Bonds can't understand they're watching the greatest player in the history of baseball."

Old habits are hard to break, Allen. Kids learn about Babe Ruth. He had the image. He hit home runs for dying kids in the hospital. He had the nicknames: the Sultan of Swat, the Bambino. If Bobby Bonds did one thing wrong in bringing up his young prodigy, it was the very first thing: naming him. Couldn't he have named him something that would be catchy, like Shaq? Even something simple yet ironic, like James, would have done.

The Knock on Bonds

Steroids.

It's hard to reconcile. But here it goes. First, there's no incontrovertible proof that Bonds actually took anabolic steroids, or any performance-enhancing drugs.

If he didn't partake, the world owes him a big-time apology. If he did, well, he did it to become the best baseball player he could become. John Lennon and Paul McCartney used illegal drugs—hallucinogenic drugs—to create music that has lasted for 40 years, and will be remembered for 400 more. If I studied art history, I would have found many great artists who did the same. Does it mean we dismiss the music and art because the artists had an "unfair" advantage over everyone else who created works sober? I don't approve of the mind-altering drugs that helped songwriters create the soundtrack of my life; but I am damn grateful that they did whatever it took to entertain and inspire me and my kids and my children's children. I'm not going to knock Bonds because he isn't a great role model to children—there are too many ghosts in many of the old-timers' closets.

My arguments are threefold: first, Bonds was a great player—a *great* player—before anyone ever accused him of bulking up and using steroids to gain advantage. Next, if steroids were responsible, then everyone taking them would have numbers like Bonds. But they don't. No other player has increased his own production like Bonds has. I've shown how Bonds has towered over the competition—even over the other players accused of doing steroids. Finally, if he did do steroids, I'm not sure it would matter in my ranking of Bonds for this book. I believe what Bonds has accomplished—even if we reasonably deduct from his score for the possibility of cheating—exceeds what the great Babe Ruth and every other player in major-league history has done.

Babe Ruth projected an image of drinking and smoking and eating too much. Mickey Mantle projected a similar image, saying in retirement that he wished he would have taken better care of himself during his playing days. In contrast, Barry Bonds has always looked like the picture of health. From the beginning, his was the story of an athlete who pushed himself in the weight room and in the batting cage. If he went too much in that direction—to the point of risking his future health—then I wish to thank him for playing in an era that I can witness, unlike Babe Ruth.

How many of you look the same at 38 as you did at 22? Most of us put on pounds; Bonds put on muscle.

Is it cheating if you take every advantage that is legal? Then there is a distinction between the legal and the illegal human growth hormones that may have been used by Bonds. Well, cheating is as old as the game. Gaylord Perry won enough games to gain entry into the Hall of Fame, and he used an illegal pitch (the spitball) by doctoring up baseballs before he threw them. Are his statistics "tainted"? For one hundred years, teams have stolen signs, grooved pitches, soaked down infields, even manipulated games for betting purposes—but now all of a sudden we're going to question the integrity of baseball statistics because a certain percentage of players were found to have engaged in taking steroids (through anonymous testing)! Many of my colleagues view spitballs and stealing signs as *gamesmanship* as opposed to outright cheating. I'm sorry, but that argument doesn't make it with me. So much of this is personality-driven. We look the other way when a popular star like Sammy Sosa gets caught corking a bat (to make his batted balls travel farther). People look to discredit Bonds because (a) they don't like him, and (b) he's exceeded every known parameter.

This is a study in ethics, and I prefer not to engage in the holier-than-thou argument. Should managers not use computerized charts to help them make decisions, since earlier generations didn't have computers at their disposal? Players have millions of dollars at stake in their careers. Hitting a baseball is the single hardest thing to accomplish successfully in sports. Pitchers have gotten bigger and stronger. Batters never face a fatigued pitcher, as specialists have evolved. Babe Ruth never had to face a fresh Mariano Rivera coming out of the bullpen.

Other Knocks on Bonds

His Armpads

Body armor takes away the fear of being hit by a pitch and may energize a batter's muscles (as it is said to do with some power lifters). Hmm. Bonds has been hit by 93 pitches, a surprisingly low number considering how he crowds the plate, daring the pitcher to come inside on him. Bonds has made a living turning on the inside pitch and belting it out. Again, if the umpire allows him to go up to the plate in a Tin Man costume, then who are we to judge? It's either legal or illegal. If we enforce a rule that says a player cannot wear protective gear, then fine. Otherwise, lay off Barry. We allow pitchers to intimidate and scare the batters, but batters can't do the same back? Barry has dug in and crowded the plate without fear. For this, I tip my hat to him.

His Personality

Former teammates (Pirates outfielder Andy Van Slyke, Giants second baseman Jeff Kent) have blasted Bonds in print. "On the field, we're fine, but off the field, I don't care about Barry and Barry doesn't care about me. Or anybody else," Kent told *Sports Illustrated*'s Rick Reilly in 2002. "Barry does a lot of questionable things . . . I was raised to be a team guy, and I am, but Barry's Barry." Uh, I'm missing something. If Jeff Kent were Lou Gehrig, then Bonds might have a couple of World Series rings, as Ruth did. He might not have Ruth's seven, but he would have more than zero. What more could you possibly do for your team than what Bonds did for the Giants? Well, many teammates, scribes, and fans wanted him to walk *less* because all the walks took away precious at-bats from Barry.

You can't swing at bad pitches just because you're the only player capable of driving in runs for your team. At some point, your teammates have to help out. Do you think Babe or Mickey Mantle were knocked for taking too many pitches? Strictly by his on-field performance, there couldn't have been a better teammate than Barry Bonds. If teammates object to an abrasive me-first personality, well, there's validity to that, but big movie stars get their private trailer and surround themselves with their people. Baseball is entertainment in this day and age. So what if Bonds is standoffish and a jerk to reporters?

Media members have regularly criticized this home run artist. The two most prominent long-form pieces were in *ESPN Magazine* in the summer of 2000 with Dan Patrick, and a 2002 *Sports Illustrated* piece by Rick Reilly. Both articles just killed Bonds.

Following the 2002 season, Bonds was awarded his fifth (of seven) MVP awards. At this point, it became logical to compare him to icons in other sports. Kareem Abdul-Jabbar won six MVP awards. Bill Russell and Michael Jordan won five MVPs. Wayne

Gretzky captured nine MVPs in the NHL, and Gordie Howe had six. When Bonds was asked to compare himself to some of those players, he said the following:

"I probably wish I was liked as much as them. That would be nice. I wish I had the same form of respect that they have. They're all very admired. People admire their achievements and accomplishments. Everyone has had their ups and downs through the media. I wish my career could be respected as much as theirs. Unfortunately, that's never going to happen."

Dan LeBatard wrote in a 2003 article that "Jim Leyland used to say Bonds wasn't nearly as good a player when calm, that Bonds needed anger, tension and chaos swirling around him in order to summon the camera-lens clarity that would erase all blur and bring that baseball into just the right focus. Poisonous journalists, jealous peers, head-hunting pitchers, distant teammates, booing fans, contract issues, Jeff Kent, manufactured slights—they've all worked together over the years to turn the chalked confines of that batter's box into a go-to-hell shell. That's where a career loner like Bonds could always escape to the perfect calm at the storm's center and be all alone with his excellence."

He's Never Won a World Series

That's the problem with baseball. As great as one player is, he needs teammates to perform. Willie Mays, Hank Aaron, and Ted Williams combined have two World Series rings.

Bonds had some bad postseasons early in his career, for which he took a lot of criticism. In the 2002 World Series, the Giants were three innings away from winning Game 7 against the Angels, a Series in which Bonds did everything humanly possible to help his team (getting on base 70 percent of the time and hitting four home runs!).

He Wasn't That Good Early in His Career

Bonds did a lot early in his career, winning MVP awards three times in four seasons. He won in 1990, 1992, and 1993.

In 1991, he was robbed. The voters selected Braves third baseman Terry Pendleton, who batted .319 with 22 home runs and contributed to the Braves' division-winning season. Bonds batted .292, but hit 25 home runs, drove in 116, and stole 43 bases for the Pirates.

His numbers didn't look like Ruth's in the early '90s, but no one put up bigger numbers than Barry. When new ballparks became smaller, pitching became diluted, and weight training was supplemented (?) with whatever, then everyone's numbers went up—none more so than Barry's.

I never thought I would live to see anyone bat 73 home runs in a single season, or get on base with his frequency and slug with his power. Bonds himself has called the 73 homers "freakish." Even that record was bittersweet for Barry, who had 63 homers by September 9, 2001, but had his chase put on hold when the tragic events of September 11 occurred. When the games resumed, Bonds prospered despite being walked in record numbers. He overtook McGwire's record 70 in early October against the Dodgers—in a loss that eliminated the Giants from playoff contention. As significant a record as 73 home runs is, there's an important distinction to be made. This Bonds was no one-trick pony. Even if he had never hit more than 59 home runs in a season, he would be ranked number one on this list of greatest players ever.

Barry Bonds is the only player to surpass 600 career home runs in over 30 years. Frank Robinson fell a little short. Mark McGwire faded from view. Bonds not only went over 600, but zoomed past Willie Mays and his 660. That is quite an achievement to pass his godfather and the man many consider the greatest player of all time. Bonds enters 2005 with 703 home runs.

Bonds had tremendous expectations put upon him when he arrived in the National League in 1986, and he exceeded all of them. He made 12 All-Star teams. He won six MVP awards and finished second in two other seasons. There were no MVPs awarded in the early '20s when Ruth played, but no one besides Barry has won more than three since they began awarding it in 1931.

Mays had a (then) record 11 years between his two MVP seasons (1954 and 1965). Bonds won his first MVP in 1990 and his seventh in 2004. He won MVP honors 14 years apart.

Bonds may be the greatest defensive left fielder of all time. He won eight Gold Gloves for his fielding excellence.

Rick Sutcliffe: "I'm telling you right now. If I had to pick a left fielder for defensive purposes, I would pick Barry Bonds. Tony Gwynn had to change his bat—find a longer one—to figure out a way to change his approach to hitting, when Bonds was in left. Bonds would play him so shallow that balls that would drop in on every other team would be caught by Barry."

Bonds is among the best at the most important of all baseball stats. Only one man has drawn more walks. Only two men have hit more home runs. Only eight men have scored more runs. He has stolen over 500 bases.

In his only World Series appearance, he had 30 plate appearances. He made exactly nine outs in the seven games. He had 13 walks and eight hits. In that series, his on-base average was .700. Four of his hits were home runs.

He broke the record for most home runs in a season, considered the top record in sports.

Who's Better, Who's Best
Barry Bonds or Babe Ruth?

"Willie's number is always the one that I've strived for," Bonds said during the 2003 All-Star break of his godfather, Willie Mays. "And if it does happen, the only number I care about is Babe Ruth's. Because as a left-handed hitter, I wiped him out. That's it. And in the baseball world, Babe Ruth's everything, right? I got his slugging percentage and I'll take his home runs and that's it. Don't talk about him no more."

Columnists (who have always crucified Bonds, although they didn't want blood on their hands) nailed Barry for this. Did Barry really want to pass Ruth because he was a left-handed batter, or did he want to pass the white man, content to have Aaron remain as number one?

"To suggest that those feats are somehow capable of 'wiping out' Ruth illustrates a complete disregard for the history and tradition of our national game, and its greatest player and star," Michael L. Gibbons, executive director of the Babe Ruth Museum (located in Baltimore, Maryland), said in a statement in response to Bonds's infamous words. Bonds said later that week he meant what he said as a compliment, and that he would consider it a huge accomplishment to pass Ruth on the all-time home runs list.

"Babe Ruth is symbolic of baseball," Bonds said.

Gibbons's statement concluded, "Can Bonds 'wipe out' Ruth? Not today, not forever."

Not so fast, Mr. Curator. First off, my argument for Bonds over Ruth has everything and nothing to do about race. It was Ruth who grew up in an orphanage, while Bonds was the privileged son of a major leaguer, hanging out at a young age with superstars like Willie Mays. Bonds was raised like an elite Republican, while Ruth was raised in the ghetto.

But race also has everything to do with this argument of mine concerning the two men. Bonds should be justifiably proud of his accomplishments over the best baseball players in the world now. Ruth was the giant among a sizable subset. Segregation allowed a select few players who pushed the scales of human limits to dominate (some might say artificially) the sport. We'll never know, but it's my guess that Ruth would have dominated play in his era even if everyone had been allowed to play. If a kid is a valedictorian in a private school, he probably would have done okay in a public school, as well.

Yes, Barry, Babe Ruth is symbolic of baseball—but then, so is racism and segregation. The fact that Ruth faced his own form of racism—there were rumors about his true blood lineage (see the Ruth chapter following)—is even more ironic.

Of course, Barry is not equipped to fight the Babe and his 80-year head start on publicity. Writers like ESPN's Adrian Wojnarowski wrote, "Bonds made us suspicious of steroid use. Until there is legitimate testing, we'll be left to wonder about his biceps and skull growing so late in his career, about the rapid power explosion that dramatically elevated in his late thirties."

But Adrian and the others fail to appreciate the total picture of Barry's power explosion in the early 2000s. It is a lot more than home runs. Bonds has become so selective at the plate that he gets on base at a historic pace. And his slugging percentages are equally historic. Look at the following lists of the greatest single-season marks for on-base average and slugging percentage.

On-Base Average, Single Season

1. .609 Barry Bonds, 2004
2. .582 Barry Bonds, 2002
3. .551 Ted Williams, 1941
4. .542 Babe Ruth, 1921
5. .529 Barry Bonds, 2003

Slugging Percentage, Single Season

1. .863 Barry Bonds, 2001
2. .847 Babe Ruth, 1920
3. .846 Babe Ruth, 1921
4. .812 Barry Bonds, 2004
5. .799 Barry Bonds, 2002
6. .772 Babe Ruth, 1927

Both Bonds and Ruth dominate those statistics, but remember, all of the great slugging marks took place either between 1920 and 1932 or between 1994 and 2003. There have been 28 instances where a player slugged .708 or better in a season, and 26 of them took place in those two eras. Only Ted Williams slugged .730 or better in a season between 1940 and 1993.

But my point is this: Babe Ruth towered over his competition, and Barry Bonds has towered over his.

Slugging Percentage, 1920–1924

1. .777 Babe Ruth
2. .650 Rogers Hornsby
3. .591 Harry Heilmann

Slugging Percentage, 1998–2003

1. .719 Barry Bonds
2. .683 Mark McGwire
3. .635 Sammy Sosa

Bonds has the single-season records for slugging and on-base average, and set them in different seasons. He has the single-season home run record, with 73 home runs. He passed Willie Mays with his 661st home run in April 2004, and now trails only Aaron and Ruth in career home runs. Ruth does hold the record for career slugging percentage at .690, and that's 56 points higher than runner-up Ted Williams. But Bonds has done better than .690 for a seven-year period—and that's damn impressive, considering the competition, relief pitchers, and everything else the modern ballplayer has to contend with.

Since 1941, only two ballplayers have ever batted .390 or better in a single season. Barry Bonds batted .370 at the age of 38 to win his first batting title. He batted .362 at 40.

Besides, this guy didn't sneak up on us. He was a great player for a long time. For a perspective from the Bay Area, I called upon a man who has been close to the San Francisco sports scene for over 40 years.

Jeff Trager (a S.F. Giants fan): "People here are not critical of Barry. People either bury their heads in the sand or blame the company that supplies the steroids. They are not even that critical of his personal trainer and old friend. It's strange because people are excited to see the long ball, it's the ultimate, especially in the new ballpark that is always full. How can you not love those soaring drives into McCovey Cove? Barry is the Bay Area's own, he's homegrown, from down the Peninsula. His dad played here and what he went through with his dad dying during the [2003] season and the way Barry handled that very sad event . . . and playing the way he did . . . they appreciate and understand his desire to win a World Series. . . . He is really the only guy that I turn the radio up to hear if he hits a home run and look up at the television when he is up to bat. . . . That's what Barry Bonds does to almost everyone. Sure, he is surly with most of the media, but he plays the game with a passion, like almost no one else. I have seen it firsthand because I have been in the locker room before a game and Barry just locks himself into the upcoming game. He doesn't want to talk to anyone unless it's his close group that he works with, like his trainer. It's really funny, he could have this town in the palm of his hand, like Joe Montana does. Montana is revered like a god, as the guy who won all those championships we never had before, and as a regular guy, with a great radiant smile for everyone; someone you would like to play golf with and that laughs at your jokes. Barry just doesn't get it . . . he will always be someone you don't want to get to know—that's just him—he has always been that way. He has a bad rap and it's really his doing, but in the end, his intentions are real and honest. He wants to play baseball, a game he totally loves and does so well. You can't really fault him one bit. It's just great to have someone that great to watch. . . . One thing, for sure, people do respect what he has accomplished on the field, and remember, this is a DiMaggio town and McCovey's town, and there's another Willie who played here who many think is the best ever."

Bobby Bonilla (16-year major-league veteran, Bonds's Pittsburgh teammate for six years): "There's no one better in the history of the sport. If you're a historian, you simply can't come to any other conclusion. I knew he was great when I played with him. I didn't know he was legendary. If he didn't walk so many times, he might have hit 90 home runs in a season."

Toward the end of his father's life, Barry could be found sleeping next to his father Bobby's bed every night, also helping him shower and pushing him around in a wheelchair with oxygen tanks. Bobby Bonds was like a lot of Americans who were born in post–World War II America. They wanted their children to do better than they did. They wanted their children to have it easier. By any measure, Bobby Bonds was successful.

BABE RUTH

He is so legendary that he not only has the greatest nickname of all time, he claims three of the best. He was the Babe. He was the Bambino. He was the Sultan of Swat. (Those weren't even all his nicknames. Teammates sometimes called him "Jidge"—a take-off on how some pronounced his real first name, George—and opponents sometimes called him "Monkey" or "Baboon.")

His exploits were so well known that more people knew 714 as Ruth's career home run total than their own area code. He was one of the first players ever to wear a number on his back—No. 3. He set the single-season record for home runs—eventually topping off at 60, the number sluggers aimed at for over three decades.

When he was just a Babe, he was no Babe in Toyland. He was not the product of a stable household. Neither of his parents devoted much time to him. When he was eight, he was placed in St. Mary's, a reform school for boys. He remained there until he entered professional baseball at age 19. (In some accounts, Ruth was often labeled an orphan who was adopted by the Ruth family. This too remains part of the enigma of the man.)

Ruth would dominate the game, both offensively and defensively (with his early career pitching). Although everyone associates Ruth with the 1920s, he had some big years before then.

Many articles hinted in February 2004 that the Yankees' acquisition of Alex Rodriguez was the biggest since they traded for Ruth in 1920. Dave Anderson of the *New York Times* wrote that the signing of Rodriguez had an even bigger magnitude because "When sold, Babe wasn't the Babe yet."

Ruth's biographer, Robert W. Creamer, disputed that in a phone conversation I had with him shortly after Anderson's article was published.

Robert W. Creamer: "The Babe was the Babe long before he came to New York. The fame he acquired with his tremendous pitching for the Boston Red Sox in 1915, '16, '17 was hyped by the nine home runs he hit as a pitcher in those three dead-ball seasons. Ty Cobb had only 14 homers as a full-time player over the same three seasons, Shoeless Joe Jackson only 13, Tris Speaker 4. Imagine a pitcher hitting nine! By 1918, the year Ruth began the transition from full-time pitcher to full-time hitter, he was being called the Home Run King. A 1918 newspaper headline called him 'The Mightiest Slugger of Them All.' He was certainly the Babe by 1918, and in 1919 he topped all he had done before by hitting an utterly sensational 29 home runs, destroying all existing home run records."

Why are Ruth's pre-1920 accomplishments being downgraded? It's almost like Barry Bonds being downgraded for his early career with the Pirates. The Babe and Barry reached such levels of excellence later that their early careers are almost passed over. Babe was a special player with the Red Sox (as Barry was truly magnificent with the Pirates). Ruth wasn't just a pitcher; he was one of the best. Ruth's pitching record against the Yankees alone was 17–5. He was a Yankee killer before he was a Yankee savior.

Robert Creamer: "The Yanks had never won a pennant before Babe. Yet they won three pennants in his first four seasons with them, six in his first nine. Their biggest season's attendance before Ruth was 619,000. With him in 1920, they doubled that to 1.2 million. It was nearly 30 percent better than the old major-league record for attendance. . . . In fact, New York was the perfect stage for Ruth, but it wasn't New York that made the Babe. He was the Babe long before he arrived."

Ruth's home runs, with their ability to draw crowds, helped usher in the livelier ball and an offensive explosion that helped popularize the game.

But look at his production in the 1910s as a hurler for the Red Sox. He was 89–46, and was also 2–0 in the World Series with an ERA of 0.87. (Ruth would pitch five games for the Yankees in his career, always as an attendance booster at the end of a season, and he won all five, giving him a career pitching mark of 94–46 with an ERA of 2.28.)

1918 World Series

In the Red Sox' World Series championship victory against the Cubs, Ruth threw a 1–0 shutout in Game 1, then pitched 7.1 innings of shutout ball in the fourth game. That extended his scoreless-inning streak in Series play to 29.2 innings, a mark that would stand until 1961, when Whitey Ford broke it. The Series was almost suspended prior to the fifth game when players from both teams demanded more money. The players agreed out of patriotism (World War I was going on at the time) to continue the Series. The Red Sox won the Series, their fifth and last championship of the 20th century.

In 1919, Ruth's last as a pitcher, he was 9–5 with a 2.97 ERA. He also set the single-season home run record with 29 homers (breaking Gaavy Cravath's record of 24) and led the league with 114 runs batted in. Boston owner Harry Frazee sold the outfielder-pitcher to New York for $100,000 plus a $350,000 loan. Frazee's defense of the deal was that not even Ruth had prevented Boston from finishing in sixth place.

The Curse of the Bambino

With Ruth gone, the Red Sox suffered 15 consecutive losing seasons. They did not even sneak back into fourth place until 1934. Much of Ruth's legend is that the team he was traded to began a winning tradition that has lasted for generations. The team he was traded from (the Red Sox) did not win another World Series until 2004.

The Babe Ruth Era

So, Ruth began his Yankees career at the same time the country came back from World War I. It was a time of great prosperity in the United States. It was the Roaring Twenties. The 1920s didn't just belong to Ruth. There was growing optimism in America, and the United States was becoming a world power. Radio broadcasts and motion pictures were just getting started. All of these elements helped create and perpetuate the Ruth legend that has many people to this day believing Babe was the greatest ballplayer of all time.

Not everyone was dancing the Charleston, however. A wave of immigrants threatened to take work from the established white Anglo citizens, and the KKK boasted five hundred thousand members. This was also the era of segregation, and the time in history when the baseball commissioner banished off-season "exhibitions" between major leaguers and Negro League teams. This, too, helped Ruth, as it kept talented sluggers like Josh Gibson and Oscar Charleston in separate leagues from Ruth.

Of course, in the majors, the "lively ball" era was under way, brought about not only by Ruth's power but a combination of things, including a pitch from Yankees pitcher Carl Mays in 1920 that killed Cleveland's Ray Chapman. Soon after that, spitballs were outlawed, and a conscious effort was made to keep a clean, fresh, dry baseball in play (as opposed to using a ball until it was gray, and harder to see). That, too, helped Ruth "see" every pitch better and helped usher in the era of the home run.

Ruth with the Yankees

In his first year with the Yanks, the team came within three games of capturing their first American League pennant. That would come a year later. Ruth hit more home runs in 1920 than any other American League *team*. He hit 54 homers that year, after breaking the record the previous year with 29. So began a decade of dominance that no player before or since has duplicated.

Ruth hit 467 home runs in the 1920s, the most by a player in any decade. In the entire American League, there were 4,684 home runs hit in the period 1920–1929. Ruth hit 10 percent of the home runs in the entire league for a ten-year period! That included the 1925 season, when Ruth missed 50 games over a "stomachache" and feud with manager Miller Huggins.

The Yankees fell a few games short in 1920, but they made the World Series in 1921 for the first time. After losing consecutive World Series in '21 and '22, the Yankees' first World Series championship was largely due to Ruth. In the 1923 World Series, Ruth hit three home runs and reached safety 15 of 26 times. All told, Ruth slugged 15 World Series home runs in 129 at-bats.

The House That Ruth Built

In 1923, Yankee Stadium opened and Fred Lieb, a writer, dubbed the stadium "the House that Ruth built." By the way, it was the first time a major-league team played in some-place called a "stadium." Yankee Stadium always had a short right field, and many people felt that Ruth greatly benefited from it; but Ruth always preferred the Polo Grounds, where the Yanks played prior to 1923. The Polo Grounds had a shorter left-field fence, but a deeper one in right field. Ruth's greatest seasons were actually in 1920, 1921, and 1922.

Rules Changes

Until 1930, a fair ball that bounced into the stands was counted as a home run. That year, the American League changed the rule to make the hit a ground-rule double, and the National League followed a year later. Baseball historian Bob Davids estimates that some 10 to 20 "bounce" homers occurred each season. According to the historians, Ruth never "bounced" a homer into the stands.

Actually, the scoring rules in 1918 deprived the Babe of a 715th homer. In the bottom of the ninth inning in a tied game with Cleveland on July 8, Ruth hit a ball into the right-field seats. Because a runner who had been on first base scored, the Babe was credited with only the bases necessary (three, a triple) to push the tie-breaking run across the plate. This was standard at the time, and actually is a rule that makes some sense. I'm sure some of the other early baseball heroes lost home runs that way, as well.

Some Incredible Numbers

In his career, Ruth drove in a run every 3.79 times at bat. Do the math—that's almost the equal of driving in one run per game. There are only three men who have ever averaged more runs batted in per game than Ruth. The leader is Lou Gehrig, who had the incredible fortune of batting behind (and driving in) Ruth. The other two superior players in runs batted in are Hank Greenberg and Joe DiMaggio.

Some More Stats

Ruth was quoted as saying that he could have batted .600 if he went for those tiny singles. He may have been right. Even swinging for the fences, Ruth had a career batting average of .342. In the first 19 years of his 22-year career, Ruth had a career mark of .349. Let's not get too excited. As impressive as those numbers were for a slugger, batting averages were generally higher in Ruth's era.

Because he walked so much (2,062 times in 2,503 games) his career on-base average was .469. That's second-best all-time, behind Ted Williams. He led the league in walks 11 times. He led the league in total bases six times. He led the league in slugging percentage 13 times—including seven years in a row. His lifetime slugging percentage of .690 is miles ahead of second-place Ted Williams (.632). He led the league in runs eight times. He led the league in home runs 12 times.

Obviously, there's so much more to Ruth's dominance than the home runs. This is a slugger who finished among the top 10 in stolen bases for a couple of seasons. This is a slugger who, as a pitcher, led the league in earned run average, games started, and hits allowed per nine innings for the 1916 season—a year he finished third in striking batters out.

Babe's Training and Diet

According to former *Sporting News* publisher J. G. Taylor Spink, Ruth generally drank a quart mixture of bourbon whiskey and ginger ale at breakfast before attacking a steak, with up to six fried eggs and potatoes on the side.

What Black People of the Time Remember About the Babe

Art Rust Jr. was a journalist and broadcaster who grew up in Harlem in the early 1930s. In his 1985 book, *Recollections of a Baseball Junkie*, Rust wrote about the continuing argument between his father and friends about the racial "purity" of Babe Ruth. "Ruth certainly wasn't acknowledging it. In fact, he went out of his way to deny the almost constant harassment about his heritage that plagued him throughout his career. . . . Any opposing team could get his goat. The bench jockeys had a field day with him. Bench jockeys would yell from the dugout, 'Hey, nigger, can't you play today?' 'Say, nigger, what part of dark town you gonna be in tonight?' Stoically, Ruth would respond with an amazing calm. 'Listen, guys, call me anything, but don't call me nigger.'"

Remember, being biracial in Ruth's day would have meant one thing: he couldn't have played major-league baseball. Roy Campanella had an Italian father and black mother, and wasn't signed until the color line had been broken by Jackie Robinson.

Of course, the question of Babe's lineage is at the heart of one of the most famous home runs in baseball history, Ruth's "called" shot in the 1932 World Series against the Cubs. Some people speculate that Ruth "called" his shot to get back at the Chicago players for taunting him constantly.

Robert Creamer: "In 1932, the Cubs were calling Ruth the 'n-word' from their bench. The Yankees weren't much better; they would heckle Cubs pitcher Guy Bush, who had a dark complexion and curly hair, and say, look at your guy Bush. The anti-black prejudice was just so strong in America then, it's hard to imagine the inferior place in society black people occupied. Calling someone the 'n-word' was a common epithet."

When I asked Mr. Creamer what his research found on the subject of Ruth being biracial, he was straight to the point: "I never found any evidence of it. If there was, it was back 100, 150 years before he was born. Ruth's family was from the Pennsylvania Dutch country, and in that part of the country, interracial relations were not likely."

The Knock on Ruth

Some people dwell on his fielding. He had a great arm, but he couldn't catch up to a lot of balls. Some people focus on his baserunning. Ruth was a better fielder and base runner than people might guess, but clearly he wasn't at the top of the list in either of those categories.

It is my contention that Ruth cannot be the greatest player of all time because of the era he played in. The baseball game Ruth played was a different game than most of his contemporaries were playing. It took a few years for them to catch up with Ruth. Ruth was going for home runs in an era when few teams had players going for the fences. Ruth never faced pitchers such as Negro League star Satchel Paige or Cuban great Martin Dihigo. He never faced fireballing relief aces late in games. Instead, he faced tired starting pitchers who may have been losing effectiveness. Or worse, he faced starting pitchers who paced themselves in the early innings, knowing they would be needing their very best in the late innings. Ruth didn't have to fly cross-country to play games. He didn't have to face a print or electronic media that sought to bring him down. He didn't even have to train that much in the winter.

Plus, none of the other contenders for greatest player ever had such support from teammates as Ruth did. Babe had Lou Gehrig hitting behind him during the back nine of the Bambino's career. Ruth hit in favorable home parks—including Fenway, the Polo Grounds, and Yankee Stadium.

The Case for Ruth

That he was a superior pitcher, and could have remained one for a long time, adds to his mystique. Ruth won close to 100 games as a pitcher, and slugged over 700 home runs. Since none of the great pitchers were as accomplished on offense, and since none of the other great offensive players served so much time on the pitching mound, Ruth is the automatic choice as greatest ever for some people.

Without broadcasters, the most prominent opinion-makers in baseball were the writers in Ruth's and Cobb's day. The one who carried the most influence was Ring Lardner, who viewed Cobb as the paramount player. There were a lot of old sportswriters who resisted the change in style brought about by the Babe. They would believe until their dying day that Cobb was better than Ruth, for instance.

Cobb was a symbol of the first part of America's history. He had an embedded self-important attitude that assumed he was better than everyone else. By his baserunning, he "stole land" that wasn't his.

Ruth didn't want to steal a base here or there. He wanted to become a superpower, launching bombs when no other players (or nations) had the means to do so.

Barry Bonds is the symbol for the United States in the early 2000s. He is the lone superpower left, after other opponents (like McGwire and Griffey Jr.) broke down. Never before in history have shortstops or catchers been able to bomb home runs like today. Never before in history have there been as many long home runs or opposite-field homers. It is the powerful Bonds that everyone scrutinizes, however.

Ruth was an exceptional pitcher and batter. He played for the best team in the biggest city in what was becoming the superpower of the world. He became world-famous. Everything else seemed small in comparison.

When the Babe retired in 1935, his 714 home runs seemed unapproachable. No other major-league player had ever batted in 400. Only Gehrig had more than 300 (Hornsby had exactly 300). If people want to cling to Ruth as the number-one player of all time, I certainly understand that. I just don't agree with it.

People who write that Babe Ruth is the best of all time want to believe that. Historically, history has been written by the winners. The Babe was a winner. Everyone could root for him. He was America's symbol to the world. Even minorities rooted for him because he could even be one of them.

It's not possible that someone is actually better than the Babe, is it? And, does race have to play a part in how people feel about the greatest ever? Does one have to be accused of racism to cling to the past and maintain that Ruth was the greatest of all time?

My feeling is that Bonds—especially over the last third of his career—was better than the Babe, and everyone else. Of course, Ruth was the consensus choice as the game's all-time great for almost 75 years. It will be interesting to see if Bonds will hold the title for subsequent generations.

WILLIE MAYS

The trouble with Willie Mays was that he spoiled the fans. He played the game with a flair for excitement. He made sensational catches and cloud-stirring slides. He was majestic. He had a great style. He had a great personality. He had a great nickname, the "Say Hey Kid." It is easy to see why he has such a hold on anyone who saw him play. I wish I had seen him in his prime.

He also had great demographics. He was the best player in the game in the 1950s. He was the best player in the game for much of the 1960s. He excelled playing in New York, on the East Coast. He was the first Bay Area superstar on the West Coast.

His career also had that all-important factor, longevity. He played in the World Series four times, including his first season, his 11th season, and his 22nd and final season. He won two MVP awards, spaced 11 years apart (1954, 1965).

He played a key position (center field) for a key franchise (the Giants) in the dominant league (National League) at a time in history when football and basketball had not yet overtaken baseball as the most popular sport in the country.

Those who favor him as the all-time greatest ballplayer point to the fact that Mays was a baseball genius, superior in the following skills: hitting, hitting for power, running, catching, and throwing. What a fantastic player he was! There were those who had higher batting averages, hit more homers, stole more bases, and were better fielders. But few have ever matched Mays in excellence in all these categories.

On May 6, 1931, Willie Mays was born in Alabama. His father, Willie, was an exceptionally fine center fielder who played semipro ball. Willie was close to his dad and bore a startling resemblance to him. His dad said that Willie was actually a better football player than baseball player as a boy. The elder Willie told his son to go into baseball, because he always liked it better. Besides, Willie didn't want his son hurting his knees.

Willie grew up to be just like his dad. He was basically a quiet man, not the least bit egotistical about who he was. When Mays was growing up near Birmingham, Alabama, his dad worked in the steel mill. "I used to tell him all the time, 'Don't go into the steel mills,'" the elder Willie told UPI's Milton Richman in 1969. Fortunately, he never had to. Willie went to high school and was signed to play baseball as soon as he finished.

Mays joined the Birmingham Barons of the Negro Leagues at age 17, and the New York Giants purchased his contract two years later. In the summer of 1950, Mays left Alabama to play integrated professional baseball in Trenton, New Jersey.

He started the 1951 season with the Giants' Triple-A team in Minneapolis, where he batted .477 before being called up in late May. He joined a Giants team that was near the bottom of the standings, having recently lost 10 consecutive games. The New York manager was Leo Durocher, who showed an enormous amount of patience with his young phenom. Mays went hitless his first few games, and had only one hit (a home run off future Hall of Famer Warren Spahn) in his first 25 major-league at-bats. Mays asked out of the lineup, but manager Durocher refused him. "You're my center fielder if you don't get another hit the rest of the season," said Leo. Smart man, that Durocher.

The Giants, down 13.5 games to the Dodgers in mid-August, caught Brooklyn by the end of the season, forcing a three-game playoff for the pennant. One of the main reasons the Giants made their comeback was Willie Mays. On August 15, 1951, his catch of a long smash off the bat of Brooklyn's Carl Furillo and Mays's 325-foot throw to double up Billy Cox at home plate had most observers at the time calling it the greatest catch-and-throw play ever made. Mays always maintained that it was his best-ever defensive play. Mays was the National League Rookie of the Year, hitting 20 home runs in his first 121 games. Willie was the on-deck batter when Bobby Thomson hit "the Shot Heard Round the World" to give the Giants the pennant.

Only a month into the 1952 season, Mays was drafted into the army, and wouldn't return to the Giants until the 1954 season. The Giants, who finished first with Mays in 1951, fell to second place and fifth place in the two years that Mays missed. In 1954, with Willie back from the army, the Giants won the pennant and returned to the World Series.

In 1954, Mays was at the absolute peak of his game. He batted .345 with 41 home runs, drove in 110, and made only seven errors in 151 games in the outfield. In the World Series against Cleveland, he made an unbelievable catch of a ball off the bat of Vic Wertz. Mays raced to deep center field, about 460 feet from home plate, stuck up his glove, and made the catch that people still talk about more than 50 years later. They still talk about it because it was so stirring; because it appeared Mays had eyes in the back of his head. The Giants swept the Indians, who had won a record 111 games during the season. It would be the only time in Mays's 21-year career that his team would win the World Series.

The most famous sportswriter of baseball's first half-century, Grantland Rice, wrote in 1954 that he had seen all the great center fielders of the previous 40 years, including

DiMaggio, Tris Speaker, and the rest; but none he had ever before seen was able to uplift a club like Mays.

Tim McCarver: "Mays is still the best I've ever seen. In so many ways he could beat you. Aaron resigned himself to more or less just be a hitter, but Mays never did that. He took tremendous pride in his baserunning, for example. He would use intimidation and mind games. He once told me when I was catching, that he cut Del Rice from his left knee to his left cheek once sliding home, but not to worry, that he didn't do that anymore. Remember, catchers used to plant that left leg, and were vulnerable from the knee to the ass. You bet he tried to use intimidation. He told pitcher [and opponent] Ray Sadecki that he would never get blocked off a base. Never. Willie had an interesting slide into catchers: not leaping, but he left his left foot up a little bit. It was a cross between a straight-in slide and hook slide, and boy, he had it down. The detail was so far ahead of other guys as far as baserunning, in a day when things were more conventional . . . nobody ran the bases like Mays."

I can't get off the fact that Mays missed those two seasons due to the army commitment. When one looks at his 1954 numbers, you can assume that Mays lost about 70 home runs while he was in the army. He would have been the one to break the Babe's career record of 714. (Hank Aaron was three years younger than Willie. He entered the majors in 1954 and never served in the army.)

Following 1954, Mays continued to put up excellent numbers, with no one watching him. The New York Giants played in the Polo Grounds in Harlem, and attendance was low. After the 1957 season, the Giants moved to San Francisco.

In his four full seasons in New York, Mays averaged 41 home runs per season. Willie would have padded his 660 career total plenty if the Giants had stayed in New York, moved to Minneapolis (where their Triple-A team was), or played almost anywhere else. Candlestick Park in San Francisco opened in 1960, and it did Willie no favors. The Polo Grounds had a lot of room in the outfield gaps, which helped Willie lead the league in triples each of the four full seasons he played there. Mays also led the league in stolen bases four straight seasons (1956–59).

The financially strapped Giants were not a good team in those final seasons in New York, but the addition of some good young players (Orlando Cepeda in 1958, Willie McCovey in 1959, and Juan Marichal in 1960) made the Giants annual contenders.

In his first year at Candlestick, Mays hit just 29 home runs. It was not like he had a bad year. His .319 average was still the third highest in the league, and he finished third in the MVP voting.

The 1961 Giants improved from fifth place to third, as McCovey and Marichal began complementing Mays. In 1962, with one game to go in the season, the Giants trailed the Dodgers by one game. Willie Mays hit his 47th home run of the season in the eighth inning to give the Giants a 2–1 victory over the expansion Astros. A few minutes later, the Cardinals' Gene Oliver hit a ninth-inning homer to defeat the Dodgers. That forced (like 11 years earlier) the Giants and Dodgers into a tie for the National League pennant, to be decided in a best-of-three playoff series.

In the first game of the series, Mays hit two home runs off of Sandy Koufax to lead the Giants to a 6–4 victory. In the second game, the Dodgers defeated the Giants 8–7, to once again set up a climactic final game.

In that deciding game, Los Angeles took a 4–2 lead into the ninth inning, but the Dodgers relievers issued four walks and the Giants scored four times to win the pennant.

The Yankees defeated the Giants in the World Series, winning Game 7 when Bobby Richardson caught a line drive off the bat of McCovey. Surprisingly, neither Mays nor the Yankees' Mickey Mantle did much in the Series.

Mays and the MVP

Willie was the best player in the National League in the late '50s and early '60s, but only won MVP honors in 1954 and 1965. He did finish second and third a few years. He should have won at least two more times.

1958 N.L. MVP Vote
1. Ernie Banks (.313, 47 HR for Chicago shortstop) 283 votes
2. Willie Mays (.347, 29 HR, 31 SB in first year out west) 185 votes

1960 N.L. MVP Vote
1. Dick Groat (.325 for Pittsburgh shortstop) 276 votes
2. Don Hoak (.282 for Pittsburgh third baseman) 162 votes
3. Willie Mays (.319, 29 HR, 25 SB) 155 votes

1962 N.L. MVP Vote
1. Maury Wills (record 104 stolen bases for L.A. shortstop) 209 votes
2. Willie Mays (49 HR, 18 SB) 202 votes

Mays lost MVPs to three different shortstops (Banks, Groat, and Wills). This was when outfielders in the National League included Hank Aaron, Frank Robinson, and Roberto

Clemente. No one had ever seen a shortstop belt almost 50 homers, or another one steal more than 100 bases. Maybe seeing Mays, Aaron, Robinson, and Clemente at the same time cancelled out their greatness in the minds of the voters.

The other factor for lack of votes, of course, was that Mays never really put together that one, singular signature season. Think about it. Babe had his 1927. Ted Williams had 1941. Mickey Mantle had 1956. Willie never had a bad season, but never did one season stand out apart from any of his others. He didn't have partial seasons due to injuries, or spectacular ones that stood out from the rest.

Also, unlike Mantle's Yankees, the Giants became bridesmaids. The Giants finished in second place in 1965, 1966, 1967, 1968, and 1970.

In 1965, Mays's second and final MVP season, the Giants went on a late-season 14-game winning streak and were 87–59 with 16 games to play. They had a four-game lead on September 20, but lost the pennant to the Dodgers.

Who's Better, Who's Best
Willie Mays or Mickey Mantle?
Career numbers:

	Batting Avg.	On-Base Avg.	Slugging Pct.	HR	RBI	At-Bats
Mays	.302	.384	.557	660	1,903	10,881
Mantle	.298	.421	.557	536	1,509	8,102

Following the 1965 season (each had played exactly 2,005 games):

	Batting Avg.	On-Base Avg.	Slugging Pct.	HR	RBI	At-Bats
Mays	.314	.389	.593	505	1,402	7,594
Mantle	.306	.426	.576	473	1,344	6,894

Both Mantle and Mays were born in 1931. Both were rookies in 1951. Following the 1965 season, they had both played the same number of games. Mantle walked about 500 times more than Mays, giving him a much higher on-base average. But the Mick also struck out a lot more than Willie, about 500 times more. Mays had 276 stolen bases at the time, to Mantle's 145. Mantle, however, had a better success rate stealing bases, and grounded into far fewer double plays than Willie.

Willie went through his career in good health. Mantle was basically done at 34 years old by the time that 1965 season was finished. Mickey had osteomyelitis, a bone disease, in one leg, even before he reached the majors. His Yankees career had been upset by serious injuries to both knees and one shoulder, a broken foot, and countless severe muscle tears.

Mantle had a Triple Crown season in 1956, reaching marks that not even the Say Hey Kid could touch: .353 batting average (Mays's best was .347), .464 on-base average (Mays's best, .425), and .705 slugging (Mays's best, .667). In that season, Mantle slugged 52 home runs and drove in 130. Mays never drove in more than 127 runs in a season.

Of course, Mantle had all those first-place finishes, as well. Mickey Mantle's teams won 12 pennants in his first 14 seasons. Mickey not only played in many World Series, he dominated them, setting several Series records.

Willie Mays played in 20 World Series games and batted only .239, without a single Series home run in his 71 at bats.

It's not so clear-cut, however. Mantle played his entire career in Yankee Stadium, which helped him. Willie Mays played from 1960 to 1972 in Candlestick Park in San Francisco, which hurt him. Mantle lost time to injury, but Mays lost those two seasons in the army.

Mickey Mantle did little following the 1965 season. In his last three seasons, he batted just .254 to bring his career average below .300. He did hit another 63 home runs, to push him past Jimmie Foxx on the all-time list and give him a career mark of 536.

Willie, on the other hand, kicked Mantle's ass at the back end of their careers. Following the '65 season, Mays added 155 home runs to give him 660 in his career. Mays also had 62 additional stolen bases in his late 30s. Mays only batted .274 in his last 3,200 at bats, which pushed his lifetime average down to .302.

In August of 1966, Mays hit his 535th home run, passing Jimmie Foxx, and trailed only Babe Ruth among career home run hitters. In September of 1969, Mays became the second player ever with 600 homers. In January of 1970, the *Sporting News* named Mays the Player of the Decade.

The finishing kick in Mays's career would have been more impressive, but Hank Aaron had an even more dramatic late-career flourish and wound up breaking Ruth's home run record. Aaron didn't catch Mays until June 1972, when they both had 648. A quarter-century later, Willie's good friend and godson Barry Bonds upped his own Hall of Fame production even further at a later age. It doesn't take away what Mays did.

A Closer Look at Mays's Stats

The numbers have changed in baseball, with an exponential jump in homers and slugging beginning in the 1990s. When Mickey Mantle (.593) and Willie Mays (.576) finished the 1965 season, their lifetime slugging percentages were topped only by Babe Ruth, Ted Williams, Lou Gehrig, and Jimmie Foxx. When Mays retired, he was seventh all time in slugging (dropping his last few years behind Rogers Hornsby and Stan Musial, while jetting past Mantle). Following the 1994 season, Mays was still seventh all-time in career slugging.

Following the 2004 season, Mays was 22nd in slugging, trailing such players as Jim Thome, Larry Walker, Albert Belle, and Juan Gonzalez. All I can say is . . . yechhhh.

Mays was the ideal ballplayer for fans, managers, teammates, and boys looking for heroes. He was the symbol of eternal youth, a man who played baseball because it was fun and gave people who watched him the same feeling of excitement and fun that sport is all about. Fans who remembered seeing pictures of an adult Mays playing stickball in the Harlem streets had trouble seeing Mays in the 1973 World Series falling down chasing a fly ball. Mays should never have grown old or had his abilities diminish. After all, he was Willie Mays. Like I said, he spoiled everyone for so many years.

A Better Analogy

Willie Mays and Oscar Robertson Oscar Robertson and Willie Mays were of the same generation. They starred in the 1960s, and were instrumental in paving the way for athletes after them to earn the really big money. Robertson played his last games in a losing 1974 NBA Finals series. Mays played his last games in a losing 1973 World Series.

When I did *Who's Better, Who's Best in Basketball?* almost every expert I talked to over a certain age told me that Oscar was the best of all time—better than Michael Jordan. The same thing happened to me this time around with baseball. I only saw Oscar and Willie play the last three or four years of their careers. They were not the same players they were in their prime, obviously, and I have to take the word of good friends like baseball historians Seymour Siwoff and the late Leonard Koppett about Mays's greatness.

Curt Gowdy: "Willie Mays was the best player I ever saw. He did everything well. I'd compare Willie to other athletes I covered like Jim Brown and Joe Montana and Oscar Robertson."

Bill White: "Willie Mays was the greatest player. When people talk about Mays, it's pretty clear they're talking the best all-around player. He could run, throw, hit for power . . . what couldn't he do?"

Bob Costas: "Mays was the best player I've ever seen. The most devastating force is Bonds of the last few years, but given everything, I'm not sure how to evaluate it."

Joe Buck: "My dad always told me that Mays was the best player he ever saw."

I respect the Big O, and I respect Willie Mays. They're not Michael Jordan or Barry Bonds. Sorry.

4

HANK AARON

As late as 1976, there was a player in major-league baseball who had played in the old Negro Leagues. Hank Aaron started his professional career with the Indianapolis Clowns in 1952.

He ended his career as the most underappreciated star in team sports history.

On the night that Aaron ended his great chase and passed Babe Ruth to become the leading home run hitter in baseball history, the baseball commissioner (Bowie Kuhn) was missing, pleading that a "previous commitment" required his presence in Cleveland.

In the final week of the 1973 season, when Aaron was at 712 home runs—two short of the Babe—he played before forty thousand empty seats a night in his home stadium in Atlanta.

When people did pay attention to Aaron's pursuit of the Babe, it was too often with racist letters, remarks, and threats. Aaron always felt that Mickey Mantle would have been the people's choice to hit number 715, had he stayed healthier.

Did the Braves appreciate him, after his 21 years of greatness? They didn't offer him a front-office position until after Aaron's retirement when new owner Ted Turner bought the team. The Braves traded him on November 2, 1974, to the Milwaukee Brewers for two nondescript players, Roger Alexander and Dave May. Milwaukee, where Aaron started his career with the Braves, was one of the few cities that Hank would approve a trade to. Aaron said in his autobiography that, with few exceptions (mainly an extended and impromptu ovation on the final day of the '73 season), there was no real warmth between the city of Atlanta and him. For the final game of the 1974 season, which was announced and understood to be Aaron's final game with the Braves after 21 years and 3,076 games, only eleven thousand fans showed up. Following his trade to Milwaukee, an exhibition game the following June in Atlanta was cancelled due to the fact that only a couple of hundred tickets were sold.

When he finally hung up his spikes for good following the 1976 season, he held most of major-league baseball's most important batting records. He had hit the most home runs (755). He had hit the most extra-base hits (1,477). He had 3,771 hits—which was second only to Ty Cobb at the time and is still third all-time nearly 30 years after his retirement. No one in history ever accumulated more total bases, or hit 30-plus home runs in as many seasons (15).

Hank Aaron never had peaks and valleys in his career. He had a long standard of excellence. He led the Braves to two pennants and the 1957 world championship. He won the MVP Award in 1957, but Stan Musial finished a very close second, meaning that Aaron almost went his entire career without ever being voted the best player in his league in any year.

Hank Aaron was born in Mobile, Alabama, in 1934. According to his wonderful 1991 autobiography, *I Had a Hammer*, when Aaron left Mobile to play with the Indianapolis Clowns, it was the first time he had ever been around white people. "I was barely 18 at the time, a raggedy kid who wore my sister's hand-me-down pants and had never been out of the black parts of Mobile." He was a skinny kid who batted cross-handed. He didn't play baseball in high school for a simple reason: his school didn't have a team. He caught the attention of a man named Ed Scott while playing in the recreation league. Scott managed a semipro team called the Mobile Black Bears. That was in 1951. Aaron's mom wouldn't let Hank travel with the team, but every Sunday they were home, he was their shortstop. Scott also did some scouting for the Indianapolis Clowns of the Negro American League. Aaron jumped at the chance to play for the Clowns for $200 a month, figuring he might never get a chance from the white scouts. Ed Scott's scouting report to the Clowns on the teenager: "Forget everything else about this player. Just watch his bat."

The Clowns played serious baseball, but had a few clowns on the squad to help them live up to their name. They were the Harlem Globetrotters of baseball, and when the Negro Leagues died out during the '50s, the Clowns stuck around by entertaining with gimmicks. Aaron was soon their cleanup hitter and drawing card, and the Milwaukee Braves offered him a contract.

In 1954, two months after his 20th birthday, Aaron earned the left fielder's job with the Braves after starter Bobby Thomson broke a leg. Aaron became the cleanup hitter, and hit the first 13 home runs of his career (12 on the road, only 1 at home) before breaking his ankle in early September, ending his season.

The next year, Aaron hit 40 home runs, his first of 15 seasons of 30 or more. Beginning in 1955, his second season, he batted .323 for the next 10 years—which led the major leagues over that period.

Highest Batting Average, 1955–1964

1. .323 Hank Aaron
2. .315 Willie Mays
3. .314 Mickey Mantle

Aaron won his first batting title in 1956, his third season. He came close to the Triple Crown in 1957, leading the league with 44 home runs and driving in 132 runs; but he trailed Stan Musial and Willie Mays in batting average. Aaron probably could have won the batting title as well, but he slumped after twisting his ankle when he stepped on a bottle thrown onto the field. He was a hitter, not just a home run hitter. Of all the players who hit as many as 500 home runs in their careers, only two others besides Aaron (Ted Williams and Mel Ott) never struck out 100 or more times in a season.

Commissioner Bud Selig: "I saw Hank Aaron play a lot in his early days in Milwaukee. He was truly one of the greats. In my generation, Aaron was the greatest ballplayer. When he came up in the '50s, he was a 175-pound guy—you never saw such quick wrists and power. It is hard to articulate if you never saw him play then, but I guarantee you never saw a better defensive player. He had a great arm. He had great instincts for the ball."

Aaron only went to two World Series in his career, and they were in back-to-back seasons, 1957 and 1958. In the 1957 Series, he led the Braves to victory over the Yankees by batting .393 with 3 home runs and 7 RBI.

Hank always felt 1959 was his best season. He slugged 39 home runs and drove in 123. That year, the Braves lost a three-game playoff with the Dodgers in a bid to win their third consecutive National League pennant. In 1959, Aaron led the league in slugging for the first of four times, duplicating the feat in 1961, 1963, and 1965. Now, let me tell you what's impressive about that. He led the league in slugging percentage four times *before* his Braves moved to Atlanta and began playing at Fulton County Stadium, otherwise known as "the Launching Pad."

Hank Aaron: Home/Road Breakdown

Milwaukee County Stadium	Atlanta's Fulton County Stadium
1954–65, 1975–76 (14 years)	1966–74 (8 years)
193 home runs	192 home runs
225 home runs hit on road	145 home runs hit on road

Aaron moved with his team from a stadium in Milwaukee that didn't do him any favors into a stadium that was standing a thousand feet above sea level in Atlanta, the highest park in the majors until the Colorado Rockies came along. Aaron's new stadium favored offense, especially long balls. When Atlanta moved its fences in, in 1969, Aaron was already 35 years old and seemingly past his prime. He then proceeded to hit 245 additional home runs. No other batter before Aaron ever hit as many late-career home runs, although Barry Bonds and Rafael Palmeiro have done it and then some in recent years.

Hank Aaron was a great ballplayer, and adjusted to the stadium that he played in. If the Braves had moved to a city with a ballpark that aided high batting averages, Aaron might have challenged Ty Cobb's record for most hits in a career, rather than Ruth's home run record.

Going into the 1969 season, Aaron's career batting average was .314, the highest of all active players.

Tony Kubek: "Aaron was not a pull hitter when his Braves played my Yankees teams in the World Series in 1957 and 1958. In his last seven or eight years, however, he became almost a dead-pull hitter. He did not hit those long home runs, but that's because he was a line drive hitter, not an upper-cutter."

In 1969, Aaron hit 44 home runs and led the Braves back into the postseason. He hit a home run in each of the League Championship Series games against the Mets. He followed that up with 38 homers the next year, and then 47. He still trailed Ruth and Willie Mays. Aaron said in his autobiography, "I had to work at not being envious of Willie. I always told myself that my time would come. There were certain things he did that I couldn't do as well, but I felt there were some things I could do a little better. I've never seen a better all-around ballplayer than Willie Mays, but I will say this: Willie was not as good a hitter as I was. No way."

Prior to the 1972 season, the Braves signed Aaron to a two-year contract that made him the first player in history to earn $200,000 in a season. On May 31, 1972, Aaron finally caught Mays at 648 career home runs. It took Aaron until June 10 to pass Willie for good. It was just a matter of time before Aaron would climb Mt. Ruth and stand alone among the home run leaders. Aaron finished with 34 home runs in '72, leaving him 41 shy of the record.

In 1973, Aaron hit 40 home runs, one of three Braves (Darrell Evans and Davey Johnson were the others) to do so. It left him one shy. The Braves planned to have Aaron break the Babe's record in Atlanta, which would mean sitting him for the first three games of the 1974 season. Commissioner Kuhn stepped in and ordered the Braves to start Aaron in at least two of the three games in Cincinnati.

Aaron hit a three-run homer off the Reds' Jack Billingham in his first swing of the 1974 season. That set the stage, a few nights later, for a Monday night game in April played on national television.

In the fourth inning of the Braves' home opener, before 55,775 fans in Atlanta, the 40-year-old Hank Aaron hit his 715th home run. It came 39 years after Ruth hit his

714th. One of the night's biggest heroes was Atlanta relief pitcher Tom House. House made a dazzling one-handed catch in the bullpen of the historic homer, and clutched it for dear life. Reports of the ball being worth $25,000 (a huge sum in 1974) meant little to House, who delivered the ball immediately to Aaron.

A few months later, Aaron would say that his breaking Babe Ruth's record probably was one of the greatest moments in the history of sports. He said this because the great majority of people thought that the record would never be broken. Aaron told Milton Richman of UPI in 1974 that "Ruth's record was one thing. What was more important to me, what I wanted to prove to everybody, was that a black player can play ball and function well under extreme pressure. I read that blacks can't think, that they don't have the mental equipment to think properly and perform during periods of great stress. Some of the ballplayers during Jackie Robinson's time—I remember who they were—held that belief I'm talking about. That's why I'm so happy for breaking it."

Commissioner Bud Selig: "Aaron's accomplishments have grown over time, over the last three decades. There is no doubt about it."

Aaron spent his final two seasons playing for Selig's Milwaukee Brewers, a recent franchise in the American League. In 1975, Aaron moved past Ruth in career RBI. On June 18, 1976, Aaron became the first player to hit 750 home runs. He retired with 755, which means he has held the record for 28 years (following the 2004 season).

He retired with numbers that surpassed—by a lot—those of men like Mays and Mantle and Musial. He wasn't flashy. He didn't hit the most impressive home runs. His cap didn't fly off. He just performed at a consistent level for so long that people didn't notice how good he was until it was nearly time to say good-bye. In the 1960s, Aaron hit more home runs, drove in more runs, scored more runs, and had a higher slugging percentage than anyone else. Throw in the fact that he had his greatest years in the 1950s and broke every meaningful record in the 1970s—and you can make a case that Aaron should be among the top five players of all time. His long quarter-century journey in baseball had him start as a Clown, and finish as the King. You just don't see that too often.

Most 30+ Home Run Seasons
1. 15 Hank Aaron
2. 14 Barry Bonds
3. 13 Babe Ruth
3. 13 Mike Schmidt

Career Extra-Base Hits
1. 1,477 Hank Aaron
2. 1,377 Stan Musial
3. 1,356 Babe Ruth
4. 1,343 Barry Bonds

Career RBI Leaders
1. 2,297 Hank Aaron
2. 2,210 Babe Ruth
3. 1,995 Lou Gehrig
4. 1,951 Stan Musial
5. 1,933 Ty Cobb

Who's Better, Who's Best
Hank Aaron or Sadaharu Oh?

People don't realize that Oh hit his 868 home runs in only 9,250 at-bats in Japan, compared to 12,364 major-league at-bats by Hank Aaron. If Oh had come up to the plate as often as Aaron, he'd have hit over 1,000 home runs. Oh's Japanese teams played only 130 games a year. Players in the U.S. get an extra 25 percent more games each year to compile numbers. And Oh walked more than any man in history. He never had as many as 500 at-bats in a season. In his best home run season, he slugged 55 home runs in only 390 at-bats. Don't forget, when Ichiro, Nomo, Shinjo, and Yoshii came to the majors, they pretty much duplicated their Japanese numbers. Oh would have had a tremendous major-league career, had he been so inclined.

On the other hand, Aaron faced better pitching. Hank did play in a hitter-friendly ballpark in Atlanta, but Aaron never had a short 288-foot wall to shoot for, as Oh did.

The fact is, Aaron did play in the major leagues, and he amassed numbers that were mind-boggling.

He won the Most Valuable Player Award in 1957, and was in the top three in voting no less than seven different seasons. He was in the top ten no less than 13 seasons.

He won two batting titles and was in the top ten in batting 12 different seasons. He led the league in total bases eight times, and is the all-time career leader. He scored 2,174 runs—third all-time. No one in major-league history had more home runs (755), extra-base hits (1,477), or runs batted in (2,297).

He had other skills as well. He won the Gold Glove for fielding excellence three times. He was in the top ten in stolen bases eight different seasons.

He even beat the great Japanese slugger in a home-run hitting contest, staged in Japan in 1974. Aaron wrote that Oh was much more of a national hero in Japan at the time than Aaron was in the States. Oh was 34 at the time, coming off a pair of Triple Crown seasons. Aaron was 40. Oh hit nine home runs in his 20 swings. Aaron hit his 10th on the 18th swing.

A Better Analogy

Hank Aaron and Sidney Poitier It is impossible to overstate the influence that ballplayer Henry Aaron and actor Sidney Poitier had on African-Americans and all Americans in the 1950s and 1960s. They arrived on the scene when racial tension was overt. They both had an integrity about them and handled themselves with dignity.

Poitier starred in dozens of movies, but was only nominated twice for an Academy Award and won only once (nominated for 1958's *The Defiant Ones* and won in 1963 for *Lilies of the Field*).

Aaron won only one MVP Award (1957), and made only two appearances in the World Series (1957, 1958).

Aaron wasn't the first black to win an MVP, and Poitier wasn't the first to win an Oscar; but they were both groundbreaking and active in their fields, and in the growing civil rights movement. They both made their voices heard. Poitier often refused parts that were demeaning to him and his race.

As influential as they both were in previous decades, their presence as elder statesmen today links them further.

WALTER JOHNSON

Not only is Walter Johnson the greatest pitcher the game has ever produced, but he was also one of the classiest men to ever grace the sport. Sportswriters from the late 1920s could not recall a single complaint he ever made over any umpire's decision. He played in the days before free agency and was forced to labor for some of the worst ball clubs in history. His Senators were so weak, they inspired a popular expression: "Washington—first in war, first in peace, and last in the American League."

Johnson was big for his time (6′1″) and threw his fastball with a submarine, or sidearm, delivery. Of course, he pitched before speed guns, but he was universally regarded as throwing the fastest ball in the game. Despite his sidearm delivery, he had very good control—almost too good for such a gentleman. Most fastballers have to instill a little fear into batters, right? Ty Cobb crowded the plate against Johnson, confident that he would never purposely hit a batter. Johnson was almost exclusively a fastball pitcher. Ty Cobb once said Walter's idea of a changeup was to just throw harder.

When he finished in 1927, he had averaged almost 39 starts per season for 21 years. He won 413 games and lost 280. Six seasons he led the league in complete games and victories. In 1912, he won 16 consecutive decisions. He struck out 3,497 batters—which stood as a record for decades, until the free-swinging modern days inflated pitchers' strikeout totals. He led the league in ERA five times and led the league in strikeouts 12 times. Just as I gave Ruth credit for being a tremendous pitcher, Walter Johnson gets positive marks for being a good-hitting pitcher. He batted .433 in 1925, at the age of 37. In his career, Johnson belted 24 home runs, drove in 255 runs, and had a career batting average of .235.

The Big Train completed 531 of the 666 games in which he started. And then, of course, there are his legendary shutout records.

Walter Johnson pitched in 175 shutout games in his career. He won 110 of them, but he lost 65. He lost 10 shutout games in 1909 alone. In fact, there was one month when Johnson lost five games in which his team didn't score a single run.

If the Senators gave Johnson a single run, he often made it stand up. He pitched in more 1–0 games than any other player ever. He won 38 games by a 1–0 score. He lost 26 more by the same score. He lost three of those 1–0 games to a Boston left-hander named Ruth. Anyway, Walter pitched in 64 games in which just a lone run was scored.

You deserve some comparison to judge how magnificent Johnson's 38 1–0 victories really are. The next winningest pitcher of 1–0 games was the great Pete Alexander. He won 17 games by a 1–0 score. Sandy Koufax won 10 by that score.

They didn't give out MVP awards or Cy Young awards in Johnson's day, but many historians believe that Johnson would have accumulated a lot of hardware: probably two MVP awards and seven Cy Youngs.

Reading about the early years of Walter Johnson is a little like reading *The Grapes of Wrath*. He was the son of Swedish farmers who had moved to Kansas by wagon train from Pennsylvania. In 1901, when Johnson was 14, the family moved to California hoping to strike it rich in the oil fields.

Late in the summer of 1907, Johnson reported to the Senators. He won only five games that rookie season and lost nine. It was not until 1910 that he began winning more than losing. By 1912, he was reaching a peak that no pitcher has reached since.

The Senators finished second in both 1912 and 1913, as Johnson went 69–19. It was the first time the franchise had ever finished higher than sixth place. The team won 56 more games than they lost those two seasons (181–125), and Johnson alone had won 50 more than he had lost.

In 1913, he won the pitcher's Triple Crown—leading the league in wins, ERA, and strikeouts. That year, he struck out 243 and walked only 38. In 1918, he again won the pitcher's Triple Crown, winning 23 games in a war-shortened season.

The Senators hired a player-manager named Bucky Harris and won their first pennant in 1924, when Johnson was 23–7 as a 37-year-old hurler with 18 years in the majors.

He got the nickname "the Big Train" from sportswriter Grantland Rice, who compared the speed of his pitches with the fastest transportation around at the time. I can only imagine what his career would have been like if he had played under modern conditions. He might have been made into a relief pitcher and devastated hitters with his fastball in the late innings. He most certainly would have played out his contract and played for a winning team earlier in his career.

The First Memorabilia Collection
Walter Johnson started a record 14 opening days for the Washington Senators, throwing seven shutouts and winning nine opening-day assignments. In 1910, President William

Howard Taft started a tradition by throwing out the first ball on opening day. Johnson collected the autographed "first" baseballs of Presidents Taft, Wilson, Harding, Coolidge, and Hoover. The entire collection was given to the Hall of Fame by his son after Walter died in 1946.

The Reward for All the Losing: The Perfect Ending

The Senators won the 1924 pennant and advanced to the World Series against the New York Giants. The nation's baseball fans pulled mightily for Johnson to get a chance at pitching in a Fall Classic. He had pitched his heart out for 18 long years, always with the same team, pitching as hard and as brilliantly when the team was bad as in the rare days they contended. During Johnson's long career, he never complained. He probably was the reason the nation's capital still had a baseball team. Going into the Series, the only question was if Johnson was past his prime. Although he was 23–7 during the season, he completed "only" 20 of his 38 starts.

Johnson started the first game of the Series, and pitched all 12 innings of the extra-inning tilt, but lost 4–3. It wasn't vintage Big Train. He allowed 14 hits and walked six in the 12 innings. Four days later, he started the fifth game and lost 6–2, pitching another complete game. In this one, Johnson fared even worse, allowing 13 hits over nine innings. Fortunately, fate reversed itself in a classic (and perhaps baseball's most theatrical) Game 7.

Walter Johnson was called on in relief in the ninth inning of Game 7, with the score tied 3–3. After he retired the first batter, Frankie Frisch hit a triple. Johnson got out of trouble by retiring the next two batters.

The 3–3 tie continued until the bottom of the 12th inning. With one out, the Senators' Earl McNeely grounded to third and the ball took an inexplicable hop over Giants third baseman Freddie Lindstrom's head, driving in the winning run. Fittingly, Johnson was the winning pitcher in this 4–3 game, which gave Washington its first title.

The Washington fans went crazy. In the twilight of Johnson's great career, the good guy caught a lucky break. No one deserved one more.

The Next Season: Reality Bites

Johnson didn't end his career with his Game 7 win in the 1924 World Series. In fact, Johnson came back and won 20 games in 1925, finishing fourth in the league in ERA at 3.07. The Senators made it back to the World Series, this time against the Pittsburgh Pirates. Johnson started, completed, and won the first and fourth games of the Series. The Senators led three games to one. At the time, no team had ever rebounded from that deficit to win.

Pittsburgh won the next two games, and Walter Johnson had the ball in his hand for Game 7, with a chance to win consecutive championships in his late 30s, after a frustrating career (shades of John Elway, anyone?). The Senators even staked Johnson to a four-run lead in the first inning. Walter didn't have his best stuff, though, and the lead was just 6–3 by the fourth inning. The Pirates scratched for another run and trailed 6–4 going into the seventh. Washington shortstop Roger Peckinpaugh muffed a pop fly off the bat of Eddie Moore. He would score on a Max Carey double. With two outs, Pie Traynor tied up the game with a triple, but was thrown out at the plate attempting to stretch it into an inside-the-park home run.

Peckinpaugh went from goat to hero when he hit a rare home run to give the lead back to Washington. Johnson retired the first two batters in the bottom of the eighth inning, but then he ran out of gas. He lost the lead for the second time in two innings. This time, there would be no miracle bad hop or storybook finish.

Johnson would return to pitch through 1927, allowing him to surpass 400 wins. He was one of the first five players inducted into the Hall of Fame.

Who's Better, Who's Best
Walter Johnson or Cy Young?

Cy Young won 511 games, which is a lot more than Johnson, but I have Johnson ranked well above him. Young was born just after the Civil War and was 17 years older than the Big Train. Cy Young was finished in the majors by 1911, when Johnson was just beginning his brilliant career. Young won most of his games before 1900, when the rules of the game and playing conditions were just not as demanding. Johnson not only pitched in the teens, but for much of the 1920s, facing the likes of Cobb, Ruth, and Gehrig.

A lot of people have compared Tom Seaver with Walter Johnson—mainly because of their wholesome images and likeability, but also because both had winning percentages that far exceeded those of their teams. I loved Tom Seaver as a pitcher, but he is not in Walter Johnson's company. Nobody is. Nobody has ever combined his success with his longevity and reputation.

TY COBB

Ty Cobb was baseball's best hitter. He couldn't pitch like Walter Johnson, hit home runs like Babe Ruth, play the outfield like Willie Mays, live up to enormous expectations like Mickey Mantle, or blaze trails like Jackie Robinson. But he was the greatest batter in baseball history. Only Pete Rose has more career hits than the Georgia Peach. Rose's final hit was number 4,256—putting him only 67 hits ahead of Cobb. But Rose also batted 2,619 more times than Ty. Like Rose, Cobb was not a super athlete; rather, he had a great desire to win.

The nation's first famous sportswriter, Grantland Rice, began receiving letters boasting how good a 17-year-old prospect named Ty Cobb was during the summer of 1904. "This Cobb has great talent and may be one of the coming stars of baseball," wrote Rice. It turned out that the letters Rice received were written by Ty Cobb himself. Cobb became a Detroit Tiger in 1905, just three weeks before Cobb's mother was arrested for the fatal shooting of his father (Cobb's dad, a Georgia state senator, attempting to catch his wife in an unfaithful act, climbed through the bedroom window of his home and was shot to death by his wife, who mistook him for an intruder).

It's a good thing Ty was a tireless self-promoter, because his friends were few and far between. He played with a chip on his shoulder and was extremely disliked.

How Disliked Was Cobb?

In the 1907 season, when Detroit manager Hughie Jennings took over the reins, his first plan of action was to move Cobb from center to right field so he and the left fielder, Marty McIntyre, would be separated. Sam Crawford was another teammate with an open dislike of Cobb, saying, "He's still fighting the Civil War, and he sees us as just damn Yankees."

Researchers Nicholas Acocella and Donald Dewey wrote that "Cobb's defensiveness about being a southern Protestant on a Detroit team filled with Irish and German Catholic northerners led to the conflicts."

In 1907, Cobb got into an argument with a black groundskeeper about the condition of the spring-training field in Augusta, and he wound up choking the man's wife when she sought to intervene. In 1909, he slapped a black elevator operator in Cleveland, eventually getting into a brawl with knives. In 1914, Cobb attacked a Detroit butcher for reputedly insulting his wife and then used the butt of his gun against a black shop assistant. By the end of one of his earlier seasons, Cobb was granted a couple of weeks' leave from the Tigers after he suffered a nervous breakdown and entered a Detroit sanitarium, where he remained for a month.

Jimmy Cannon, who wrote for New York papers beginning in 1936, frequently with the lead, "Nobody asked me, but," once wrote: "He was the strangest of all our national sports heroes. But not even his disagreeable character could destroy the image of his greatness as a ballplayer. Ty Cobb was the best. That seemed to be all he ever wanted."

The incorrigible Cobb was not only hated by teammates, but by opponents. The most sensational example of the contempt that surrounded Cobb is probably the controversial 1910 batting race. In 1910, the American League batting title came down to Cobb versus Cleveland's Nap Lajoie in the final days of the season. On the season's last day, St. Louis played a doubleheader in Cleveland. Cobb was sidelined that day, but had a comfortable lead in the batting race. In a very suspicious defensive move, St. Louis manager Jack O'Connor ordered his third baseman, Red Corrigan, to play on the rim of the outfield grass against Cleveland. In response to that strategy, and accepting St. Louis's invitation, Lajoie collected eight hits in the doubleheader, six bunt singles down the third-base line and a "triple" that was lost in the sun, bringing Lajoie the batting title.

Now Ty Cobb, he wasn't too pleased about losing out on the batting title. The matter was investigated, and the St. Louis manager was barred from the game, though Lajoie's average stood at .384 and the eight hits were allowed to count. The story of Cobb and Lajoie took a few more twists afterward: a recount of Cobb's stats revealed that a scorer's error had deprived him of two hits; those hits were restored to his season total, and American League president Ban Johnson officially recognized Cobb as the batting champion.

In 1981, *Sporting News* researcher Paul MacFarlane came across a hit erroneously attributed to Cobb in 1910 that, when subtracted, returned the batting title to Lajoie. Despite the evidence, Commissioner Bowie Kuhn rejected the arguments and insisted that Cobb was still the batting champ of 1910. Still, baseball encyclopedias like *Total Baseball* credit Cobb with 11 batting titles, but the plaque in the Hall of Fame reads that he has 12.

More on the Character of Ty Cobb

You didn't want to heckle Ty Cobb. In 1912, Cobb climbed into the stands and began punching and kicking a heckler. Cobb reached his limit, he told reporters afterward, when the fan called him "a half-nigger." Informed that the heckler had lost four fingers in a printing press accident, Cobb shrugged that he didn't care "if the guy has no feet." When Cobb was suspended before an investigation into the matter, all 19 of Cobb's teammates staged a walkout before the next game at Philadelphia's Shibe Park.

Faced with a $1,000 fine for forfeiting a game, Tigers manager Hugh Jennings immediately signed eight students from St. Joseph's College of Philadelphia and one sandlotter. The nine replacement Tigers went down to a 24–2 defeat in Philly to the Athletics. Cobb actually lessened his sentence after convincing his teammates to take the field and end their boycott the next day.

Given what we know about Cobb, would we guess that in World War I he volunteered for service in the U.S. Army's chemical warfare division after the 1918 season?

Given what we know about Cobb, would we guess that Ty Cobb was the first baseball player to get rich off endorsements? He endorsed a chewing gum, a brand of suspenders, and underwear. In September of 1907, with Cobb's Tigers on their way to the World Series, Coca-Cola began running an advertising campaign featuring the 20-year-old Cobb. An ad showed the Georgian at the plate and claimed that "Coca-Cola will put you back into the game—relieve the thirst and cool you off."

It was the beginning of a lifelong association with the soft-drink company for Cobb. Another ad read: "Ty Cobb says: On days we play a doubleheader, I always find that a drink of Coca-Cola between the games refreshes me to such an extent that I can start the second game feeling as if I had not been exercising at all, in spite of my exertions in the first."

Cobb took a loan against future baseball earnings to buy his first stock in the Coca-Cola Company in 1918 at the suggestion of Robert Woodruff, who would run the company for six decades. He became one of the first athletes to become independently wealthy. According to Dan Holmes, the Web manager of the National Baseball Hall of Fame, the Hall has a special 1986 Coca-Cola bottle that was put out celebrating the 100th anniversary of Cobb's birth and the birth of Coca-Cola.

As much as Cobb was hated by teammates, opponents, and fans, he had to have undying support from an equal amount of people. Among southerners, many of whom shared his views, he must have been quite the pitchman.

Given what we know about Cobb and the fact that many of his teammates hated him, would we guess that in 1920 he was made the manager of the Tigers? After all, in all his years as a player, he never once played on a team that won the World Series.

Given what we know about Cobb, would we guess that in his later years he helped to establish scholarships and funded a medical center in his father's name in Royston, Georgia?

Not everything is black and white, although it might have appeared that way to Ty.

Who's Better, Who's Best
Ty Cobb or Walter Johnson?

Ty Cobb played for 24 seasons, from 1905 to 1928. Cobb was almost exactly two years older than Walter Johnson, who played from 1907 to 1927. They were two of the original five players enshrined in baseball's Hall of Fame. So which of the early stars should be ranked ahead of the other?

I found the following note on Cobb's performance against Johnson by accident, from the May 30, 1915, *New York Times*:

> Walter Johnson has faced Cobb in the capacity of pitcher just 133 times, and of that many times at bat the champion batsman of the American League has been sent back to the bench 109 times hitless, the gentleman from Georgia failing to swat the ball in his usual consistent and blithesome manner when facing the consistent Mr. Johnson. So Walter Johnson has the honor of being about the only hurler to hold the fiery Cobb in subjugation. In the 133 times that Cobb faced the Washington star, he made 31 base hits, 9 runs; just six of the hits were better than singles (3 doubles, 3 triples). These figures give Cobb a batting average for the eight seasons a palling acquaintance of Mr. Johnson of .233.

Now, it is impossible to figure out how Cobb did against Johnson after that, but the point is this: in Cobb's peak years, he couldn't figure out the fastballing ace of the Senators.

Ty Cobb Versus Walter Johnson, 1907–1914

Cobb's eight-year batting totals	4,182 at-bats	1,578 hits	.377 average
At-bats versus anyone but Walter Johnson	4,049 at-bats	1,547 hits	.382 average
At-bats versus Walter Johnson	133 at-bats	31 hits	.233 average

In the official Ty Cobb website, one can find the following quote from Cobb concerning his first meeting with Johnson:

> On August 2, 1907, I encountered the most threatening sight I ever saw in the ball field. He was only a rookie, and we licked our lips as we warmed up for the first game of a doubleheader in Washington. Evidently, manager Pongo Joe Cantillon of the Nats had picked a rube out of the cornfields of the deepest bushes to pitch against us. . . . He was a tall, shambling galoot of about twenty with arms so long they hung far out of his sleeves and with a side arm delivery that looked unimpressive at first glance. . . . One of the Tigers imi-

tated a cow mooing and we hollered at Cantillon: "Get the pitchfork ready, Joe—your hayseed's on his way back to the barn." . . . The first time I faced him I watched him take that easy windup—and then something went past me that made me flinch. The thing just hissed with danger. We couldn't touch him . . . every one of us knew we'd met the most powerful arm ever turned loose in a ball park.

Who's Better, Who's Best
Ty Cobb or Honus Wagner?

Wagner was the dominant player for the decade between 1900 and 1910. Cobb was the best in baseball between Wagner and Ruth. As great as Cobb was, Wagner was considered the better player. Honus had the ability to play anywhere defensively but spent most of his time at shortstop, making him a more valuable commodity than the outfielder Cobb.

In 1907, Cobb won his first batting title, hitting .350 and leading the Tigers to the American League pennant. In the World Series, Detroit fell in five games to the Chicago Cubs, with Cobb held to only four hits in 20 at-bats. The Tigers (with an outfield of Cobb, Sam Crawford, and Davy Jones) won the pennant and represented the A.L. in the World Series in 1908 and 1909 as well.

In the 1909 season, Cobb batted .377. The Series that fall featured a classic matchup between Cobb and the Pirates' Honus Wagner, another of the original five Hall of Famers. Cobb was quoted as saying, "I'll show that Kraut," and threatened to spike Wagner on the base paths. Wagner was 35 years old at the time; Cobb was 22. Can you guess what happened?

Wagner hit .333 in the Series. The brash Cobb hit only .233 as the Tigers lost their third consecutive World Series.

Ty Cobb, 1907–1909
Regular Season: Cobb batted .350 in 1,759 at-bats
Three World Series: Cobb batted .262 in 65 at-bats

Wagner was already 29 years old by the time the first World Series was played in 1903. At the age of 35, his performance in the 1909 Series helped the Pirates defeat the Tigers for the championship (he got on base 12 times in the seven games, drove in six runs, and stole six bases). Wagner won the battle, but Cobb's play the next 20 years (against increasingly superior competition) pushes him just past Wagner in these pages.

A Better Analogy

Ty Cobb and Babe Ruth Ty Cobb played baseball one way, and Babe Ruth came along and played it entirely differently. The two coexisted for a while, but by 1920 the people had made a choice for Ruth's brand of ball. You should think of it like this: Cobb (and his style of play) was like cassette tapes. Ruth (and his style of play) was like compact discs. Within a few short years, everyone wanted compact discs.

In 1919, Babe Ruth began to come on strong as a home run hitter, the very first of the kind that baseball had ever known. Cobb abhorred Ruth's power game, and when he saw fans becoming enamored with the Babe, he was afraid that the "inside style" of bunting, taking the extra base, and hitting the ball to gaps that he had perfected would fall by the wayside.

When Ruth broke the home run record in 1919 with 29, and started 1920 on pace to destroy his own record, it meant trouble for Cobb and his "brand" of baseball. When Cobb and the Tigers showed up in New York to play the Yankees for the first time that season, the writers billed it as a showdown between two stars of competing styles of play. Ruth had two homers and a triple in the series; Cobb got only one single the entire series. One *New York Times* reporter wrote, "Cobb was in eclipse for the first time since he began to show his remarkable ability. Ruth has stolen all of Cobb's thunder."

As Ruth's popularity grew, Cobb became increasingly hateful of the Sultan of Swat. Cobb saw Ruth not only as a threat to his style of play, but also to his style of life. While Cobb preached ascetic self-denial, Ruth gorged on hot dogs, beer, and women. Cobb stole home a record 50 times. Ruth just walked home, jogging lightly after a powerful blast. Perhaps what angered Cobb the most was that despite Ruth's total disregard for his physical condition and traditional baseball, he was still an overwhelming success and brought fans to the ballpark in record numbers to see him set records.

Rob Neyer wrote in 2003 in his *Big Book of Baseball Lineups* that "For something like a half a century, it was Cobb—and not Ruth—who was considered the game's greatest player ever; when he was passed, it was by Willie Mays." First of all, let's think about that.

Cobb came up in 1905, and had a 10-year head start on Ruth. Babe came into his prime as an everyday player in the early 1920s. But that's nonsense that Cobb was considered the best ever for 50 years. Cobb was not considered the best in the game until about 1909. Ty Cobb was the gold standard until Ruth pulled into the station. By the mid-'20s, Ruth had pulled nearly even (at the very least) with Cobb.

In early 1936, when the first-ever voting for the Hall of Fame was announced, five players were enshrined: Cobb, Ruth, Wagner, Christy Mathewson, and Walter Johnson.

Cobb had seven votes more than Ruth and Wagner. This is how the Associated Press reported it:

> Of 226 ballots cast by players and writers, the Georgia Peach received 222, or four less than a unanimous vote. Ruth and Wagner received 215 each. . . . The committee in charge of the vote tabulation, figured the struggle for ballots among the moderns (players who starred from 1900 on) would be a two-man battle between Cobb and Ruth. When the first 100 votes were counted, both Cobb and the home run king were unanimous. Ruth was the first to fall out, losing a vote from a writer who had watched him hang up some of his greatest records. The committee was amazed. Vote counting stopped momentarily for a discussion on how anyone could leave the great Ruth off the list of immortals.

Does that make it sound like Cobb was widely considered clearly the best player over Ruth?

What I guess happened is one of two things (or perhaps both). Certain writers (and/or players) might have wanted Ruth to wait, as they wanted to enshrine the earlier stars first (that would also explain the support for Mathewson and Johnson). Everyone voting knew that the *same* names would be submitted in another poll the very next year. The other possibility is that the last images of Ruth to players and writers in 1936 were closer to an exiting Dennis Rodman than to Superman.

Cobb was an unfriendly bigot, a racist who was suspended for everything from going into the stands and beating a physically disabled fan to conspiring to fix the final game of the 1919 season. Whatever he did, though, he took baseball seriously. Cobb spent his final years in a Philadelphia Athletics uniform after being picked up by legendary manager Connie Mack. Cobb received an opportunity to manage in the majors, unlike Ruth. By the end of his career, Ruth was just a sideshow attraction hired to boost attendance.

Ruth and Cobb were clearly the two best players of the first half-century of the major leagues. But there is no way that Cobb was a better player.

(I'm not looking forward to defending my position on this matter to Cobb one day. After all, it will be hot enough down there.)

TED WILLIAMS

He couldn't pitch like Babe Ruth. He couldn't run and throw like Willie Mays. He didn't have the versatility of Honus Wagner. He couldn't run the bases like Ty Cobb. He couldn't play left field like Barry Bonds.

He couldn't stay healthy like Gehrig, losing time late in his career to broken collarbones and assorted injuries. He couldn't switch-hit like Mantle. He couldn't handle the media or switch positions for someone else like Alex Rodriguez.

All he ever wanted, though, was to walk down the street and have people comment, "There goes the greatest hitter that ever lived."

Ted Williams was from San Diego, California. He practically raised himself while his mother devoted practically all her time to the Salvation Army and his father kept busy night and day in his photo shop. Williams was a left-handed batter, and was signed at the age of 17 to play in the Pacific Coast League. Hall of Famer Eddie Collins made a trip to the West Coast to sign Williams for his Boston Red Sox.

Williams developed his theories on hitting early on. He emulated Lefty O'Doul, whom he first saw take batting practice through a knothole. He listened to Rogers Hornsby, who briefly managed him in Minneapolis in the spring of 1938. He listened to Collins, a career .333 batter. In his early life, all Williams did was practice hitting. He made a science out of it.

Williams worked at baseball, played it, and lived it. He knew more about opposing pitchers than any of the other players or managers. He studied the wind and air currents. He studied the different pitching mounds around the league.

He did have talent to work with his desire. He also had incredible vision. Navy doctors who gave him his entry examination said his eyesight would occur only six times in one hundred thousand people.

Then called simply "the Kid," Williams made his debut on April 20, 1939. That was also the first year that a major-league game was televised. Like *The Wizard of Oz*, which also debuted that spring, Williams's career began in black and white and soon turned to color. Lou Gehrig retired in June of Williams's rookie season, and a new modern era was under way. Williams was called lanky. He wasn't built like a power hitter, like Babe Ruth or his teammate Jimmie Foxx.

In his rookie season, Williams batted .327 (seventh in the league), had an on-base average of .436 (sixth), and slugged .609 (fourth). He hit 31 home runs and drove in 145 runs in 149 games. He was fourth in the voting for the Most Valuable Player Award—at the age of 20.

A funny thing was happening to baseball. Williams came in as the golden age of hitting was coming to an end. Ted swam against the tide, as you can see from the following table:

	American League Batting Average	**Ted Williams**
1939	.291	.327
1940	.284	.344
1941	.278	.406
1942	.269	.356

After four years in the majors, Williams was 23 years old and had the following numbers:

Ted Williams: First 4 Seasons		
.356	127 HR	515 RBI
4th in MVP voting in 1939		
14th in MVP voting in 1940		
2nd in MVP voting in 1941		
2nd in MVP voting in 1942		

He came into baseball as a 19-year-old rookie, and was the best player behind only the great DiMaggio, Foxx, and Feller. In 1941, Williams batted .406 to become the first .400 batter in the majors since Bill Terry in 1930.

1941

Williams played 143 games in 1941. Despite being walked 147 times, he got hits in 121 games—meaning he went hitless in only 22 games. He batted .406 with 37 home runs, 120 RBI, and 135 runs scored.

He was the last batter to hit .400 in a single season, but he did so much more than bat .400. He got on base over 55 percent of the time. His .551 on-base average that season set a major-league record that would stand for more than six decades, until Barry Bonds broke it. He hit a game-ending home run to win the All-Star Game.

Not only did Williams hit over .400—he did it the honorable way, by not sitting out to protect his average. He came into the final day of the season batting .39955, which could have been rounded off to .400. He played in both games of the season-finale doubleheader, getting six hits in eight at-bats against left-handed pitchers he had not seen before.

But at the end of the season, MVP voters preferred Joe DiMaggio (.357, 30 HR, and a record 56-game hitting streak) over Williams's .406.

I can't overstate how proficient a hitter Williams was. Try this on for size, however: in 1941, Williams walked 147 times and struck out only 27 times.

1942

Williams followed his .400 season with a .356 average, which once again led the league. In many ways, he had as good a season as the year before. Williams led the league in batting, home runs, and RBI to win the Triple Crown.

	Runs	Hits	HR	RBI	Walks	Batting Avg.	On-Base Avg.	Slugging Pct.
1941	135	185	37	120	147	.406	.551	.735
1942	141	186	36	137	145	.356	.499	.648

Williams somehow finished second again in the MVP voting, this time to Joe Gordon, who batted .322 with 18 home runs as a middle infielder for the Cleveland Indians.

Then, following that 1942 season, Williams missed the next three seasons due to World War II.

1946

Williams, now 27 years old, returned from overseas in his prime. He won his first MVP Award, and the Red Sox won the pennant for the only time in his career. In 1946, Williams batted .342 with 38 HR, 123 RBI, and a slugging percentage of .667. Put another way, over 47 percent of his hits were for extra bases. Plus, he got on base 50 percent of the time. Again, he did it his way, by refusing to let the defense dictate to him how to hit.

On July 14, in the first game of a doubleheader against the Indians, Williams thumped three homers and drove in eight runs. When Williams went to bat in the second game, Cleveland shortstop-manager Lou Boudreau concentrated six men in right field. This is how the defense shifted: Boudreau moved from shortstop to the normal second-base position. The second baseman moved closer to first base, but played on the outfield grass. The third baseman played right on second base, while the left fielder moved in to about 30 feet beyond the normal shortstop position. With the shift, Cleveland dared "the Splendid Splinter" to bunt or punch the ball to left, something Williams stubbornly refused to do.

Curt Gowdy (former Red Sox announcer): "Ted Williams could hit to left field, and hit the Green Monster consistently—but he said that if he did that, all he would hit were singles. Williams thought that if he did hit to left field, it would soon harm his swing—and people didn't come to the park to watch Ted Williams hit singles.

"He had a natural hitting style, and it worked for him. He didn't care if they packed eight fielders to one side. He was still going to pull the ball."

Williams, the son of a gun, refused to give in to the shift, which other teams then copied. Only once did Williams take advantage of the strategy. In one famous at-bat in September 1946, when the Sox and Indians were locked in a scoreless duel, and Williams punched the ball over the head of left-fielder Fat Pat Seerey and chugged around the bases, sliding home with the game's only run. Williams's one and only inside-the-park homer clinched the pennant for the Red Sox.

In the World Series against the Cardinals, however, Williams suffered a slump and collected only five singles in 25 at-bats. The Red Sox lost in seven games to St. Louis.

Only DiMaggio and another Cleveland middle infielder (this time, Lou Boudreau) finished ahead of Williams in MVP voting in 1947 and 1948: in 1947, just Joe D., and in 1948, Boudreau and DiMaggio. In 1947, the Splendid Splinter once again won the Triple Crown (.343, 32 HR, 114 RBI), but lost the MVP voting, 202–201, to DiMaggio. The papers called Williams Boston's temperamental "problem child." The *New York Times* reported, "The scribes apparently estimated DiMaggio the more valuable team worker."

In 1948, the Indians and Red Sox finished tied after the regular season, and played a single-game playoff to see which of the clubs would represent the American League in the World Series. The game was played in Boston, and Williams only managed one single in four at-bats. To add to that, he capped his day by muffing a fly ball that gave the Indians an insurance run in the eighth inning of a 6–3 game.

Williams had his best power numbers in 1949, when he hit 43 home runs, drove in 159 runs (in 155 games), and won his second MVP.

Williams just missed winning the batting title on the final day of the 1949 season, the same day his Red Sox lost the pennant to the Yankees in a dramatic showdown at Yankee Stadium. In Boston's 5–3 loss, Ted went hitless to finish the year at .3428. Meanwhile, Detroit's George Kell went 2–3 against St. Louis to finish at .3429 and win the batting crown.

At this point, Williams had played eight full seasons and had won two MVP awards, finished second three times, and finished third once. He led the league in batting four of those seasons, and finished second in 1946 and 1949.

Despite missing three seasons, Williams still led all major leaguers in home runs in the 1940s. Of course, most of the other big stars also missed time because of World War II, including DiMaggio, Johnny Mize, and Hank Greenberg.

In 1951, Ted once reached base in 16 consecutive plate appearances (two singles, four homers, nine walks, and one hit-by-pitch).

He was the only major-league star to lose time to both World War II and the Korean War, when the 33-year-old left-fielder was once again sent overseas, forcing him to miss virtually the entire 1952 and 1953 seasons. Williams returned to play the final 37 games of the 1953 season, and pounded out 12 home runs in his first 75 at-bats following 16 months in the service. He hit a home run as a pinch hitter in only his second at-bat, exactly a month after he landed in the United States after flying jet planes over Communist territory in Korea.

In 1954, Ted broke his collarbone within minutes of taking the field in spring training, and the 35-year-old slugger did not return until May 16, missing the first five weeks of the season. He wasted no time, collecting eight hits in his first nine at-bats and driving in seven runs in a doubleheader at Detroit. Williams hit .345 for the season, higher than league leader Bobby Avila's .341, but Williams was walked 136 times in 117 games and had only 386 at-bats. He was 14 short of the 400 at-bats required to qualify for the batting title. Because of the controversy, the rule was later changed to 400 plate appearances rather than times at bat.

Williams was 36 years old, the age when most of his contemporaries had retired. He contemplated retirement, until a fan pleaded with him not to, explaining that his career numbers did not guarantee him entry into the Hall of Fame, certainly not on the first year of eligibility.

Ted Williams, 1955–1957					
1955	.356	28 HR	83 RBI	.703 slugging	4th in MVP voting
1956	.345	24 HR	82 RBI	.605 slugging	6th in MVP voting
1957	.388	38 HR	87 RBI	.731 slugging	2nd in MVP voting

Williams began his career in the shadow of Yankee Joe DiMaggio, finishing second to him in the MVP voting the year he batted .406. He ended his career in the shadow of Yankee Mickey Mantle, finishing second to him in the MVP voting the year he batted .388 at the age of 38.

In August of 1956, Williams was fined $5,000 (tying the largest sum a player had ever been fined to that point) for spitting at fans and newspaper writers during a game with the Yankees. At the end of the 11th inning of the game, Williams first missed a fly ball and then made an outstanding catch for the third out on another drive. He started spitting as he neared the Red Sox dugout. The United Press reported Williams as saying, "I'm not a bit sorry for what I did. I'd spit again at the same fans who booed me today. If I had the money, I wouldn't be out there tomorrow."

Interestingly, umpires were never one of his targets. He was always one of their favorites. He never squawked at a call. Umpires respected his eyes, and probably were more than a little intimidated by "the greatest hitter in the world."

His one regret in his career was that his team, the Red Sox, only made it to the World Series once while he was in the lineup—in 1946. He played poorly in the Series. Still, he was the dominant athlete in Boston in the 20th century, more so than greats such as Bill Russell and Bobby Orr.

Williams retired in 1960, going out hitting .316 in his final season and hitting a home run in his final at-bat ("Hub Fans Bid Kid Adieu," wrote John Updike).

Was Ted Williams the greatest hitter of all time? Curt Gowdy, who has been around baseball for 60 years, claims he was the greatest he ever saw. Tony Kubek told me the same thing. Joe Cronin, who was a contemporary of Ruth's and Gehrig's, and Williams's manager in the 1950s, said, "Williams has proved beyond a shadow of the doubt he belongs in a special class with Babe Ruth and Lou Gehrig. He is as great as the Babe when it comes to combining batting average with slugging. Ruth hit more homers, but struck out more. You must remember that Ruth, as well as Gehrig, played in parks that fitted their special talents. Yankee Stadium had that short right-field fence. It can never be said that Fenway Park, with the most distant right field in the majors, was built for Ted Williams."

Who's Better, Who's Best
Ted Williams or Barry Bonds?

Tim McCarver: "Barry Bonds is a top-five player of all time. . . . I think he has his detractors personally. . . . The biggest reason Barry is not voted higher in most people's eyes is people don't like him . . . they do it begrudgingly and reluctantly because of the way he treats people. Ted Williams, unlike Barry, was impish . . . both terribly insecure people, and that accounts for so much of their personalities. In terms of personality, they were frenetic, in the way that the late Judy Garland was. In other words, Judy Garland was frenetic; you could see when she performed, she was nervous . . . you could see how Williams and Bonds treated people, how insecure they were as well. Williams was more of a little-boy personality. Barry Bonds had the bitterness . . . not the truculence. . . . I said in the early '90s that Bonds was a better left fielder than Williams overall . . . and now it's hands down, not even close."

The Elias Sports Bureau used a complex calculation in 1999 to figure out how much Williams lost by his time spent in service to his country. By restoring what he lost in those periods, they figure that Ted would have wound up with 3,024 games played, 3,617 hits, 712 home runs, 2,589 RBI, and 2,916 walks. Of course, one has to assume that (a) he would have remained healthy in those five lost years, and (b) he wouldn't have retired earlier than 1960, having attained his career goals.

But let's not get carried away with the possibilities. Williams was better than Bonds and Ruth and Cobb at on-base average. He got on base over 48 percent of the time (.483). He led the league in this stat 12 times. In 1941, Williams had an on-base percentage of .551. That remained the record for 61 years, when Barry Bonds broke it.

Since 1901, there have been 14 seasons in which a player had an on-base average of .499 or better. Babe Ruth did it five times, Ted Williams four times, and Bonds did it four times. Mickey Mantle did it once.

Ruth, Williams, and Bonds are the top three all-time in slugging percentage above league average. That's how they rank in OPS (on-base average plus slugging), too. Bonds and Ruth did other things better than Williams, and that is why I rank them ahead of him.

HONUS WAGNER

Honus Wagner has been romanticized for nearly one hundred years, a tribute to his character as well as his stellar play on the baseball diamonds. He didn't look anything like a great athlete should look like. He didn't hit a lot of home runs, and he sure made a ton of errors, especially for a shortstop. They called him "the Flying Dutchman" because of his speed. He led the league in stolen bases five times, but at 5'11", 200 pounds, he certainly didn't look like the fastest ballplayer. He was stocky, if not downright heavy. He was bowlegged.

He was also the most dominant player of his era, towering over the competition as much as Bonds, Ruth, and Mays did over theirs.

He was born John Peter Wagner in February of 1874, and he was the greatest player in the history of the National League for its first 60 years (let's say until the mid-1950s, when a mature Musial and a young Mays could lay serious claim to the throne). One legend has it that Ed Barrow (a scout at the time who would become famous as a manager for turning a Red Sox pitcher named Babe Ruth into an outfielder and then joining Ruth with the Yankees and building their dynasty) discovered the 18-year-old Wagner flinging rocks across the Monongahela River and signed him on the spot. Honus began his professional career in Steubenville, Ohio, and moved up the ranks, eventually joining the National League Louisville team for three seasons. After the 1899 season, the National League contracted from 12 teams to 8, and Wagner's Louisville team was disbanded. Louisville owner Barney Dreyfuss became president of the Pittsburgh Pirates, and brought his star with him. For the next 17 seasons, Wagner was a fixture on the Pirates.

Wagner was positively the greatest shortstop in baseball's history for a century, from 1896 to 1996. Only in recent years has anyone posed a serious threat to that title, but even that threat (by Alex Rodriguez) has been squelched with A-Rod moving to third base for the 2004 season. Wagner's contemporaries—like rival New York Giants manager John McGraw—used to say that Wagner could have been number one at any of the nine positions on the diamond! Wagner showed his versatile talents by playing all four infield positions, spending time in the outfield when needed, and even pitching a few games.

Wagner was so well respected that Ty Cobb, when picking his all-time great team in 1945, chose Honus as his shortstop. Cobb didn't like Wagner—going back to the 1909 World Series—but he sure respected him.

Wagner was considered the best-fielding shortstop of his era, which is one reason that you have to throw stats out the window when considering players from 1900 to 1920.

Honus Wagner: Fielding at Shortstop

1901	61 games	36 errors	.918 fielding percentage
1902	44 games	28 errors	.893 fielding percentage
1903	111 games	50 errors	.933 fielding percentage
1904	121 games	49 errors	.929 fielding percentage
1905	145 games	60 errors	.935 fielding percentage
1906	137 games	51 errors	.941 fielding percentage
1907	138 games	49 errors	.938 fielding percentage
1908	151 games	50 errors	.943 fielding percentage

Now, compare that to Alex Rodriguez, who never had more than 24 errors in a season playing shortstop in the late 1990s and early 2000s. Look at the way Wagner's fielding percentage at shortstop improved throughout the decade. Conditions must have gotten better for the fielders. By 1914, Wagner was 40 years old. He played 132 games at shortstop that season, and committed only 39 errors and had a .950 percentage. Was he that much better a fielder at 40 than he was at 28, when his fielding percentage was only .893?

Wagner played in an era where the fields had no lighting, the balls were kept in play until they were black, and the gloves were very little help. Honus had a lot in common with singer Michael Jackson. They each wore a glove for no apparent reason. In one instance, Honus was caught with his glove hand in his back pocket, so he fielded a sharp grounder with his bare throwing hand and threw the runner out. Stories abound about how Wagner played shortstop like an octopus. It was often said that Wagner threw out runners lying on his back. Wagner played his position better than the average shortstop in his day (as Rodriguez did in his), and therefore should get credit for his fielding.

Wagner's hitting statistics can help us understand why folks one hundred years ago raved about him. He led the league in batting eight times, seven times in doubles, six times in slugging, and won multiple times in runs, hits, runs batted in, and on-base average. He hit at least .300 for 17 consecutive seasons—and those were seasons that he faced (then legal) spitballs and other trick pitches used in the "dead-ball" era. His lifetime batting average was .329 (the average batting average of his time was .268).

Who's Better, Who's Best
Honus Wagner or Alex Rodriguez?

Rodriguez had batted 5,587 times following the 2004 season, about half of Honus Wagner's career total of 10,430. But one can't just double Alex's total numbers and do justice to Wagner. The 10,430 at-bats include Wagner's last five seasons, when Honus was clearly past his prime.

I have stated that Wagner batted about 60 points higher in his career than the league average at the time. Rodriguez batted about 35 points higher than the league average. Wagner's slugging percentage was 115 points higher than the league average (he slugged .466 when the average was only .351). Rodriguez has a monster slugging average of .574, which betters the league average by about 140 points.

Wagner, however, stole 722 bases (leading the league five times). Rodriguez—in a league that doesn't place as much value on the stolen base—stole 205 in the first half of his career, but never finished among the top three in the league.

Both were considered the best players in the game, and both were considered among the most likeable guys in the game. Even when Ty Cobb and Barry Bonds surpassed Wagner and Rodriguez in production, they weren't nearly as loved by fans, teammates, and the media.

In the end, although I lean toward the modern-day player and the increased competition he faces, I had to choose Wagner over Rodriguez.

Honus Wagner led the National League in extra-base hits in 1900, 1902, 1903, 1904, 1907, 1908, and 1909. In five of those seasons, he also led the league in stolen bases! Rodriguez never had a year to compare with Wagner's 1908 season, but then again, neither did Bonds, Ruth, Mays, or Aaron. Wagner batted .354 that year (league average .247) and led the league in every batting statistic except home runs. He was second in homers, with 10.

How the Game Was Different in Wagner's Day

On June 20, 1901, Wagner became the first player in the new century to steal home twice in a single game. In August of 1902, Wagner stole second, third, and home in the same inning. He did it twice more in his career, as well.

In a 1906 game, Wagner had one of the longest hits in club history, but only made it to third base. Rounding first, he was clipped by first baseman Kid Gleason, and Wagner limped to third. He was replaced by a pinch runner, and the opponent (the Phillies) allowed Wagner to return to shortstop in the next inning.

In 1916, at the age of 42, Wagner hit an inside-the-park homer. Today, it's rare to see a youngster, let alone a 42-year-old man, hit an inside-the-park home run.

Wagner retired with a then-record 27 steals of home.

Honus would have been considered peculiar, in some regards, no matter what era he lived in. He didn't like to have photographers snapping pictures of him. Like many ballplayers, he had superstitions, and believed that a photograph taken of him while handling his favorite bat might have a disastrous effect on his batting average.

The Hall of Fame

Wagner was one of the first five players inducted into the Hall of Fame, and was the third leading vote-getter, trailing only Cobb and Ruth. If the players and writers of the 1930s thought that Wagner was better than almost everyone else—including Walter Johnson, Christy Mathewson, and Tris Speaker—who are we to argue?

What Wagner Is Most Famous for These Days

Honus Wagner baseball cards are among the most valuable in existence. They were recalled in 1909. At the time, cards were in packages along with tobacco, and Wagner, a nonsmoker, objected to being included because he didn't want to set a bad example for children. (If I discover a way to go back in time, I'm going back as Honus Wagner's agent!)

By 1991, at Sotheby's in New York, a 1909 Wagner tobacco card in mint condition sold for $451,000 to hockey star Wayne Gretzky and L.A. Kings owner Bruce McNall. By 1996, a Wagner card sold for $640,000. On July 25, 2000, a Wagner card was auctioned for a record $1.1 million dollars on eBay.

A Better Analogy

Honus Wagner and Davy Crockett Honus Wagner was one of the nation's first heroes of the 20th century. Crockett was one of the first heroes of the 19th century. There were tall tales about both of them. I have a 40-year-old *Baseball Joke Book* that attributes this story to Honus: "Way back when I played, they didn't have stadium lights and when it got dark, you couldn't see what you were doing very well. One time, I was playing in the outfield and the ball was hit my way, but I lost it in the darkness. Fortunately, a rabbit was running by and I grabbed it and threw to first for the out. It was the first time anyone was thrown out by a hare."

Well, did Davy Crockett really "kilt him a bear when he was only three?"

The nation snapped up Wagner's rare baseball card, and Crockett's coonskin hat. In fact, that's what those two are most known for in these times. One was "the King of the Wild Frontier," and the other was "the Flying Dutchman." It's difficult to distinguish fact from fiction with all the tall tales told about each of them. But it's not difficult to place Wagner high among the greatest players in baseball history.

ALEX RODRIGUEZ

After only nine full seasons in the major leagues, Alex Rodriguez has established himself as one of baseball's all-time greats. There are only a handful of players with higher career lifetime slugging averages. Of those ten sluggers, five of them were outfielders (Ruth, Williams, Bonds, Manny Ramirez, and Joe DiMaggio), four were first basemen (Lou Gehrig, Jimmy Foxx, Hank Greenberg, and Mark McGwire), and one was a second baseman (Rogers Hornsby). There has never been a shortstop or third baseman who has had the power of the man they call "A-Rod." I give him a great chance at eventually hitting 700 home runs, possibly even 800.

Ken Griffey Jr. (a former teammate of Rodriguez in Seattle) once said he hoped that when Rodriguez batted .330 with 25 home runs, people wouldn't say he had a bad year. Actually, in 2004 people said Alex had a bad year when he batted .286 with 36 home runs and 28 stolen bases.

He had raised the bar so high that anything less than a 50-home-run season wouldn't suffice.

Alex was traded from the Texas Rangers to the New York Yankees for Alphonso Soriano and cash on February 16, 2004. The Yankees received a 28-year-old superstar who was coming off an MVP season. They asked him to change positions and play third base for the first time in his career.

Rodriguez played a flawless third base, becoming one of the best defensive players at that position. He drove in 106 runs. He scored 112 runs. He led his team to 101 wins and the best record in the American League. He did it all in a year when he "bottomed out" and suffered the worst season in his nine-year career.

The most important statistic of all in baseball is runs scored. The object of the game, after all, is to score the most runs. Over a nine-year period, Alex Rodriguez averaged 122 runs scored per season—the most in the majors.

Most Runs Scored, 1996–2004

1. 1,102 Alex Rodriguez
2. 1,071 Barry Bonds
2. 1,071 Jeff Bagwell
4. 1,032 Derek Jeter

One way that Alex scores so many runs is to put himself into scoring position. I'm not even talking now about the 28 stolen bases in 2004 (and the 205 in his career). I want to mention all the extra-base hits.

Most Extra-Base Hits, 1996–2004

1. 701 Alex Rodriguez
2. 697 Barry Bonds
3. 689 Sammy Sosa
4. 675 Jeff Bagwell

How many people realize that A-Rod has been pounding out more extra-base hits than Barry Bonds or Sammy Sosa over the greatest stretches in their careers?

Most Home Runs, 1996–2004

1. 442 Sammy Sosa
2. 411 Barry Bonds
3. 376 Alex Rodriguez

In the greatest nine-year stretch of Barry Bonds's career, he out-homered A-Rod by just 35 home runs (less than four per season). Rodriguez has averaged close to 42 home runs per season for nine seasons.

In Hank Aaron's best nine consecutive seasons (1957–1965), he hit 332 home runs. In Willie Mays's best nine (1954–1962), he hit 344 homers.

Alex Rodriguez grew up in Miami, the right city to play a lot of baseball, and he took advantage. He dominated high school competition like a man among boys. His team lost only 13 of the 100 games that Rodriguez played in. Alex batted .419 with 17 homers, 70 runs batted in, and 90 steals in those 100 high school games. He was first-team prep All-American as a senior, hitting .505 with 35 steals in 35 attempts in 33 games. He was the first high school player to ever try out for Team USA, and was the USA Baseball Junior Player of the Year.

He was the first overall pick of the 1993 draft, by the Seattle Mariners. Unlike the basketball and football drafts, the baseball drafts are always risky crapshoots. Rodriguez was anything but a high-risk selection, however.

Alex Rodriguez made his major-league debut in July of 1994, becoming just the third 18-year-old shortstop in the majors since 1900. The Mariners started Alex for 17 games at shortstop before he was sent to Triple-A Calgary on August 2 (a few weeks before the majors ended their season prematurely due to a player's strike).

The 20-year-old Rodriguez began tearing up the league in 1996. He wasn't just selected to the All-Star team; he finished a close second in the MVP voting to Juan Gonzalez. He led the American League in batting with a .358 average. How good was that average? Consider this: he was the first right-handed batter to hit for such a high average in the American League since Joe DiMaggio's .381 in 1939. He was the first American League shortstop to win a batting title since Lou Boudreau did it in 1944. He was the first shortstop in the majors to win a batting title since Dick Groat accomplished it in 1960. He led the league in runs with 141. He led the league in total bases. He led the league in doubles. His slugging percentage was an astronomical .631.

In 1997, Rodriguez had the worst season of his career. He batted "only" .300 and hit "only" 23 home runs. He missed 14 games after he got into a collision with Roger Clemens. It would turn out to be the only one of his first nine seasons in which he would fail to hit at least 36 home runs.

In 1998 Rodriguez broke through to become a major superstar. He hit 42 homers and stole 46 bases to join Jose Canseco and Barry Bonds as the only players in history with 40 homers and 40 steals in a single season. Despite playing on a team with two other all-time greats (Griffey Jr. and Johnson) the Mariners went 76–85 and finished in third place.

The Mariners let Randy Johnson leave in the final months of the 1998 season, for three prospects. They let Griffey Jr. leave as a free agent following the 1999 season. They couldn't reach an agreement on a contract with A-Rod during the 2000 season, and allowed him to leave as well.

The Mariners, who finished in third place in 1998 and 1999, went to the American League Championship Series in 2000, but lost to the Yankees despite Rodriguez batting .409 in the Series.

It worked out all right for the Mariners. Seattle won 116 games in 2001 without any of their former three superstars. They had paid Rodriguez $4.3 million dollars in the 2000 season, and received one of the greatest bargains in baseball. They were then unwilling to pay market value for him. So, how did Lou Piniella's Seattle team win so many games in '01? They actually increased their payroll (from $59 million to $74 million) and spread the wealth around, paying several starters (like John Olerud and Mike Cameron) what it would have cost to keep A-Rod around.

The problem for Rodriguez was that he was pricing himself out of all but a few places. His agent, Scott Boras, negotiated a historic deal with the Texas Rangers. He signed a seven-year contract with player options for three additional seasons on December 11, 2000. He signed with a team that had won the American League West as recently as 1999. In the 2000 season, the Rangers dropped to 71–91.

Texas owner Tom Hicks was thrilled with the signing, and he should have been. Recently signed deals with local cable sports networks had upped the value of his franchise. By signing the popular Rodriguez, he was able to ink additional marketing deals with companies.

In some respects, Hicks got exactly what he paid for from Rodriguez. Alex hit 52 home runs, slugged .622, and finished sixth in the MVP voting in 2001. In addition to his great baseball skills, he was a true "mensch." In the 2001 All-Star Game, Rodriguez insisted that Cal Ripken Jr. (who was playing in his final All-Star Game) move over and play his old position of shortstop. A-Rod then played third base, later proclaiming that playing alongside Ripken, his boyhood hero, was one of the most thrilling moments of his life.

Things didn't turn out so great for the Rangers. Texas finished in last place all three seasons that Rodriguez was to play for them. While the Rangers had an $88 million payroll in 2001, 25 percent of it went to one man, Rodriguez.

This was what the Rangers allocated to their starting pitching rotation:

2001 Texas Rangers Pitching Staff

Kenny Rogers	5–7	6.21 ERA	20 starts	$7.5 million
Ricky Helling	12–11	5.19 ERA	34 starts	$4.5 million
Darren Oliver	11–11	6.02 ERA	28 starts	$7 million
Doug Davis	11–10	4.45 ERA	30 starts	$250,000
Rob Bell	5–5	7.18 ERA	18 starts	$250,000

That is a total of $19.5 million for five men who started 130 games for the Rangers that season—less than the total they paid the shortstop. The Rangers spent all their money on 37-year-old first baseman and designated hitter Rafael Palmeiro, star catcher Ivan Rodriguez, and A-Rod.

The ironic thing was that people blamed Alex for his contract and made him defensive about talking about it. All anyone wanted to talk to Rodriguez about that 2001 season was the contract. Even "60 Minutes" asked him if he felt embarrassed by the $252 million contract. A-Rod answered, "Somebody wins a lottery and they're a national hero. Somebody works their butt off and he's a devil. I've made the progression to this point and I can't feel guilty." Despite that, Rodriguez batted 52 home runs and drove in 135 in 2001.

Here are some of the more fascinating numbers of Alex Rodriguez's career. During the three years he played in Texas, he won three consecutive American League home run titles—that's only been done two other times since Babe Ruth stopped winning the damn title (by Harmon Killebrew and Ken Griffey Jr.). Rodriguez topped the league in homers, runs, and slugging in the same year—becoming only the fifth player to do so in 50 years (joining outfielders Mickey Mantle, Carl Yastrzemski, Albert Belle, and Ken Griffey Jr.). In 2003, he won his second consecutive Gold Glove for fielding excellence. That year, he led American League shortstops in double plays and was among the leaders in putouts and assists.

Alex hit 40 home runs in a season in six consecutive seasons, matching Sammy Sosa (1998–2003) for the second-longest streak in major-league history. Only Babe Ruth (seven straight 40-plus home run seasons from 1926 to 1932) tops A-Rod. Only a handful of players have ever had six seasons of 40-plus homers, much less consecutively. Their names are all well known: Babe Ruth, Hank Aaron, Harmon Killebrew, Barry Bonds, Ken Griffey Jr., Sammy Sosa, Willie Mays, Mark McGwire, and Rodriguez.

All of those home run sluggers except A-Rod were outfielders or first basemen. None of the other most prolific home run hitters ever had to play the demanding defensive position of shortstop.

Rodriguez took plenty of heat for signing with Texas, a team that had no chance to win a World Series because of their pitching. That argument (that Alex shouldn't have even considered signing with a team that wasn't a contender) held so little water with me. These same critics were harsh with free agents who signed with the best, wealthiest, big-market teams like the Yankees (saying they were just after a ring). Shouldn't an athlete as great as Rodriguez be confident that no matter which team he signed with, that team would contend for the title? Shouldn't signing an athlete as great as A-Rod have a ripple effect among other top free agents, causing them to consider any team with Rodriguez on it?

Apparently, after three fruitless years in Texas, Rodriguez and Rangers owner Tom Hicks agreed that their partnership wasn't working. By now, Rodriguez's contract had priced him out of most major-league teams' payrolls. The players' association even refused to let Rodriguez take less money from a new team (their job is sometimes to protect players from themselves). The Boston Red Sox—who had finished in second place to the Yankees seven consecutive seasons—stepped up to the plate to arrange a trade involving the Sox's Manny Ramirez and Rodriguez, the two $20 million players. The deal came apart when the players' association rejected Boston's proposal to restructure Alex's $252 million contract. Baseball commissioner Bud Selig gave the Red Sox and Rodriguez 72 hours to again restructure the contract. Boston asked that he slash his contract by $28 million to $30 million, which the union blocked. The union and Boras tried to make the Boston deal work. It was to no avail.

It looked like Rodriguez would remain the captain of the Texas Rangers.

The Yankees and Rangers worked out a trade a few months later. The Rangers agreed to assume $67 million of the contract, which the commissioner approved. In sending Soriano to Texas, the Rangers were acquiring a talented player with many of the same skills as Rodriguez. Alex Rodriguez, meanwhile, would try to lead the Yankees to a World Series—something that had eluded A-Rod his entire career.

Alex Rodriguez accomplished every individual goal in baseball. He was the youngest player ever to hit 300 home runs (he did it at 27 years, 249 days). He was the youngest to bat 350 home runs.

Alex Rodriguez has never been afraid of a challenge. At the peak of his career, he changed positions to the less glamorous third base to accommodate the Yankees' all-star shortstop Derek Jeter. Having to give up his longtime uniform number 3, he chose number 13 to honor another boyhood hero, Dan Marino. The athlete he admired most when he was young is the one that makes the best analogy with A-Rod, however.

A Better Analogy

Alex Rodriguez and Michael Jordan Each of them was born in New York but raised in the south—Jordan in North Carolina and Rodriguez in Miami. Each worked their butts off—even after they made millions and millions of dollars—and dominated their team sports like few others in history. Each of them have gained the respect of most of their sport's greatest legends. Each of them has gained the adoration of young fans. Each of them has physical features that make them attractive to females all over the world. They both have always dressed impeccably off the field, almost looking like they came off the pages of a fashion magazine. Of course, not all of this is coincidence. Alex idolized Jordan growing up. Rodriguez is a virtual god in Latin America. He is very well known in South America, where he has a lucrative endorsement deal with Nike. Hmmm, if I remember right, Nike has been synonymous with Michael Jordan as well. Jordan's popularity knows no boundaries on the earth. As players, both dominated their sports both offensively and defensively. Jordan and Rodriguez were both the best defensive players at their position.

Jordan, of course, enhanced his popularity and legend by winning a number of NBA championships. For Rodriguez to be included in any comparison with Jordan, he must win a World Series or two.

JOSH GIBSON

There is no way of proving this, but many people in the 1920s and 1930s accepted as fact that Josh Gibson was a better slugger than Babe Ruth. Gibson led a tortured life, and was screwed. His sport, baseball, was segregated, so he performed basically in anonymity. Boxing and running were considered suitable sports for blacks. In 1936, when Gibson was 25 years old, Jesse Owens's remarkable victories at the Berlin Olympics in the face of Adolf Hitler's German dictatorship rallied all Americans behind a black athlete. That same year, Joe Louis was the heavyweight champion of the world, and he became an American hero for the entire nation, especially when he defended his championship in 1938 against German superpower Max Schmelling. Josh Gibson didn't get to play on the world's premier stages or compete against the very best. Instead, he played for two of the Negro Leagues' finest teams, the Pittsburgh Crawfords and the Homestead Grays. Then again, any team Josh suited up for would have been one of the league's premier teams. In 16 seasons, playing upwards of 200 games a year, there was no batter more feared, and no athlete more anonymous and underpaid, than Gibson.

Josh Gibson was born in 1911, in Georgia, the son of sharecroppers. In search of a better life for his family, Gibson's father migrated north, and Josh and the rest of the family joined him shortly before Josh entered the sixth grade. Josh was known to have called the move from the South the greatest gift his dad ever gave him.

By the age of 16, Gibson weighed over 200 pounds and was catching for black semiprofessional teams in the Pittsburgh area. When he was 17, he married 18-year-old Helen Mason, who died in labor while delivering their twins, Josh Jr. and Helen. Gibson wasn't home much to be a father, as he had to earn a living playing baseball. He established quite a reputation as a young slugger. Wherever there was a baseball game in the area, there was Gibson. He was willing to strap on roller skates in order to travel six miles to play in a sandlot game. Word of Gibson was spreading, slowly at first and then rapidly throughout western Pennsylvania semipro baseball circles.

Josh even helped organize the schedule of the Crawford Colored Giants of Pittsburgh, a semipro team. He got so good as a hitter that the Homestead Grays—a team started twenty years earlier in a steel town about 20 minutes north of Pittsburgh that was beginning to emerge as a black baseball power—heard about Gibson's gift at the plate.

Gibson got his lucky break in 1930. The Kansas City Monarchs came to town to play the Homestead Grays. It was the best of the East versus the best of the West, and Forbes Field in Pittsburgh hosted thirty thousand fans that night with a rudimentary portable light system the Monarchs brought with them. Smokey Joe Williams pitched for the Grays, and—depending on whom you listen to—(a) either catcher Buck Ewing injured his hand or (b) Ewing walked off the field rather than handle Williams's fastballs in the poor lighting. Grays manager Judy Johnson asked one of his outfielders to take over behind the plate, and he was refused. Eighteen-year-old Josh Gibson was literally called out from the stands (many of the Grays had seen Gibson play semipro ball), and the crowd waited while Gibson put a uniform on. Although Josh didn't get any hits that night, the appreciative Grays did sign the unpolished Gibson to a contract for the remainder of the season.

He stayed with the Grays for two seasons (1930–31) and then jumped to the crosstown rival Pittsburgh Crawfords when owner Gus Greenlee offered him more money. He won home run titles in 1932, 1934, and 1936 while wearing Crawford red. Gibson rejoined the Grays and their power-hitting first baseman Buck Leonard in 1937. The '37 edition of the Grays split their home games between Washington, D.C., and Pittsburgh. Before the season ended, Gibson and several teammates ran off to play for the Santo Domingo dictator Rafael Trujillo.

Gibson returned to the Homestead Grays and picked up where he left off. He won home run crowns in 1938 and 1939, and his first batting title in 1938 with an unbelievable .440. Asked about Gibson's long-distance drives, teammate Buck Leonard responded, "Nobody hit the ball as far as Gibson."

In 1940 he once again jumped from the Negro Leagues, this time to Venezuela. That league collapsed midseason, so Josh found his way to Veracruz of the Mexican League. Gibson made $6,000 for his 94-game season with Veracruz in 1941, $2,000 more than he had been offered by the Homestead Grays in the United States. Josh returned to Mexico the following year and won the home run and RBI crowns. He batted an amazing .480 in the Puerto Rican winter league in 1941. However, after two years south of the border, health and legal problems drew Gibson back to the States. By playing the 1941 season in Veracruz, Josh had breached a contract with the Grays. Management went to court and had a $10,000 lien placed upon Josh's house. In exchange for dropping the claim, the owners of the Grays got Gibson's name on a two-year contract.

Gibson had become very ill in Mexico before returning to the Grays in 1942. Despite intermittent health problems, Gibson won home run crowns in 1942, 1943, and 1946, plus a batting title in 1943, hitting .521.

In the States, Gibson and his teammates would play two or three league games a week. They might play a doubleheader on Sunday in New York, then train down to Baltimore for a Tuesday game. I've read that only Sunday games used to count in standings, so the better teams didn't get too far ahead. How did Gibson and his teammates earn a living the rest of the week? They would play each off-day against white semipro teams within driving distance.

Sure, Josh padded his numbers in those semipro games—but the fact that he played at a consistently high level in All-Star games and exhibitions with the top major leaguers justifies his ranking here. Gibson didn't just destroy Negro League pitchers, he also beat up on white major leaguers. In 61 recorded at-bats against the likes of Dizzy and Daffy Dean, Johnny Vander Meer, and others, Josh hit .426 with five home runs. This guy could have hit anybody.

Josh was known for his short, compact swing and his long, Ruthian drives. At the end of the 1930 season, Gibson slugged a ball over Forbes Field's center-field wall—the first man to ever hit a ball over that fence (457 feet away). Shortly after that, with his Grays playing the Monarchs in New York, Gibson belted one of the longest balls ever hit at Yankee Stadium. The *Sporting News* from June 3, 1967, credited Gibson with a drive that hit just two feet from the top of the stadium wall circling the bleachers in center field, about 580 feet from home plate. Both Ruth and Gibson played before the era of the tape-measure home run. While there is some mythology associated with both men, it can be assumed that the two of them were the premier power hitters of their day. They called Josh "the Brown Bambino," and not even the Babe might have been able to hit a baseball farther.

In late 1942, Gibson began to suffer from recurring headaches and dizzy spells. On New Year's Day of 1943, he was hospitalized for ten days after doctors discovered a brain tumor. Josh refused to allow an operation. He returned to baseball, while the headaches and blackouts continued, eventually eroding his herculean skills. That summer, he was in and out of a mental hospital, possibly suffering from high blood pressure, drug abuse, or alcoholism. Sometimes he would leave the hospital to play a game, then return to the hospital after the game was over.

During the off-season between 1942 and 1943 Josh Gibson gave an interview in which he listed the greatest thrills in his baseball career. Interestingly, he listed winning the MVP trophy in the 1941 Puerto Rican winter league as his greatest moment. It has been suggested that this is because the Negro Leagues never had any types of awards other than for the East-West game, and that this was one of the few times that Josh was given official recognition.

Josh Gibson had great years in 1944 and 1945 despite his failing health, and he actually thought he should have been the first black man to break the color line in the major leagues. He was still only 34 years old in 1945, but he was an old 34.

By 1946, Gibson had bad knees and was having difficulty catching his usual workload. At the end of the season, he began drinking heavily. He died before the 1947 season started, so he never lived to see Jackie Robinson play for Brooklyn. Gibson died before reaching his 36th birthday and was buried in Pittsburgh.

His reputation as a player was rock solid. Pitching great Walter Johnson said, "There is a catcher that any big-league club would like to buy for $200,000. His name is Gibson. He can do everything. He hits the ball a mile. And he catches so easy, he might as well be in a rocking chair. Throws like a rifle."

Robert Peterson, a noted Negro League author and historian, called Gibson "probably the preeminent power hitter in history, not excepting Babe Ruth."

How good would Josh Gibson have been if he'd played in the majors? Well, the major-league record for home runs by a catcher was Gabby Hartnett's 209, which stood from the '30s to the late '50s, until Roy Campanella and then Yogi Berra passed it. Do I think that Josh Gibson would have hit 300 home runs in the majors, if he'd been a rookie in 1930? I think he would have hit 300 by 1936.

In the majors, Gibson would have benefited from less travel and fewer innings behind the plate. There is no doubt in my mind that he would have been better than the premier catchers of his era (Mickey Cochrane, Bill Dickey, Gabby Hartnett). He would have been somewhere ahead of them, but behind Ruth. Even if Gibson had exceeded Ruth's 714 home run total (entirely possible), he would have trailed Ruth in this book for a number of reasons. Ruth was a fabulous pitcher, and as an outfielder he led the league in assists with his cannon arm. By all accounts he was a selective hitter, and, at times, not a bad base runner. Gibson had mixed reviews on his catching ability, but almost all accounts point to his early trouble with pop-ups. I'm sure he was at least a serviceable catcher, if not a remarkable one. If Gibson had played in the major leagues, perhaps he would have had a manager wise enough to let him play a less demanding defensive position in order to extend his career.

Gibson might not have earned Ruth's salary (more than the U.S. president's), but he would have gotten a heckuva lot more than $500 a month, which is what Gibson earned in 1940 at the age of 29.

With so many major-league stars in military service in the early 1940s, it must have been tempting for a major-league team to sign a star of Gibson's magnitude. There were talks—especially concerning the Washington Senators—but nothing materialized.

Roy Campanella began playing in the Negro Leagues in 1937, when Gibson was at his peak. Campy said that Gibson was not only the greatest catcher but the greatest ballplayer he ever saw.

Campy saw something most of America never did see. As for the comparisons with contemporaries Jesse Owens and Joe Louis, it's not like they didn't also suffer from prejudice. There were no endorsements for Jesse Owens following the Olympics. For a while he was a runner for hire, racing against anything from people, to horses, to motorcycles. The Negro Baseball League often hired him to race against Thoroughbred horses in an exhibition before every game. Jesse even raced against some of the fastest ballplayers in the major leagues, always giving them a 10-yard head start before beating them. And Joe Louis was broke by the age of 37, and lived out his days as a casino host.

A Better Analogy

Josh Gibson and Charlie Parker Josh Gibson died early, after a personal life filled with poverty, despair, tragedy, and alcoholism. At times, he had fits of rage and rambling outbursts. His legend grew after his death, and while he never had a chance to play in the major leagues and draw mainstream appeal, he was eventually enshrined in the Baseball Hall of Fame. His death is clouded in mystery. An old teammate, Jimmy Crutchfield, often said Gibson died of a "broken heart."

Charlie Parker was born in 1920 in Kansas City, Kansas. He was given the nicknames "Bird" and "Yardbird." By age 15, he was serious about the alto saxophone. Soon, Parker was playing with local bands, and in 1935 he left school to pursue a music career.

While Parker was still as good as ever, drugs started to consume his daily life. He died in 1955 at the age of 35. He was an amazing saxophonist who gained wide recognition for his innovative improvisations. He was one of the most influential and talented musicians in jazz history. His stature has grown in death. He was arguably the greatest sax player of all time. Like Gibson, he didn't live long enough to reap the full benefits of his talent.

LOU GEHRIG

"Today, I consider myself the luckiest man on the face of the earth." When Lou Gehrig said those words at a packed Yankee Stadium, he was a dying and courageous man. With or without the early tragic death and emotional speech, he would be considered—hands down—the greatest first baseman in the game's history.

When I was growing up in Southern California in the late 1960s, it was well before the days of cable television and hundreds of television channels, and there were certainly no VCRs so kids could view their favorite movies as many times as they wanted. Maybe that's why I remember a week in the fourth grade, when KTLA-Channel 5 broadcast the movie *Pride of the Yankees* each night for a week. The 1942 classic starring Gary Cooper made a deep impression on me. Was it the fact that my whole family watched it together, even reenacting the corniest of scenes (the Gehrig family in a conga line chanting "Geh-rig, Geh-rig, Geh-rig" to celebrate a home run)?

Everything kids need to know about Gehrig is portrayed in the movie. He was born in 1903, on 94th Street in New York City. His parents had immigrated to this country in 1900. His father was a janitor and his mother a cook. His mom even worked in the fraternity house that Lou pledged at Columbia. Just like the movie showed, in Gehrig's first game of his famous streak, he was struck by a ball in the forehead trying to break up a double play, and refused to be taken out of the game.

Lou lived with his parents—buying them a house in the suburbs in the late '20s—until he married wealthy debutante Eleanore Twitchell at the end of the 1933 season.

Gehrig's story is inspiring, but what was most inspiring was his play on the field. Gehrig was a fabulous baseball player, driving in at least 100 runs for 13 straight seasons and establishing an American League record with 184 RBI in 1931 that still stands. He compiled a .340 lifetime batting average and belted 493 home runs in a career shortened by terminal illness. Gehrig was a supreme run producer. Only three men in history drove in more runs. One of them—Hank Aaron—had 4,363 more at-bats than Gehrig. Another one—Cap Anson—played between 1871 and 1897. The only other man to drive in more runs than Lou was Babe Ruth. If Gehrig's career hadn't been cut short, he might have driven in more runs than the Babe.

Lou Gehrig had 1,995 RBI in 8,001 at-bats. That's an average of 1 RBI every 4 at-bats (or 150 RBI per 600-at-bat season). Barry Bonds has played 19 brilliant seasons, and won't catch Gehrig's RBI total even in a superlative 20th. Bonds is 152 RBI from Gehrig's total following the 2004 season.

There are only two men in history with a higher slugging percentage than Gehrig. Their names are Babe Ruth and Ted Williams. There are only two men with a higher OPS (on-base plus slugging). Their names are Babe Ruth and Ted Williams.

What makes Gehrig's story so compelling and sad? Only Gehrig, among the truly legendary baseball stars, faced a terminal illness during his playing days. The manner in which Gehrig handled it—with class and dignity—gives his story a moral compass that seems almost religious.

Of course, Gehrig was a popular and respected player long before he got sick. He was most famous for his 2,130 consecutive games played. He pinch-hit on June 1, 1925. The next day, Yankee first baseman Wally Pipp went to manager Miller Huggins complaining of a headache. Huggins suggested that Pipp take the day off, and Miller gave the 22-year-old Gehrig the start. Lou didn't leave the lineup for 14 seasons. He didn't play all 2,130 games at first base, however. The streak at first base ended at 885 games in 1930, when he appeared in the outfield. He played another game in the outfield in 1933, and in 1934 he was in the lineup as the shortstop and leadoff hitter just long enough to single in the top of the first and be removed for a pinch runner.

In 1927, the Yankees had their most celebrated lineup, nicknamed Murderers Row. Babe Ruth hit 60 homers to break his single-season record, but Gehrig won the MVP Award. Of course, the rules of the time prohibited Ruth from winning that year (he had already won one). Gehrig hit .373 with 47 home runs and 175 RBI that summer.

In October 1928, Gehrig just destroyed St. Louis Browns pitchers with a .545 average (11 at-bats, four homers, one double, one single). Everyone has heard of Ruth's "called shot" against the Cubs in the 1932 World Series, when Ruth "pointed" to center field and then hit a home run in that direction. In that same game, Gehrig hit two homers.

Gehrig finished in the top five in the league in batting average eight times. He led the league in home runs three times, but he finished in the top three no less than 10 different seasons. He led the league in RBI five times, and finished in the top three in 10 different seasons. He won the Triple Crown in 1934, playing for months with a fractured toe.

"The Iron Horse" was reliable, despite a list of injuries that would debilitate most mortals. In one game, he was knocked unconscious by a wild pitch. The next day, he was in the lineup and had four hits. When Lou's hands were x-rayed late in his career, they were found to have 17 assorted fractures that had healed by themselves. He had broken every finger in each hand, and didn't even tell anyone about it.

In 1927, Gehrig was neck-and-neck in homers with Ruth until mid-August, when Lou went into a slump.

Gehrig and Ruth were a terrific tandem for 10 years, from 1925 to 1934. They were better friends than people realized, although they didn't talk for four years after Ruth made an insulting remark about Mamma Gehrig's cooking. The Babe was Lou's boyhood idol, and Ruth took great pride in his young teammate.

Ruth was gone from the Yankees in 1935, and just a year later, the great Joe DiMaggio appeared in the Yankees lineup with Gehrig. By 1938, something was wrong with Lou, although no one knew what.

Lou Gehrig, 1937–38

	AB	HR	RBI	BB	K	Batting Avg.	On-Base Avg.	Slugging Pct.
1937	569	37	159	127	49	.351	.473	.643
1938	576	29	114	107	75	.295	.410	.523

Gehrig was only 35 years old in 1938, so he wasn't particularly old to show such a sudden steep decline. His slugging average went down more than 100 points, and his batting average was down 56 points. He drove in 45 fewer runs.

Manager Joe McCarthy of the Yankees gave so much respect to Gehrig that he refused to bench him early in 1939, even when it was clear something was wrong. Gehrig batted only .143 (four hits—all singles—in 28 at-bats) in the first eight games before he asked out of the lineup. Gehrig's final 604 at-bats produced only a .288 batting average— about 65 points below his career average.

If Gehrig's career had ended after 1937, his final numbers would have looked like this:

Lou Gehrig, 1923–1937

7,397 AB	2,547 hits	.344	464 HR	1,880 RBI

That .344 batting average would have put him even with Ted Williams. Even with his final 604 at-bats included, Gehrig's .340 average is one of the greatest ever. His career basically took place in the first 12 full seasons that he played (1926–1937). Gehrig averaged 37 home runs and 150 RBI for those 12 seasons.

In *Pride of the Yankees*, Gehrig keels over while lacing his spikes in the locker room, as his teammates looked away, so as not to embarrass him. Supposedly, it really happened. "The Iron Horse" spent his last months working at a desk for the City of New York as a parole commissioner, going to work even when he was unable to move his arms.

He played his entire career in an era of skyrocketing batting averages and home run totals. But then, there have been skyrocketing numbers since 1994, too. Gehrig didn't have the advantages that modern players have, including therapists, luxury suites, charter plane travel, and so on.

As a man and as a player, Gehrig won the hearts of America before and after his illness. He was a great sportsman and baseball player who rose from poverty to extreme success. Ruth was "the Babe," but Gehrig was "the Man."

A Better Analogy

Lou Gehrig and Kobe Bryant, Art Carney, and Michael Imperioli Lou Gehrig was the second banana to Babe Ruth on the celebrated "Murderers Row" of the New York Yankees for almost a decade. Even after Ruth left the Yanks, Gehrig took a backseat to Joe DiMaggio, a star from the moment he set foot in center field. Gehrig was one of the greatest players in baseball history, but he played behind a fat man—Babe Ruth—in the prime of his career.

Kobe Bryant played second fiddle to Shaquille O'Neal from 1997 to 2004 with the Los Angeles Lakers. The NBA equivalent of the two stars of the 1927 Yankees, Shaq and Kobe have performed up to Ruth and Gehrig's accomplishments. Fittingly, Kobe might be the best ever at his position—but he's never been as dominant as the heaviest man in his lineup (O'Neal).

Art Carney was the second banana to Jackie Gleason on the 1950s situation comedy "The Honeymooners." As Ed Norton, the sewer worker, Carney won five Emmy awards for playing behind a famous fat man—Jackie Gleason ("the Great One")—in the prime of his career.

Michael Imperioli plays Christopher Moltisanti on the HBO series "The Sopranos." He has been the second banana to James Gandolfini's Tony Soprano. Like the 1927 Yankees, or the 1955 Honeymooners, the Sopranos show and cast is the greatest of its time. Much of the credit goes to Chrissie, Tony's nephew and Carmela's first cousin. Under Tony's tutelage Christopher became a cugine and eventually, a made man—but his ascent wasn't smooth. Playing behind a fat man (Tony Soprano), Moltisanti is the best second option in an all-star family.

MICKEY MANTLE

I grew up believing that if you looked up the word *hero* in the dictionary, there would be a picture of the Yankee great Mickey Mantle. He was born in 1931 and rose from being a miner to a major hero for all of America. He was handsome. He combined incredible power with ridiculous speed. He had flawless baseball instincts. He was the symbol of youth and vitality, even while battling injuries and alcoholism. He played 18 seasons weak-kneed and in need. For much of his career, he was the best-loved, most-renowned athlete in the nation. But before fans really got to know him, at the beginning of his career, they called him "coward," "draft dodger," and "Commie." It was only after some of his best years that fans turned him into a legendary and heroic figure. But, even in the prime of his career, when the fans wanted to embrace Mick, he made little effort to connect with them, never tipping his hat or acknowledging the fans after hitting a home run. It was just his personality.

Not having lived through the Mickey Mantle years, I had to figure out why there were such strong reactions to the Yankees center fielder. Was this a legend that was more style over substance? Or was he, as my friend Bob Costas thinks, actually underrated and more than a little underappreciated?

Mantle was born in Commerce, Oklahoma, in 1931 during the country's Great Depression. Mick's dad, Mutt Mantle, worked his entire life at the mine. Mutt didn't want the same for his son, who he named after Mickey Cochrane, the Hall of Fame catcher. Mutt determined that his son should play baseball, and began working with him on hitting when Mickey was only five years old. Mutt would work all day in the mines and then come home and work with his son, teaching him the art of switch-hitting. Mickey would tell author Pete Golenbock in his 1975 *Dynasty* that his father "was a shoveler when he first went into the mines, and when he died, he was the ground boss. Dad was a real good semi-pro player. He was the one that said that someday there's going to be platooning, and that's the reason he taught me to be a switch-hitter."

Mick was a great athlete in high school, but once he was kicked in the ankle during a football game and shortly thereafter developed osteomyelitis, a serious, sometimes deadly bone disease. He was hospitalized for treatment in 1947 and again in 1948. It kept him out of the army, as service doctors who examined him found his condition serious enough to merit a 4-F classification. Mantle couldn't understand the negative reaction of the public. He always maintained that he would be glad to fight for the army, or play ball for the army. The army told him no, repeatedly. The Yankees told him yes, and he signed with them.

Mickey worked with his dad in the mines his last two years of high school. In 1951, Mantle's rookie year, the Yankees sent him to their minor-league team in Kansas City for additional seasoning. Mickey was so humiliated that he considered quitting and going home. Mutt Mantle told him, "If that's all the guts you have, then come home."

Mantle stayed, hit well in his short stint in the minors, and returned quickly to the Yankees.

The Yankees made it to the World Series in 1951, with Mantle playing right field to accommodate retiring Yankee center fielder Joe DiMaggio. Mantle had covered for DiMaggio—literally, covered ground that the aging Joe D. couldn't cover anymore. On October 6, in the fifth inning of Game 2 of the Series, Giants rookie Willie Mays hit a short fly ball to right-center field, between DiMaggio and Mantle. Mickey heard DiMaggio call for the ball at the last second. Mantle tried to stop, but his right shoe landed on a sprinkler head. In one of his books, Mantle described the moment like this: "There was a sound like a tire blowing out and my right knee collapsed."

Mantle hadn't yet played 100 games with the Yanks when he injured his knee. And in 2,000-plus games to follow, he would never again play another game for the Yankees without pain.

The stretcher came for him, and his father—at the Series game—escorted him to the hospital. When Mick tried to lean on his father to get out of the cab in front of the hospital, Mutt collapsed on the sidewalk. Mickey learned how gravely ill (with Hodgkin's disease) his father was. They wound up in the same hospital room. Mutt would survive another few months—even going back to the mines, before dying at the age of 39.

Mickey's father and his two uncles all died before they reached 40 years old. By the time he was 20, Mick had lost his best friend, who would never see Mickey inherit the center-field job from DiMaggio.

By the 1952 season, his manager and father figure, Casey Stengel, called Mick the greatest switch-hitter in history. Since counterpart Mays was in the army, some people were already calling Mick the most exciting player in the game, and had forgiven him for not serving his country. Of course, he had a lot to deal with besides learning to play his position. He had married, and was the sole support for his wife, his mother, two brothers, and a sister. It didn't stop him from batting .311 and finishing third in the MVP voting, though. After the World Series (in which he batted .345 with 2 home runs), the 20-year-old Mantle had to go back to work at the mines to make money for his family.

Early in the 1953 season, Mantle hit one of the longest home runs in history. He was batting right-handed against Washington when he drove a pitch 565 feet over the bleachers at Griffith Stadium.

Batting left-handed in 1956 at Yankee Stadium, he smacked a ball that was still rising when it crashed into the façade fixed to the roof of the third deck. Mantle maintained that the guys always thought that was his best shot.

He was entering his prime, and although statistics can't do justice to his dominance and greatness, let me give you a few.

Mantle's 1956 season was the single greatest season any player had between Ruth's seasons in the 1920s (pick one) and Barry Bonds's seasons in the early 2000s (pick one).

In 1956, Mantle won the Triple Crown and the MVP, and the Yankees won the World Series. He led the league in runs (132), home runs (52), home run percentage (9.76), RBI (130), batting average (.353), slugging percentage (.705), on-base average (.464), and total bases (376). He drew 112 walks (second in the league) and even stole 10 bases (seventh in the league).

Mantle's peak was 1955–1957, a three-year stretch where baseball was still the nation's number-one sport. Mickey slugged .661 in those three seasons, almost 50 points better than everyone not named Ted Williams.

Major-League Leaders in Batting Average, 1955–1957

1. .364 Ted Williams
2. .341 Mickey Mantle
3. .325 Stan Musial
4. .321 Hank Aaron

Mantle averaged .314 for the 10-year period from 1955 to 1964, tops in the American League in an era when only one other batter (Kaline, .310) averaged as much as .300. Mantle finished in the top seven in batting no less than eight different seasons.

Most Home Runs in American League, 1955–1963

1. 362 Mickey Mantle
2. 268 Rocky Colavito

In the 10-year period from 1954 to 1963, Mantle had a better home run percentage than everyone in the majors. He missed much of 1962 and 1963 with an injury.

Home Run Percentage in Major Leagues, 1954–1963

1. 7.67 Mickey Mantle
2. 6.51 Willie Mays
3. 6.43 Eddie Mathews
4. 6.18 Ernie Banks
5. 5.99 Frank Robinson
6. 5.76 Hank Aaron

Mantle was superior to all the great sluggers in the National League, and had a percentage *twice* what the next closest American League slugger had in those years (Al Kaline hit a home run 3.94 percent of the time to Mick's 7.67 percent).

Mantle was the dominant slugger of his time, leading the league by incredible margins. In 1956, he hit 56 home runs—no one else in the American League even had as many as 37 home runs. Mantle slugged .705 that season, a full .100 points higher than Ted Williams, who finished second.

Mantle won the American League MVP Award in 1956, 1957, and 1962. The fact that he didn't win in 1961 (when he batted .317 with 54 home runs and 128 RBI, and slugged .687) remains criminal. Mickey's teammate Roger Maris won the MVP in 1961, in large part because he broke Babe Ruth's single-season home run record.

In the years following his 1951 knee injury, Mantle suffered a host of other injuries. There was torn knee cartilage in 1952; torn left thigh muscles in 1953; a cyst behind the right knee in 1954; a pulled right thigh muscle in 1955; a tonsillectomy and sprained left knee in 1956; a torn right shoulder in 1957; a broken finger in 1959; a hip abscess requiring surgery in 1961; pulled left thigh muscles in 1962; torn rib cartilage, torn left knee cartilage, and a broken bone in his left foot in 1963; and more leg ailments in 1964. In the 1961 World Series, Yankees manager Ralph Houk had to order Mantle out of the game because an injury to his thigh had abscessed and the blood was soaking through Mantle's uniform.

Bob Costas (from his 1995 eulogy for Mantle): "Mickey Mantle had those dual qualities so seldom seen, exuding dynamism and excitement but at the same time touching your heart—flawed, wounded. We knew there was something poignant about Mickey Mantle before we knew what poignant meant. . . . There was greatness in him, but vulnerability too."

Mantle's Faustian bargain had him deal with the injuries, the grief over losing his father so young, and the impending doom of his (certain) early demise—but it also gave him immediate rewards, such as 12 pennants in his first 14 seasons. Number 7 won seven

World Series championships. He did it with his friends and drinking buddies, he did it with a manager he adored, and he did it spectacularly. Plus, by 1961, Mantle had finally won over the public. He had made everyone forget the great DiMaggio. When Roger Maris began threatening to break Babe Ruth's record of 60 home runs in 1961, the public made their intentions known: they wanted Mickey to break the record.

He never did surpass Babe's single-season record, but Mantle did break Babe Ruth's World Series record with 18 home runs.

His last three Series homers came in 1964, at the end of his last good season.

Bob Costas: "Mickey will be underrated in future generations because he really was done in October 1964, when he was just turning 33. After that, he played four more seasons, and all it did was lower his lifetime average. Because he had only 14 seasons through '64, and some of those were only 154-game seasons, and because of games missed due to injuries, he didn't have the number of career at-bats to offset the declining four years. If Mantle had retired after 1964, he would have left a .309 average and a plus .580 (actually .582) slugging average. Mays has long been considered the best position player after Ruth. Yet, through the prime cut of their careers, Mantle was every bit Mays's equal or very close to it. Now, with the explosion in offense, many players who weren't nearly as good as Mantle will have higher career numbers. As time passes, fewer people will have an appreciation for how great he was at his best, and how good he was relative to his peers."

Who's Better, Who's Best
Mickey Mantle or Joe DiMaggio?

As early as 1951, the New York press had begun comparing Mantle to DiMaggio. Yankees manager Casey Stengel would spur Mantle on by saying after the 1956 season—Mick's Triple Crown year—that DiMaggio, because he was a right-hander playing in a park that didn't give him any advantages—was the better player. Mantle, in a 1994 *Sports Illustrated* article chronicling his lifelong addiction to alcohol, said, "When I retired at the age of 37, Casey Stengel had said that when I came up, 'This guy's going to be better than Joe DiMaggio and Babe Ruth.' It didn't happen. I never fulfilled what my dad had wanted, and I should have. God gave me a great body to play with, and I didn't take care of it. I blame a lot of it on alcohol."

Despite the alcohol and the injuries, and the high expectations from the start, Mantle does surpass DiMaggio in this book.

Bob Costas is right—Mantle should have retired at the age of 33 following the 1964 season. Remember, DiMaggio retired in 1951, after only 13 seasons—so he never had that period of decline. Here is how their numbers look after each had played 13 seasons:

	At-Bats	Runs	Hits	HR	RBI	Batting Avg.	On-Base Avg.	Slugging Pct.
DiMaggio	6,821	1,390	2,214	369	1,537	.325	.398	.579
Mantle	6,533	1,473	2,016	454	1,298	.309	.429	.582

Now, DiMaggio was as graceful a fielder as there ever was. His teams were 9–1 in 10 World Series appearances. In DiMaggio's first seven seasons, he batted .323, .346, .324, .381, .352, .357, and .305. He drove in between 114 and 140 runs every year. He almost never struck out.

But Mantle walked a lot more, giving him a higher on-base average. Mantle hit more home runs and had a higher slugging average. DiMaggio batted much higher—but in an era when batting averages were 20 points higher than they were in Mantle's day.

DiMaggio: .325 career average when league average was .276 (49 points better)

Mantle: .298 career average when league average was .256 (42 points better)

If you take away Mantle's final four seasons—when his average was just .254 (and the league average was .242)—he and DiMaggio are a virtual wash.

Mantle's final four seasons were not a total waste. In May of 1967, he hit his 500th career home run in his 7,300th at-bat, which was faster than everyone but Ruth and Jimmy Foxx at the time. Mark McGwire and Harmon Killebrew would beat that, as will Alex Rodriguez if he stays healthy. At the time of Mantle's retirement, only Babe Ruth, Willie Mays, and Hank Aaron had hit more home runs. No one had ever played more games with the Yankees, despite the myriad of injuries Mantle suffered.

Although by a hair, Mantle was better than DiMaggio.

Bob Costas: "For decades, every scout would tell you that Mantle was the greatest raw talent they had ever seen, with his combination of speed and power."

Jim Bouton: "The best player I ever saw—either as a teammate, as an opponent, or on television . . . was Mickey Mantle. He had tremendous power from both sides of the plate and had incredible speed. You don't see that combination."

Tony Kubek: "Ted Williams was the best hitter I ever saw. But I'll say that with a caveat. One man—Mickey Mantle batting right-handed—was better even than Williams. As a left-handed batter, Mantle was a low-ball hitter, and an upper-cutter. But Mick batting right-handed was as good as there was."

Mantle had a difficult time with his father's early death in 1951, and began drinking to escape the pain. He always maintained that if he had known he was going to live so long, he would have taken better care of himself. He didn't follow rehab assignments or keep himself in shape during off-seasons. After he retired at the age of 37, his drinking habits became worse. He had biblical disappointments in his life—his son Billy came down with Hodgkin's disease when he was only 19, and died at 36. Mantle blamed himself for not fulfilling his father's dreams. He blamed himself for not doing more for his four sons, particularly Billy. Finally, he checked himself into the Betty Ford Clinic. In June of 1995, he received a liver transplant, prompting a sharp increase in the number of organ donors nationwide. In his last months, he was once again a hero.

In the end, he wasn't a hero because he had a magical name that rolled off the tongue. He wasn't a hero merely because he was white, in a predominantly white country, playing baseball at a time when it was becoming integrated and dominated by blacks. He wasn't a hero because he played the glamour position on the glamour team in the most glamorous city. In the end, he was a hero for all the right reasons.

He had the highest of highs and lowest of lows. What killed him was a bad liver. He died young, but he lasted longer than the other males in his family and achieved so much and impacted so many, despite what he believed, whether he truly understood that or not.

CHRISTY MATHEWSON

Many people in this country have one recollection of what life was like at the turn of the 20th century in America. That image is Walt Disney's sanitized version. Think about it. Walt Disney recaptured his childhood, or what he wished his childhood was like, and his Disneyland (and later, Disney World) became every youngster's idea of that era. What was Main Street USA, if not Disney's Midwestern sensibilities about life in the early 1900s? Ice cream parlors, general stores, and parades were the order of the day. Blatant disease and bigotry were the norm everywhere but in Walt's moneymaking mind.

One thing ol' frozen Walt had correct was that the heroes of his youth were represented correctly. Check out the Abe Lincoln and the Hall of Presidents display on Main Street. Other heroes reside in places like Frontierland (Davy Crockett), and Adventureland. Idols were politicians, war heroes, inventors, and writers. In Disney's youth, there were no heroes who made their living singing or dancing or throwing a baseball. A 1974 *Playboy* interview with a very old Groucho Marx asked him who his idols were growing up. Groucho responded that "I used to have a girl in Montreal." "Was she an idol?" the interviewer asked. "She was idle a good deal, but she made a pretty good living anyway," was Groucho's reply. The interviewer tried one more time. "Who did you like when you went to the theatre?" Groucho responded, "President Roosevelt." That was probably an honest answer from the rascally old vaudevillian. There were no stage or athletic heroes at the turn of the century.

Christy Mathewson was one of the first.

Ballplayers then were mostly young and uneducated. Many were off the farms or had worked in factories, and arrived mostly from the South. Among college graduates, baseball players were the ones too lazy or uneducated to work for a living.

"Matty," or "Big Six," as he was known (Big Six, because he was a "big six-footer"), became America's first baseball hero. He captured the heart of the nation in a way that few ever have. He was born in Factoryville, Pennsylvania, in 1880 (that sounds like a rejected idea for one of Mr. Disney's parks, doesn't it?).

He actually had a comfortable upbringing. His father was a gentleman farmer, and his mother was wealthy. His father played on Lincoln's team and fought for the Union.

In 1895, Christy was 15 years old and earned $1 a game playing for the Factoryville semipro team, pitching to kids three or four years older than him. Mathewson's grandmother had established Keystone Academy, and Christy played baseball, football, and basketball there—graduating from the high school and enrolling at Bucknell University.

At Bucknell, Christy starred in the three main sports, was elected class president, participated in glee club, and was a member of two literary societies. He was headed for a career in the ministry or forestry, but he loved playing baseball in the summer, and left Bucknell in 1899 to sign his first pro contract, with Taunton in the New England league. There he learned his famous pitch, the "fadeaway" or the "reverse curve." The rest, as they say, is history. (If you're wondering what happened to the fadeaway, later pitchers would use it and call it a different name: a "screwball.")

The New York Giants acquired Mathewson in 1900 for $2,000. Christy did not have much success that summer. New York wanted him to go back to the minors, which meant other teams could sign him. The Cincinnati Reds did so, and the Giants quickly traded pitcher Amos Rusie, the so-called "Hoosier Thunderbolt," to Cincinnati to get Mathewson back. Let's just say New York got the better of the deal. Rusie had won over 30 games in a season three times for the Giants, but that was before the pitcher's mound was moved back to 60 feet 6 inches. Rusie failed to win a single game for the Reds. Mathewson went on to win 373 in his career.

Mathewson was the first of many baseball stars to realize that New York was the place to be. From Mathewson to A-Rod, the biggest stage in baseball has always been New York. At the age of 21, in 1901, Mathewson pitched in front of as many as ten thousand per game, and became a star.

In 1901, he won his first eight games, with four of those games being shutouts. At the end of the season, his record was 20–17, as he completed 36 of his 38 starts. He had an earned run average of 1.99. His Giants were 52–85 that year, only 32–68 when Mathewson wasn't on the mound!

The Giants finished last in '02, with Mathewson suffering a "sophomore slump"—ironically, since he was the first college star to be in the majors.

In 1903, Mathewson won 30 games. New York found another good pitcher—Iron Man McGinnity—and the two combined to pitch nearly every day, elevating the Giants. Matty and McGinnity appeared in 100 of 139 games that season, and they combined for 61 victories.

By the following season, the team was a juggernaut. The Giants won 53 of their first 71 games, and Mathewson would win 33 games in 1904. They won the pennant, but wouldn't play the American League champion Red Sox in the World Series because Giants ownership (and manager John McGraw) so hated Ban Johnson and the American League.

"That's a minor league, why would we play them?" said McGraw. Of course, the Giants were upset that the American League put a team in New York (that would become the Yankees) to compete with the Giants.

McGraw and the Giants would change their tune a year later—in part to prove that they had the best team, and in part because the players wanted their share of some World Series money.

1905 World Series

There was enough intrigue to go around before this Series ever started. The managers were the two biggest names in the sport: Connie Mack of the Philadelphia Athletics and John McGraw. The cities were two of the biggest in America. Philadelphia had a 26-game winner, Rube Waddell, who would not pitch in the Series, as he had injured himself in an off-field confrontation with a teammate. Rumors were rampant that Waddell was approached by gamblers and told not to play. According to Ray Robinson's *Matty: An American Hero*, among the eighteen thousand crammed into Philadelphia's ballpark to see Game 1 were every big entertainer, saloon owner, gambler, and restaurateur from New York.

It was against this backdrop that Christy Mathewson started Game 1 for the Giants. He pitched a four-hit shutout. He also started Game 3, thanks to a well-timed rainout. He pitched another four-hit shutout. McGinnity started the fourth game and won, giving the Giants a 3–1 lead. Mathewson pitched the fifth game, and recorded his third shutout of the Series.

In the three victories over which he presided, he threw 27 innings. Not only didn't a Philadelphia batter score a run, not one got as far as third base in the three games. He struck out 16 men, while walking one and hitting one batter. His almost superhuman accomplishments ring loudly a full century later.

Here is what the *New York Times* reported in part of its game story following the fifth and final game. It speaks to Mathewson's personality and magnetism and sportsmanship.

> Mathewson was the last to arrive on the scene and got a magnificent reception. He was applauded for a full minute and the crowd yelled for him to doff his cap. Instead of doing so, however, he walked over to McGinnity, the conqueror of yesterday, and ostentatiously removed Joe's headgear. McGinnity returned the compliment.

The Series cemented Mathewson's reputation. He was a hero to the nation, sold to kids as someone who didn't smoke or drink (although he occasionally did).

1908

In the 1908 season, Mathewson won a career-high 37 games. It remains a National League record (post-1901). It was also a season the Giants were locked in a pennant race with the Cubs and Pirates. On September 23, the Giants led the other two teams by percentage points, with New York facing Chicago. One of the most famous games in history was played, and Mathewson was on the mound for the Giants. The score was tied 1–1, heading into the bottom of the ninth inning. New York had runners on first and third with two outs, when 18-year-old Fred Merkle (running from first base) failed to touch second as the winning run scored from third. Merkle was ruled out, the run was taken away, and the game called on account of darkness. The incident became famous as "Merkle's boner." The Giants and their fans had won a hard-fought game, only to have it snatched away by the umpire (later, the National League upheld his ruling). The Giants would finish the season tied with the Cubs and lose the "replayed" game of September 23. Years later, in his *Pitching in a Pinch*, Mathewson said losing the game to the Cubs was an event that stood out like "the battle of Waterloo and the assassination of Abraham Lincoln."

New York still had plenty left, and won three consecutive National League pennants in 1911, 1912, and 1913. Mathewson lost two games of the '11 World Series, and two more in the '12 Series. Although Christy had a World Series ERA of 1.51 in those three years, he lost five very big games.

In 1913, Mathewson went 68 innings without issuing a walk on his way to 25 wins. The next season was the 12th consecutive year that Big Six won as many as 20 games.

By 1916, Mathewson was 36 years old and had pitched way too many innings. His friend John McGraw traded him to the Reds, so that Mathewson might begin a managerial career.

From 1901 to 1914, Christy Mathewson won 361 games, 152 more wins than anyone not named Eddie Plank (who had 284 victories).

What Makes a Hero?

On August 28, 1918, Mathewson (at the age of 38) entered the army voluntarily to join the troops fighting the First World War. While in action overseas, he inhaled poisonous gas, which permanently damaged his lungs and left him with a serious cough. Within a few years, his cough got so bad that he entered a sanitarium in upstate New York. He died just before the first game of the 1925 World Series—when he was still just 45 years old.

Who's Better, Who's Best
Christy Mathewson or Tom Seaver?

Matty has been compared to Tom Seaver, who made his major-league debut in 1967, and according to sportswriter Maury Allen their careers, appearance, and personalities were similar. But as great as Seaver was, he was never considered the best pitcher ever. Mathewson was most certainly the best along with Cy Young and Walter Johnson in the first part of the 1900s.

Mathewson was one of baseball's first heroes, and one of its most enduring.

A Better Analogy

Christy Mathewson and Pat Tillman   Pat Tillman, who in the early 2000s gave up the glamorous life of a professional football star to join the Army Rangers, was remembered as a role model of courage and patriotism after military officials reported he had been killed in action in Afghanistan. Mathewson sacrificed for his country in World War I when, unlike Tillman, he was at the end of his career and the biggest star in his sport. That gives just a glimpse of the impact Mathewson had on baseball.

14

LEFTY GROVE

You can win a lot of bar bets posing the following question: Which Baltimore pitcher won 108 games (while losing only 36) for an Oriole team that won five straight pennants?

The answer is Robert Moses (Lefty) Grove, and it's a bit of a trick question. Grove pitched for the Baltimore Orioles of the International League in the early 1920s. At the time, the rival league had attracted quality players by paying them salaries equal to or greater than the major-league teams were paying. Grove was a local kid from Maryland, and was happy to pitch for Baltimore. It's the equivalent of Long Island, New York, basketball star Julius Erving playing for the ABA New York Nets for the first five years of his pro career.

Grove was born in 1900, and by 1915 he was working in the coal mines at 50 cents a day to help his family. Fortunately, he found sandlot baseball a few years later, and was signed by the Orioles. In 1920 he won 12 of his first 14 games for the Orioles. Next year, his record was 25–10. Two years later, it was 27–10, with 330 strikeouts. He was, by all accounts, a polished pitcher except for an annoying lack of control, leading the league in walks three different seasons. In the fall of 1924, Baltimore owner and manager Jack Dunn sold Grove for $100,000 to Connie Mack's Philadelphia Athletics. That was a lot of money at the time, especially for Mack. After five years and more than 100 victories, Grove was finally in the major leagues at the age of 25. Grove then won exactly 300 games in the majors, pitching until 1941. Eight times he won 20 or more games, including his masterpiece 1931 season, when he won 31 games.

Mack's $100,000 investment would pay dividends, but it took some time. In his rookie year, Grove was 10–12 with an earned run average of 4.75. The next season, Grove abandoned his sidearm delivery and began pitching overhand. It helped his control. Grove's style was to appear in a near-stop as he reached the top of his swing, instead of a quick follow-through. The result was a 1926 season that saw him win the first of nine ERA titles.

Mack and Grove had a mutual admiration. The legendary manager (who piloted the Athletics for 50 years) always maintained that Grove was his greatest pitcher. And Grove, in turn, had this to say about Mack: "He was like a fifth infielder or a fourth outfielder, using his scorecard to shift the players for certain hitters. He knew exactly how to set the defense in all situations."

In the 1928 season, Grove had not one, but two different innings where he struck out the side on just nine pitches. Midway through the 2004 season, Milwaukee Brewers pitcher Ben Sheets did this feat (something I first saw cartoon character Bugs Bunny do in a classic short), and it represented just the 37th time in history it had been done. Only two other pitchers besides Grove, however, have ever had more than one "super-perfect" inning. Sandy Koufax did it twice in the 1960s. Nolan Ryan did it twice in the 1970s.

The stock market may have crashed in 1929, but Grove's stock continued to rise. In 1929, the A's won their first of three consecutive pennants, with Grove leading the way. Lefty was 20–6 and led the league in winning percentage, ERA, and strikeouts. In 1930, Grove won 28 games and saved an additional 9 others. He again led the American League in winning percentage, ERA, and strikeouts.

Lefty's career season came the following year, in 1931. He won the MVP Award over Ruth, Gehrig, Foxx, and everyone else. In the greatest offensive year in baseball history, Grove was 31–4. The four games he lost were by scores of 2–1, 7–5, 1–0, and 4–3. I'm sure he won some lucky games, but this sucker came close to 34–1 or 35–0. His ERA of 2.06 that year led the league by a whopping 57 points.

Lefty took a 25–2 record (including a record-tying streak of 16 straight victories) into an August 23 game that 1931 season against the St. Louis Browns. The game was scoreless until a backup center fielder for the A's misplayed a two-out fly ball into a double, which scored the game's only run. Grove never forgave regular center fielder Al Simmons for taking that day off due to a doctor's appointment.

In June 2004, Richard Lederer's weekly column on the Internet posted an article called "The Grooviest Lefty of All Time." Lederer refuted an earlier column by ESPN.com writer Rob Neyer, who had written that Grove was rarely allowed to pitch against the Yankees for a stretch in the early 1930s.

Based on Lederer's research, Lefty faced the Yankees 69 times out of a total of 457 games started. In other words, Grove went against New York in 15.1 percent of his starts. Given that there were eight teams in the league throughout Grove's career, it would be expected that he would start one-seventh, or 14.2 percent of his games against each of his opponents. Grove started more than his fair share of games against the Yankees. In 1927, he started five games against them. In 1928, he started seven games. Only in 1930, when he started only two times against them in 32 starts, was the number really low (he should have started four or five games against New York). Lederer wrote that Grove was

30–25 with an ERA of 3.82 as a starting pitcher against the Yankees, including 18–16, 4.34 with the Athletics and 12–9, 3.11 ERA with the Red Sox.

Those numbers are well below Grove's numbers versus the rest of the league, but he still did damn well against the most feared offensive lineup in baseball history. I seriously doubt he would ever have called the Yankees "his daddies."

Max Silverman, Philadelphia Athletics Society historian: "Lefty Grove: He was the best left-hander there ever was. He certainly was the best of his time. He was mercurial in temper. He could certainly be an unpleasant individual. He got along formally with manager Connie Mack. Mack never called him by his first name. Called him Groves, which was actually his real name (they dropped the "s" later on). Lefty was given to fits of temper. It was not an unusual thing to see him tear the clubhouse apart whenever he lost."

By 1934, Grove had been sold to Boston. The Athletics had stopped winning and weren't drawing fans, and Mack sold off his stars. The Red Sox would gain dividends from their $125,000 investment, but it again took some time. In Grove's first year at Fenway, he was only 8–8 with an ERA of 6.52. He bounced back with a 20-win season in 1935, and won 34 the next two years. Now relying more than ever on his curveball, Grove won back-to-back ERA titles in 1938 and 1939 while going a combined 29–9. That left him with 286 victories. He limped to the finish line of 300 wins, needing two more seasons to achieve the goal. He was elected to the Hall of Fame in 1947.

In 1969, baseball named an all-time team to commemorate its centennial. Lefty Grove was named the greatest left-handed pitcher of all time. That says a ton about Grove in relation to two men who had been active in the previous decade: Warren Spahn and Sandy Koufax.

According to author Pete Golenbock's *Fenway*, Grove was an extremely difficult person. He wouldn't autograph baseballs. He didn't like kids. He didn't like rookies. He didn't like fans. But he could sure pitch. Thankfully, as historian Max Silverman told me, his catcher with the Athletics, Mickey Cochrane, was a great catcher and could handle Grove's personality as well as his fastball. Grove threw as fast as anyone in history. A 1933 newspaper article examining the issue concluded that Walter Johnson probably topped Grove, but tests can't be too accurate. During the 1931 World Series against the Cardinals, Paul Gallico, sports editor of the *New York News*, attempted to time the fastballer with a split-second stopwatch. Gallico timed a number of Grove's pitches at .46 second for the 60 feet 6 inches between the mound and home plate. If Grove threw a ball 60 feet 6 inches in .46 second, the ball would be traveling at 131 feet a second.

Of course, even in 1933, they noticed the obvious fallacies in Gallico's study. The first factor to be considered is that Grove, in delivering the ball, took a tremendous stride, which cut down distance to the plate. John McGraw said of Grove's pitching motion,

"Grove follows through better than any pitcher I've ever seen. The result is the ball does not have as far to travel when he releases it. When a good golfer hits a ball he keeps the face of the club in contact with the ball as long as possible. That is what Grove does."

Now, if my math is correct, 131 feet a second would be 89 miles per hour.

131 feet in one second
7,800 feet in 60 seconds (1 minute)
471,600 feet in 60 minutes (1 hour)
471,600 feet divided by 5,280 = 89.3 miles per hour
(there are 5,280 feet in a mile)

My conclusion is that this means either that today's pitchers really don't throw as fast as we think they do, or that stopwatches have improved considerably since 1931.

Who's Better, Who's Best
Lefty Grove or Sandy Koufax?

Grove won 300 games in the majors despite pitching five years in the International League, where his stats didn't count toward his career totals. Koufax never spent a day in the minor leagues, and won just 165 games. Grove had nine seasons in which he led the league in ERA. Koufax had only five great seasons, leading the league in ERA each of those five years. Both were hard-throwing southpaws who had trouble controlling their wildness early in their careers. Both of them had wicked curveballs, which made their fastballs even more devastating.

World Series Numbers

Grove	Koufax
4–2	4–3
1.75 ERA	0.95 ERA
5 starts	7 starts
4 complete games	4 complete games
2 saves	
36 strikeouts	61 strikeouts
6 walks	11 walks
51⅓ innings	57 innings

That is as close as you can come.

Let's not judge Grove or Koufax before they found their control and learned to win. Both Lefty and Sandy had their first 20-win season in the majors at age 27.

Performance at Age 27

1927 Grove	20–13	9 saves	3.19 ERA (league ERA 4.26)
1963 Koufax	25–5		2.54 ERA (league ERA 3.63)

Notice that both Grove and Koufax were a little more than one run better than the league ERA.

Best Four-Year Stretch

Lefty Grove	1930–1933	108–27	27 saves
Sandy Koufax	1963–1966	97–27	3 saves

In those four seasons, Grove and Koufax each won two World Series championships. Both led their league in victories three times in those four seasons. Each won an MVP. Grove led the league in saves one year. Koufax and Grove were the winningest pitchers, the stingiest pitchers, the ones with the most strikeouts, shutouts, and everything else. It's a virtual statistical toss-up.

Why Grove Gets the Advantage Over Koufax

Sandy Koufax pitched in an era when even ordinary pitchers put up outstanding numbers. Lefty Grove, on the other hand, had his dominating seasons smack in the middle of the offensive-happy Roaring Twenties and early 1930s. Grove faced the Yankees teams of Ruth and Gehrig. He faced them in 1927, when the Yankees lineup was known as "Murderers Row." Lefty gave up only six homers in 262 innings that entire season. One of them was to the Babe.

The other reason Grove is ahead of Sandy is longevity. Both men suffered arm injuries, but Grove worked through his, and remained an effective pitcher into his 40s. In fact, not only did Grove allow a Ruth homer in 1927, but Joe DiMaggio kept his 56-game hit streak alive in 1941 with a hit off of Grove. Remember, in the beginning of Grove's career, he won 108 games in the International League. Maybe major-league baseball doesn't count his accomplishments from those five seasons, but I do. Grove won over 400 games while being the meanest, fastest, most ornery pitcher there was. It may have been Bugs Bunny striking out three consecutive lumberjacks in that famous short, but Grove was actually closer in personality to Yosemite Sam.

Sandy Koufax matched Grove's 1931 season. He almost matched his four-year run in the early '30s. When one looks at the complete scorecard of both men, it becomes obvious that Grove beats Koufax—and all other left-handed pitchers.

Grove led the league in ERA a record nine seasons, including four straight. He topped the league in strikeouts in each of his first seven seasons in the majors.

That's all, folks.

SATCHEL PAIGE

He pitched against Babe Ruth and Ty Cobb in the 1920s. He outdueled fellow hurlers Dizzy Dean in the 1930s and Bob Feller in the '40s, when they were in their prime. In the '40s, he finally was able to sign with a major-league team, and pitched in the World Series. In the 1950s, he was used in relief for the hapless St. Louis Browns, and twice made the American League All-Star team. He made a brief comeback in the mid-'60s. Finally, in the early '70s, he became the first Negro Leaguer to be inducted with his fellow baseball immortals into the Hall of Fame. He died in the '80s, after teaching us all to "not look back, because someone may be gaining on you." He's been gone over 20 years now, and no one has yet gained on him.

He was born in Mobile, Alabama, definitely—and in 1906, possibly. Some reports have his birth around 1900, which would have made Paige 48 years old upon reaching the majors.

He started his career in 1924, when he had a tryout with the Mobile Tigers, a semipro baseball team.

There were no records kept of his individual appearances—there wasn't even a reliable birth certificate for this cat. We can't judge him on statistics, like most of the other greats. This is what Paige said he did in the Negro Leagues: He reckoned that he pitched around 2,500 games and won around 2,000. According to him, he pitched around 100 no-hitters. He even said that he played for around 250 different teams. We don't have to believe everything he said, but I'm sure there's a kernel of truth in the ageless wonder. It is documented from the newspapers at the time that in 1933 he went 31–4, winning 21 consecutive games and at one point hurling 62 consecutive scoreless innings.

He pitched for pay and caught heat for it. His teammates felt they couldn't count on him because he never hesitated to jump from one team to another if the price was right. He played from 1937 to 1939 in the Dominican Republic, Mexico, and Puerto Rico. And in 1935, Paige pitched for an integrated semipro team in Bismarck, North Dakota. The Bismarck team allowed Paige to hire himself out to other teams in the area. He took advantage, and was worth every penny to Bismarck. Bismarck won 95 of 100 games that year. Paige claimed he started 29 games one month for Bismarck, and won 104 games that year.

He was skinny and tall, with most accounts telling us he was 6′4″. So much of Paige's exploits are the stuff of legend, but this we know: he threw very fast and he had pinpoint control. He could warm up by throwing strikes not over home plate, but over a match-book. Sometimes, he put a gum wrapper over a part of home plate to indicate where he intended his pitch to go.

Joe Garagiola: "In 1972, I did my show, 'The Baseball World of Joe Garagiola,' and I did a show with Satchel. I said, 'Satch, I've heard so much about your control, and how you could get the ball over matchbox covers. What I want to do is catch you from the regulation 60 feet 6 inches away, with a real umpire—and you have to get the ball over the matchbox cover.' I told Satch he probably couldn't get 5 out of 10 pitches over. He answered that 5 out of 10 would be a bad day. He threw 8 of 10 over the little match-box—and the other two just barely missed!"

He got his excellent control from throwing rocks at birds and butterflies as a kid. Although he normally threw overhand, Satchel sometimes pitched with a submarine or sidearm delivery. He had an assortment of pitches. Satchel named his pitches, calling his fastball "Long Tom," "Bee Ball," "Jump Ball," or something else. He also threw an unhittable curveball, which he named the "Bat Dodger," the "Hurry-Up Ball," the "Midnight Creeper," and the "Nothin' Ball." One thing he didn't throw was the spitball. He also didn't hit batters. His precision assured that he always had control of where his pitches were going.

Bob Wolff: "Satchel Paige was fantastic. He had a variety of windups. The first time a batter came up, he would pump the ball over his head, using a windmill motion. The next time up, the same batter might see Satch's famous "hesitation pitch." The commissioner eventually banned that pitch—it was so unfair to the batter. He was not only fast, but had unerring control. In the Negro Leagues, it was said that he would throw three straight balls on purpose, and then would come back with three consecutive strikes. He could always put the ball where he wanted it."

Joe Garagiola: "I batted against Satchel in an exhibition game when I was with the Pirates and he was with the St. Louis Browns. It had to be 1952, and so he was old. . . . I had heard so much about him, I couldn't wait to hit against him. I figured that I would take his first pitch and see how fast it was. I took what must have been around a 92-mile-per-hour heater. I thought to myself that he could still bring it. The next pitch came in even faster. Although there were no radar guns, of course, it must have been about 95 miles per hour. I wanted to catch up to his fastball, so I timed his release point and began my swing. He threw me his hesitation pitch. He froze me completely, and all I could do was watch it float by. He threw me three strikes that must have timed out at 92, 95, and 53 miles per hour. He had me hypnotized—there was no way I could hit that guy."

Curt Gowdy: "Some people thought that Satchel Paige should have been the first black player in the majors. He'd been a legend for twenty years in the Negro Leagues, the greatest pitcher of his day. Maybe that was why Branch Rickey (who signed Jackie Robinson to be the first black ballplayer) bypassed him—because Paige's time had passed."

Joe DiMaggio said that Paige was the greatest pitcher he ever batted against, but that was in the late '30s and early '40s. When Jackie Robinson was signed by Brooklyn, it must have been very hard for Satchel to take. "Somehow I'd always figured it would be me," Satchel wrote in his 1962 autobiography, *Maybe I'll Pitch Forever*. Robinson, though he was 27 when signed, spent a year in the minor leagues. Other Negro League veterans, including Roy Campanella, did the same. Satchel, rightly, did not want to subject his body to time in the minor leagues, after earning more than most major leaguers over the years. Cleveland Indians owner Bill Veeck—a noted promoter whose primary function was to attract fans to the park—wanted Paige as a spot starter and reliever. He held off hiring him in 1947, because he didn't want the signing to appear to be one of his promotions.

After Veeck hired him midway through the 1948 season—first having him audition for 31-year-old manager Lou Boudreau, whom Paige referred to as "Mr. Lou" in his autobiography—the Indians won their first pennant in more than 20 years. Paige went 6–1, becoming the seventh black to play in the majors. He was also the first black American League pitcher.

Paige became the biggest draw in the American League—and the pitcher that put Cleveland over the top. Boudreau passed him up for a World Series start in a move that startled many, and his lone relief appearance in that World Series—in a mop-up role—was Paige's crowning moment according to his 1962 autobiography. Paige had one more year in Cleveland before he was released. But he was far from finished, thanks to the fact that Veeck had moved on to the St. Louis Browns.

In 1952 (remember, he was at least 45), he won 12 games for Veeck's Browns. He saved 10 games, which was second in the league. He made the All-Star team in 1952 and 1953, after which no team gave him another chance until Charlie Finley's Kansas City A's did in 1965. In between, the master entertainer and pitcher continued to barnstorm the country. He never really retired or stopped pitching.

Satchel was by far the biggest showman and quite possibly the best pitcher in the Negro Leagues. He was definitely the greatest ambassador. He was, like the Frank Sinatra song goes, "A puppet, a pauper, a pirate, a poet, a pawn, and a king." He was up and down, and over and out. He was part Michael Jordan, part Meadowlark Lemon, part Donald Trump, and part Babe Ruth. He was nearly as famous as the other great "Satch" of his time—Louis Armstrong. When you listen to the stories and read the accounts, you can't help but think he very well may have been the greatest pitcher ever.

Puppet

Said Paige, "Quite a few people told me if I was white I would be playing in the major leagues. But I never did feel no bitterness. I was satisfied in my own world."

Sure, he was. And when he was told he was entering the Hall of Fame, he said what the commissioner and old-world owners wanted to hear: "When Jackie went in, they asked me if I was bitter and I wasn't. They said then they had to have a college boy as the first black player in the majors, and in my soul, I believe Jackie should have been the first."

Pauper

Mark Ribowski's 1994 biography of Paige, *Don't Look Back*, quoted Satchel as saying, "I was no different than any other kid, only in Mobile I was a nigger kid. I went around with the back of my shirt torn, a pair of dirty diapers or raggedy pieces of clothing covering me. Shoes? They were somewhere else." Is it any wonder that he was a thief by the age of 10, and was caught stealing jewelry from a store a few years after that? Satch put a bunch of rings in his mouth, and the guard saw it and hit Satch in the mouth and the rings flew out. The 12-year-old was committed to the Industrial School for Negro Children just outside of Montgomery, Alabama. He was locked up at night, and during the day he was forced to pick potatoes and cotton.

Pirate

Satchel Paige indeed lived like a pirate, long after he was a child thief. He was never that popular with teammates. Of course, how could they trust him? He could not be counted on to show up on time, and never hesitated to jump from one team to another if the price was right. When real pirates returned from their plundering escapades, they were ready for fun. Pleasures such as rum, food, wine, and gambling made poor tavern masters rich overnight. In short, the pirates wasted in the taverns all they had earned, by giving themselves to all manner of voluptuousness they could afford. Similarly, after reading Paige's 1962 autobiography, we discover that Paige spent every dime he ever made.

Poet

Satchel's famous rules for living, published in *Colliers* magazine in the 1950s, included the advice to "Avoid fried foods, which angry up the blood," and "Don't look back, someone might be gaining on you." His words were poetic in their simplicity and their directness. Some of his legendary sayings are so beautiful, it boggles my mind that no one has turned them into songs or shows. "How old would you be if you didn't know how old you were?" "Work like you don't need the money. Love like you've never been hurt. Dance like nobody's watching."

Pawn

The two baseball owners who were hucksters and promoters intent first and foremost on getting fans into the park were Bill Veeck and Charlie Finley. They were the owners that hired Paige long after his prime. Finley bought the Kansas City Athletics in 1965 and signed the famous pitcher, who happened to live in Kansas City. Paige may have been as old as 60. Satchel sat in the bullpen in a rocking chair and was served coffee by a "nurse" between innings for a September 25 game against the Red Sox. No matter that Paige pitched three scoreless innings before nine thousand fans that night. He served as a human "bobble-head" doll, designed to bring people in the front gate, as opposed to having a role on the team. To some in those racially charged days, he was a "Stepin' Fetchit" for allowing himself to be demeaned for a payday.

King

In 1971, Satchel Paige became an immortal. He was enshrined in the Baseball Hall of Fame. He went in as the first member from the Negro Leagues, with Josh Gibson and Buck Leonard to follow the next year.

In my opinion, he was better than Bob Feller and other contemporaries. If he had played in the majors all along, I believe he would have been ranked behind Walter Johnson and ahead of all others. He was that good.

16

OSCAR CHARLESTON

According to the late Hall of Famer Judy Johnson, Oscar Charleston "was Ty Cobb and Tris Speaker rolled into one." Johnson was a teammate of Charleston's in 1930 on the Homestead Grays, and played against him for a number of years.

Charleston began playing professionally in 1915, and was often compared to Cobb, at least offensively. They played the same aggressive kind of baseball. The writers and athletes of the time, however, insist that Charleston had much more power than Cobb and was better defensively. Oscar was six feet tall and had that combination of blazing speed and tremendous power. The speed allowed him to play a very shallow center field, just like Speaker.

He was born in Indianapolis in 1896. The local professional baseball team, the Indianapolis ABC's—a black team—hired him as a batboy. In 1910, shortly before his 15th birthday, he joined the army and was made a member of the black 24th Infantry, stationed in the Philippine Islands. In the Philippines, he had the opportunity to run track, and records show that he ran the 220-yard dash in 23 seconds. He also played service ball, and by 1914 was the only black player in the Manila League. Oscar was discharged in 1915 and joined the Indianapolis ABC's, where he began one of the most legendary careers in the Negro Leagues.

Oscar was a left-handed batter and had the five skills that make a great baseball player: he could hit, hit for power, run, throw, and field. Charleston also had a temper. A brief article on Charleston in the November 26, 1915, edition of the *Indianapolis Star* carried the headline: "Charleston dropped by the ABC Club. Colored Outfielder who Assaulted Umpire Scanlon Here is Dismissed by Taylor While Team is in Cuba."

Oscar, like many players of the time, played winter ball in Cuba, making baseball a year-round job. The Indianapolis team had been playing Cuban teams for a number of weeks when one day, Oscar apparently got into a fight with an umpire. He was held by police on $1,000 bond. The article from the *Indianapolis Star* concluded, "Only prompt action by the police prevented a race riot." Charleston was suspended by the team owner, C. I. Taylor.

By 1916, Charleston was back with the ABC's when they beat the Chicago American Giants to capture the Black World Series. Charleston changed teams in 1919 to the Chicago American Giants, run by a man named Rube Foster. A year later, the league put Charleston back in Indianapolis to maintain a competitive balance in the league. In 1921, Charleston was at the peak of his physical skills. He led his league in batting (.426), triples (10), home runs (14), and stolen bases (28) in a 50-game season.

If he had been allowed in the major leagues, would he have done better than American League batting champ Harry Heilmann, a line drive hitter with no speed? I believe there is little doubt that he would have won several batting titles, stolen base titles, and hit his share of home runs.

Charleston began his managerial career as early as 1925, when he became the player-manager of the Harrisburg Giants of the Eastern Colored League. In 1928, he joined the Philadelphia Hilldale club for two seasons, and reportedly batted .396 with 99 hits in 250 at-bats, including 37 extra-base hits.

He joined the Homestead Grays in 1930, teaming with Judy Johnson, Josh Gibson, and Smokey Joe Williams to lead the Grays over the New York Lincoln Giants in a 10-game Black World Series.

By then, Charleston was a first baseman with an expanding waistline. The Grays were an outstanding team, and during the down-and-out days of the Great Depression, the team functioned as entertainment in addition to sport. The Grays would receive several hundred dollars for each contest with local semipro teams. The more money they were to receive, the closer they permitted the local team to make the score. They reportedly offered an Indiana coal mining team a close game for $200. They were told that they would get their $200, but they would have to earn every penny, as the local team planned on winning. Charleston took that as a challenge, and offered an additional wager of a steak dinner to play the entire game one-handed! As the local pitcher threw his hardest in his warm-up before the game, Charleston said, "If the kid has a fastball to go with his slowball, he might do okay."

Charleston won his bet, as surely he must have won many in those years.

In 1932, financier Gus Greenlee raided the Grays and moved Charleston and other stars to his Pittsburgh Crawfords. Charleston became the player-manager, batting .363 with 19 triples and 13 home runs. That was second best on the team to Josh Gibson. That legendary Crawfords team also boasted Satchel Paige and Cool Papa Bell.

Oscar was close to 40 years old, but he still played first base and appeared in three East-West All-Star Games between 1933 and 1935. In 1941, at the age of 45, he started managing the Philadelphia Stars. He still took some turns at bat.

Charleston signed with Branch Rickey in 1945 to play for the Brooklyn Brown Dodgers. Rickey formed the United States League as a way to evaluate black players for possible integration into the major leagues. Charleston was born 20 years too soon, for he would have been Rickey's choice to integrate baseball in another era. He was reliable (he wasn't a late-night partier), and he was a hard slider like Cobb who could take and give punishment.

Rickey's relationship with Charleston provided big dividends to Brooklyn for many years, as Charleston had Rickey's ear. A July 1951 article by Joe King in *The Sporting News* provided a few clues as to how Roy Campanella became a Dodger:

> Clyde Sukeforth was one of the masterminds of the organizational meeting when Campanella was first discussed in 1945. Our general opinion, from what we had learned, was that Campanella was too old. But Mr. Rickey said, "Before we decide, let's hear what Charleston has to say."

That was Oscar Charleston, one of the great hitters whom Mr. Rickey had hired because Charleston could get in clubhouses and find out facts in the Negro Leagues. Charleston told us, "That boy's not too old; he started early."

Campanella was signed by the Dodgers and became the catcher on their pennant-winning teams for a glorious decade.

Charleston's career spanned virtually the entire history of the Negro Leagues. Following Robinson's debut with Brooklyn, Charleston returned to the Philadelphia Stars as the Negro Leagues began to fold. Oscar spent some time managing the Indianapolis Clowns, baseball's answer to the Harlem Globetrotters, and he took a team of all-stars on a tour of Canada, rooming with Satchel Paige to make certain Paige was around to pitch the games.

In 1949, Charleston took a job in the baggage department of the Pennsylvania Railroad Station. He worked there for several years. He suffered a stroke in 1954, at the age of 56, and died a few days later.

Charleston was, with Paige and Gibson, the greatest of Negro League stars.

Who's Better, Who's Best
Oscar Charleston or Ty Cobb?

In 2000, in an off-Broadway production of *Cobb*, playwright Lee Blessing had Cobb confront Oscar Charleston. Charleston's character asked Cobb how he would like to be known as "the white Oscar Charleston." Cute.

If Charleston had been able to play in the major leagues in the 1920s, when he was thin and fast, and the ball was lively, there is no telling how good he would have been compared to Cobb. As an excellent center fielder, he would have been more valuable defensively than Ruth. As a base runner, with his spikes aiming for certain players, he would have been Cobb's equal.

Timing is the only thing that prevented Oscar from achieving major-league glory. Legend has it that he once pulled the mask off of a Klansman and began punching him. Even if that's not true, it's fairly safe to assume that, like Cobb, he had plenty of rage bottled up inside him. It's not hard to see why. He was born in the period of Reconstruction and died before the Civil Rights Act. He wasn't a slave, but he wasn't afforded the opportunities of other Americans.

MIKE SCHMIDT

In the 1950s and '60s, the National League dominated baseball, but by the early 1970s, the familiar dinosaurs that had ruled the terrestrial grass fields were becoming extinct. Ernie Banks played his last game in 1971. Roberto Clemente died prematurely following the 1972 season. Willie Mays hung up his spikes in 1973. Hank Aaron was finished with the Braves in 1974.

The landscape changed, with many of the teams moving to cookie-cutter stadiums with Astroturf. It was at that time that Michael Jack Schmidt emerged in Philadelphia. He was one who hit more homers than any other third baseman before or since. One whose fielding would qualify him for Hall of Fame entry. One who provided speed and durability and would walk nearly 1,400 times.

Mike Schmidt was a rookie in 1973, Mays's final season. He bridged the gap in the National League between Mays and Barry Bonds. There wasn't a whole lot to get excited about in the Schmidt era, unless you liked disco, bell-bottom jeans, and "Laverne and Shirley."

Schmidt was worth getting excited about, if you were a baseball fan, however. Was he ever!

Michael Jack Schmidt was born in 1949 in Dayton, Ohio. After an outstanding collegiate career at the University of Dayton, Schmidt was drafted in the second round of the June 1971 draft by the Philadelphia Phillies.

The shortstop on the College All-America team for 1971 became the Pacific Coast League's all-star second baseman in 1972. He came up to the last-place Phillies at the end of the season and played third base in 11 games. He hit his first home run in his 34 at-bats that season.

In the 1972 off-season, the Phillies traded their starting third baseman, Don Money, and made Schmidt their starter at the hot corner. Money had batted only .223 and .222 the previous two seasons, so it would be hard for Schmidt to do worse.

He failed miserably in his rookie season, batting only .196 with 18 homers in 132 games. It was the major leagues' lowest batting average among regulars that season.

Schmidt had been touted as having unlimited potential before that 1973 season, but at that point in his career he couldn't hit a breaking ball.

Following the season, he played winter ball in Puerto Rico and changed his hitting approach while facing hurler Pedro Bourbon. He found himself relaxed at the plate, and for the first time he didn't try to muscle the pitch. After that, he found he was a better hitter.

In the next five seasons, he hit 171 home runs. That might not sound like much in today's Sosa/Bonds/McGwire days, but it was 20 more home runs than anyone else hit from 1974 to 1979.

Through the 1979 season, Schmidt's career batting average was only .255. However, he walked 621 times in the six years from 1974 to 1979. He placed in the top 10 in on-base average four of those six seasons, despite the anemic batting average.

Even before his brilliant eight-year run from 1980 to 1987, Schmidt was a terrific player. In 1977, he scored 114 runs on his .274 batting average. That's the record for most runs scored on a sub-.280 average in baseball history.

It wasn't just the home runs that earned Schmidt a six-year, $3 million contract in 1977, making him one of the highest-paid players in baseball at the time. Phillies general manager Paul Owens credited Schmidt with saving the team 15 to 18 runs on defense. Even if the number of runs is debatable, Schmidt's defense most certainly was beyond questioning. Owens said that while Brooks Robinson may have been better defensively to his right (getting balls hit down the line), Schmidt was better to his left. He made shortstop Larry Bowa's job easier by allowing Bowa to cheat a little more to *his* left.

Tim McCarver: "Mike Schmidt was the best third baseman in the history of the game. . . . I have all the respect for Brooksie, but he played on a high infield grass in Baltimore, while Schmidt had to play deeper, had to have a better arm. . . . His base running was exceptional . . . he stole 32 bases one year. . . . When you look at his runs scored and runs driven in, Schmittie has to be the best third baseman of all time."

Was Schmidt consistent? Beginning in 1974, he hit 36, 38, 38, and 38 home runs in four consecutive seasons. He hit at least 30 home runs in 13 of 14 seasons, missing only in 1978. In 1974, he was second with 116 RBI and led the league with a .546 slugging percentage. He hit into just four double plays. He led the league in home runs for the first of eight times. On April 18, 1976, Schmidt hit home runs on four consecutive at-bats against the Cubs. At one point in that game, the Phillies trailed 13–2. Led by Schmidt's four drives, Philadelphia won the wild game 18–16.

He played in Philadelphia, so he got booed a lot. He got booed in 1973, when he failed to live up to expectations. He got booed after signing the big contract in 1977. He got booed when the Phillies lost playoff series in 1976, 1977, and 1978. Never mind that Schmidt (along with pitching ace Steve Carlton) was most responsible for making the Phillies division champs during the regular season.

In the 1977 League Championship Series against the Dodgers, Schmidt managed just one single in 16 at-bats. In the 1978 League Championship Series against the Dodgers, Schmidt had just three hits in 15 at-bats. In the three consecutive years that the Phillies lost postseason series, Schmidt played in 11 postseason games and had 44 at-bats without hitting a home run.

In 1979, the Phillies spent spring training actually playing Schmidt at second base—where he hurt his throwing arm while making double-play pivot throws. What were they thinking? Luckily for Schmidt, the Phils traded for second baseman Manny Trillo, and the move allowed Schmidt to move back to third base before the season started.

Despite the booing, and the occasional attempt by the Phils to tinker with his defensive position or his batting swing, his game continued to improve dramatically.

Mike Schmidt

First 2,115 at-bats	618 strikeouts	29.2 percent of his at-bats
Last 6,237 at-bats	1,265 strikeouts	20.2 percent of his at-bats

Schmidt also improved his batting average. Through 1979, his career average was .255. In the 1980s, his average was .277.

Everything came together in his game in 1980, his first of three MVP seasons.

Mike Schmidt, 1980

.380 on-base average (4th in league)

.624 slugging average (1st in league)

104 runs scored (2nd in league)

48 home runs (1st in league, a record for third basemen)

121 RBI (1st in league)

.286 batting average

He won a Gold Glove that year (his fifth in a row). He batted .381 in the World Series against the Royals to help Philly to the World Series title.

He was even better the next year.

No third baseman has ever won the Triple Crown (leading the league in batting average, home runs, and RBI), but Schmidt came close in a strike-shortened 1981 season. He finished fourth in batting (.316), and led the league in home runs (31) and RBI (91).

That was in 102 games and only 354 at-bats. He hit a home run once every 11 at-bats that season. Since the strike cost him about 200 at-bats, it is safe to assume Schmidt might have hit a career-high 50 home runs that season. He was certainly on pace.

For the record, the closest a third baseman has ever come to winning the Triple Crown was Al Rosen in 1953, when he finished second in batting and led the American League in home runs and RBI.

Schmidt was 33 years old in 1983, old by baseball standards but young for his Phillies team, which began coveting experienced players to make a run at capturing another title. They already had 42-year-old Pete Rose and 38-year-old Steve Carlton; and they figured Ben Franklin was even older than that when he opened the first library and started flying kites. The team went out and got 41-year-old Tony Perez and 39-year-old Joe Morgan. The ace reliever, Tug McGraw, was 38. Schmidt was the baby of the bunch.

Schmidt hit 40 home runs, drove in 109, and finished fourth in the MVP voting in 1983. The attempt at winning one more title by signing a bunch of old veterans on their way to the Hall of Fame worked about as well as the 2004 Los Angeles Lakers' attempt at the same plan. It worked up until the World Series, where the Phils bowed out meekly in five games (sounds familiar). In the 1983 World Series, Schmidt had just one single in 20 at-bats.

Over the next four seasons, Schmidt batted .277, .277, .290, and .293. He cut his strikeouts way down. He still hit 30 home runs or more each season.

In 1985, at the age of 35, Schmidt moved to first base for 106 games so a man named Rick Schu could play third base. The Schu didn't fit, and Schmidt returned to third, where he played the majority of his games his last four seasons. Back at third base, Schmidt produced his third MVP season in seven years in 1986. He won his 10th Gold Glove that season. He was first in the league in slugging, and fourth in on-base average. He scored 97 runs, third most in the league. He led the league in home runs (for the eighth time) and RBI (for the fourth time).

In 1987, players started hitting more home runs, and Schmidt's 35 was only sixth in the league. He suffered a rotator cuff injury the following year, and never did recover. He retired in May of 1989 with 548 home runs, then seventh on the all-time list.

Most Home Runs Between 1972 and 1992

1. 548 Mike Schmidt
2. 436 Dave Kingman
3. 432 Dave Winfield
4. 431 Reggie Jackson
5. 414 Eddie Murray

Even when we include a year or two before Schmidt came on the scene, and extend for a few seasons after Schmidt left (to show a 20-year period), we can see Schmidt's dominance in home run hitting.

Who's Better, Who's Best
Mike Schmidt or Harmon Killebrew?

	AB	HR	RBI	Batting Avg.	On-Base Avg.	Slugging Pct.
Harmon Killebrew	8,147	573	1,584	.256	.376	.509
Mike Schmidt	8,352	548	1,595	.267	.380	.527

Killebrew is one of the top one hundred players in baseball history, and was a premier slugger in the 1960s. Although Killebrew hit a few more homers (in a few less at-bats), and their on-base average is virtually the same, Schmidt was probably a touch better as a hitter. Schmidt had a higher slugging percentage. "Killer" stole only 19 bases in his career. Schmidt stole 174. Killebrew scored 1,283 runs. Schmidt scored 1,506.

Killebrew never led his team to a postseason series victory, and Schmidt did. In the field, though, Schmidt far exceeds Killebrew. Schmidt played 2,212 games at third base. Killebrew played 791 games at third, with the majority of his games at first base, but also some in the outfield and as designated hitter. Killebrew was a below-average fielder who didn't get to as many balls as the league average.

If Schmidt's glove raised him above Killebrew, it was his bat that separated him from other great glove men at third base, players like Brooks Robinson and Graig Nettles and others.

George Brett and Eddie Mathews are the closest to Schmidt, but Schmidt remains alone as the greatest third baseman in history.

A Better Analogy

Mike Schmidt and Michael Jordan As great a player as Jordan was offensively, he was better defensively. At one point in his career, he was the best offensive and defensive player in the NBA. One could make the same case for Schmidt in baseball.

ROGERS HORNSBY

What should you know about Rogers Hornsby? For one thing, his first name was Rogers (his mother's maiden name) and not Roger. The other is this: since the mid-1920s, he has been regarded as the greatest right-handed batter in the game's history. That means he's regarded as a better batter than DiMaggio, Aaron, and anyone else you want to name to hit from the right side. He was also considered as distant and aloof as Barry Bonds is now. He might have been a brilliant manager if he had learned a little diplomacy along the way.

He had a famous and distinct hitting style. Hornsby stood in the farthest corner of the batter's box with a heavy bat held at the end. He stepped into the ball. Many pitchers suspected that Hornsby could not hit an outside pitch with his stance, but Hornsby managed to destroy pitching with his unorthodox batting style.

He was born in 1896 in Winters, Texas. He was 19 years old, and playing in Class D baseball, when the St. Louis Cardinals bought him for a mere $500. Hornsby was no more than 135 pounds, with skinny arms on his 5'11" frame, and his manager, Miller Huggins, urged Rogers to choke up on the bat. He put up a .246 mark with the Cardinals in 18 games in the 1915 season, and then gained 25 pounds over the winter, returning at 160 pounds and able to switch back to the swing that would bring him fame and fortune.

In his career, Hornsby would play 1,561 games at second base. He played just one game there in his first four seasons. It was not until 1920 that Hornsby became a full-time second baseman (having played just 25 games at second previous to that season). An accomplished shortstop, he could have played any position. His only reported weakness at second base, oddly enough, was in the fairly routine play of going back on a pop fly. But Hornsby was skilled at making the double play. When he moved to second base in 1920, Hornsby became a great player.

Starting in 1920, everything clicked for the man they called "Rajah." Umpires started discarding older baseballs once they became harder to see, replacing them with new, white baseballs, which made things easier for hitters. Hornsby's manager with the Cards, Branch

Rickey (yes, the same Branch Rickey that you will read about in the Jackie Robinson and Robert Clemente chapters), encouraged Rogers to push his weight close to 200 pounds. It wasn't fat, it was muscle. Hornsby went from 32 extra-base hits in 1919 to 73 extra-base hits in 1920. I wonder if people commented on his neck size. Meanwhile, the extra weight couldn't be responsible for his batting eye, could it? Rajah went from being a .318 hitter getting on base 38 percent of the time to a .370 batter getting on base 43 percent of the time. Whatever the reason, Hornsby won the batting title by a whopping 19 points. He led the National League in hits, runs batted in, and doubles.

Hornsby hit 36 home runs in his first five full seasons. He then hit 21 home runs in 1921 and 42 homers the next year. His stretch from 1921 to 1925 was the best five-year offensive output for 80 years, until Barry Bonds. Some people might still prefer Hornsby's half-decade.

He won the batting title all five of those seasons, posting averages of .397, .401, .384, .424, and .403. He led the majors with a .402 average and 1,078 hits in those five seasons. He led the league in doubles in three of those years, triples one year, and home runs two years. His single-season .424 average remains the highest of the 20th or 21st century.

Hornsby was improving on Ty Cobb's numbers. He had more total bases than even Babe Ruth in that five-year period. Hornsby led the National League in slugging percentage eight times in a nine-year period. He led in on-base average seven times in an eight-year span.

This guy was brash and outspoken, and it got him into trouble sometimes. He became the Cardinals' player-manager in 1925, his 10th year with the club. In 1926, St. Louis captured their first pennant, advancing to the World Series against the Yankees. In the Series, Hornsby brought in 39-year-old Pete Alexander to strike out Tony Lazzeri in the seventh inning of Game 7, and the Cards went on to win the world championship.

Hornsby played on five different teams and managed five different franchises. He would've fit in nicely with modern free agency, as his style grated on people, who were happy to move him every few years. Following that 1926 season, Hornsby was traded to the New York Giants, essentially for their great second baseman Frankie Frisch. Hornsby couldn't get along in St. Louis with Rickey or owner Sam Breadon, and wouldn't be able to get along with Giants owner Horace Stoneham, either. After a year, Rogers was traded to the Boston Braves.

The 1920s were really Hornsby's great decade. He was fired in 1932 by the Cubs, and they went on to win the pennant. He lost a reported $100,000 in the 1929 stock-market crash. He managed the St. Louis Browns from 1933 to 1937. After that, he spent 15 years in exile, coaching and managing in the minor leagues. As a manager, trouble always found Rajah. No one could appraise a player like Hornsby, yet he couldn't hold a job.

There were always reports about him gambling on racehorses, but he always blamed his dismissals on front-office interference. Briefly, in 1938, Hornsby had the chance to tutor a young lad from San Diego named Ted Williams, who lapped up everything about hitting from Hornsby. Williams soaked in Hornsby's theories on hitting (essentially, waiting for one's pitch) and began a brilliant career in Boston. Hornsby finally returned to the majors in 1952 to again manage the Browns. He had a brief run managing the Reds, and then coached for the Cubs and Mets.

Hitting was his obsession. And he did everything to take care of his body to ensure he performed to the max. He refused to read books or watch movies for fear of damaging his eyes. He never read on trains. When asked to account for what made him a batting champion, Hornsby usually replied, "Them juicy steaks." He never smoked or drank, and reportedly slept up to 12 hours a day.

One of his contemporaries who did drink, Pete Alexander, had this to say about Hornsby: "There was the finest right-handed hitter of all time. I'll never forget the first time I saw him. I said to myself, 'Here's a recruit. Guess I'll let him hit one.' He did, and I spent the next 15 years trying to get him out."

It was Alexander whom Hornsby waved in from the bullpen to retire Tony Lazzeri with the bases full and give the Cards the 1926 World Series.

Who's Better, Who's Best
Rogers Hornsby or Ted Williams?

One is considered the greatest right-handed batter, and the other the greatest left-handed batter. One might be the greatest National League hitter, and the other the greatest American League hitter.

	Batting Avg.	On-Base Avg.	Slugging Pct.
Ted Williams	.344	.482	.634
Rogers Hornsby	.358	.434	.577

Hornsby batted 76 points better than the league average over the course of his career. Williams batted 67 points better than the league average. Of course, Williams walked so much (leading the league eight different years) that his on-base average was a lot higher. Ted also swung for the fences, and his slugging percentage is higher. Both Hornsby and Williams ended their careers ranked among the leading home run hitters of all time.

Williams would have gone over 600 easily if he had not lost five years of playing time due to his military service.

It's interesting to compare these two players in World Series competition.

Postseason

Ted Williams	1946 Series	Lost	5 hits	25 at-bats	.200 (no extra-base hits)
Rogers Hornsby	1926 Series	Won	7 hits	28 at-bats	.250 (1 double)
	1929 Series	Lost	5 hits	21 at-bats	.238

How about that? The two greatest batters in history play a combined 41 years in the majors and combine to bat 17–74 (.230) in the World Series!

Williams was better, but not by all that much. Hornsby was the Barry Bonds or Ted Williams of his era.

19

TRIS SPEAKER

When Nomar Garciaparra was traded by the Boston Red Sox in midseason 2004, he represented another in a long line of unhappy stars Boston was forced to deal. Many fans know about Carlton Fisk's departure from the Red Sox. Even more know about the circumstances that forced Babe Ruth's exodus from Boston. But the very first Red Sox star to force a trade was the man they called "the Gray Eagle."

Tristram Speaker was one of the greatest outfielders in baseball history, and in 1915 was the highest-paid player in the game's history. Two years earlier, when the upstart Federal League was seeking his services, he'd signed a two-year pact with the Sox worth $18,500 a year. With the folding of the Federal League two years later, the Red Sox attempted to sign Speaker for $9,000 a year. Speaker became so mad at Boston owner Joseph Lannin that he refused to report to spring training. At the time, Speaker had played nine seasons, and helped Boston to a pair of World Series championships. As a defensive player, he had no peer. As a batter, he was second to Ty Cobb in his era.

The Red Sox found a buyer for Speaker in the Cleveland Indians. Boston—which would trade Babe Ruth three years later—received pitcher Sad Sam Jones, third baseman Fred Thomas, and $55,000 for Speaker. Boston, the World Series champs of 1915, with a record of 101–50, had other contract problems that off-season besides Speaker's. Smokey Joe Wood held out the entire 1916 season, until Boston dealt him to Cleveland.

P.S. The year after he was traded, Speaker hit .386 to win the batting title.

Boston's loss was Cleveland's gain: I hope the Red Sox enjoyed Sad Sam Jones, Fred Thomas, and that $55K they got for Speaker. This is what the Indians received: 11 years of a marvelous center fielder who batted .354, led the league in doubles six times, and managed the Tribe to the pennant and a World Series victory over the Brooklyn Dodgers in 1920.

Speaker's career spanned from 1907 to 1928, virtually identical to Ty Cobb's. How good was Speaker? His career batting average of .344 is seventh best all-time, but he is much more famous for his defensive abilities.

He was born in 1888 in Texas, and his father died 10 years later of "consumption." Tris played semipro ball for a couple of years in the North Texas League and was sold to the Boston Red Sox in September of 1907—the very first year the Boston American League franchise was known as the Red Sox.

At the plate, Speaker batted from a semi-crouch, standing deep in the batter's box with his right foot (he was a left-handed batter) a few inches in front of the left. He held his bat rather low, almost seeming to rest his hands on his left hip. He was also a bat-waggler, moving the bat up and down slowly in preparation for the pitch.

It was in the field, however, that he was best remembered. He played so shallow in center field that he was able to execute unassisted double plays at second base. Sometimes, he took pickoff throws from the catcher.

You have to inspect this guy's offensive numbers, though. They're simply outstanding. No one in history—before or since—has belted as many doubles.

Most Doubles, Career
1. 792 Tris Speaker
2. 746 Pete Rose
3. 725 Stan Musial
4. 724 Ty Cobb
5. 665 George Brett

In 1923, Speaker pounded out 57 doubles—which broke a record that had stood for 24 years (Ed Delahanty set the previous record back in 1899). Speaker led the league in doubles no less than eight times. The Gray Eagle also ran his way to 223 triples—sixth all-time.

The only players who had a higher career batting average than Speaker's .345 were Ty Cobb, Rogers Hornsby, Joe Jackson, Lefty O'Doul, and Ed Delahanty. Now, Jackson was limited to under 5,000 career at-bats because of the Black Sox scandal. O'Doul had even fewer at-bats (3,264). And Delahanty played from 1888 to 1903. In the last one hundred years, of all the players with at least 5,000 major-league at-bats, only one right-hander (Hornsby) and one left-hander (Cobb) hit for a higher lifetime average.

Only a handful of players—most of them ranked ahead of Speaker in this book—had more career extra-base hits. They include the usual suspects—Aaron, Musial, Ruth, Mays, Bonds, Gehrig, Frank Robinson, Yastrzemski, and Cobb.

For many years, only Ty Cobb had more career hits than Speaker.

Who's Better, Who's Best
Tris Speaker or Joe DiMaggio?

In 1957, the Baseball Writers Association of America voted on their all-time team. With Joe DiMaggio fresh on their minds, they selected DiMaggio to be one of the three outfielders with Ruth and Cobb.

With the objectivity afforded by the passing years, and never having seen either of them play, of course, I would select Speaker over DiMaggio.

In a nine-year period from 1910 to 1918, Speaker (competing yearly against Ty Cobb) finished in the top four in the league in batting eight out of nine years. He had seasons where he batted .383, .388, .380, and .389.

DiMaggio had no flaws in his game. He was a graceful wonder in center field. But, obviously, so was Speaker. Tris Speaker set major-league records 90 years ago for most career outfield assists (448) and double plays (139).

The Yankee Clipper's teams had a sparkling postseason mark, winning 9 World Series in 10 attempts. But Speaker's teams won each of their three appearances in the World Series (1912, 1915, 1920).

Speaker lasted a long time. He batted .327 in 1927, at the age of 39. DiMaggio's career was cut short due to World War II and injuries. DiMaggio had almost 4,000 fewer at-bats, and played only until the age of 36. By the slimmest of margins, justified by Speaker's longevity, he ranks ahead of DiMaggio.

On January 19, 1937, in the second year of Hall of Fame balloting, three players were elected to follow the original five: Nap Lajoie, Tris Speaker, and Cy Young. If the players and writers of the mid-'30s slotted Speaker as one of the eight best players of the first quarter-century (and trailing only Cobb and Ruth among outfielders), then he deserves to be slotted very high even today.

GROVER CLEVELAND ALEXANDER

What is it about these guys who were born before 1900? It seems so many of them were named after presidents. And while this Grover Cleveland wasn't leading the country in the early 1890s, Alexander the great pitcher made a different contribution to society. He stood up to the Yankees in the World Series, despite being hung over.

Let's start at the beginning, because this guy Alexander is one of the most fascinating figures in baseball history.

Born on a Nebraska farm in 1887, Alexander may have learned his great control by hunting birds with rocks as a youngster. He had several imaginative nicknames, including "Pete," "Grove," "Alex," "Ol' Pete," and "Ol' Grove."

He was discovered while throwing baseballs at a county fair, and signed to a contract in the Illinois-Missouri League. In his first season, he had a record of 15–8. Late that season he suffered a near-fatal injury when, running to second base, he was hit squarely on the head by a throw to first, knocking him unconscious for 56 hours (that being the record until many years later when another pitcher was unconscious for 56.2 hours). The injury left Alex—or Ol' Pete, or choose your favorite nickname here—with double vision. His team took immediate action. They sold him to the Indianapolis team. With Alex's first practice pitch for his new club, he broke the ribs of his new manager, thus alerting his new team to his vision problems.

Amazingly, his vision cleared up, and he pitched so well in the 1910 season for Syracuse (International League) that he earned a promotion to the Philadelphia Phillies. In his rookie season of 1911, he led the National League with 28 wins, including four consecutive shutouts. He also led the league with 31 complete games and 367 innings pitched. He would have won the Cy Young Award had there been one; instead, he pitched a shutout against the 44-year-old Cy Young in Young's last season.

Alexander had incredible success with the Phillies, despite pitching his home games at Baker Bowl, with a right-field wall only 272 feet from home plate. Alexander was 190–91 with an ERA of 2.18 for the Phillies from 1911 to 1917.

Fearing that their pitching ace would be drafted into the U.S. Army, the Phillies sprung into action and dealt Pete to the Chicago Cubs for $60,000 and two bad players. Alexander pitched three games for the Cubs in 1918 and then was sent to France as a member of the 89th Infantry Division. In France, shelling cost him the hearing in one of his ears and the first signs of his epilepsy appeared. The trauma of the war, coupled with the disease, was later blamed for Alexander's alcoholism.

His drinking habits didn't bother his pitching. In 1919, he returned to the Cubs and led the league in ERA. In 1920, he led the league in wins, ERA, and strikeouts. That was the fifth straight season (not counting the 1918 World War I season) he led the National League in earned run average. In fact, it was the third time he won the pitcher's equivalent of the Triple Crown (leading the league in wins, strikeouts, and earned run average).

Following the 1925 season, he entered a sanitarium for his drinking.

In 1926, he was waived by the Cubs and picked up by the St. Louis Cardinals. Alexander won nine games for St. Louis down the stretch, and the Cards easily won the National League pennant. In the World Series, Alexander started Game 2 against the Yankees' Murderers Row. He defeated the Yanks 6–2 in that game, and came back to win Game 6 as well, this time by a score of 10–2. Believing his season was over, Alexander had a little too much to celebrate after the Game 6 victory.

Game 7 was at Yankee Stadium. The Cardinals led 3–2 in the seventh inning. The bases were loaded, two men were out, and wouldn't you know that St. Louis manager Rogers Hornsby decided to relieve pitcher Jesse Haines, and called in Alexander. Alexander fanned Tony Lazzeri on four pitches in one of the most dramatic moments in Series history. He then pitched a one-two-three inning in the eighth and retired the first two batters in the ninth before walking Babe Ruth. The Series ended with Ruth getting thrown out attempting to steal second base.

That was the highlight of Pete's career, but heck, it remains one of the highlights of World Series play. Alexander went back into a sanitarium for part of the 1929 season. He spent most of that last season attempting to break Christy Mathewson's National League record of 372 wins. Very late in the season, he finally got the record number 373 by pitching five scoreless innings in relief against the Phillies. He was unable to get a 374th victory, despite pitching in nine games in 1930, including six starts.

He lost sole possession of the record win total when, in 1946, Mathewson was credited with one more victory (from a 1902 game that was previously disallowed), which pushed his total to 373, tying him with Alexander for the most wins in National League history.

Who's Better, Who's Best
Grover Cleveland Alexander or Nolan Ryan?

In 1999, Nolan Ryan was named to the All-Century Team, and Grover Cleveland Alexander was not. That is just hard to justify.

Grover Cleveland Alexander is second all-time with 90 shutouts. Only Walter Johnson pitched more. In the 1916 season, Alexander pitched 16 shutouts.

Alexander led the league in wins six times. He led the league in ERA five times. He led the league in strikeouts 12 times. He pitched 437 complete games.

Alexander became the ninth player enshrined in the Hall of Fame, and the fourth pitcher. He followed Walter Johnson, Christy Mathewson, and Cy Young.

Nolan Ryan never led the league in wins. He never finished in the top three in that most important of categories. Ryan led his league in earned run average twice (1981, a strike-shortened season, and 1987). Most of Ryan's accolades are wrapped around his 5,714 strikeouts.

Hey, I'm not saying it's not close. Ryan pitched 222 complete games and 61 shutouts—outstanding totals for any era, but especially his.

But Alexander pitched for lousier teams. He pitched in smaller ballparks. Ryan, remember, spent nine very productive years playing in the pitcher-friendly Astrodome in Houston.

In 1991, the Elias Sports Bureau introduced a technique for measuring the number of victories a starting pitcher was worth. A pitcher's value to his team was defined as the difference between the number of games he won and the number that would have been won by whomever would have pitched in his place had he not been there. It was estimated that Alexander won 141 more games than a "replacement" on the same team would have. In his best four seasons (1914–1917), he won 52 more games than a "replacement" would have won. Only one pitcher—Walter Johnson—betters that. The fact is, Alexander won more than a third of all the Phillies victories those seasons.

Ryan won 32 more games than he lost in his 27 seasons. Alexander had more wins, a better winning percentage, a better earned run average, better control, and performed better in his postseason appearances than Ryan.

A Better Analogy

Pete Alexander and Vincent van Gogh Vincent van Gogh painted some of the world's most renowned paintings. He also went a little crazy. He quit school when he was 15 years old and began a career as an art dealer. Finally, beginning in 1880, van Gogh painted 872 paintings. He had a 10-year period (like the pitcher Alexander) of artistic talent that was just mind-boggling.

Van Gogh also suffered from severe depression and was admitted to an asylum in December 1888, after chopping off his own ear. He would be in and out of asylums for the next year. It is thought that Vincent was actually epileptic, and that is why people thought he had fits of insanity throughout his life. While in the asylum Vincent painted one of his best-known paintings, *Starry Night*. In 1890, Vincent left the asylum and spent the last few months of his life in France. On July 27, 1890, he shot himself in the chest with a revolver.

Alexander's life didn't have a good ending either. His two marriages (both to the same woman) ended in divorce. He wound up pitching for the barnstorming House of David team, and later appeared in a sideshow in Times Square. He sank deeper into alcoholism, had additional problems with epilepsy, was hospitalized for cancer, and had an ear removed.

In 1950, at the age of 63, he died alone and penniless in a rented room back in Nebraska.

JOE DiMAGGIO

Joseph Paul DiMaggio's story was the story of America. He was the eighth of nine children born to Giuseppe and Rosalie DiMaggio. His parents had emigrated from a small island off the coast of Sicily to America and remained for a short time in New York before settling in San Francisco.

Joe grew up in the streets around Fisherman's Wharf, and his dad made a living as a fisherman. Joe wanted to see more in his life than Fisherman's Wharf.

DiMaggio's pro career began in 1932 while his brother Vince was an outfielder for the San Francisco Seals of the Pacific Coast League. Vince suggested his brother for the final three games when one of the Seals outfielders left the team early to play in Hawaii on a barnstorming tour. Joe played the last three games of that '32 season, and earned a serious look by the Pacific Coast League team (just a notch below major-league ability) the next season in 1933.

DiMaggio was an 18-year-old outfielder with the Seals when he got a hit in 61 consecutive games. Most minor-league players give an indication of how they'll perform in the major leagues, but this is ridiculous. He ended the season with a .340 average and 169 RBI in 187 games.

DiMaggio played with effortless grace in the outfield. He ran down fly balls that other fielders would not have gotten to, or would have had to slide to catch. DiMaggio never lost his hat, like Willie Mays. He didn't make any catch look difficult. He was a good base runner, although he had only 30 stolen bases in his career because the Yankees were reluctant to risk injuries to his legs. He made contact with the ball—in fact, he struck out only once every 18.5 at-bats, a great ratio for a power hitter.

By 1936, he was with the Yankees. He had a sensational rookie year, hitting 44 doubles and 15 triples, while belting 29 homers and driving in 125 runs. That was in spite of missing 16 games to injury.

In 1937, the 22-year-old DiMaggio did something that most of the great power hitters in baseball never accomplished: he collected 400 total bases in one season. Ted

Williams never did it. Mickey Mantle never did it. Barry Bonds never did it. Mark McGwire never did it.

DiMaggio had 418 total bases in 1937 (119 singles, 35 doubles, 15 triples, and 46 home runs). The all-time record is held by Babe Ruth, who had 457 total bases in 1921. Since 1933, only Stan Musial (429 in 1948), Sammy Sosa (425 in 2001), and Luis Gonzalez (419 in 2001) have topped DiMaggio's 418.

Joe had an amazing sophomore season. He drove in 167 runs, and scored 151 in his 151 games. He hit 46 home runs, and struck out only 37 times.

DiMaggio's Homers and Strikeouts

In his rookie season, DiMaggio hit 29 homers, but struck out 39 times. In 1937, DiMaggio had nine more home runs than strikeouts. That's incredible, as most home run hitters strike out at least twice for every home run.

There are over one hundred players in history who have struck out more than 1,200 times. Reggie Jackson struck out 2,597 times. Even the great hitters of DiMaggio's day struck out more (Musial struck out 696 times to DiMaggio's total of 369). Even the hitters with the most selective eyes (Barry Bonds and Ted Williams) struck out more than DiMaggio.

Vladimir Guerrero struck out more than DiMaggio did in his first seven years, by the age of 28.

Sammy Sosa struck out 345 times in a two-year period (1997–1998). DiMaggio struck out 369 times in his 13-year career!

After Joe's 12th season in 1950, he had 349 home runs and just 333 strikeouts. In his final season of 1951, when he was 36, he had 12 homers, but struck out 36 times, to end his career with just eight more strikeouts than home runs. DiMaggio had a record seven seasons of more homers than strikeouts.

Joe and His Annual Trip to the World Series

Before DiMaggio's rookie season, the Yankees had been out of the World Series for a while. They finished in second place in 1933 (seven games behind Washington), 1934 (seven games behind Detroit), and 1935 (three games behind Detroit).

In DiMaggio's rookie year, they won the World Series.

In his second year, they won the World Series.

In his third year, they won the World Series.

In his fourth year, they won the World Series. No team had ever won four consecutive World Series until the 1939 Yankees. In DiMaggio's first four years, his Yankees were 16–3 in World Series games.

In his career, DiMaggio's teams were 9–1 in the World Series.

Joe and the Batting Titles

In 1939, DiMaggio won the batting title with a .381 average. In 1940, he repeated as batting champ by batting .352. It was hard to defeat Ted Williams in the batting race after that.

Joe's 56-Game Hitting Streak

During DiMaggio's famous batting streak, a disc jockey, Allen Courtney, wrote some lyrics on a nightclub tablecloth. He showed his poem to Les Brown, leader of the Band of Renown. In turn, Brown gave the lyrics to Ben Homer (what an appropriate name to write a baseball song!). Homer wrote the music to the words, and "Joltin' Joe DiMaggio" became a hit.

In the 56 games, DiMaggio had 91 hits (56 singles, 16 doubles, 4 triples, 15 homers), with 55 runs scored. He walked 21 times, and struck out just seven times in 223 at-bats!

After the streak was stopped, DiMaggio hit safely in another 16 games.

1941 MVP Vote

DiMaggio had won his first MVP Award in 1939. The summer of '41 saw two amazing players at their all-time best. Who would you have voted for?

In one corner was Ted Williams. He batted .406 for the season, which no one had done in more than a decade. He had 37 home runs and slugged .735. No one except Ruth, Gehrig, Hornsby, and Foxx ever slugged higher in a season prior to 1941. Only four players—Bonds, McGwire, Bagwell, and Sosa—would slug higher in a season in the next 60 years.

In the other corner was DiMaggio. He had a 56-game hitting streak that captivated the nation. He batted .357, with 30 home runs and a .643 slugging percentage. His Yankees won the pennant with 101 wins, finishing 17 games in front of Williams's second-place Boston Red Sox.

DiMaggio received 15 first-place votes and 291 points. Williams finished a distant second, with 8 first-place votes and 254 points.

Soon after the vote was taken came December 7, 1941, and the country was at war.

DiMaggio played the 1942 season, and the Yankees made it to the World Series for the fifth time in his six seasons. The St. Louis Cardinals won the Series that year, the only time in 10 trips to the Series that DiMaggio's team would lose.

"DiMaggio Does Good Turn for Himself and Baseball"

That was the headline of an AP story from February 19, 1943. "The big, shy guy is doing the game a favor by leaving it. He is eliminating one of the vulnerable spots that would be a natural target for malicious barbs hurled by those who resent any game for profit in war time," the story said.

DiMaggio was vulnerable because he was making $42,000 a year. The big draft board hadn't even called his number yet, but there was pressure on him to enter the service.

In his first six years, he had averaged .345 and 33 home runs a year. He didn't return to the Yankees until the 1946 season.

1947 MVP Voting

In 1947, the Yankees won the American League pennant (finishing 12 games in front of Detroit) and went on to capture the World Series. DiMaggio batted .315 with 20 home runs. Ted Williams won the Triple Crown, leading the league in batting (.343), home runs (32), RBI (114), on-base average, slugging, runs scored, and total bases.

DiMaggio edged out Williams again for the MVP, by a count of 202 to 201. Williams lost MVPs to DiMaggio when he batted .400, and when he won the Triple Crown.

That was the third of DiMaggio's MVP awards. He probably deserved one in 1937 that he didn't get (Charlie Gehringer won it), and received an MVP in 1947 that Williams should have won.

Injuries

The Greek god had an Achilles heel. The Italian god had a DiMaggio heel. In 1947, a bone spur was taken from Joe's left heel. Before the 1948 season, doctors removed bone chips from his throwing arm. At the end of the 1948 season, his right heel began giving him problems. They removed bone spurs from his right heel. In 1949, he was hospitalized for the pain in his heels, missing the first 65 games of the season. Then he returned in June and played the final 76 games, leading the Yankees to another pennant. He batted .346 with 67 RBI in his 76 games.

He played two more seasons, but he was clearly not the same player he once was. He retired at 36, in part "because he wasn't Joe DiMaggio" anymore.

One Final Amazing Streak

DiMaggio captivated the nation in the '40s with a 56-game hitting streak. He had the attention of the country in the '50s when he stayed married to actress Marilyn Monroe for an amazing 274 consecutive days.

Retirement

DiMaggio was named the game's "Greatest Living Player" in 1969, and had the title 30 years, until he died in 1999 at the age of 84. His reputation seemed to grow 20 years after he retired. That's because he was remembered in song and in literature (Hemingway's *The Old Man and the Sea*), and the hero worship people had for him was sky-high. In his later years, DiMaggio showed up to old-timers' games, but didn't play in them, never allowing the public to see him at anything less than his best. He was the sport's diva. Was he the game's greatest player?

Bob Costas: "There has been a DiMaggio revision going on in recent years, and much of that can be attributed to the perception of his personality. People have actually said he's been 'overrated.' He's no worse than the second or third greatest player of an entire generation. He was better defensively than Williams. He was a great and elegant player and was hurt by the park in which he played. He's obviously one of the ten greatest outfielders of all time."

STAN MUSIAL

Stan Musial was born in November 1920 in Pennsylvania's coal-mine country. Out of that soot would arise one of the greatest major leaguers of all time. At 19 years old, he was an 18-game winner in Class D ball (the low minor leagues). A year later, he seriously injured his pitching shoulder diving for a ball, and when he reported in 1941, the pitching arm was still not healthy, and he was through as a pitcher. He zoomed from Class C to the majors as a slugging outfielder after he led his minor league in home runs. By the age of 22, Musial was a starter on the St. Louis Cardinals. He remained there for 22 seasons (missing only the 1945 season due to World War II). He broke many of Honus Wagner's National League records, and later had his marks smashed by Hank Aaron.

The Nickname

"Stan the Man" might not seem like an original nickname by today's standards, but that wasn't the case in the 1940s. Musial was given that nickname by Dodger fans for his pounding of the Brooklyn team at Ebbets Field.

The Best Team He Ever Played On

When Musial was a 21-year-old rookie in 1942, his St. Louis Cardinals team went 106–48. Musial joined an outfield that already featured Enos Slaughter and Terry Moore. The pitching staff was led by Mort Cooper (22–7, 1.78 ERA) and Johnny Beazley (21–6, 2.13).

1946 World Series

This was about two superstars, Ted Williams of Boston and Stan Musial of the Cardinals. The Series went seven games, with the Cards winning. But Musial hit only .222, which was actually better than Williams hit in the Series (.200). The Series will forever be remembered for a play in the eighth inning of the seventh game. Enos Slaughter singled to open the bottom of the eighth of a 3–3 tie. With two outs, Harry Walker lashed a 2–1 pitch into left-center field that was bobbled momentarily. Slaughter's mad dash home was the winning run of the game, Series, and season.

The Stats

Here is a top-10 list of the most impressive stats about Stan Musial:

10. He played in 24 All-Star games.
 9. He finished with 3,630 hits—exactly half at home and half on the road.
 8. He led the league in doubles eight times, and in triples five times. He never led in home runs.
 7. He never struck out more than 46 times in a season.
 6. He won seven batting titles—and finished in the top five in 17 different seasons.
 5. He won three MVP awards in his first six full seasons.
 4. He had 1,377 extra-base hits, but less than 35 percent of them were home runs.
 3. In 1948, Stan led the league in doubles and triples, and finished one home run short of the leaders.
 2. He played over 3,000 games, all for the same team.
 1. He had 6,134 total bases, more than anyone ever except Hank Aaron.

There were many career highlights sandwiched in his nearly quarter-century of baseball. There was the 474th home run of his career—hit on the same day he became a grandfather. There was the 1955 All-Star Game in Milwaukee, when Stan hit a solo home run in the bottom of the 12th inning to give the National League a 6–5 win. There was the 1957 All-Star voting by fans, which was stuffed by Cincinnati fans to such extent that Musial was the only non-Reds player elected to start the All-Star Game (the commissioner stepped in and eliminated three Reds from the starting lineup).

1948

Musial was a rookie in 1942. He led the league in batting and won the MVP Award in 1943. He was away in the service in 1945. In 1946, he again led the league in batting, and again won the MVP. He was slowed in 1947 by appendicitis. That set the stage for one of the greatest single seasons anyone has ever had.

In 1948, Musial batted .376, with 39 home runs, 135 runs scored, and 131 RBI. He had 18 triples among his 230 hits. No National Leaguer has won the Triple Crown since Joe Medwick in 1937, but Musial came closest. He led the league in batting and RBI. He finished one home run short of the lead. He even lost a home run that season in a rainout. In that 1948 season, Musial became the first National Leaguer to slug .700 or better since 1930 (Hack Wilson).

Musial was the only National Leaguer between 1930 and 1996 (Mark McGwire) to slug .700 in a season. Neither Mays nor Aaron ever did it. Barry Bonds did it for the first time in 2001.

Musial almost set the record for total bases (Rogers Hornsby in 1922) and extra-base hits (103 by Chuck Klein in 1930) in 1948. He also became the first National Leaguer ever to capture three MVP awards.

Following an off-season in 1949, Musial won batting titles in 1950, 1951, and 1952.

In 1957, he came within nine votes of winning his fourth MVP (and stealing Hank Aaron's only MVP victory).

The only real career lowlights were these: Musial batted only .256 in his 23 World Series games, and didn't get to a World Series in his last 17 seasons.

In 1956, *The Sporting News* named Musial the Player of the Decade (1946–1955) in a poll of 260 players, officials, umpires, and media members. But that's a little unfair to Ted Williams. Musial had 5,891 at-bats in that 10-year period. Williams had only 3,789 at-bats, missing virtually the entire 1952 and 1953 seasons. Williams only played 98 games and had 320 at-bats in 1955, when the vote was taken. Williams was a superior player to Musial from 1939 to 1942, and again from 1956 to 1960. If the vote had been taken just a year or two later, then Willie Mays would have zoomed past everyone.

Why Musial's Ranking Isn't Higher

Bob Costas: "Musial—what comes to mind? When you look at some of the other great players of his era, something immediately springs to mind. . . . Ted Williams—you think of the man who batted .400. Willie Mays—you think of the Say Hey Kid making that catch in the '54 World Series. Mickey Mantle—one thinks of a flawed but poignant man. Hank Aaron—we all remember 755 home runs. DiMaggio—we have the 56-game hitting streak. Stan Musial [Bob's voice now rising like a preacher's] stands for nothing but excellence and decency. He won seven batting titles—of all the living players, Musial is the most underrated and least appreciated, at least to those outside St. Louis.

"He was a very fast runner, with a huge number of doubles. He played past 40 . . . one of the most decent, beloved guys, and his stats speak for themselves. Before Aaron and Mays, Musial was second or third in most of the important categories."

Musial played from 1942 to 1963. Before Jackie Robinson broke the color line, Musial's Cards won four pennants in four seasons. After the color line was broken, Musial played 17 seasons and never played on a team that finished first. The Cardinals didn't win again until they had the services of Lou Brock and Bob Gibson and Curt Flood.

Musial won batting titles in 1943, 1946, and 1948. You wonder if he would have won them if blacks had been allowed in the majors earlier. Even by 1950, only nine blacks and nine other Latin players were in the major leagues.

Stan the Man led the National League in slugging percentage in 1943, 1944, and 1946—before Jackie broke the color line. He also led the league in 1948, 1950, and 1952. After Duke Snider led the league in 1953, the National League leader in slugging percentage was a black man 21 times in the next 23 years.

Stan Musial's Last Game

It was August 1963, and Musial was 42 years old. Stan finally decided that '63 would be his final season. Before the final game of the season, Musial's every move in batting practice was cheered. There was a stirring pregame ceremony. After the first pitch to Musial in the first inning, the ball was taken out of play to be displayed at the Hall of Fame. In the fourth inning, Musial got a base hit up the middle. In the sixth inning, Musial drove in a run with another base hit and was taken out for a pinch runner.

Bill White: "Stan Musial: He was the best hitter I ever saw. Willie was the best player, but Stan was the best hitter. He played in a park conducive to lefties hitting it out, but he was a complete batter—not just a home run hitter. Since you don't face your own teammates, you tend to overlook them when talking about the best you ever saw. But Musial was the best batter.

"He played first base when I came to the Cardinals. They put me in left field, and I screwed up. They put me in center field, and I screwed up. They put him in left field, and he screwed up. Eventually, it worked out."

Tim McCarver: "He wasn't the same hitter when I joined the Cardinals (in 1959)."

Stan Musial	AB	Hits	Batting Avg.	On-Base Avg.	Slugging Pct.	HR	RBI
1942–1958	9,158	3,116	.340	.426	.578	398	1,634
1959–1963	1,814	514	.283	.369	.466	77	317

Those last five seasons Musial's career batting average dropped from .340 to .331. This seismic shift dropped him from the more exclusive neighborhood where Ted Williams (.344), Babe Ruth (.342), and Lou Gehrig (.340) live for eternity to a less-pricey subdivision, with occupants like Heine Manush (.330), Wade Boggs (.328), and Rod Carew (.328).

Who's Better, Who's Best
Stan Musial or Hank Aaron?

Tim McCarver: "Stan might have been the best low-ball hitter I ever saw. Aaron hit more balls on the fat part of the bat than anyone. . . . (Lew) Burdette told me a story that several of the Braves picked up Aaron's bat in June, and they could find no marks near the end of the bat . . . all the indentations were on the sweet spot. Joe Buck said he had heard the same thing about Musial. One thing about Musial, he could run in his earlier days. He could fly. Aaron could run too. . . . You know, Aaron was a great right fielder . . . he charged the ball . . . superb. . . . A lot of people just look at his offense, they think he couldn't be a great defensive player. They are wrong. He wasn't Clemente, but he was terrific. Hank had power to all fields. I called pitches that Aaron hit over the right-center field roof. One thing about Stan, he could lift the low pitch . . . that set him apart. He never fouled it off, he never missed it. When he was fooled, he caught up with the pitch, his stride would go forward. Another thing about Musial was his strength. The muscular shape of his back—the clumps of his muscles—they were centered. Man, he was strong. Mays was like that, too.

"I was asked quite frequently when I retired who the greatest player was I had ever seen, and I said Mays over Aaron. Now that time has passed, it's not so automatic. I appreciate what Aaron did to an even greater extent now. Aaron over Musial."

GEORGE BRETT

There might have been better places to grow up than Southern California in the late 1960s, but I doubt it. George Brett was the youngest of four boys all spaced two years apart from Hermosa Beach, California. Don't think that Brett had it easy—he had to shag flies for his brothers and wait for his turn at bat.

George spent much of his life trying to please his father, who was a tough World War II veteran and lavished little praise on any of his kids. George inherited his happy-go-lucky spirit from his loving mother.

Brett idolized his brothers, especially his oldest brother, Ken, who was drafted by the Boston Red Sox in 1966. Ken Brett was a phenom who could pitch and hit. He became the youngest pitcher to ever play in a World Series, when he appeared in the 1967 World Series. Joe Stephenson, the scout who signed Ken Brett for the Red Sox, wanted Boston to draft George Brett in 1971. But the Red Sox, who were frustrated with Ken's development and had drafted another Brett sibling two years earlier, passed on George in the first round.

The Red Sox cannot be faulted. They made a sensational pick with the 15th overall pick in the 1971 draft. They selected Jim Rice, who would play 16 seasons for Boston, making eight All-Star teams and hitting close to 400 career homers. But he wasn't George Brett.

The Kansas City Royals came into existence in 1969, and their second-round selection in the June 1971 draft was Brett, then an 18-year-old shortstop from El Segundo High School. That draft produced some other pretty fair players, including Mike Schmidt, Ron Guidry, and Keith Hernandez.

George Brett's major-league debut was on August 2, 1973, in Chicago. Brett batted eighth in that game. He played 13 games that season for injured third baseman Paul Schaal, and had only five hits in 40 at-bats.

He opened the 1974 season in the minors, but the Royals traded Schaal on April 30, and the left-hand-hitting Brett was recalled for good. He didn't get off to a good start.

Then something happened to turn around his career. Here is what Brett said in his 1999 Hall of Fame induction speech:

> Charley Lau was my hitting coach in 1974. At that time I was hitting .200 with 200 at-bats at the All-Star break. He put his arm around me and he said, "George, I think you've got a chance to hit, but you're going to have to change a few things." I said, "Well, what do you have in mind?" He said, "We'll try to figure out a philosophy and a theory that will work for you." Well, we got out there and we looked at video of players that he helped before and other players that he wanted to, maybe, model me after, and we started to take batting practice each day, extra batting practice.

In the final 53 games of the 1974 season, Brett hit .340. It raised his season average to .282, and Brett finished third in the Rookie of the Year voting.

In 1975, the 23-year-old Brett began wearing out American League pitchers, none more so than California Angels right-hander Ed Figueroa. Brett had 13 consecutive hits off of Figgy that season, getting 14 hits in 16 at-bats against that one very good pitcher. Brett finished the season with a .308 average, his first .300 season.

The first of Brett's batting titles came in 1976, although it came with a lot of controversy. George collected three hits on the final day of the season against Minnesota, to win the title with a .333 average. It's more impressive than it looks, as the American League average that year was a paltry .257.

This batting title not only came down to the last game but also to the last inning of the season. Teammate Hal McRae led Brett by .00005 with one game to go. The Royals had clinched their first division title the night before the season finale. Brett and McRae were each two-for-three in the final game heading into the bottom of the ninth inning. McRae was at .33269. Brett was at .33229. Brett needed a hit to surpass McRae. Brett hit a routine fly ball to medium left field. Twins left fielder Steve Brye (who was white) seemed to stop and let the ball bounce in front of him, and then the ball went over Brye's head. Brett circled the bases for an inside-the-park home run. McRae had one final at-bat to win the batting title. He grounded out to shortstop. As McRae returned to the Royals dugout, he made an obscene gesture to Twins manager Gene Mauch. Mauch charged McRae, and players had to separate the two. After the game, McRae claimed the Twins and manager Mauch had ordered Brye to let the ball drop so McRae would not win.

The interesting thing about that is that Brett was so unselfish as a player.

Rick Sutcliffe: "When I think of George Brett, I think of the incredible amount of energy for the game he had. I compare him in this way to Michael Jordan. When Michael was winning scoring titles, his team didn't win at first . . . in fact, they didn't win until he got others involved in the Bulls offense. George Brett also had a way of keeping others involved in the Royals offense. He was unselfish, and a real team player. If he knew Hal McRae was slumping and batting behind Brett, George would expand his strike zone. . . . He would change his zone. If the batters behind him were hot, he might take more pitches. He was like Michael . . . because of that, the Royals franchise was competitive for many years."

George Brett had a batting title under his belt and a trip to the playoffs. He had a great playoff series against the Yankees, batting .444 and slugging .778 (getting 14 total bases in 18 at-bats). It might have been enough to get them to the World Series, but Chris Chambliss hit a home run that put the Yanks into the World Series. Brett finished second in the MVP voting in 1976. In 1977, he increased his home runs from 7 to 22. His Royals won their division, and again met the Yankees. The Yankees dashed Brett's World Series hopes for a second straight year. In 1978, the Yankees came from 14 games behind the Red Sox to overtake Boston in a thrilling playoff game. The Royals, winners of their division a third straight season, awaited the Yanks. Brett slugged three homers off of Catfish Hunter in Game 3 at Yankee Stadium. It didn't matter. The Yankees ended the Royals' season for a third straight year. In that 1978 series, Brett accumulated 19 total bases in his 18 at-bats, slugging over 1.000.

Brett had a truly magnificent season in 1979. Among his 212 hits, he had 42 doubles, 20 triples, and 23 home runs. He stole 17 bases, and struck out only 36 times in 645 at-bats. He scored 119 runs and drove in 107. His stats that year wouldn't look out of place on Joe DiMaggio's career record. No matter how great 1979 was, though, it was nothing like his 1980 season.

1980

This was Brett's MVP season. Because of assorted injuries, Brett missed 45 games. In the 117 games he did play, he batted .390—the highest in the majors since Ted Williams batted over .400 in 1941. No third baseman had ever batted as high as .350 previously. Brett drove in 118 runs in 117 games and slugged .664. As late as September 19, he was batting .400. With 11 games remaining, he was at .394. The Royals then went on a road trip, where Brett had just four hits in 20 at-bats. The killer was an 0–4 night against Minnesota left-hander Jerry Koosman. For the fourth time in five seasons, the Royals met the Yankees in the American League Championship Series. They finally advanced, eliminating the Yankees, as Brett provided the signature shot, a home run off relief ace Goose Gossage.

In the World Series, Brett's Royals met Mike Schmidt's Philadelphia Phillies, a matchup of the two greatest third basemen of their time, and in my estimation, the two best ever.

In the 1980 World Series, Brett suffered with . . . hemorrhoids. Brett always joked afterwards that after that, he was always ridiculed at ballparks about that ailment. Let's just say baseball was filled with bigger assholes, but none more famous. Because Preparation H didn't work, the Phillies won their only World Series. Despite the pain in the ass, Brett batted .375 in the six-game Series.

Pine Tar

On July 24, 1983, the Royals were playing the Yankees in New York. Brett's two-run homer off Goose Gossage gave Kansas City a 5–4 lead. Immediately after Brett touched home plate, Yanks manager Billy Martin approached the home plate umpire. Soon Tim McClelland summoned Brett's bat from the dugout and conferred with the rest of the umpiring crew. A moment later, McClelland thrust his arm in the air and signaled that Brett was out for excessive use of pine tar on his bat. Brett stormed from the dugout, going crazy because a possible game-winning home run was taken away from him.

The Yankees won that game 4–3, but the Royals protested the game and the decision was overturned by American League President Lee McPhail, who reinstated Brett's homer. The game was resumed three weeks, four hours, and 14 minutes later, when Dan Quisenberry took 12 minutes to retire the Yanks in the (now necessary) bottom of the ninth. The scene of a charging Brett when he found out his home run was called back has been replayed countless times. It remains my single most vivid memory of Brett. He was one of the greatest batters I ever saw, but I remember him wanting to beat Billy Martin and the Yankees so bad that he exploded in that "Pine Tar Incident."

1985

The Royals finally won the World Series championship in 1985, and George Brett had another big season. He was MVP of the American League Championship Series, batting .348 in the seven games with the Toronto Blue Jays. He hit three homers, and slugged over .800 for the Series. In the seven-game World Series, he batted .370.

Postseason Career

George Brett was not a home run hitter. In his career, he averaged a home run every 32 at-bats. In his 43 postseason games (166 at-bats), however, he hit 10 home runs, a home run every 16.6 at-bats. He improved his batting average during postseason play as well.

The Move to First Base

Beginning with the 1987 season, the Royals moved Brett to first base in an effort to extend his career.

George Brett				
First 13 years	1,677 games at 3B	6,675 AB	2,095 hits	.314
Last 7 years	15 games at 3B	3,674 AB	1,059 hits	.288

Brett got his 3,000th hit at the end of the 1992 season, in a game where he had four hits. He finished up in 1993, having finally married and started a family toward the very end of his career.

George Brett had a storybook career, and was one of the greatest players in history. Unfortunately for George, he couldn't share it into old age with the three men most responsible. Charley Lau, the coach who turned his career around, passed away from colon cancer in 1984. His father, Jack, passed away in 1992. Sadly, his 55-year-old brother Ken died of a brain tumor in late 2003. "All I wanted was to be as good as my brother," said George.

Maybe it does rain in Southern California.

Who's Better, Who's Best
George Brett or Mike Schmidt?

Rick Sutcliffe: "Brett versus Schmidt: Schmidt was the most complete player I saw in my time. Schmidt's the guy at the top of every list I ever had, but George would be not far from that."

Who's Better, Who's Best
George Brett or Wade Boggs?

Wade Boggs had 9,180 at-bats and a .328 batting average. George Brett had 10,349 at-bats and a .305 average. But Brett had a higher slugging average, with many more extra-base hits. Brett won a Gold Glove and an MVP Award.

Tony Kubek: "Unlike Wade Boggs at Fenway Park, George Brett was a left-handed batter in a *big* ballpark. Teams could pitch him in a variety of ways. Brett, though, had more extra-base hits than Boggs. He was a good runner. He had great range at third base. He not only walked, but he often would go after bad balls to drive in runs—something Boggs really didn't do too much. That was someone else's job."

24

JIMMIE FOXX

They called him "Double XX" as well as "the right-handed Babe Ruth." It seems wrong for the encyclopedias to list Jimmie Foxx at only 6 feet tall and less than 200 pounds. The numbers point to a bigger player. The stories point to a bigger player. He played from 1925 to 1944. At the time of his retirement, only Babe Ruth had hit more home runs. At the time of his death in 1967, only Ruth and Willie Mays had hit more homers. Following the 2004 season, the slugging percentage of Foxx (.609) was bettered only by Ruth, Ted Williams, Lou Gehrig, and Barry Bonds. They were all left-handed batters, meaning Double XX was first among right-handers. Joe Cronin always said that "if Foxx were a right-handed hitter, he'd hit between 70 and 80 homers a year." Foxx drove in 1,922 runs, a feat bettered only by Hank Aaron, Ruth, Cap Anson, Gehrig, Stan Musial, and Ty Cobb.

Legend has it that Jimmie received his first dollar for playing baseball when he was only 14 years old. The next season, he joined a club for $6 a week playing third base. Not yet 16 years old, Foxx signed with the Easton Farmers of the Eastern Shore League, then managed by Frank (Home Run) Baker, the former Philadelphia Athletics star.

Foxx, a free-swinging, clumsy teenager who nonetheless showed an enormous amount of power, became a catcher for Baker. Before anyone ever used the word *networking*, Baker was showing off his 16-year-old prodigy to his former Athletics manager, Connie Mack.

Mack had little need for a catcher, with Mickey Cochrane on the team already, so he began experimenting with Foxx at different positions, particularly third and first base.

By 1927, when Foxx was 19, Mack had played him 32 times at first base. Foxx would play over 1,900 games there before he was through. Foxx was nothing if not versatile, however. "Double XX" caught 37 games in the 1920s, 29 games in the '30s, and was even behind the plate for 42 games in the 1940s.

In an effort to extend his career, he pitched for the Philadelphia Phillies in 1944, when the young major-league talent was off fighting World War II.

The best example of Foxx's versatility was demonstrated in 1934, the year of the very first All-Star Game. Lou Gehrig was the American League first baseman and played all nine innings. Foxx started at third base for the A.L., in order to get his heavy bat in the lineup.

It's doubtful any man ever hit the ball harder and farther. It was Foxx who, in the days before official measurements of home runs, held each ballpark's "unofficial" record for longest home run. Twice he hit pitches completely out of Comiskey Park in Chicago.

In 1932, only five years after Ruth's record for 60 home runs in a season, Foxx belted 58. Jimmie would have beat Roger Maris by three decades, except that twice that 1932 season Foxx belted home runs in the early innings of games that were rained out before they could be considered official. On three other occasions that year, he hit balls against screens in St. Louis and Cleveland which were not in place when Ruth was hitting 60 in 1927.

In 1933, Foxx hit "only" 48 home runs and averaged .356. The Philadelphia A's then cut his salary from $16,000 to $11,000. It was during the Depression, and his team just didn't have any money to pay their star players.

The Athletics had one of the greatest teams of all time, but they couldn't keep the team together for long because of money problems. Mack eventually had to sell off his best players, and Foxx never made it to a World Series after the age of 23.

When Foxx was 19 years old in 1927, he played in only a handful of games. On June 11, he played in one game in which seven future Hall of Famers played on the field at the same time during the ninth inning. The outfield consisted of Ty Cobb in right, Al Simmons in center, and Zack Wheat in left. Jimmie Foxx played first base, with Eddie Collins at second. Lefty Grove pitched the ninth inning in relief. Mickey Cochrane was the catcher that last inning as well. Not even the 1927 Yankees (or the modern Yanks) could match a team like that.

By 1928, Foxx was able to break into the lineup for 118 games and 400 at-bats. His first big year came the following season, at the age of 21. Beginning in 1928, Foxx averaged 39 homers and 134 RBI over 13 seasons.

Seeing the numbers Foxx put up, it's no wonder that the Athletics captured the American League pennant in 1929, 1930, and 1931. They won back-to-back World Series titles in the first two of those seasons, as well.

Jimmie Foxx, 1929–1931

1929	.354	33 HR	118 RBI	123 runs
1930	.335	37 HR	156 RBI	127 runs
1931	.291	30 HR	120 RBI	93 runs

The 1929 Athletics won the pennant by 18.5 games over the Yankees, and then defeated the Cubs in seven games in the World Series. The best of those pennant-winning Athletics teams was probably the 1931 team, which went 107–45 despite Foxx having a sub-par season (for him) and the team failing to win the Series.

After that, Connie Mack was hamstrung by finances. He tried to keep his team together, but eventually had to sell off his best players. Following 1933, Grove was gone, as were Simmons, Cochrane, George Earnshaw, and Rube Walberg, the foundations for the team that dominated the American League. But Mack held onto young slugger Foxx. Former Athletics star Jimmy Dykes said in 1967 at the time of Foxx's death, "I always regarded Mr. Mack, our manager, as one of my greatest friends. But I disagreed with him about Foxxie's salary in 1934. It was none of my business, either. He offered him a salary of $11,000, a 30 percent cut from the three-year contract he had just completed. Foxxie had 48 homers and batted .356. He hit 58 homers the year before. Yet, Mr. Mack still wanted to cut him."

Foxx's achievements in the early '30s were incredible. In 1932, he won the MVP Award over Lou Gehrig. In 1933, he won the MVP again, as well as the Triple Crown (leading the league in batting, home runs, and RBI). He won the batting title by 20 points.

Jimmie Foxx, 1932–1933

1932	.364 batting avg.	.469 on-base avg.	.749 slugging pct.
1933	.356 batting avg.	.449 on-base avg.	.703 slugging pct.

To put those numbers in perspective, Foxx slugged over .700 in 1938 with the Red Sox, his third such season. Only three other players (Babe Ruth, Barry Bonds, and Lou Gehrig) have slugged better than .700 in three or more seasons. Those four players have accounted for 19 of the 35 seasons in history that a player slugged for such a high percentage.

Foxx's batting average is the most impressive aspect of his 1932 and 1933 seasons. Foxx won the Triple Crown in 1933, and should have won it in 1932. They awarded the batting title to Dale Alexander, though he didn't even have 400 at-bats.

Following the 1935 season, the 27-year-old power-hitting Foxx was sold to the Red Sox for $150,000 and two inconsequential players. He wouldn't play on a pennant winner in Boston, but at least owner Tom Yawkey was a good and generous owner, and Foxx was able to get paid for his abilities.

In Boston, the one-time teammate of Cobb would wind up as a teammate of Ted Williams. Williams loved Foxxie, as did most other contemporary players and media members. Jimmie was always willing to lend a hand and spent half of his time helping other players out of scrapes while working himself into one.

Foxx nearly won another Triple Crown in 1938, batting a league-best .349 with 50 homers (second to Hank Greenberg) and leading the league with 175 RBI. He had two more good seasons, then fell off in 1941. In that season, he hit just 19 homers with 105 RBI. That was a major dropoff from the 35- and 36-homer seasons he'd had the two previous years.

In June of 1942, the Red Sox sold Foxx to the Cubs for little more than the $7,500 waiver price. He was still in his early 30s, but he probably was old for his age, especially with a habit for drinking.

Foxx retired a Cub following the 1942 season. Cubs owner Philip Wrigley had unique plans for Jimmie. The United States was well into World War II when Wrigley received word from President Franklin Roosevelt that the 1943 major-league baseball season might be suspended due to the manpower shortage. Roosevelt wanted Wrigley to do something to keep baseball going until the men got home from service. Wrigley joined forces with Branch Rickey and others to create the first professional baseball league for women. Four teams were formed, and the league started its first season in 1943. One of the managers was Jimmie Foxx.

Perhaps you've seen the 1991 Penny Marshall movie *A League of Their Own*. The manager in the movie, Jimmy Dugan, was played by Tom Hanks and is based on Foxx. Like Dugan, Foxx had a shortened career due to alcoholism, forcing him into managing in the women's leagues.

The league was short-lived, as the war soon ended and the men came home. Foxx was persuaded to return in 1944 with the Cubs and 1945 with the Philadelphia Phillies. But basically, he was finished in 1942, at the age of 34.

In 1951, he was elected to the Hall of Fame. At the time, he was a salesman for a Doylestown, Pennsylvania, trucking company. Just two years later, reports began to circulate that Foxx was broke and out of a job. His former roommate with the Red Sox and Phillies, Johnny Peacock, explained why in a 1953 article: "If Jimmie is broke, it is because his heart was a revolving door that was never locked. Anyone could walk in—and frequently did. Jimmie always used to pay the whole room bill, no matter who his roommate was. He'd pay all the telephone, valet, room service—everything. I don't believe the fellow had an enemy in the world—even though he did squirt tobacco juice on the shoes of his teammates in the dugout."

A former business manager disclosed to the press in 1958 that Foxx had become ill and lost his job with a "transfer company" in South Florida. Foxx had missed out on baseball's player pension plan by one year. Foxx also lost large amounts of money in various ventures, including a $50,000 investment in a Florida golf club before World War II. Apparently, he was an easy target and people took advantage of him.

He died in 1967 at the age of 59.

Who's Better, Who's Best
Jimmie Foxx or Lou Gehrig?

Foxx really was the right-handed Gehrig, with a few differences.

Gehrig played one position for one team—the Yankees—and played in the World Series no less than seven times. His teams won six of the seven World Series that he played in. While Gehrig played with Ruth and DiMaggio, Jimmie Foxx played with Cobb and then Ted Williams. Foxx played in three World Series, with his team winning twice.

If one compares Foxx's stats with Gehrig's, they are very, very close.

	Games	Batting Avg.	HR	RBI	Slugging Pct.
Foxx	2,317	.325	534	1,922	.609
Gehrig	2,164	.340	493	1,995	.632

Both players managed to squeeze most of their career numbers into 13 solid seasons. Gehrig—four years older—did his best work from 1925 to 1938. Foxx did the majority of his damage from 1929 to 1941. Both players were magnificent in postseason play. Both players were popular leaders on their squads. In 1934, for the very first All-Star Game, it was Gehrig who batted fourth and played first base. Foxx batted fifth (behind Ruth and Gehrig) and played third base that day to accommodate Gehrig.

Both these men played in the very large shadow of Babe Ruth. Both of these guys were finished by age 35. Foxx hit only 7 homers after his 35th birthday, and Gehrig hit only about 15. Compare that to modern-day first baseman Rafael Palmeiro, who has hit 190 home runs after his 35th birthday. Barry Bonds has hit even more. Hank Aaron hit 245 homers past his 35th birthday. Gehrig and Foxx are head and shoulders above all other first basemen, including Mark McGwire (who hit 126 of his 583 homers after age 35).

If Foxx and Gehrig had a finishing kick anything close to that of the more recent stars who are bred for longevity, their records—particularly the RBI records—would be unreachable by Aaron, Bonds, and everyone else.

Both Gehrig and Foxx took advantage of the era in which they played, with favorable ballparks and inflated averages. Gehrig was a smidgen better than Foxx, but that's still enough to place him as the second-greatest first baseman of all time. On the big screen, Gary Cooper played Gehrig and Tom Hanks played Foxx. Cooper is better than Hanks by an even slimmer margin.

SANDY KOUFAX

Sandy Koufax was unhittable. There were few National Leaguers from the 1960s that differed from this general opinion. Willie Stargell said being up at bat against Koufax was like drinking coffee with a fork. Bill White told me that he was 0-for-about-100 against Koufax: "His fastball rose, and his curveball, I never could hit." Ernie Banks said, "He's the greatest pitcher I ever saw."

Despite compiling only 165 victories, Sandy Koufax was one of the greatest pitchers of all time. He retired at 30, and was the youngest member to be elected into the Hall of Fame, at the age of 36.

He connected with fans the way only certain superstar athletes can. Christy Mathewson had that magic in the early 1900s. Mickey Mantle had that spell over a generation. Koufax had it.

The young Brooklynite Koufax earned a basketball scholarship to the University of Cincinnati. He continued to play baseball "just for the fun of it," and the result was that when he enrolled at Cincinnati, he made the varsity basketball and baseball squads in his freshman year of 1954.

He began to get attention from major-league scouts. The Reds thought he was too wild. In his tryout for the Giants, his first pitch soared over the catcher into the third-row seats. He auditioned for three other teams, but it was the Brooklyn Dodgers who signed him to a two-year contract at $6,000 a year. The $14,000 signing bonus meant that Koufax would spend at least his first two years on the Dodgers' major-league roster.

In 1955, Sandy appeared in only 12 games for Brooklyn, throwing 41.2 innings. He did show signs of his future stardom, throwing two shutouts, including a 14-strikeout performance against the Reds in late August. He was principally remembered for having slipped and fallen on his face while walking out to start his first game at Ebbets Field. In October, the Dodgers defeated the Yanks in the World Series for Brooklyn's first (and only) championship.

There wasn't much progress for Koufax in either of the next two seasons. He won two games in 1956 (10 starts), and made only 13 starts in 1957, the Dodgers' final year in Brooklyn.

Koufax was 22 years old when he and the Dodgers moved to Los Angeles. He continued to frustrate the team with his inability to control his fastball. In 1958, he was 11–11 in 26 starts, striking out 131 but walking 105. Issuing six walks per nine innings was entirely too many. He showed just enough promise for Los Angeles to hold out hope.

In 1959, Koufax was only 8–6 in 23 starts, cutting his walks to 5.4 per every nine innings. He did strike out 16 batters on June 22, then a record for night games. Two months later, he tied Bob Feller's major-league record with 18 strikeouts against the Giants. In the World Series, he made his first appearance in relief in Game 1. Sandy entered the game in the fifth inning, with the Dodgers trailing 11–0. He pitched two scoreless innings. That earned him the start in Game 5, with the Dodgers leading the Series 3–1.

He allowed only one run and five hits. He walked only one batter in his seven innings. The run scored on a double play, but it was the only run of the game, and the Dodgers lost.

Koufax was only 8–13 in 1960 as the Dodgers fell to fourth place. After six seasons in the majors, his record was just 36–40. The following spring training, backup catcher Norm Sherry advised Sandy to ease up on his speed to achieve control. Koufax figured he had nothing to lose, and pitched seven no-hit innings in the exhibition game.

That 1961 season was Koufax's first overpowering year. He struck out 269, while walking just 96. His walks were down to a manageable 3.3 per nine innings. That season set up one of the greatest five-year runs in baseball history.

For the last five years of Koufax's career, he became an immortal.

Sandy Koufax					
First 7 years	54–53	138 starts	37 complete games	7 shutouts	3.94 ERA
Last 5 years	111–34	176 starts	100 complete games	33 shutouts	1.95 ERA

Koufax won the MVP Award in 1963. He finished second to Willie Mays in 1965, and a narrow second to Roberto Clemente in 1966.

He led the National League in ERA in each of his last five seasons, giving up less than two runs per nine innings over that five-season period.

He led the league in wins in 1963, 1965, and 1966. He was fourth in 1964, and circulatory problems in 1962 kept him out of action for two months.

He led the league in strikeouts four of those seasons, and his 382 strikeouts in 1965 set a new major-league record. He pitched a no-hitter in four consecutive seasons, including a perfect game in 1965.

He was at his best with the season on the line. From 1963 to 1966, he was 14–2 in September, with a 1.55 ERA.

1963 World Series

Game 1 was a dream matchup of Whitey Ford (24 wins during the season, and a 10–5 World Series mark going into the game) against Koufax (25–5 during the season).

Sandy struck out the first five batters he faced, en route to a Series-record 15 for the game. Dodgers catcher John Roseboro hit a three-run home run, and Koufax won 5–2 at New York.

A few days later, Koufax clinched the Series sweep for Los Angeles by besting Ford again, this time 2–1. Ford allowed only two hits—both to Frank Howard—but the Dodgers needed only two runs for Koufax.

1965 World Series

The Dodgers were heavily favored this time against the Minnesota Twins. On October 6, 1965, Sandy Koufax observed the Jewish holiday of Yom Kippur instead of pitching Game 1 of the World Series. Don Drysdale started the opener instead, and lost to the Twins' Mudcat Grant. Koufax then gave up a single earned run in Game 2, but was defeated by Jim Kaat. Claude Osteen's Game 3 shutout brought the Dodgers back, and Drysdale evened the Series in the fourth game. Koufax pitched a shutout in the fifth game to give the Dodgers a 3–2 lead. Mudcat Grant hit a three-run homer and pitched the Twins to victory in Game 6, setting up a seventh game.

Dodgers manager Walt Alston had a huge decision to make. He had a well-rested Don Drysdale available, or he could come back with Koufax on two days' rest for Game 7. Instead of playing it safe, Alston chose Koufax. Sandy rose to the challenge and won 2–0, striking out 10 Twins while allowing just three hits.

Koufax was the MVP of the World Series. He started three of the last six games, pitching 24 innings and allowing just one earned run (0.38 ERA). He struck out 29 and walked just five.

The southpaw star was an iron man the whole season, despite an arthritic elbow that had threatened to (and eventually did) curtail his career. Including his World Series achievements, Koufax made 44 starts in 1965, completed 28, pitched 359 innings, and struck out 411.

It is easy to look back and wonder why Alston allowed Koufax to work so many innings. Following Game 7 of the 1965 World Series, Koufax admitted he was tiring as early as the fifth inning. "Alston told me not to reach back and throw too hard," said Sandy after the game. Koufax must have thrown 400 pitches that week in his three starts.

Before the 1966 season, Koufax and Drysdale teamed up to gain leverage in salary negotiations. This was before teams allowed agents to negotiate player contracts. Koufax and Drysdale asked for a little more than a million dollars over three years—for both of them to divide as they saw fit. Eventually, Sandy signed for $130,000 and Drysdale for $105,000.

Here is what the Dodgers got for their $130,000 in 1966: They drew an unprecedented 2.6 million fans to their home games—with extra spikes every time Koufax pitched. Sandy was 27–9 with an ERA of 1.73. He was in such pain that he couldn't straighten his left arm—it was curved like a parenthesis. His elbow was shot full of cortisone several times, which would leave him queasy.

Koufax told reporters in August 1966 that "they said the traumatic arthritis would get progressively worse, and it has." He learned of the condition in March 1965. Over his last two seasons, he was allowed to pitch almost 700 innings. Tom Verducci's 1999 *Sports Illustrated* article on Koufax reminded us that "in the last 26 days of his career, including the loss in the 1966 World Series, Koufax started seven games, threw five complete-game wins, and had a 1.07 ERA. He clinched the pennant for a second straight year on two days' rest."

In Koufax's last game, he lost 6–0 in the World Series to a 21-year-old pitcher for the Baltimore Orioles, Jim Palmer. He gave up only a single earned run, however.

Koufax: World Series Career

4–3
0.95 ERA
7 starts
4 complete games
2 shutouts
61 strikeouts
11 walks
57 innings

There are few athletes that retire at the top of their game. Koufax was forced to.

Who's Better, Who's Best
Sandy Koufax or Warren Spahn?

Spahn, like Koufax, was one of the greatest left-handed pitchers of all time. Spahn won 20 or more games 13 different seasons. Koufax had only three such seasons.

Koufax was only dominant his last four to five years, and then the arthritis cut short his career. Spahn was never as dominating, but man, did he have staying power. He won three ERA titles, and hurled two no-hitters. In 1963, at the age of 42, Spahn won 23 games and lost only 7.

Spahn then gave lasting memories of the wrong kind in 1964 and 1965, pitching way past his prime. Koufax—not exactly by choice—left the game before anyone could see him past his peak.

Sandy reminds me of Joe DiMaggio. He was an ethnic American hero whose grace was everywhere admired, but whose life was all mystery. DiMaggio and Koufax each had short careers that were filled with memorable World Series moments. Neither suffered the Willie Mays/Warren Spahn indignity of allowing people to see them play well past their prime. There is an ever-growing number of players who surpass Koufax's victory total and DiMaggio's home run tally. It doesn't take away from their dominance.

Koufax is one of the greatest. Spahn is one of the winningest. Sandy was better for one season, for two, and for a five-year period. They are both on the short list of greatest left-handed pitchers of all time.

A Better Analogy

Sandy Koufax and J. D. Salinger J. D. Salinger was one of the greatest authors in American literature, despite a body of work that included only six books. Koufax and Salinger are similar in that both are recluses who live mostly in New England. Each chose a different path than most talented artists. Both went through a couple of divorces, and both had houses that burned down. They influenced generations of fans and then stayed out of the public eye. On a personal level, my wife, Amy, is an even better analogy to Sandy. They are both Jewish, from Brooklyn, born on December 30, and were wild in their early 20s. I'm also fairly certain that Amy wouldn't pitch on Yom Kippur.

ROGER CLEMENS

Frank Sinatra sang, "It was a very good year," the story of a man who is in the "autumn of the year" and thinking back on his life. He concludes with the last line of the song: "It was a mess of good years."

There's no better way to describe Roger Clemens's baseball career. It was, simply, a mess of good years. There were 21 seasons of indelible memories, some that have aged like fine wine. There were other regrettable incidents and poor performances. It all added up to a career superior to all but a few pitchers in the history of the sport.

One doesn't have to be Columbus—merely pass through it—to get from Cambridge, Ohio, to Dayton, Ohio. In 1962, a real American hero from Cambridge, NASA astronaut John Glenn, climbed into his *Friendship 7* Mercury capsule and lifted off on an Atlas-6 rocket. Glenn became the first American to orbit the Earth and became an instant national hero. That same year, a baseball hero was born in Dayton. Roger Clemens would be called "Rocket Man" for the speed that he threw baseballs.

Some artists are born with the gift for painting images. Other artists are born with heavenly voices. Roger was born with the gift to throw—with incredible velocity and accuracy—a baseball. Like many great artists, he had a rough childhood; in this case not knowing his birth father, losing his stepfather by the time he was 10, and moving often.

He was drafted by the Minnesota Twins out of high school, but they tried to pressure him into signing for less than he wanted, and he elected to go to college instead. Two years later, he had a tryout with the Mets and their manager at the time, Joe Torre. When nothing came of that tryout, Clemens chose to pitch at the University of Texas, where he went 25–7 over two seasons and won the 1983 College World Series championship game. He was drafted in June 1983 by the Boston Red Sox, and tore through their minor-league system over the next 12 months.

By August 1983, the *Boston Globe*'s Bob Ryan was writing, "I haven't seen him pitch yet, so the only thing I can tell you about the hallowed Roger Clemens is that he has the same body as (1) Robin Roberts, and (2) Tom Seaver."

Only 13 months removed from the College World Series, Clemens was called to make his debut for the Red Sox in May of 1984. His manager was Ralph Houk, who was nearing the end of a career that spanned nearly 50 years. In earlier days, Houk had managed Mickey Mantle, Yogi Berra, and Whitey Ford with the Yankees. Almost immediately, Houk and the devoted members of Red Sox Nation were impressed. In his rookie season, Clemens had a 4:1 ratio of strikeouts to walks when 2:1 was considered outstanding. In one game, he struck out 15 and walked none. He had 119 strikeouts in only 129 innings. Clemens entered the major leagues with a simple game plan. He was going to go strength against strength. "Rocket" was a fastball pitcher, and he was going to throw it by hitters. There was no trickery or off-speed pitches necessary. He was 9–4 (and winner of six consecutive games) when the team shut him down for the season on August 30 to undergo shoulder surgery.

The next season was even more frustrating. His shoulder problems from the previous season forced him to the sidelines after just 15 starts, and Clemens feared that he would have to alter his style and become a "junk-baller" rather than a fastball specialist. He never did have to change his style.

When Clemens was 23, it was a very good year. It was a very good year for Red Sox fans, who stared at the Fens. Clemens won his first 14 decisions. In one game, he broke the all-time record for strikeouts with 20. Not only did Roger strike out 20, he didn't walk a batter in the game.

He finished the season 24–4 with an ERA of 2.48. When one considers the league batting average and the ballpark adjustment for the hitter-friendly Fenway Park, Clemens's ERA was minuscule. He was the MVP of the All-Star Game and the MVP of the regular season.

The 1986 postseason did not go exactly as planned. In the first game of the American League Championship Series, Clemens was roughed up by the California Angels and lost 8–1. He came back on three days' rest and took a 3–0 lead into the ninth inning in Game 4. Calvin Schiraldi couldn't save the game, and the game went into extra innings. Again on short rest, Clemens came back and easily won 8–1 in Game 7, sending the Sox into the World Series for the first time since 1975.

Clemens made his first World Series start in Game 2 against the Mets, but he lasted less than five innings. The Mets' ace, Dwight Gooden, was hit even harder, though, and the Red Sox took a commanding 2–0 lead as they attempted to win their first World Series since 1918.

Boston took only one of three home games at Fenway Park, setting the stage for Clemens—the MVP of the season and the pitcher who won Game 7 of the League Championship Series—to wrap up the Series in Game 6. Boston even had the luxury of giving Al Nipper a start in Game 4, so they could pitch a well-rested Clemens. But that plan didn't exactly work out the way Boston intended. Clemens had a 3–2 lead late in Game 6, and was only a handful of outs from delivering a gift to all of New England, but Clemens developed a blister and gave way to reliever Schiraldi. Schiraldi gave up the tying run in the eighth inning. The Red Sox scored twice in the top of the 10th inning, and Schiraldi retired the first two Mets in the bottom of the 10th. Boston was one out away from winning the World Series. They never got the out. The Mets made a memorable comeback in Game 6, and then won Game 7 as well.

Clemens, at this point the best pitcher in baseball, bolted from training camp the next spring in a contract dispute and vowed to sit out the season. He signed just before the 1987 season opened, and started poorly. On June 12, he was only 4–6, and was only 8–6 at the All-Star break. After June 12, he went 16–3 to end the season. He was 5–1 in September, with an ERA of 1.78. On the last day of the season, he threw a second straight shutout, a two-hitter against Milwaukee. He finished 20–9, with an ERA of 2.97, which was third in the league. He finished with seven shutouts, and it was enough for him to capture a second consecutive Cy Young Award.

The next season saw the Red Sox return to the postseason, and Clemens led the way with 18 wins (including eight more shutouts). In the postseason, the Rocket Man lost to Oakland, giving him just one win in his first six postseason starts.

Clemens was steadily going downhill following his spectacular liftoff.

Roger Clemens, 1986–1989
1986: 24–4
1987: 20–9
1988: 18–12
1989: 17–11

Roger Clemens was just getting started in his series of orbital missions around the American League. In 1990, he won 21 games (his third 20-win season). His ERA was 1.90. He lost the Cy Young Award to A's pitcher Bob Welch, who won 27 games. Clemens was more overpowering, but missed five starts due to injury. In the postseason, however, he lost his composure as well as a huge game.

Clemens was ejected by plate ump Terry Cooney in the second inning of Oakland's 3–1 victory that completed the A's sweep of the Red Sox. Trailing 1–0, with a runner already on base, Clemens issued a walk on a close pitch to Willie Randolph. Clemens shook his head at ball four, and heard Cooney tell him, "I hope you're not shaking your head at me." Clemens then responded with, "If you want to talk to me, take your mask off." Several witnesses said that Clemens used profanities. The Red Sox would lose, and the A's finished off a four-game sweep of the ALCS. American League President Bobby Brown suspended Clemens for the first five games of the next season, for making significant physical contact with an umpire, for threatening Cooney, for verbally abusing the ump with obscenities, and for not leaving the dugout immediately.

All that didn't stop the Red Sox from offering Clemens a contract in early 1991 that made him the highest-paid player in baseball. He led the league in ERA for a third time, and shutouts for the fourth time. He won the Cy Young Award for the third time. He had another dominating season in 1992, but finished third in the Cy Young voting behind reliever Dennis Eckersley and starter Jack McDowell.

Then, for no apparent reason, Clemens went into a four-year period of mediocrity. And then it came undone . . . when he was 31.

In June of 1993, Clemens stopped a six-game Red Sox losing streak by stopping the Orioles. It made Roger's record 7–5. It also pushed Clemens's career record following a Boston loss to an outstanding 96–32.

Following that game, Clemens went 4–9 the rest of the season. Although there was no discussed injury, Clemens won only 40 games over his last four seasons in a Boston uniform.

Roger Clemens, 1993–1996
1993: 11–14
1994: 9–7
1995: 10–5
1996: 10–13

There would be only one more highlight from his time in Boston. On the night that Clemens tied the immortal Cy Young for the Red Sox team lead for most career victories—in the final week of the 1996 season—he also tied his major-league record for most strikeouts in a game. In a showcase to solicit attention from other teams who were interested in the soon-to-be free agent, Clemens showed what he was capable of. He struck out 20 Detroit Tigers in gaining his 38th career shutout and 192nd win. It would be his last win in a Red Sox uniform.

He had done everything for Boston except deliver them the World Series. In nine post-season starts for the Red Sox, he had one win.

Clemens had said that he wanted to play closer to home, and that made the Texas teams the favorites to land him in 1997. That made it more surprising when Clemens accepted an offer from the Toronto Blue Jays.

He won his first 11 games for them. In 1997, Clemens became the first pitcher to lead the American League in wins, ERA, and strikeouts since Detroit's Hal Newhouser did it in 1945. Clemens was 21–7 with a 2.05 ERA. He joined only two other pitchers, Greg Maddux and Steve Carlton, as four-time Cy Young Award winners, and he was just getting started. He would leave them in the dust soon after that year, winning a record fifth Cy Young Award with Toronto in 1998. No pitcher had ever won Cy Young awards 11 years apart, but that is exactly what Clemens did (his first was in 1986, his fourth in 1997).

In 1998 Roger led the league in ERA for the sixth time. He led the league in wins for a fourth time. He had a career season in strikeouts, striking out 10.39 batters per nine innings.

In spring training of 1999, Clemens was at the top of his game, having won consecutive Cy Young awards. He also had two years remaining on his contract, with the Blue Jays owing him more than $16 million. In a move that stunned everyone, the New York Yankees—coming off a record-setting 125-win season (counting postseason)—traded Homer Bush, Graham Lloyd, and David Wells for Clemens. The Rocket Man was always one of George Steinbrenner's favorite players. Clemens said at the time of the trade, "I met my match in a guy who wants to win." Clemens was 36 years old when he was traded to the Yankees to begin the 1999 season.

The Yankees didn't need Clemens to make the World Series; they already had a well-established team that was expected to win. In that 1999 season, Clemens was just one of five starting pitchers to win between 11 and 17 games for the Yankees. Despite finishing just 14–10 with a 4.60 ERA, Clemens turned in his best postseason performances to that point in his career. I remember working the 1999 American League Divisional Series, when Clemens completed the Yankees' sweep of the Texas Rangers with a dominating performance—his first postseason win in 13 years (and only second ever in 10 starts). I was there a few weeks later when Clemens completed a sweep of the Atlanta Braves in the World Series, with a dominating performance in Game 4.

How ironic that Clemens had put up incredible regular-season numbers in his first 15 seasons, only to blow up with blisters or temper tantrums in October. Then, in 1999, he had a disappointing regular season, but came up huge in those two postseason victories.

Of course, when Clemens is bad, he can be very bad. In the American League Championship Series of 1999, Clemens pitched against Pedro Martinez in one of the most anticipated games in Fenway Park history. Roger lasted only two innings. The Red Sox prevailed easily, 13–1. It would be their only win of the Series.

The 2000 season was much like 1999 for the Rocket. Clemens won only 13 games during the season, and lost twice in a best-of-five series with Oakland in the first round of the playoffs. The Yankees won the other three games that Clemens didn't pitch, and Roger owed the Yankees some big games in the League Championship Series and World Series. He delivered.

Clemens, Last Two Rounds of 2000 Postseason

LCS versus Seattle	9 innings	1 hit	0 runs	2 walks	15 strikeouts
World Series versus Mets	8 innings	2 hits	0 runs	0 walks	9 strikeouts

The one-hitter against Seattle was a very special performance. I was there, and it was one of the best games anyone will ever pitch. I remember Tino Martinez coming awfully close to catching Al Martin's double. It hit off his glove in the seventh inning, for the Mariners' only hit. Roger came within inches of a postseason no-hitter against a Seattle team that featured Alex Rodriguez and Edgar Martinez.

Of course, everyone remembers something else about Clemens from the Mets game in the World Series. Clemens flung the jagged stump of a sheared-off bat toward Mets batter Mike Piazza, narrowly missing him. Earlier that July, a Clemens fastball hit the bill of Piazza's batting helmet. Piazza suffered a concussion, and Roger was fined $5,000. Clemens was still throwing fastballs, and still throwing inside, and still creating both positive and negative headlines.

Finally, Clemens would earn the respect of the temperamental Yankees fans by finishing 20–3 and winning his record sixth Cy Young Award with the Yankees in 2001. Following his overdue outrageous season with the Yanks, Clemens was again brilliant in the World Series against the Arizona Diamondbacks. The Yankees were down 2–0, but Clemens (and Mariano Rivera) got them back in the Series in Game 3. Clemens started Game 7, with the season on the line. He matched Arizona's Curt Schilling for the first five scoreless innings, then left in the seventh inning of a 1–1 game. The Yankees took a 2–1 lead on Alphonso Soriano's homer, but Mariano Rivera blew his first save opportunity in 23 postseason attempts, and the Diamondbacks denied Clemens a third World Series championship ring.

Clemens won 30 games over the next two seasons, including his 300th career victory. He announced that he would retire following the 2003 season. At the end of that season, there was another remarkable postseason performance.

Clemens started Game 4 of the 2003 World Series, and gave up three runs in the first inning. Then he regained his edge and didn't allow another run through the seventh inning. At the conclusion of the seventh, when it became apparent that Clemens was leaving the mound for the final time, the players and fans of both teams stood up and applauded this great competitor. He had thrown over 4,000 innings, striking out more than 4,000 batters and starting 26 postseason games.

Once again, Clemens surprised people by saying hello after he had said good-bye. He signed with the Houston Astros, and won his first nine decisions in 2004. He finished 18–4, with an ERA of 2.98. He struck out 218 batters. He started the All-Star Game, this time for the National League, and won his record seventh Cy Young award. Clemens has won 328 games, and has won 136 times since leaving the Boston Red Sox. His accomplishments place him among the best pitchers of all time.

Bob Costas: "I loved Seaver, but you have to put Clemens ahead of him. He's on a short list of being one of the greatest of all time. In my lifetime, no one was better than Koufax at his best. I would pick Sandy for one game. But Clemens was ahead of Gibson and Seaver at their best."

Who's Better, Who's Best
Roger Clemens or Pedro Martinez?
Joe Buck: "Roger Clemens over Pedro Martinez. I'd say that based on 2004. For Clemens to do what he's done for as long as he's done it, is pretty remarkable. Pedro Martinez had a pretty severe drop over a three-year period, and with his body type, it's unlikely he'll return to his dominance."

A Better Analogy
Roger Clemens and John Glenn In 1998, NASA announced a return to orbit for John Glenn, the first American to orbit the Earth, and later a U.S. senator. In November of 1998, Glenn showed the world that he still had "The Right Stuff."

The other "Rocket Man" announced a return to active pitching duty shortly after announcing his retirement after the 2003 season. Both Glenn and Clemens were both role models for a generation as young men, and then in later years. They both pushed beyond boundaries thought impossible to break. Both men took risks in going back.

There really was no reason to fear that Clemens would somehow "tarnish" his legacy by continuing to pitch. After all, when you look back, it was a mess of good years.

JOE MORGAN

Of the players who spent at least 75 percent of their careers at second base, Joe Morgan is the greatest to play the position.

Now, I'll add the qualifier. Rogers Hornsby played 1,561 games at second base. He played 2,164 games, so only 71 percent of his games were at second. He spent 356 games at shortstop, 192 at third base, and some time in the outfield and first base. Joe Morgan played 99 percent of his games at second base. There are others close (Nap Lajoie and Eddie Collins are ranked almost immediately following him), but no one better.

I will make full disclosure on my feelings on Joe. He was the best player in the game when I was twelve years old. Of course most people will remember their childhood heroes as being "the best." Also, I worked with Joe for five consecutive Octobers, sitting on airplanes and in press boxes with a man who was as great an analyst as anyone I've ever worked with in any sport. When calling him the best second baseman ever, I am being as fair as possible. I was also greatly influenced by another one of the all-time greats (Johnny Bench), who told me that Morgan was the greatest player he ever played with.

Joe Morgan is a little guy, standing only 5'7"; he weighed less than 160 pounds when he started in the major leagues. He was born in Bonham, Texas, in 1943. His father got him interested in baseball. He was drafted by the Houston Astros (then the Colt-45s) and was second in voting for Rookie of the Year in 1965 (to the Dodgers' Jim Lefevre). He might have been small, and younger-looking than his 21 years, but he wasn't intimidated when facing Sandy Koufax, Bob Gibson, Juan Marichal, or anyone else.

There wasn't a kid that didn't imitate Joe's "chicken-wing" flapping at the plate, awaiting the pitch. He had patience at the plate. He had speed on the bases. He hit for power.

Tony Kubek: "I told Ted Williams a long time ago, 'There's a guy in the National League that hits exactly like you.' Of course, Joe wasn't six-four and 225 pounds. He backed off the plate versus left-handed pitchers. Still, he was quite the batter—quite an excellent batter."

Bob Costas: "Joe Morgan—the argument you make against him was that although he had a very long career, his period of greatness was less than half of it. For about six years, he was one of the greatest of his generation at any position."

Johnny Bench: "Joe Morgan was as good as anyone I ever played with. In fact, he was the best. He didn't become a great player until he came to us in 1972. What made the difference? He had a tendency to get into a funk. But whenever he started to go into a slump, Tony Perez would make him laugh and get out of it. And if Tony didn't make him get out of it, someone else did. Joe was the ultimate pro, and was so serious all the time. He could win games with a walk, or with a stolen base, or with a home run. He had all the dimensions. If he had a weakness, it was that he didn't have the greatest range or throwing arm. He had so many tools, however, that it would have been unfair if he had a stronger throwing arm to turn the double play."

One of Joe Morgan's nicknames when he played was "Sweet Pea." When he played with Houston, he was one of several young stars, among them Rusty Staub and Jimmy Wynn ("the Toy Cannon"). As a rookie, Morgan hit 14 homers and stole 20 bases for a ninth-place team in the absolute worst ballpark for hitters. The Astros might not have had the best team, but they sure had good nicknames.

In 1966, the Astros improved, and moved up in the standings. On June 25, Morgan was hit by a line drive during batting practice, shattered his kneecap, and missed 40 games. Houston immediately lost 28 of their next 31 games without Morgan.

The next season, Morgan started off in a terrible slump, until he began pounding the ball in July. In 1968, he missed all but ten games. During the season, Harry Walker took over as manager of the Astros. Morgan and Walker did not see eye-to-eye on things. It probably held Morgan back. From 1969 to 1971, Morgan began showing glimpses of his talent. He stole 131 bases. His batting average and power were well-kept secrets, courtesy of the Astrodome, Walker, and a weak lineup around him. That would change when the Cincinnati Reds traded for him following the 1971 season.

Morgan clicked with Reds manager Sparky Anderson. Morgan, the consummate pro, popped the ball up to the infield early in 1971, and failed to run hard to first base. Sparky, privately, told Joe after that that he had too much class to make himself look bad like that. Joe appreciated the way Sparky approached him—quietly and gently. He never had to be told again.

Morgan became a team leader on the Reds, both on and off the field.

Johnny Bench: "If you could put Joe Morgan, Pete Rose, and Willie Mays on a team, then you could put any other collection of guys out there and you wouldn't worry. You know everyone would play hard. Those three guys always hustled, always ran everything out, always played the game correctly."

In the 1975 season, Morgan led the Reds to the National League pennant and World Series title. He batted .327 (fourth in the league), scored 107 runs (fourth), stole 67 bases (second), walked 132 times (most in the league), hit 17 homers, and drove in 94 runs.

The next season, he was even better. He led the league in slugging percentage (.576). He led the league in on-base average (.444). He scored 113 runs (second in the league), drove in 111 (second), and stole 60 bases (second).

Did Morgan make the Reds the most potent lineup in decades, or did the other MVPs in the Cincinnati lineup make Joe become the player he was?

"The Big Red Machine" had Tony Perez at first base, Morgan at second, Davey Concepcion at shortstop, and Pete Rose at third base. Johnny Bench was the catcher. George Foster, Cesar Geronimo, and Ken Griffey Sr. were starting outfielders, rounding out a lineup that featured four players (Bench, Rose, Morgan, and Foster) who between them won six MVPs over an eight-year period.

Over a quarter-century after the Reds' halcyon days, Morgan was the national broadcaster of the World Series when the Yankees were winning three consecutive World Series and a record 114 games in 1998. Morgan made his feelings known that the Yankees were not as good as his Reds.

Johnny Bench: "I don't disagree—I don't think any of us from those Reds teams would—that the Reds of the mid-'70s were better than the 1998 Yankees. But, we all had great respect for the Yankees and the way they approached the game. I admire Joe Torre, and what he and his team accomplished."

My opinion is that the Yankees had a clear advantage with their pitching staff. The Reds didn't have a Mariano Rivera in the bullpen. The Reds didn't have starters like Andy Pettite or Roger Clemens. The Yankees might have even had a small advantage at center field (Bernie Williams) and right field (Paul O'Neill), but outside of the pitching staff, the only clear advantage the Yankees had was at shortstop. You don't want to compare Concepcion to Derek Jeter.

Joe Morgan became a catalyst for winning teams. Although he didn't win in his first seven seasons with Houston, he became one of the greatest winners after that. His team finished in first place in 1972, 1973, 1975, 1976, 1979 (with Cincinnati), 1980 (in a second tour with Houston), and 1983 (with Philadelphia).

He would have been an excellent manager; he was able to see things on the field that other people don't see. He knew, for example, when pitchers were getting tired, or when base runners should steal bases. Instead of managing, he became a proud and disciplined professional announcer.

Again, there's little doubt that Hornsby deserves to be ranked ahead of Morgan in this book. But Morgan played longer and more exclusively at second base. He ranks closely with some of the legendary second basemen of yesteryear, and some of the modern second basemen (Ryne Sandberg, Lou Whitaker, Craig Biggio, perhaps even the active Alphonso Soriano) aren't too far behind him.

If Morgan had played in the early 1930s or the late 1990s, his offensive numbers would have made everyone salivate. He played in an era when offensive numbers were down. He was almost too dignified—and too late—for the appropriate nicknames. He should have been nicknamed "Sparky" with the Reds—not the manager. He should have been "the Toy Cannon" with the Astros—not roommate Jimmy Wynn. In fact, he should have been Joe Wynn. That's what Morgan did over and over in his 20-plus years in the majors.

Who's Better, Who's Best
Joe Morgan or Ryne Sandberg?

Morgan played 22 years, and Sandberg played 16. The two of them were very good players for a long time, but dominant for nine years each: Morgan from 1972 to 1980 and Sandberg from 1984 to 1992.

Morgan won his two MVP awards in 1975 and 1976. In addition, he was fourth in MVP voting in 1972, fourth in 1973, and eighth in 1974.

Sandberg was MVP in 1984. In addition, he was fourth in 1989 and fourth in 1990.

Morgan went to eight All-Star games and won five Gold Gloves in his best nine-year stretch. In the other 13 years of his career, he went to two All-Star games and didn't win a Gold Glove.

Sandberg went to nine All-Star games and won nine Gold Gloves in his best nine-year stretch. In the other seven years of his career, he went to one All-Star Game, and won one Gold Glove.

Morgan went to the playoffs seven seasons, including six times between 1972 and 1980. Sandberg went to the playoffs twice, both in his best nine-year stretch.

For career totals, Sandberg hit 277 home runs as a second baseman, which broke Joe Morgan's major-league record. He hit 282 total homers, 14 more than Joe.

Sandberg also batted 14 points higher than Joe (.285 to .271), and slugged 25 points higher than Little Joe.

Ryno went to as many All-Star games, and even won a few more Gold Gloves than Joe. So why is Morgan ranked so high, and Sandberg is not even in my top 100?

Joe Morgan played the first third of his career playing home games at the Houston Astrodome in the era of the pitcher. This has to be accounted for. Ryno played his entire 16-year career with the Cubs, where he played at hitter-friendly Wrigley Field.

Morgan was the central figure on one of the greatest teams in history—the Big Red Machine of the mid-'70s. Joe also led other teams to the postseason. He went to four World Series, which is four more than Ryno.

Joe Morgan walked a ton more than Sandberg, among the most of all time. His on-base average was almost 50 points higher than Sandberg's. Morgan also stole 689 bases—345 more than Sandberg.

Morgan was the best player in the game in the 1970s. Pete Rose was a singles hitter with no speed, power, or defensive excellence. Mike Schmidt was not on the scene at the beginning of the decade, and Bench wasn't the same at the end of the decade. Reggie Jackson had some big years and big postseason moments, but Morgan provided leadership, stability, defense, and more versatility in his game than Jackson.

NAP LAJOIE

There are a couple of things one should know about Nap Lajoie. The first is how to spell his surname, and the second is how to pronounce it. Spelling it is easy if you remember to buy a vowel from Vanna White—his name is the rare bird with only two consonants, plus an *a, e, i,* and *o.* The proper pronunciation of his name was "LaJwa," but he was sometimes called "Laj-away."

This is all you need to know about Lajoie's batting ability: On May 23, 1901, Nap came to the plate in the ninth inning with the bases loaded, with his team ahead 11–7. Fearing that Lajoie, who led the league with a .422 average, would hit a game-tying grand slam, Clark Griffith, then a pitcher-manager working in relief, walked Lajoie intentionally with no outs. The next three batters were retired, and the move worked. Now that's respect!

Lajoie was born in 1875, about one hundred years before some of the youngest players in this book, in Rhode Island, the youngest of eight children. His earliest heroes were among the first baseball stars, players like King Kelly and Hoss Radbourne. Lajoie joined the Philadelphia Phillies in 1896, when he was only 21 years old. He batted a very impressive .357 that season. Did he go on and have a successful career? Well, he was the very first second baseman elected to baseball's Hall of Fame, and the sixth player ever to be inducted. Playing in the dead-ball era, Lajoie was not a home run hitter. He was, however, a powerful right-handed pull hitter, and his smashes down the left-field foul line were legendary. His 648 doubles rank tenth all-time and he hit 10 or more triples in seven seasons. He finished his career with 3,244 hits. In the field, the 6′1″ 195-pound Lajoie was known for his grace despite being considerably bigger than most infielders of his day. He had excellent speed and good hands.

In the 1950s, the question everyone argued was who was better, "Willie, Mickey, or the Duke?" In the 1960s, it was "Ginger or Mary Anne?" Well, in the first years of the 20th century, the question was "Wagner or Lajoie?"

Honus Wagner dominated play in those years, and earned a spot in the early pages of this book. It stands to reason that there were other great players in his time. None were better than Nap, who held or established 70 batting records. Lajoie finished with 3,244 hits. Of the players from his era, only Wagner had more hits (they both played from 1897 to 1917).

In 1901, Lajoie created a huge controversy when he became the first superstar to jump to the newly formed American League. If not for that move, the American League might not have made it financially. Today's World Series format owes much to Lajoie. He had spent the years before the turn of the century in Philadelphia, with the Phillies. Connie Mack, owner and manager of the new American League Philadelphia Athletics, persuaded Lajoie to jump leagues. Nap went from $2,400 a year to a four-year contract at $6,000 per season. He became the first star and gate attraction for the junior circuit.

In that inaugural A.L. season of 1901, Nap batted .422, with 229 hits, 13 home runs, and 48 doubles—all league-leading totals. Let's not get excited about that .422, which still stands as the best single-season batting average in American League history. Foul balls weren't considered strikes yet, which would seem to help hitters enormously.

The Phillies weren't going to lose Lajoie without a fight, however. They obtained a court injunction, effective on Opening Day 1902, prohibiting Lajoie from playing with any other club in Philadelphia. Connie Mack didn't want to hurt the new American League, so he traded Nap to Cleveland so that he could play every game (except those road games in Philadelphia). In 1904, Lajoie hit .381 when only five other players hit as high as .300. He led the league in slugging four times, and was in the top five in slugging eight times.

Other learned baseball scholars have studied the impact Lajoie had in his time. Bill Deane selected "hypothetical" award winners beginning in 1900, for *Total Baseball* (1989). He "felt a certain responsibility to make my selections consistent with the perceptions and voting trends of a particular era. . . . They are the ones which can be best justified with the available evidence." STATS, Inc., selected "retroactive" annual award winners from 1876 onward for *The All-Time Major League Baseball Sourcebook* (1998). "We didn't try to guess what the voting trends might have been in a particular era. We concentrated on individual statistics (offensive and defensive) and team performance." The findings: Deane awarded American League MVP awards to Lajoie for the years 1901, 1903, and 1906. STATS, Inc., agreed with the selections in 1901 and 1903.

And it's not that Lajoie dropped off in production after those years, it's just that Ty Cobb entered the American League.

After a stint as manager of the Indians (when they were known as the Naps), Lajoie hit .384 in 1910, losing a controversial batting title to Ty Cobb. Nap was 35 years old, but far from done.

After he was released from the majors at age 40, he hit a league-leading .380 with Toronto in the International League. For those who wonder why I rank Lajoie behind

Wagner but ahead of Eddie Collins, consider the Hall of Fame voting of the time. Honus Wagner was elected to the Hall in 1935, one of the original five players to go in. Lajoie and Collins, both eligible, weren't selected by the required 75 percent of voters in the first year. Lajoie made it in 1937, Collins in 1939. I'll slot them the same way. Lajoie lived to the ripe old age of 84, passing away in 1959.

A Better Analogy

Nap Lajoie and Roy Orbison The first class of performers to enter the Rock and Roll Hall of Fame were familiar names all: people like Elvis Presley, Chuck Berry, James Brown, Ray Charles, and Little Richard. The next year, the list of performers who were enshrined had a little less cachet: the class included Roy Orbison, Bo Diddley, Carl Perkins, and Smokey Robinson.

Lajoie didn't enter the Baseball Hall of Fame with Cobb or the Babe. He went in as a second-tier guy, the baseball equal of Orbison or Perkins. Nothing wrong with that. He was one of baseball's biggest stars in the early 1900s and remains one of its all-time great second basemen.

PEDRO MARTINEZ

I anticipate what many people will be saying when they read that Pedro Martinez is ranked 29th all-time—ahead of contemporary pitchers like Greg Maddux and Randy Johnson and old-timers like Bob Feller and Warren Spahn. They will think that I got plunked by a Martinez fastball in the head. Fear not. I will make my case for Martinez, 33 years old at the conclusion of the 2004 season. I will point out how many experts thought that Roger Clemens was done at a similar age. I will show how Pedro's prime was, in many ways, superior to that of Sandy Koufax. I will defend the proud Dominican, who is one of the greatest pitchers of all time.

I'll start with cross-examining the opening arguments for Pedro's critics. They'll point out the fact that the Yankees have "owned" him in recent years, to the point that Pedro Martinez said, in late September of 2004, "Call the Yankees my daddy . . . I wish they would disappear. I would probably like to face any other team right now. . . . I just have to give them credit and say, 'Hey, you guys beat me. You're not my team.' And let it go. They're that good."

Pedro made those statements immediately following another frustrating loss to the Yankees. To that point, in his last 23 starts against New York, his team had only won six times. Boston was only 11–19 in the 30 starts Martinez made against New York. Ouch.

Martinez then had to return to Yankee Stadium for a start in Game 2 of the 2004 League Championship Series just a few weeks after uttering those remarks. Taking more verbal abuse than any visiting player has ever taken, Martinez allowed only one run in the first five innings before surrendering a two-run homer to John Olerud in the sixth inning. The Yankees took the game, 3–1. The taunting that Martinez received made it one of the most memorable nights in the history of Yankee Stadium. After the game, Martinez told reporters that he enjoyed the jeers.

"I actually realized that I was somebody important. Because I caught the attention of 60,000 people, plus the whole world watching a guy that if you reverse the time back 15 years ago, I was sitting under a mango tree without 50 cents to pay for a bus. And today I was the center of the whole city of New York."

While he could have phrased the "daddy" remarks differently, those statements were not those of a quitter. They weren't the remarks of a loser. They were the honest feelings of a proud pitcher who is the winningest pitcher in baseball history (by percentage).

Pedro Martinez has won more than 70 percent of his career decisions (182–76 following the 2004 season). In his first six years in a Red Sox uniform, he won 78 percent of his decisions (101–28). Of all the pitchers with 250 decisions or more, no one has ever been better. The two men directly below him in that category—two of the greatest "winners" of all time—are Whitey Ford and Lefty Grove. Yankees manager Casey Stengel protected Ford and kept him from pitching in Brooklyn's Ebbets Field to the dangerous right-handed-hitting Dodgers lineup. Lefty Grove had problems with the Yankees' "Murderers Row" of Ruth and Gehrig.

Did Ford openly object to Stengel's maneuvers to keep Ford out of harm's way by not pitching him in small, bandbox National League stadiums in the biggest World Series games? Did Grove publicly call the Yankees his "daddy"? Probably not, but they certainly didn't take the ball as much as one would expect against their archrivals.

Now, contrast that with Martinez, who has never hidden from the Yankees or anyone else. He's always taken the ball against the Yankees in their latest dynasty. In regular-season play, Pedro's record is 10–10 against New York (172–66 for a .722 winning percentage against all other teams). At times, he has been unhittable when facing New York. Their best strategy against him was to keep the game close and extend his pitch count until he was relieved. Pedro got the better of Roger Clemens not once, but twice in postseason matchups. In 1999, he held New York scoreless and gave the Yankees only two hits in seven innings, as the Sox defeated Clemens and the Yankees in Game 3 of the League Championship Series. In Game 7 of the 2003 League Championship Series, Clemens was knocked out in the fourth inning, trailing 4–0. Martinez took a 5–2 lead into the eighth inning of that memorable game. (In four postseason starts against the Yankees, Martinez has 33 strikeouts and only 8 walks.)

Boston manager Grady Little was fired for believing this marvelous pitcher could get him five more outs in Yankee Stadium on an October night in 2003 when the entire city of New York was working against him.

I believe Grady Little did the right thing. Little had options in the bullpen. Relievers Mike Timlin, Alan Embree, and Scott Williamson had combined to allow New York only one run in 11 innings, and had given up just five hits in 36 at-bats. In that spot—on the road, in New York, in the eighth and ninth innings, desperately trying to coax six outs and earn a spot in the World Series—Little did not trust anyone more than a fatigued Pedro Martinez. (In the Red Sox' very next postseason series—the 2004 divisional round against the Angels—Boston manager Terry Francona proved Grady Little correct. He pulled his Game 3 starting pitcher, Bronson Arroyo, in the seventh inning with a 6–1 lead; Timlin and Embree blew the lead, although they would be bailed out with an extra-inning walk-off home run by David Ortiz.) Grady Little at least went down with his best.

To Martinez's credit, he didn't ask Little to take him out.

He didn't ask Terry Francona to take him out after 100 pitches in September 2004, when he again couldn't hold a late lead against the Yankees.

If the Red Sox are convinced that Pedro has only seven innings (and about 100 pitches) in him, why do they continue to start him in the first inning? A real riverboat gambler of a manager (like me) would start a Scott Williamson or Alan Embree. Put Pedro in the game to start the third inning. If Martinez doesn't have enough bullets for nine innings, make sure he has some left for the crucial late innings.

It didn't bother Kevin McHale, a Boston Celtics star in the 1980s. He started every game on the bench, but played all the big fourth-quarter minutes. If his ego took a hit, he didn't make it known. He even wound up making the Hall of Fame.

The Red Sox know that the formula works. Pedro came out of the bullpen in a 1999 American League divisional playoff game with Cleveland and pitched six hitless innings.

In 2004, Martinez lost his last four starts and gave up 20 runs in the final 23 innings of the regular season. On the other side of the ledger, he still won 16 games. He still threw 217 innings, his most since 1998. He still finished second in the league in strike-outs. He still came back strong in the postseason, winning a World Series game by pitching seven scoreless innings.

Pedro Martinez was born in a small town named Manoguayabo in the Dominican Republic, where he was the fifth of six children raised by a single mother. As a boy, Martinez would play catch with rolled-up socks, fruits, and even his sister's doll heads to get a game going.

He did have one advantage: an older brother named Ramon who was signed by the Dodgers as an amateur free agent in 1984, when Pedro was only 12 years old. Ramon would win 135 games in the major leagues, including a 20-win season in 1990 for the Dodgers. It was a good career, but nothing like the one his baby brother was about to embark on.

Pedro was signed by Dodgers scouts as a nondrafted free agent in June 1988. By 1991, Pedro was recognized as *The Sporting News*'s minor-league pitcher of the year, as he went 18–8 with an ERA of 2.28. He was a hot prospect. He had a September call-up to the Dodgers in September 1992, and was the youngest player in the majors at 20 years old.

Martinez was sensational as a 1993 rookie, winning 10 games in relief and holding opponents to a .201 average. He had 119 strikeouts in 107 innings, an excellent ratio. Surprisingly, and regretfully for Los Angeles, the Dodgers traded him in the off-season to Montreal. The Dodgers obviously felt that Martinez was too frail for long-term success, and they needed a second baseman.

Now a starting pitcher, Martinez started his fifth-ever major-league game on April 13 and took a perfect game into the eighth inning. He hit Reggie Sanders with a pitch in the eighth, precipitating a brawl. He still had his no-hitter in the ninth, until Brian Dorsett led off with a single.

Martinez was 11–5 in 23 starts when the strike ended the 1994 season. In 1995, his 14 wins was fifth most in the league. He threw nine perfect innings against San Diego on June 3 at San Diego, losing his bid for perfection when Bip Roberts led off the 10th with a home run. The game had been scoreless after nine innings.

In 1996, he made the All-Star team for the first time, but his greatness was shown in flashes. It wasn't until 1997 that Martinez began making his case for being one of the top players of all time.

Everything came together in 1997. He captured his first Cy Young Award, finishing 17–8 with 305 strikeouts and a league-leading 1.90 ERA. He was the first pitcher to get more than 300 strikeouts while allowing less than two runs per nine innings since Steve Carlton in 1972. He was the first right-hander to do so since Walter Johnson.

In the 1997 All-Star Game, he pitched a perfect inning. He struck out Alex Rodriguez. He retired Ken Griffey Jr. on a pop-up, and he struck out Mark McGwire.

When Martinez won his first Cy Young Award, in 1997, he dedicated it to Hall of Fame Dominican native Juan Marichal, who never won the award.

In the off-season, the Red Sox made a trade that should have taken off the curse they incurred from selling Babe Ruth 77 years earlier. They acquired Pedro for right-handed pitchers Carl Pavano and Tony Armas.

The Red Sox needed to replace Roger Clemens, who had been their ace since the mid-1980s. They got someone just as good.

Well, almost as good. In 1998, Pedro finished second to Toronto's Clemens for the Cy Young. Martinez went 19–7 with a 2.89 ERA in 33 starts.

In 1999, he had a year that would have looked good if it were on Walter Johnson's career line. He was the unanimous choice for the Cy Young Award. He was 23–4 with a 2.07 ERA. He struck out 313 and walked (no typo) 37.

He was the starter, winner, and MVP of the All-Star Game (played at Fenway Park). Again, he struck out all but one batter he faced.

He pitched an unbelievable game at Yankee Stadium in September, defeating the Yankees 3–1 as he struck out 17 and walked none. He allowed only one hit—a home run to Chili Davis.

His ERA of 2.07 that year was 1.37 points lower than the 3.44 of league runner-up David Cone, and was 2.80 runs lower than the league average. There have been just two other occasions—Dazzy Vance in 1930 and Greg Maddux in the shortened 1994 season—when the pitcher with the best ERA was more than a run better than the runner-up. Opponents batted .205 against Pedro when the league average was .275. He completely dominated the league.

Then there was his historic performance in the American League divisional series against Cleveland. Back strain had limited his availability in that series against the Indians. In Game 1, he left after four innings and a 2–0 lead, which the bullpen couldn't hold. He didn't appear again until the deciding Game 5, when he relieved Bret Saberhagen in the fourth inning with the score tied 8–8. Pedro threw six hitless innings as Boston took the series. In the following American League Championship Series against the Yanks, Martinez wasn't able to start until Game 3, the only game in the series the Red Sox won.

In 2000, he almost topped himself. His ERA was 1.74, less than half the 3.70 that was second-best in the league, and three whole runs lower than the league average of 4.90. He only received an average of four runs per game (which is why he lost six games). There were only two games in which Pedro gave up more than three runs.

Shoulder problems limited Martinez in 2001, but he rebounded with terrific seasons in 2002 and 2003, going a combined 34–8. The problem was that he was limited to 59 starts and less than 200 innings per season, as Boston treated him like mothers treat fine china. Barry Zito took the Cy Young Award in 2002, only because voters must have gotten tired of giving it to Pedro.

Martinez, a free agent after the 2004 season, was the Boston ace between Roger Clemens and Curt Schilling. He had huge shoes to fill, and he filled them. He did it in the glare of a city that had such high expectations. He is working on the back end of his career, which will eventually surpass that of many of the legendary pitchers. Following the 2004 season, he had a career ERA of 2.71, pitching primarily in Boston and primarily in the American League (with a designated hitter). There's no better competitor. There's no one better at allowing runs. There is no one who has won a higher percentage of games.

Who's Better, Who's Best
Pedro Martinez or Sandy Koufax?

Pedro Martinez and Sandy Koufax were both signed by the Dodgers. In their first 11.5 years of major-league service, the left-handed Koufax had 165 victories, the right-handed Martinez had 166.

It is a fascinating comparison.

First 12 years	Record	Pct.	Games	Complete Games	Shutouts	IP	BB	K
Koufax	165–87	.655	397	137	40	2,324	817	2,396
Martinez	166–67	.712	355	41	15	2,079	554	2,426

	Cy Young Awards		ERA Titles		Postseason Record	
Koufax	3 (1963, 1965, 1966)		5		4–3, 0.95 ERA	
Martinez	3 (1997, 1999, 2000)		5		6–2, 3.40 ERA	

Who was better for one season? Who was better over a two-year stretch? How about over a five- or six-year period?

The Case for Koufax

Sandy Koufax pitched in an era of four-man rotations and was allowed to stay in games with high pitch counts. In his last four seasons, he threw 311, 223, 335, and 323 innings (an average of 298 innings per season). Martinez has never thrown as many as 250 innings in any season. In his best four seasons (1997–2000), he averaged 226 innings per season. The difference of 80 additional innings (over 160 games) is enormous. When one considers that the Red Sox didn't exactly have Mariano Rivera in the bullpen, Martinez's lack of complete games (21 in his first six seasons with the Red Sox) gives a big edge to Koufax.

The Case for Martinez

Martinez had an advantage in the early part of his career and is making a back end that Sandy didn't have due to injury. Koufax had one double-digit victory season in his first five. Martinez was 10–5 in 1993, 11–4 in 1994, and 13–10 in 1996. Pedro was 34–19 in those three seasons—*before* he became great.

Even if one gives Koufax a tie for the six-year total of their peak ability, then Martinez would move ahead based on the formative years and the closing ones.

I'm not sure that Koufax even draws a tie. Pedro finished first or second in his league in ERA in six of seven years (each year since 1997, except for his injury-shortened 2001). That was done while pitching a lot in Boston's Fenway Park, a hitters' park that hurts pitchers' stats.

In the end, Martinez is ranked here behind Koufax for several reasons. Sandy was dominating in the World Series, with a 0.95 ERA in his postseason career. And Pedro was unable to defeat the Yankees consistently.

If you had to give the ball to one man to win one game, you would have to give the ball to Koufax. He had more in the late innings than Pedro.

RICKEY HENDERSON

Rickey Henderson was born on Christmas Day, 1958, in Chicago, Illinois. He graduated from Oakland Technical High School in 1976, where he played baseball, football, and basketball. As a senior, he batted .465 and stole 30 bases. In football, he rushed for 1,100 yards in his senior year, and received a reported two dozen scholarship offers to play football.

He was drafted by the Oakland A's in the fourth round of baseball's June draft in 1976, and he played pro baseball for the next 29 summers. He reported first to a team in Boise, and then soon wound up in "Joisey," stealing 249 bases in 380 minor-league games.

For one season, the Oakland A's had a Double-A minor-league franchise in Jersey City, New Jersey. In the 1978 season, 19-year-old Rickey Henderson called Jersey City's Roosevelt Stadium home. It was the same Roosevelt Stadium that was home to the Brooklyn Dodgers for eight games in each of the 1956 and 1957 seasons, when Dodgers owner Walter O'Malley tested the waters of playing somewhere other than Brooklyn. The twenty-five-thousand-seat stadium was also the place on April 18, 1946, where baseball's color line was broken. Jackie Robinson made his professional debut on that date at Roosevelt Stadium as a member of the Montreal Royals (a Dodgers farm club) against the Jersey City Giants. In that historic game, Jackie stole two bases.

I wish I could say that I had the good sense to see a game at Roosevelt Stadium. I did, however, unwittingly stop and inspect (trespass) the empty stadium in the early '80s, after getting lost trying to find a train station. Jackie Robinson stole bases in that stadium. Rickey Henderson stole bases there. And if there was a base not screwed into the ground lying around that afternoon, I would have stolen a base. Roosevelt Stadium, made appropriately of steel, was demolished in 1985.

You couldn't demolish Rickey Henderson. Twenty-six years after he played his summer in Jersey City, he was still leading off and stealing bases in the minor leagues somewhere in the swamps of Jersey. Following his major-league debut on June 24, 1979, Henderson played in more than three thousand major-league games, and it wasn't enough for him. In April of 2003, he signed with the Newark Bears, an independent minor-league team in the Atlantic League. He played so well that he earned a twenty-fifth season in the majors, signing with the Los Angeles Dodgers. This cat used up his nine lives, and still wasn't through. In 2004, when the majors turned their back on Henderson, he signed again with Newark. Despite being closer to 50 than 40, he was amazingly among the league leaders in stolen bases when I showed up with two of my boys at Newark's Riverfront Stadium on the afternoon of July 11.

I told my sons more stories about Henderson: He wore number 24 in honor of Willie Mays. He batted right-handed, but threw left-handed. There were only a few players in history (notably including former Mets outfielder Cleon Jones) who did that. Rickey had played with so many famous and talented players. I made up a team of Rickey's teammates:

1B: Mark McGwire, Don Mattingly
2B: Joe Morgan, Roberto Alomar
SS: Alex Rodriguez
3B: Paul Molitor
C: Mike Piazza
OF: Tony Gwynn
OF: Dave Winfield
OF: Dave Parker

He played behind several of the premier relief pitchers in baseball history, including Dennis Eckersley, Trevor Hoffman, Goose Gossage, and Troy Percival. He played behind starting pitchers Jack Morris and Dave Stewart. If Henderson didn't play with everybody, he could be linked to almost anyone. Rickey was a teammate of Joe Morgan, who played with Don Larsen, who played with Satchel Paige.

I think of Paige when I think of Rickey. Remember, long after Paige proved himself in the major leagues, he continued to barnstorm and play well into his 50s (and even his 60s). Rickey no longer needed to play in the minor leagues in 2004, but there he was in his familiar crouch, rattling pitchers.

Henderson was a designated hitter the day we went to see the Bears. I had to tell the boys about his "snatch catches" in left field. After Rickey grounded out to end the sixth inning, my boys (dressed as hot dogs) ran a race with other kids around the bases in a corny promotion. I took my boys to see Rickey—often called "Style Dog" because of the showy way he plays—run the bases, but I noticed as he took a peek from the Newark dugout to watch the boys race, it was the other way around. He was watching my "hot dogs" on the bases. If I'd had a little sense of foresight, I would have told Wyatt and Jordan to slide into third base headfirst, Henderson style, to show homage.

Henderson's Major-League Career

He joined the A's midway through a last-place 54–108 season. In his first full season, 1980, Oakland hired Billy Martin as their manager. The A's improved from 54 wins to 83. Martin's team played his aggressive "Billyball" style, and Henderson stole 100 bases, a new American League record. Rickey was far from being a one-dimensional player, though, even winning a Gold Glove for his defense. Martin had his five starting pitchers complete 94 games, unheard of in modern times. In the strike-shortened 1981 season, the A's made the playoffs, defeated the Royals in the Divisional Series, and lost to the Yankees in the American League Championship Series.

It was in 1982 that Henderson set the major-league record for stolen bases in a season with 130. He was able to steal that many by getting on base so much. He had 143 hits and walked 116 times.

In 1983 he stole 108 bases. In his first three full seasons (in 1979 he didn't play until June, and labor strife cost him 50 games in 1981), Rickey stole 100, 130, and 108 bases.

How impressive was that?

Most Stolen Bases, Season, 1900–1984

1. 130 Rickey Henderson, 1982
2. 118 Lou Brock, 1974
3. 108 Rickey Henderson, 1983
4. 104 Maury Wills, 1962
5. 100 Rickey Henderson, 1980

Ty Cobb stole 96 bases in a season, and that record held until 1962, when Wills stole 104 bases. Neither Brock nor Wills could sustain the pounding that stealing 100 bases causes.

Lou Brock: Top Three SB Totals

1. 118
2. 74
3. 70

Maury Wills: Top Three SB Totals

1. 104
2. 94
3. 53

Now, if you include the 104 years from 1900 to 2004, there have been only three more seasons of 100-plus stolen bases—all by Vince Coleman. But Coleman stole 326 bases in his first three seasons, and then dramatically dropped off.

Vince Coleman

First 3 seasons	326 stolen bases (108 per year)
Next 4 seasons	260 stolen bases (65 per year)
Last 6 seasons	166 stolen bases (28 per year)

Coleman and Henderson stole almost the same number of bases in their first seven seasons in the major leagues: Henderson stole 573 and Coleman stole 586. But after their first seven seasons, Henderson kept on going, and going, and going, stealing 833 bases to Coleman's 166.

Most of the great base stealers steal most of their bases early in their careers. Only Brock maintained a pace in his mid-30s that was anything close to Henderson's. But Henderson is one of a kind. He has stolen over 1,400 bases in his career. No one else playing in 2004 had stolen as many as 600.

Henderson didn't just break Lou Brock's career record of 938 stolen bases—he did laps around it. He broke Brock's record by 468 stolen bases!

When Henderson broke Brock's record, Rickey's remarks were hardly modest, but correct. He said, "Lou Brock was a great base stealer, but today, I'm the greatest of all time."

Henderson stole his 939th base in 1,154 attempts (81.3 percent success rate), in 12 years.

Brock stole 938 bases in 1,245 attempts (75.3 percent) in 19 years.

Who's Better, Who's Best
Rickey Henderson or Lou Brock?

Henderson was the 1990 MVP. He was second in MVP voting in 1981, and third in 1985. The only top-five finish for Brock was second place in 1974.

Brock had a better lifetime batting average (.293 to .279), but that hardly represents anything meaningful in relation to Henderson. Henderson had a higher on-base average, thanks to his 2,190 walks. He had a higher slugging percentage.

Both players were terrific in their three World Series appearances, and both helped their teams win two World Series championships.

World Series Performances

Brock	Henderson
21 games	14 games
.391 batting avg. (34–87 AB)	.339 batting avg. (19–56 AB)
.424 on-base avg.	.448 on-base avg.
.655 slugging pct.	.607 slugging pct.
14–16 SB	7–9 SB

While those 21 games represented the best in Brock's career, Henderson was his equal in October, and superior to him from April to September.

Henderson had twice as many home runs as Brock (297 to 149), and he walked 2,190 times to Brock's 761.

Now, for the Really Impressive Stats

There have been only four men in baseball history to draw more than 2,000 walks. Their names are Barry Bonds, Rickey Henderson, Babe Ruth, and Ted Williams. That's good company.

The Most Impressive Number

Rickey Henderson scored 2,295 runs in his career. That's more than anyone who ever played major-league baseball. Only six other players have scored 2,000—and their names are Ty Cobb, Hank Aaron, Babe Ruth, Pete Rose, Willie Mays, and Barry Bonds.

Henderson may have been at his best in 1985, in his first season with the Yankees. Despite missing the first 10 games of the year (and 19 total) he led the league with 146 runs scored in only 143 games played, more than a run per game. That was the highest runs-scored total in the major leagues since Ted Williams scored 150 runs in 1949.

In the two decades since 1985, only one player—the National League's Jeff Bagwell—has topped 146 runs in a season. And Bagwell didn't score a run per game. He scored 152 runs in 159 games for the 2000 Houston Astros.

Rickey Henderson is one of the first inspirations I had for writing this book. I took Wyatt to a Mets game in April of 1999, and Henderson was the leadoff batter. I tried to convey to him what was so special about the New York left fielder wearing number 24.

I told him that he was primarily known as the greatest base stealer of all time. In addition, no one in baseball history scored more runs—the most important statistic in baseball. I told him that Henderson was 40 years old—ancient by baseball standards—yet had led the league in stolen bases the previous season. Though I knew he was a special player, one of the greatest in baseball history, I didn't know how I would rank him against the other legends of the game. It turns out, pretty high up. Among players who played mostly left field, only Barry Bonds, Ted Williams, and Stan Musial rank higher.

The most impressive aspect about Henderson's game is his durability. He is both "the Man of Steal" and "the Man of Steel." As Neil Young once sang, "Long May You Run."

Rickey Henderson is a link to Satchel Paige and a link to Jackie Robinson and a link to my youth when I got lost on my way home from Hoboken and found a historic stadium.

EDDIE COLLINS

One really has to search for great second basemen. There were great second basemen (Eddie Collins, Nap Lajoie, Frankie Frisch) who were all retired by 1938, but then the numbers dwindle in comparison to earlier eras. Charlie Gehringer played until 1942; Jackie Robinson played from 1947 to 1956; and Joe Morgan was among the best at any position in the 1970s. Ryne Sandberg distinguished himself in the '80s, and Roberto Alomar in the '90s. The great second sackers were few and far between. Even the Negro Leagues didn't produce a truly outstanding second baseman.

Today, teams move their best athletes away from second base, to protect them from injury. When the Yankees acquired Alex Rodriguez, they had to find a new position for either A-Rod or Derek Jeter. Neither one moved over to play second; Rodriguez took a crash course in third base, a position where the Yankees felt he would be farther from harm's way.

Eddie Collins was born in 1887 and raised in Tarrytown, New York. At the age of 16, he enrolled at Columbia University and was soon a baseball player as well as the quarterback on the football team—despite being only 5'8" and 165 pounds. The coach of Columbia's baseball team asked Collins if he wanted to make some money in the summer playing semipro baseball. Eddie improved enough to attract the attention of one of Connie Mack's scouts. Mack, the manager of the Philadelphia Athletics, signed Collins, and by 1908 Collins was entrenched as the A's second baseman. That was the first of 18 seasons Collins would bat at least .300. In 1910, Philadelphia breezed to the pennant, and easily defeated the Cubs in the World Series. Collins stole 81 bases that year, and batted .429 in the World Series.

He was described as modest and unassuming, yet he was given the name "Cocky" Collins, and was well known for his fiery temper and fighting spirit. Collins was part of the A's famed "$100,000 Infield," along with Stuffy McInnis (first base), Jack Barry (shortstop), and Home Run Baker (third base). That group led the A's to a second consecutive American League pennant in 1911. Connie Mack managed for 50 years, and called Collins the quickest thinker he ever saw. Mack thought no player quite matched Collins in everything.

Following the 1914 season, Mack sold his best players and decided to rebuild his team on a lower pay scale. Collins was sold to the Chicago White Sox in a deal brokered by the league to keep the great second baseman in the American League. Cocky Collins had leverage because the newly formed Federal League had made him a substantial offer. Mack tried to sell Collins to the Red Sox for $50,000. According to old-time Boston sportswriter Joe Cashman in Peter Golenbock's *Fenway: An Unexpurgated History of the Boston Red Sox*, when the league office got wind of Mack's deal with the Red Sox, A.L. President Ban Johnson told Mack, "Listen, if you have to sell your players, sell them. But you cannot sell Eddie Collins, the best second baseman in baseball, to a championship-caliber team like Boston. They are strong enough now as it is. If we give them Collins, there will be no race. Collins goes to Chicago."

Collins enlisted in the marines in the middle of the 1918 season, but World War I ended before he was sent overseas. In 1919, Eddie helped the White Sox capture the pennant. They lost to the Cincinnati Reds in the World Series, a Series infamous because bookmakers had used a bunch of Eddie's teammates to conspire to fix the Series. The 1919 White Sox became better known to headline writers as the "Black Sox."

Collins remained in Chicago, playing at a high level, until the end of the 1926 season.

He was some player. Only Ty Cobb was a better base stealer in his era. In 1912, Collins stole six bases in a single game. He repeated the trick just 11 days later. He batted over .340 in 10 different seasons, and was a part of four World Series champions. He might have had five rings if his teammates hadn't thrown the 1919 Series. As great a hitter as he was, he never won a batting title. He was second in the batting race twice, and in the top five in 10 different years. He walked a great deal, and was almost always among the on-base leaders.

Before closing his long career, Collins returned to Connie Mack as a player-coach from 1927 to 1930. Following his playing days, he became a vice president and general manager of the Boston Red Sox.

In 1936, while serving as Red Sox general manager, he made his one and only scouting trip to the West Coast. While he was in San Diego, he scouted an 18-year-old second baseman named Bobby Doerr (who later starred for the Sox and made the Hall of Fame). During the same trip, Collins noticed a tall, skinny teenager named Ted Williams. Collins was impressed with Williams's swing, and tried to buy his contract from the San Diego minor-league club. The owner wasn't ready to sell his contract at that time, but made a handshake deal with Collins to give the Red Sox the first chance at Ted Williams.

If that was all he did, he deserves praise as one of the great general managers of all time. In this book, however, he is judged as a player. An alert base runner and excellent hitter, Collins had a well-deserved reputation as one of baseball's best clutch hitters. He participated in seven World Series. He batted over .400 three times. His lifetime batting average, over 25 years, was .333.

He was the 11th player to be inducted into the Hall of Fame. He died in 1951.

Who's Better, Who's Best
Eddie Collins, Rogers Hornsby, or Nap Lajoie?

The following is an excerpt from a 1945 letter that had hung in the Hall of Fame at Cooperstown, written by Ty Cobb at the request of Mr. E. J. Lanigan, the Hall's historian at the time:

> To my way of thinking, no contest at second base. Hornsby couldn't catch a pop fly, much less go in the outfield for them; and he couldn't come in on a slow hit. Lajoie could not go out, or come in, and did not cover much ground to his right or left. Collins could do it all, besides being a great base stealer and base runner. Career average of .330 odd, I think. Also another manager on the field. . . .

So, the great Cobb voted for the base-stealing Collins over Hornsby and Lajoie.

Like they always say, Ty goes to the runner. Seriously, remember that Cobb was prejudiced against Lajoie, probably still holding a grudge from the last day of the controversial 1910 batting race. Cobb also played with Collins at the end of their careers. John McGraw and Connie Mack both rated Collins over Hornsby as well. Still, I can't put Eddie Collins over Rogers Hornsby. Collins was a great player, and he lasted for a quarter-century. But Hornsby was by far the superior offensive player. I'll take the offense Hornsby provided over the intangibles that Collins brought with his fielding and baserunning.

GREG MADDUX

In the sport of bowling, the number 300 signifies a perfect game. Baseball pitchers have a similar respect for the number. On August 7, 2004, Greg Maddux won his 300th game. In both sports, one has to throw a lot of strikes.

Maddux learned to throw strikes from his father, Dave, a military man who was a fast-pitch softball pitcher for over 20 years. Greg and his older brother, Mike, became baseball fanatics at a young age, especially in the five years they lived overseas in Spain. How appropriate that Greg Maddux would spend part of his youth calling a (military) base home.

Unlike the only other pitcher to win his 300th game since 1990 (Roger Clemens), Maddux never had an overpowering fastball or intimidating manner. He didn't have a sculpted body. He didn't scare anyone. It's not that Maddux pitches slow, but his fastball has never been the key to his success. The key is his ability to change the speeds of his pitches. He had a lively arm when he was young, but he wasn't very big, so he became more of a pitcher than a thrower, which worked out just fine for him. "We are pretty much the same kind of pitcher, we just do it at different speeds," Maddux said in August 2004 about Clemens. "We do the exact same thing on the mound. Just subtract 10 miles per hour from the radar gun."

Greg was drafted by the Chicago Cubs in the second round of the 1984 amateur draft. In 65 minor-league starts, he was 33–15. He joined the Cubs in September 1986, and made his first five starts of his career, at the age of 20. He was the youngest Cub of Don Zimmer's pack.

Zimmer let Maddux start every fifth day in 1987, and Maddux showed no sign of the pitcher that he would become. He was 6–14, and at one point was demoted back to the minors.

Greg got his groove back, and he began one of the most impressive streaks in major-league history. He won at least 15 games for a record 17 consecutive seasons. More than the 305 wins, this is the streak that best defines Maddux's greatness.

I firmly believe that Maddux's streak is more impressive than Ripken's consecutive games, which is why Maddux is ranked ahead of Cal Ripken Jr. in this book. Ripken had poor games, month-long slumps, and bad seasons, truth be told. Ripken had seasons where he led a last-place team by hitting .252 and getting on base only 33 percent of the time. Sometimes, his streak was counterproductive to his team's success. Ripken could have a bad season and not hurt the streak.

Greg Maddux, on the other hand, had a streak that had everything to do with his team's success. His teams finished in first place 10 years in a row with the Braves. His teams made the postseason 11 times in 15 seasons (there was no postseason play for anyone in the lockout-shortened 1994 season). Even when the Cubs failed to make the playoffs in 2004, it wasn't because of Maddux. He was 9–4 with a 3.48 ERA after the All-Star Game.

He was always one of the key reasons for his club's winning ways. Greg Maddux started an average of 34 games a year for 17 years. In his 572 starts from 1988 to 2004, he got a decision in 79 percent of the games (453), and won 64 percent of his decisions (297 wins). His team won over 60 percent of the games in which he appeared. That's not over a year or two. That's closer to 20 years.

He led the league in games started in six different seasons. He was in the top five in games started in 13 different years.

He showed that a pitcher could dominate without relying on the strikeout. He had exactly one season where he struck out 200 batters (204 in 1998). He used an economy of effort, throwing fewer pitches per inning than nearly every other starting pitcher. He has walked 1.87 batters per nine innings in his career, about half of what Randy Johnson issues.

Joe Buck: "Greg Maddux suffers in these comparisons from not throwing 95 miles per hour, but he's every bit as good and had seasons that rank with the best of all time. When batters face him, it's got to be frustrating. It looks comparatively easy, but they walk away saying, 'I can't hit this guy.' Maddux is the smartest pitcher of this era. He's a Vegas kid, a guy who you wouldn't want to get into a card game with, because he could outthink you. He just moves the ball, and seems to have it on a string."

Maddux was no average pitcher who compiled numbers. He had a four-year period of excellence that was better than any right-handed pitcher had all the way back to Walter Johnson.

Maddux won four consecutive Cy Young awards from 1992 to 1995.

Greg Maddux, 4 Cy Young Seasons
1992: 20–11, 2.18 ERA
1993: 20–10, 2.36 ERA
1994: 16–6, 1.56 ERA
1995: 19–2, 1.63 ERA

As good as those numbers look, he actually was better than they would indicate. In 1992, for instance, he lost 11 games—but his Cubs were shut out in 7 of them. The Cubs scored a grand total of eight runs in Maddux's 11 defeats. In the second half of the season, he was 10–3 with a 1.91 ERA. After signing with the Atlanta Braves, he continued his mastery of the league.

In 1995, he went 51 innings in a row without walking anyone. Remember, too, that the major-league seasons in 1994 and 1995 were shortened. Maddux lost 17 starts in those seasons (11 at the end of 1994, and about 6 to begin the '95 season).

The obvious person to compare Maddux to is his contemporary, Randy Johnson. The Big Unit is the only other pitcher to string together four consecutive Cy Young seasons (1999–2002), but Johnson (three years older than Maddux) has won 59 fewer games. Maddux has been remarkably healthy, needing only one trip to the disabled list in his career. Johnson was limited to just eight starts in 1996 due to a lower back injury. He was only 6–8 in 2003 due to an injured right knee that required two trips to the disabled list.

Johnson won his four consecutive Cy Young awards with a fastball so intimidating that many left-handed batters felt it was futile to even attempt to hit the ball. Maddux, on the other hand, looked a lot easier to hit. He sure wasn't, however.

Maddux's ERA in his four Cy Young seasons was 1.98. The league ERA was 3.95. He cut the league ERA in half. He was twice as good as the average pitcher in the league.

Bob Gibson's four best consecutive seasons were 1965 to 1968. In those seasons, he had a 2.33 ERA. The league ERA was 3.38. Gibson's ERA was more than a full run better than average, and only 70 percent of the league's average. But it wasn't as good as what Maddux did.

Roger Clemens led the league in ERA three straight years (1990–1992), but gave up a lot of runs on both sides of that stretch. He had more good seasons than Maddux (Clemens has led his league in ERA six times; Maddux has led the National League four times). Clemens had to work in the American League, having to face nine real batters instead of eight, because of the designated hitter. Clemens had to work in Fenway Park, conducive to hitters. But the fact is, Roger never strung together four consecutive Cy Young seasons, or years where he gave up 50 percent fewer runs than the league average.

That's not a knock on Roger. Bob Feller, Tom Seaver, and all the other great right-handed pitchers never did, either, except for Walter Johnson. For some reason, there have been a couple of lefties that have put together four consecutive seasons like Maddux—those being Sandy Koufax and Randy Johnson.

Walter Johnson, almost a hundred years ago, had a career ERA of 2.17. He had consecutive seasons of 1.36, 1.90, 1.39, 1.14, 1.72, 1.55, 1.90 (a bad year, no doubt), 1.27, and 1.49.

Clemens, Johnson, Koufax, and Feller were all strikeout pitchers. Not Maddux. Let the other guys pile up the pitch counts and labor to strike out batters.

Maddux nabbed batters with his "circle-change." He could change speeds, keeping hitters off balance. Umpires sure seemed to give Maddux a few inches off the plate, at least until 2003 (in some people's minds), when the controversial QuesTec system made umps more accountable.

The Knock on Maddux

Well, he doesn't exactly throw a lot of complete games. He's never thrown more than 10 in a season.

> Sandy Koufax: 93 complete games in his last 4 years (including World Series)
> Greg Maddux: 105 complete games in his 19 years

> Bob Gibson: 8 complete games in 9 postseason starts
> Greg Maddux: 2 complete games in 29 postseason starts

The problem isn't the earned run average, as many people like to believe. The problem is that Maddux expects—wants—to be taken out. In Maddux's 300th victory, he pitched only five innings before telling his pitching coach Leo Rothschild that the bullpen had to handle the rest. It's hard to knock a guy like Maddux, who has thrown 200-plus innings in 17 seasons (missing only in 2002, when he threw "only" 199⅓ innings). But, although he might feel that he did his job by throwing five, six, seven, or eight innings—and leaving with a lead—sometimes more is needed. It's not like his Braves had Mariano Rivera in the bullpen for Maddux's Atlanta years.

That leads me into Maddux's other problem, his postseason record. Maddux's teams lost five National League Championship Series and two World Series.

Greg Maddux in Postseason

Career	11–14	3.22 ERA
LCS Record	4–8	3.80 ERA in 14 starts

It was often John Smoltz (14–4 in the postseason) or Tom Glavine (nailing down the Braves' only World Series championship with a 1–0 gutsy performance in Game 6 of the 1995 Series) who came up big for Atlanta in the postseason. If you lump together the League Championship Series and World Series, then the pitcher from Vegas is a combined 7–11 in the 19 biggest starts of his career.

It's not the strikeout advantage, or the extra few wins that Roger Clemens has over Greg Maddux. It's his postseason record that pushed Roger and Pedro (5–1 in the postseason) over Maddux in this book.

Who's Better, Who's Best
Greg Maddux or the Other 21 Pitchers with 300-Plus Wins?

When Greg Maddux became the 22nd pitcher to win 300 games, it naturally led to speculation about his place in history. Here, he's ranked as the ninth best pitcher in history, the eighth best to pitch in the major leagues.

Of the first 21 pitchers to win as many as 300, 12 are not even ranked in this book among the top 100. Six of them (Pud Galvin, Kid Nichols, Tim Keefe, John Clarkson, Old Hoss Radbourn, and Mickey Welch) pitched well before 1900. Clarkson, for instance, went 53–16 in 1885, when playing conditions were totally different. Eddie Plank pitched between 1901 and 1917, but never led the league in wins or ERA.

Early Wynn pitched from 1939 to 1963, but didn't make my top 100, despite his 300 wins. Like Plank, he was a very good pitcher for a long time. But not great.

That is also my argument against Nolan Ryan, Don Sutton, Phil Niekro, and Gaylord Perry. Ryan and Sutton combined to pitch nearly 50 years in the major leagues. Combined, they don't have a single Cy Young Award. They never led the league in wins. They had a combined three seasons of 20-plus wins.

Niekro never won a Cy Young Award, either. He made the All-Star team only five times. Does anyone who ever saw Niekro pitch think he belongs with the all-time greats?

Gaylord Perry actually is the 300-game winner not in the book that gave me reason to pause. He won two Cy Young awards. He led his league in wins three times. He was squeezed out of the top 100 by a pair of starting pitchers turned relievers (John Smoltz and Dennis Eckersley).

Of the 10 pitchers with 300-plus wins that *are* ranked in my top 100, all are in the top 50. Five are ranked ahead of Maddux. As great as Maddux's four prime years were, they still weren't a match for the prime of Mr. Johnson, Mr. Mathewson, Mr. Grove, and Mr. Alexander. Clemens, too, was also a better pitcher, in his prime and over the course of his career.

That's not to slight Greg Maddux, who is ranked ahead of 300-game winners like Warren Spahn, Cy Young, Tom Seaver, and Steve Carlton.

Greg Maddux always knew that it didn't matter how fast the pins went down. What mattered was the location of the ball. He makes the top 35 with plenty to spare.

BOB FELLER

Bob Feller is generally regarded as the greatest pitcher of his time. If not for the timing of World War II, he might have been regarded as the best of all time. Feller is an American hero. Smack in the middle of the prime of his career, when he was the number-one gate attraction and one of the highest-paid players in the game, Feller enlisted and fought for our country. In essence, he traded about one hundred probable career victories for battle citations. Heroes like Feller did that willingly.

Of course, in this book, Feller is not ranked ahead of his contemporary, and sometime sparring partner, Satchel Paige. Paige led a very different life from Feller's and wasn't allowed in the major leagues until he was in his 40s.

Bob was born on an Iowa farm in 1918, and he credited his childhood chores—milking the cows, picking the corn, and throwing bales of straw and hay—with strengthening his arms, which allowed him to complete as many as 36 games in a season. Feller's father built him his own "Field of Dreams" back in 1932 on their farm. The elder Feller managed a team of young adults with 12-year-old Bob being the only kid on the team. After 10th grade, Feller signed his first baseball contract with the Cleveland Indians. He received a check for $1 (which was enough to legally bind the contract) and a baseball autographed by the entire Cleveland Indians team. The cancelled check still exists in the Bob Feller Museum in Van Meter, Iowa.

Teams couldn't sign a high school player back then, so Cleveland kept him hidden from other major-league teams by assigning the contract to an Indians farm club, which Feller never pitched for. This was in clear violation of the rules at the time, but for some reason Baseball Commissioner Landis ruled that Feller should remain Cleveland property. Landis prevented what surely would have been a bidding war for his services. Feller pitched in the 1936 Iowa state high school tournament and immediately afterward went to Cleveland so that Indians officials could check him out. The 17-year-old pitched the middle three innings of an exhibition game against the St. Louis Cardinals, and struck out eight of the nine batters he faced. Instead of going to a minor-league team, he went directly to the Indians.

In the 1936 season, Feller got his feet wet in the major leagues by entering games in relief when they were already out of hand. He started his first game in late August, and struck out 15. In September, he tied the single-game strikeout record with 17. He finished the 1936 season with a record of 5–3, striking out 76 batters in 62 innings. He threw a blazing fastball, and people compared it to Walter Johnson's of a long-gone era. The great *New York Times* baseball columnist Red Smith wrote about the first time Feller faced the New York Giants in a 1937 exhibition game in Vicksburg, Mississippi: "All the Giants had heard, but they had not yet seen the young man. They were taking their pre-game exercises when the kid kicked his left leg high and delivered his first warm-up pitch. All over the field, action ceased. Nobody said anything. Everybody just stood still and watched. Those who were there do not tire of describing the scene. 'That day,' they say, 'I saw a pitcher.' "

By the 1938 season, Feller won his first strikeout title, but set an American League record with 240 bases on balls. When he retired, Feller was the all-time leader, walking 1,764.

On the final day of the 1938 season, Feller struck out 18 Detroit Tigers. In 1939, he became the youngest player ever to win 20 games in a season. He remained the youngest for almost 50 years, until Dwight Gooden was even younger upon winning 20 games in 1984.

Feller's strikeouts began increasing, he issued fewer bases on balls, and became the dominant pitcher of his generation in the majors.

	Strikeouts	Walks	Complete Games
1938	240	208	20
1939	246	142	24
1940	261	118	31

In 1939, Feller was 24–9, leading the league in wins for the first time. His 2.85 ERA was third best in the league. He finished behind only Joe DiMaggio (.381, 30 home runs) and Jimmie Foxx (.360, 35 home runs) in the Most Valuable Player voting.

In 1940, he opened the season on April 16 at Chicago's Comiskey Park. Feller described the day as a cold, Norway-gray day, with the temperature of Lake Michigan at 35 degrees and the wind blowing off the lake. With his dad, mother, and sister in the stands watching, he loaded the bases on walks in the second, but retired the side. Feller pitched a 1–0 no-hitter on Opening Day. Feller went 27–11 that season, leading the league in ERA (2.61). But Cleveland fell one game short of Detroit for the pennant that year. A stranger named Floyd Giebell beat Feller 2–0 in the deciding game of the Indians' pennant race.

In 1941, Feller pitched 343 innings in 40 starts and four relief outings. He won 25 games to again lead the league, and finished third in the MVP voting—trailing only Joe DiMaggio (in the season of his 56-game hitting streak) and Ted Williams (in the season of his .406 batting average).

By the end of the 1941 season, Feller had 107 victories and had yet to celebrate his 22nd birthday. While driving to Chicago for the major-league meetings on December 7, 1941, Feller's radio was interrupted by an urgent announcement. Pearl Harbor had been attacked. He drove into Chicago, and at 8 A.M. on Monday called boxer and friend Gene Tunney, who Feller knew from running the U.S. Navy physical fitness program.

Tunney met Feller at the courthouse the next morning, and Feller signed up with the navy while newsreel cameras and microphones recorded the event. Feller joined the navy as a physical education instructor, later applied for gunnery school, and was subsequently assigned to sea duty.

Feller would not pitch the 1942 season, the 1943 season, or the 1944 season, and pitched only five games in the 1945 season. He served his country in the navy instead.

During his time in the navy, he developed his slider, which made him even more devastating in 1946, his first full season back. He pitched another no-hitter in April of '46. That turned out to be his career season.

Feller in 1946

26–15 (led league in wins for 4th straight season that he pitched full year)

2.18 ERA (3rd in A.L.)

10 shutouts

4 saves

371.1 innings pitched

348 strikeouts (then the major-league record)

That season, Feller averaged 8.43 strikeouts every 9 innings pitched. He allowed only 11 homers in those 371 innings.

Following that season, he did a few things. He became the first player to incorporate himself, making money off his name. He called teammates and opponents to play games in the off-season. He organized a team of major leaguers in the fall of 1946 to tour the country with a Negro League All-Star team headed by Satchel Paige.

Feller had seen Paige pitch for the Negro League Crawfords and Monarchs as far back as 1936, even pitching against him in Iowa. Ten years later, they formed a friendly rivalry, playing above the Mason-Dixon Line. Hall of Famer Monte Irvin always said that Feller did as much for the integration of baseball as Jackie Robinson and Branch Rickey by playing so many exhibition games with African-American players immediately after World War II. It's hard to state what his intentions were, although they probably weren't altogether altruistic. He saw a way of making some big money.

According to Mark Ribowski's *Don't Look Back*, Feller and Paige built the biggest stash of lucre that all of baseball had yet seen. As Feller couldn't wait to get on with this huge attraction, he asked for permission from the new big-league commissioner, Happy Chandler, to begin barnstorming with his Feller All-Stars even as the World Series was being played. Chandler, who had signaled his amenability to integration when he took over after Judge Landis's death, readily agreed. The Feller-Paige tour of 1946 was staged on the scale of a big media circus. With Feller footing the tab, two DC-3 planes were leased to get the players from town to town. The tour nearly trivialized the World Series in some parts of the country. Today, teams are encouraged not to announce hirings and firings of managers for the duration of the World Series. In 1946, you had all-stars playing exhibitions during the Series! Feller and Paige worked for a percentage of the gate. Feller paid his players—the white major leaguers—salaries that in many cases were almost half their yearly salary. The black players got far less, although Satchel probably did fine. Scouts came to those exhibitions, and within a few years, players like Larry Doby and Monte Irvin and Hank Thompson would be major leaguers.

Feller, in his 40-year-old autobiography, said about Satchel, "Satch and I were friends, teammates, and business associates." In Feller's 2001 memoir, he wrote, "Satchel was one of the top five or ten pitchers in the entire history of baseball."

Paige would become an Indians teammate by 1948, when Satchel's 6–1 mark down the stretch enabled the Indians to advance to the World Series.

On November 10, 1945, Feller went on record with the *Los Angeles Times* as saying he "could not foresee any future in the majors for Jackie Robinson." Feller said that Robinson had football shoulders and that he couldn't hit an inside pitch to save his neck. Of course, UCLA star and then Negro Leaguer Robinson had threatened not to play the exhibitions unless Feller's promoters gave him more money, a demand that was rejected. In the early '40s, Feller was on record saying that only Josh Gibson and Satchel Paige were big-league material. Of course, in 2001, Feller wrote, "I barnstormed against these players, and they were all major leaguers in my book." Did Feller misjudge Jackie's abilities? Or did the Cleveland great survive long enough to rewrite his own history? Feller—who in 1962 would enter the Hall of Fame with Jackie Robinson—will be forever linked with Paige and Robinson. Perhaps his barnstorming tours really did pave the way for breaking the color line.

There is no one who has ever mastered the art of hitting a baseball quite like Barry Bonds. He would be tops in any era. He would be tops in any weight class. Every one of his at-bats is an event not to be missed. (© Jed Jacobsohn/Getty Images Sport/Getty Images)

Babe Ruth and Lou Gehrig were longtime teammates, sometime friends, and two of the top dozen players in history. Together, they formed the heart of "Murderers Row." (© Hulton Archive/Getty Images)

Old-school Willie Mays, in 1962.
(©Louis Requena/Major League
Baseball/Getty Images)

New-school Ken Griffey Jr. His game
sampled and reconfigured Willie Mays's
game in much the same way that rap
music borrowed from earlier artists.
(© Brian Bahr/Getty Images Sport/Getty Images)

Hank Aaron and Eddie Mathews combined to hit 863 home runs as teammates with the Braves. (© Louis Requena/Major League Baseball/Getty Images)

In an alternate universe, it was the Homestead Grays—not the New York Yankees—that were the dominant team of the late 1920s and early 1930s. It was Josh Gibson who hit the most—and the longest—home runs. (© Sporting News/Hulton Archive/Getty Images)

Shoeless Joe Jackson (right) finished second in the batting race in each of his first three seasons—each time trailing only Ty Cobb (left). Cobb was effusive in his praise of Jackson's abilities. (© MPI/Hulton Archive/Getty Images)

Former Yankee Jim Bouton told me that Mickey Mantle was the best player he's ever seen—as a teammate, as an opponent, or on television. "He combined exceptional speed with tremendous power from both sides of the plate." Tony Kubek claimed that Mantle, batting right-handed, was a better hitter than Ted Williams. (© Hulton Archive/Getty Images)

In 1971, Satchel Paige went into baseball's Hall of Fame as its first member from the Negro Leagues, with Josh Gibson and Buck Leonard following the next year. (© Major League Baseball/Getty Images)

Bob Feller was the best pitcher in baseball 60 years ago. His numbers would have been even more impressive had he not lost years to military service. (© Major League Baseball/Getty Images)

"I have all the respect in the world for Brooksie [Robinson] . . . but Mike Schmidt is the greatest third baseman of all time," insists Tim McCarver. (© Stephen Dunn/Getty Images Sport/Getty Images)

How good was Rogers Hornsby? His five-year stretch of batting between 1921 and 1925 (.391, .401, .384, .424, and .403, while leading his league in home runs in two of those seasons) is comparable to Barry Bonds's five years between 2000 and 2004. (© Getty Images)

Former player, broadcaster, and National League president Bill White said, "Stan Musial was the best hitter I ever saw. Willie was the best player, but Stan was the best hitter." (© John G. Zimmerman/Time & Life Pictures/Getty Images)

Joe DiMaggio struck out 369 times in his 13-year career. For comparison, Sammy Sosa struck out 345 times in just two seasons (1997 and 1998). (© New York Times Company/Getty Images Sport/Getty Images)

A perfect illustration of the cool, calm captain of the Yankees: Derek Jeter holds back the fiery Roger Clemens in the 2003 League Championship Series against the Red Sox. (© Ezra Shaw/Getty Images Sport/Getty Images)

Tony Kubek: "A great many years ago, I told Ted Williams, 'There's a young hitter in the National League who hits exactly like you.'" Of course, Joe Morgan wasn't 6′4″ and 220 pounds.

(© Major League Baseball/Getty Images)

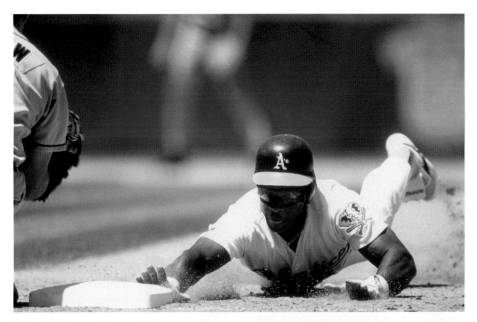

Rickey Henderson, the most prolific base stealer in history, stole 465 more bases than previous record-holder Lou Brock. Henderson perfected a head-first slide that enabled him to preserve his legs and avoid injury. (© Otto Greule Jr./Getty Images Sport/Getty Images)

According to Yogi Berra's lifelong friend Joe Garagiola, "Everyone always underestimated Yogi. They said he couldn't play. They said he couldn't catch. They said he couldn't manage. It used to make me mad."
(© Hulton Archive/Getty Images)

Pete Rose at first base following one of his record 3,215 singles. That's nearly 20 percent more than anyone in history besides Ty Cobb. Rose sure didn't maximize his 4,256 hits; players like Eddie Murray and Dave Winfield had almost as many total bases with far fewer hits. Rose was a one-trick pony, but that trick sure did impress a lot of people! (© Stephen Dunn/Getty Images Sport/Getty Images)

Beginning in 1890, Cy Young threw a record 749 complete games. No other pitcher who played after 1893 is within 200 games of that record.

(© Hulton Archive/Getty Images)

Tom Seaver practiced what he preached about leg power; he ended his pitching motion with his right knee rubbing the ground. He was Tom Terrific, but ranks behind Roger Clemens because he pitched mostly in a ballpark, a league, and an era that favored pitchers over hitters. (© Rich Pilling/Major League Baseball/Getty Images)

According to Joe Buck, in 1998 Mark McGwire was "fighting history to get to a level that had never been done before . . . and even after McGwire broke Roger Maris's single-season home-run record, he had to hit all those homers in the final days just to surpass Sammy Sosa." (© Vincent Laforet/Getty Images Sport/Getty Images)

Mike Piazza, seen here catching in the 2004 All-Star Game, is ranked just a few spots behind Dodgers catching great Roy Campanella. Campy won three MVPs; Piazza hasn't won any.
(© Jed Jacobsohn/Getty Images Sport/Getty Images)

For 50 years, catcher Yogi Berra has insisted that he tagged out Jackie Robinson as he was stealing home in the 1955 World Series. Jackie was safe in this memorable play. (© Getty Images Sport/Getty Images)

Manny Ramirez is my early-line choice to set the major-league record for career RBI.

(© Brian Bahr/Getty Images Sport/Getty Images)

NFL Hall of Famer Dan Fouts told me that Dave Winfield, had he wanted, could have been a tight end in the NFL—and as good as former Charger Kellen Winslow. Winfield was one of baseball's biggest stars in the 1970s and '80s. (© Rick Stewart/Getty Images Sport/Getty Images)

Feller had his own lost time to make up for—the years in the navy. He let himself be overused in pursuit of the 1946 strikeout record, then barnstormed immediately after the season, trying to keep up with the rubber-armed Paige. He developed arm problems, and had just a few good seasons left.

1948 World Series

It should have been the highlight of Feller's career. Instead, it turned into his toughest defeat in baseball. In Game 1 of the World Series, he was matched against the Braves' Johnny Sain. In the eighth inning of a scoreless game, the Braves' Phil Masi was ruled safe in a pickoff play at second base. Tommy Holmes then singled in the game's only run. Feller pitched a complete-game two-hitter, but lost. (If Holmes had singled in the pitcher, he would have driven in Sain, and driven Feller insane.)

Feller then took the ball in Cleveland for Game 4, before the largest crowd ever assembled to see a baseball game at that point. Feller was uncharacteristically knocked around, surrendering seven runs before being pulled in the seventh inning. His knockout also led to the appearance of Satchel late in that game, the first time an African-American pitcher appeared in a World Series game. Paige's account of getting into that game is the crux of his mid-'60s memoir, *Maybe I'll Pitch Forever*. Paige was bypassed for a start in the Series, and the fans desperately wanted him to pitch. Even after Feller was knocked out in Game 4, several other relievers had to fail before Paige was put in.

The Indians went to the World Series again in 1954 (when Feller was 35), but Feller's 13–3 record as spot-starter didn't earn him a start. He played the role that Paige played in '48.

Feller retired after going 0–4 in 1956. He was 37 at the time, not old for a pitcher in the early 2000s, but ancient in his time. No one was in the league in '56 that had played when Bob burst onto the scene in 1936. Feller—the youngest player in baseball then— had retired as one of the oldest players.

He retired with a record of 266–162, winning over 62 percent of his decisions. He retired with 2,581 strikeouts. He pitched three no-hitters, and 12 one-hitters.

Long after his pitching career ended, Feller continued to travel America, pitching in exhibitions in minor-league parks. When he was 66, he said he could still throw 70 miles per hour—more if he didn't want to comb his hair for a week. How much would you give to have seen Feller and Paige pitch against each other in the 1960s—long after their careers were over? It would have been like seeing *The Sunshine Boys*, the movie about the fictional old vaudevillians who reunite in their old age.

Who's Better, Who's Best
Bob Feller or Roger Clemens?

Bob Costas told me that Clemens is probably the best starting pitcher in baseball the last 50 years. Okay, I buy that. Was the Rocket Man better than Feller? Feller began his career in the '30s and lasted into the '50s. What I want to do is take away Clemens's four best seasons in his Red Sox prime, and see how he rates with Feller. After all, Feller has an empty void in his four prime seasons because of World War II. Let's take out those years from the Rocket Man's record.

Roger Clemens was born in August 1962, and he was a rookie with the 1984 Red Sox. His first huge year was in 1986. Imagine if Clemens had to miss the next four seasons (1987–1990).

Clemens, without those four prime seasons: 252–126   3,331 strikeouts
Feller, career: 266–162   2,581 strikeouts

Clemens has almost as many victories as Feller when one takes away the four big seasons, and yet Roger is clearly the better pitcher. He had many more strikeouts, and pitched many more innings. It's pretty close, though. If Feller had the option of free agency, he might not have pitched so many innings in exhibitions, hurting his arm and probably cutting short his career. Then again, Feller threw a lot of pitches by striking out and walking so many batters. He also pitched exhibitions for money long after he retired. Clemens had more productive seasons, and won a lot of big games late in his career. Feller was voted as the Greatest Living Right-Handed Pitcher in a vote conducted in 1969; but those who voted weren't aware of a five-year-old in Texas who would eventually be even better than Bullet Bob.

I don't believe Feller was as great as Pedro Martinez. On June 2, 2004, Martinez struck out his 2,500th batter. It was his 300th start. Feller, the premier strikeout pitcher of his time, struck out 2,581 in his career, and made 484 starts. Of course, in Pedro's day, hitters shoot for the fences and strike out more frequently. Still, when examining the body of work, Feller has to rank behind Paige of his era, and behind Roger and Pedro of the modern era.

JOHNNY BENCH

National Football League general managers have always operated under a universal philosophy. That being, a team must have a "franchise" quarterback to win. Despite that, a recent trend showed that teams could win the Super Bowl with a "caretaker" at the quarterback position. NFL teams sometimes just wanted their quarterbacks "not to mess things up."

The quarterback of a baseball team has always been the catcher, the signal caller. The best one to ever play in the major leagues, Johnny Bench, showed up first in 1967 at a time when World Series champions had "caretakers" playing quarterback.

World Series Champ	Full-Time Catcher	Batting Avg.	HR	RBI	On-Base Avg.
1963 Dodgers	John Roseboro	.236	9	49	.291
1964 Cardinals	Tim McCarver	.288	9	52	.343
1965 Dodgers	John Roseboro	.233	8	57	.289
1966 Orioles	Andy Etchebarren	.221	11	50	.293

I prefer to call the period from 1962 to 1967 the "Bob Uecker Era" in baseball history, in honor of the catcher who played sparingly in those days for a number of teams. As Bob said, "If a guy hits .300 every year, what does he have to look forward to? I always tried to stay at .190, with three or four RBI. And I tried to get them all in September. That way, I always had something to talk about during the winter."

No doubt about it—before Bench, catchers were a funny lot. Joe Garagiola and Uecker were comedians. Many catchers looked funny, including Yogi Berra, Ernie Lombardi, and Etchebarren. Even Roy Campanella was described as "roly-poly."

And then Johnny Bench came along. He was anything but funny. He was a straitlaced, short-haired, conservative, handsome kid who would play for the Cincinnati Reds his entire career.

Was he the greatest catcher to ever play in the major leagues? Well, Mike Piazza has proven to be a better hitter. Ivan Rodriguez has proven to be a better fielder. Yogi Berra certainly won more championships than Bench. Carlton Fisk lasted a whole lot longer. Of all the players in major-league history, however, I believe that Johnny Bench is the best catcher ever. Mine is not a solitary voice in the wilderness.

Tim McCarver: "Who is the greatest catcher of all time? Bench. Johnny Bench. It's not even close. The two Pudges [Rodriguez and Fisk] may have an edge on John from a physical standpoint . . . but if you consider the number of clutch hits, RBI, and add everything together, it's Bench."

When Bench was a rookie, Ted Williams signed a baseball for him, writing, "To a sure Hall of Famer." When one talks about Bench's Hall of Fame career, you have to start with his defense. He won 10 Gold Gloves for fielding excellence in his first 10 seasons.

He revolutionized the catcher's position defensively. I thought he was the first to play with one hand behind his back, but when I spoke with Bench recently, he told me that the Cubs' Randy Hundley had played 161 games in 1967 that way. Bench used the technique to protect the fingers on his throwing hand. It worked. He became the first catcher ever to catch at least 100 games in 13 straight seasons.

He was such a force defensively. In the 1976 World Series against the Yankees, Bench threw out Mickey ("Mick the Quick") Rivers attempting to steal in the first inning of the first game. Message received. No other Yankee even attempted to run on Bench the rest of the Series.

Offensively, he was in a league of his own among fellow catchers. In 1970, Bench was the MVP of the National League, hitting 45 home runs and driving in 148. In 1972, he had his second MVP season, hitting 40 homers and driving in 125—both league-leading numbers.

More important, the Reds, who won the National League pennant in 1970, won it again in 1972. Cincinnati met Pittsburgh in the National League Championship Series for the right to go to the 1972 World Series.

The Pirates were led by 38-year-old Roberto Clemente, whose home run in the fourth game of the Series helped the Pirates tie the best-of-five matchup at 2–2.

In the fifth game, Pittsburgh brought in ace reliever Dave Giusti to pitch the ninth inning and protect a 3–2 lead. The Reds were down to their final three outs when Bench led off the ninth inning with a home run to tie the score. The Reds would eventually eliminate Pittsburgh and advance.

The man had clutch hits time and again. In 1973, the Reds again won their division. This time, they faced the underdog Mets in the NLCS. In Game 1 of that series, Bench hit a walk-off home run off of Tom Seaver.

There was no other catcher like him, although in short order a few would come close. In the National League, Ted Simmons would post impressive numbers. In the American League, 1970 Rookie of the Year Thurman Munson and 1972 Rookie of the Year Carlton Fisk emerged on the scene.

Bench not only was the superior player over all three, he and his team denied Fisk's Red Sox in the 1975 World Series and Munson's Yankees in the 1976 Series.

Bench's offense began to suffer in the mid-'70s, but the Reds batted him sixth in those years at Johnny's urging, so he could concentrate on defense. Like Berra and Campanella, Bench took his role of handling the pitching staff very seriously. And when it mattered, Reds manager Sparky Anderson had all the confidence in the world in Bench. In 1976, Johnny hit only .234; but in the postseason, Bench batted .533 with two homers and six RBI in the Reds' four-game sweep of the Yanks in the World Series.

Even when Bench slumped at the plate, he did everything else well. In 1975 and 1976 combined, he stole 24 bases. He was caught just twice. He was difficult to run on and impossible to throw out. He was like a point guard in basketball who leads the league in fewest turnovers—and is also among the leaders in steals.

Rick Sutcliffe: "I only pitched to Johnny Bench at the end of his career. He was still very much feared. When we went over the scouting reports, they were filled with what you couldn't do . . . don't let Bench extend his arms on a pitch, et cetera. You would come out of those meetings and say there was no way he could be that good, have the whole package. When you think of the demands put on a catcher, it really increases the respect for what Bench did offensively."

Bench was also among the first to cash in on his name. In a late-1970s autobiography, he admitted to endorsing the following: the Batter-Up Batting Game; plastic balls and bats; instructional calendars; barbeque grills; a T-shirt design company; pewter necklaces and medallions; and countless more. He had car dealerships and interests in banks. He had his own television show.

And he was the host—with the San Diego Chicken—of a kid's show that was produced when I was an impressionable teen, called "The Baseball Bunch." It was a combination of "Pee Wee's Playhouse" and "This Week in Baseball." The highlight was when a wizard played by Dodgers manager Tommy Lasorda appeared each week.

Bench's outside interests, however, never conflicted with his play. The Reds moved him to third base at the end of his career to keep him on the field. Bench would say that playing five games in a row at third base was like playing one behind the plate.

I have worked with two of Bench's former teammates—Tom Seaver and Joe Morgan. Neither of them ever had a bad word to say about their catcher. He commanded respect.

You can win a World Series without a great catcher. It's been done. Just like NFL teams can win without a franchise quarterback. But given a choice, it's a lot easier to win with an Elway or a Bench on your side.

Major-League HR Leaders, 1970–1978
1. 268 Johnny Bench
2. 264 Willie Stargell
3. 263 Reggie Jackson

Major-League RBI Leaders, 1970–1979
1. 1,013 Johnny Bench
2. 954 Tony Perez
3. 936 Lee May

Who's Better, Who's Best
Johnny Bench or Yogi Berra?
Curt Gowdy: "Who's better, between Bench or Berra? Bench. They were both helluva catchers, but Bench had the better arm. He had a great arm. Johnny was a real threat at the plate, and probably more consistent than Yogi."

35

WARREN SPAHN

Warren Spahn was part of a generation that broadcaster and author Tom Brokaw called "The Greatest Generation." Brokaw believes Spahn's time "produced the greatest generation any society has ever produced." To me, Spahn was the perfect representation of his generation.

Spahn pitched for the Boston Braves in 1942, and legend has it that he refused to throw at the head of Brooklyn's Pee Wee Reese when ordered to. He was sent to the minor leagues for not having guts. Soon after that, he had a new employee—the United States Army. In the next three years, he won a Bronze Star, a Purple Heart, and earned a battlefield commission. He was injured by shrapnel at the Battle of the Bulge and almost lost his toes to frostbite.

He was 25 years old by the time he returned to the major leagues in 1946, although he never complained publicly about the lost time. In fact, Spahn always maintained that the time in the army made him a better pitcher. There was little pressure for Spahn on the baseball diamond, after what he had gone through.

In 1947, he won 20 games for the first time. He would have 13 seasons of 20 or more victories, tying him with Christy Mathewson. No pitcher of Spahn's generation churned out more wins, season after season.

He helped himself at the plate, hitting 35 home runs in his career, a record for pitchers. If you like numbers like I do, you may be fascinated to learn that Spahn finished his career with 363 wins and 363 hits. He was a complete player in every way.

Tony Kubek: "Warren Spahn had the best pickoff moves of any pitcher I ever saw."

Spahn was known for his high leg kick. In the beginning, he threw fairly fast, but soon mastered the slider and changeup. He adhered to the notion "Batting is timing. Pitching is upsetting timing."

There were many memorable moments in Spahn's career. He defeated Bob Feller in the fifth game of the 1948 World Series, temporarily staving off elimination for the Braves. In that game, he pitched 5.1 scoreless innings in relief, giving up just one hit. The

Braves were the second-best team in Boston in the late '40s, but Spahn took a backseat to no one. The fans wanted Spahn, and (Johnny) Sain, and two days of rain. The Braves moved to Milwaukee in April of 1953, and Spahn won a new following of fans.

In 1956, he pitched all 11 innings to win his 200th game. On the next-to-last day of the season, he lost 2–1 in 12 innings at St. Louis, in a game that knocked the Braves out of the pennant chase.

He spent a lifetime pitching tough games. Spahn won his 300th game by a score of 2–1. He knocked in the first run himself, and the game was knotted at 1–1 as late as the eighth inning. Spahn—who had become only the third left-hander to win as many as 300 games, and the first pitcher of any kind since Lefty Grove 20 years earlier—was non-chalant about winning his 300th. His goal was to win 400.

In 1962, at the age of 41, he pitched what many people consider his greatest game ever. It was against the San Francisco Giants of Willie Mays and Willie McCovey. His mound opponent was 25-year-old Juan Marichal. Spahn lost 1–0, when Mays hit a homer in the 16th inning—Spahn's 201st pitch of the game.

Spahn didn't retire on top. Instead, he went kicking and screaming, pitching for the Mets and Giants, before being released. Even then, he insisted he could pitch and attempted to hook on with teams until as late as 1967.

Spahn was elected into the Hall of Fame on his first try, in 1973. He was the only one voted in that year, as rigid standards kept legends waiting their turn. In Spahn's case, he made it in 1973, whereas Whitey Ford did not. Spahn joined Jackie Robinson, Stan Musial, Ted Williams, Bob Feller, and Sandy Koufax as players enshrined in their first year of eligibility.

Over the years, a glut of great pitchers and pitching performances—and the lasting images of Spahn pitching in his 40s—led many to drop Spahn from the list of all-time greats.

In 2001, following the death of his boyhood idol Spahn, sportswriter Thomas Boswell wrote:

> Line them up, all the best hurlers since Babe Ruth's home runs tempted baseball to juice its ball and shorten its fences in 1920. That's when the game we recognize today began. You can have Roger Clemens and Sandy Koufax, Lefty Grove and Nolan Ryan, Pedro Martinez and Randy Johnson, Tom Seaver and Steve Carlton, Bob Feller and Greg Maddux. With my one pick for total accomplishments and best entire career, just give me Warren Spahn.
>
> Not because he won more games than any southpaw ever or because, since 1900, only Christy Mathewson matched his 13 seasons with 20 wins. The reason is simpler. No statis-tic is more basic, more bedrock, more full of indisputable truth than wins by a starting

pitcher. Especially when, like Spahn, you loathe the sight of relievers and lead the league in complete games nine times. Since that 1920 line in the dirt marking the modern game, nobody has even managed to win as many as 330 games. Nobody. Except Spahn. And he won 363.

Who's Better, Who's Best
Warren Spahn or Tom Seaver?

	Wins	Complete Games	Shutouts	World Series Record
Seaver	311	231	61	1–2, 2.70 ERA
Spahn	363	382	63	4–3, 3.05 ERA
	Cy Young Awards	#1 in Wins	#1 in ERA	#1 in Strikeouts
Seaver	3	3	3	5
Spahn	5*	8	3	4

Warren Spahn in 1949: He was 21–14 with a 3.07 ERA. He led the league in wins, innings pitched, and strikeouts. There was no Cy Young awarded, but he finished higher in the MVP voting (seventh) than any other pitcher in the league. He would have won the Cy Young this season.

Warren Spahn in 1953: He was 23–7 with a 2.10 ERA. He led the league in wins and earned run average. There was no Cy Young awarded, but he again finished higher in the MVP voting (fifth) than any other pitcher in the league. This would have been his second Cy Young.

Warren Spahn in 1957: He received 15 of 16 votes and won the Cy Young Award.

Warren Spahn in 1958: He finished 22–11, and was second in the Cy Young voting to New York Yankee Bob Turley (21-7, 2.97 ERA). If a National League Cy Young ERA had been awarded, Spahn would have picked it up handily, his fourth as we are counting them.

---

*The record books will show that Spahnie only won a single Cy Young Award, in 1957. But they don't tell you that the Cy Young was first awarded in 1956, and then only to one pitcher in baseball. Beginning in 1967 (Seaver's rookie season) separate Cy Youngs were awarded to the outstanding pitchers in the National League and the American League.

Warren Spahn in 1961: He was 21–13 with a 3.01 ERA and was a close second to Yankees left-hander Whitey Ford (25–4, 3.21 ERA) for the Cy Young Award. Again, Spahn was the deserving choice in the N.L.—what would have been his fifth Cy Young Award.

Spahn was the best pitcher in the National League five different seasons (in the '40s, '50s, and '60s) and led the league in victories eight different seasons.

Seaver's first All-Star Game was in 1967, and his last in 1981. That's 14 years apart. Spahn's first All-Star Game was in 1947, and his last in 1963. That's 16 years apart.

Seaver had a winning percentage of .603. Spahn had a winning percentage of .597. Spahn had better teams for much of his career.

Seaver had a better ERA, even compared to the league averages.

Seaver had 52 fewer wins and 151 fewer complete games. Seaver had five 20-win seasons, and Spahn had 13 such seasons.

It's very close, and they are not ranked far apart from each other. Spahn was the premier post–World War II pitcher, and just behind the great players from the 1940s like Ted Williams, Joe DiMaggio, and Stan Musial. Seaver was one of the great pitchers of his era, but not appreciably better than Koufax, Gibson, and Marichal.

Spahn should be ranked ahead of Seaver.

Warren Spahn served his country, served Casey Stengel, lived to set records and see some of them broken, and lived long enough to enjoy adult grandchildren. His likes will not be seen again, or at least not often enough. Maybe he was part of the greatest generation. He was certainly one of the greatest heroes in baseball history.

RANDY JOHNSON

Randy Johnson has been the intimidating pitcher that no batter, least of all the ones who hit from the left side of the plate, wants to step into the batter's box to face. Because of his 6'10" frame and intimidating manner on the hill, people tend to overlook his achievements. They call Johnson "the Big Unit," and he has been one of the game's greatest competitors over the last two decades. He had a great fastball and a devastating slider to get batters out. With those long arms of his, the ball seemed to explode onto the plate, leaving little reaction time. Only two players (Nolan Ryan and Roger Clemens) have struck out more batters. Johnson has fanned 11.1 batters per 9 innings.

He was drafted out of high school, but elected to go to USC, where he was a teammate of Mark McGwire. He was signed by the Montreal Expos in 1985 and was called up to the big leagues in 1988. He went 3–0 in four dominating starts that gave everyone a glimpse of his talent. Of course, he was still a "Wild Thing," throwing 25 wild pitches in his first two minor-league seasons.

The Expos couldn't live with his 0–4 start in 1989 (he walked 26 batters in 29 innings), and traded him to Seattle in May for a more established pitcher named Mark Langston.

Like Lefty Grove and Sandy Koufax, Johnson needed a few years to learn to control his pitches. Johnson led the league in walks in 1990, 1991, and 1992. He was 39–35 in those three seasons, with an ERA close to 4.00. The early career wildness probably helped him in his later seasons, as batters were literally scared to face him. After his first 119 starts in the majors, he was only 46–44.

Beginning in 1993, at the age of 29, he started to compile his Hall of Fame credentials.

Among left-handed pitchers, there are only a few to be mentioned in the same breath as Johnson: Grove and Koufax and Warren Spahn and Steve Carlton. Only Spahn, Carlton, and Grove have won more games. Only Koufax held batters to as low a batting average and was as intimidating. There have been other great left-handers—including the Yankees' Whitey Ford and Ron Guidry—but they don't match up to the Big Unit.

Whitey Ford's claim to fame is his sparkling winning percentage. He won 69 percent of his 342 decisions (236–106).

Randy Johnson—despite the 46–44 start—had a winning percentage nearly the equal of Ford's. The Big Unit was 246–128 (a .658 percentage) after the 2003 season. Ford pitched his entire career for the Yankees, and had Hall of Fame teammates like Mantle, Berra, Howard, et cetera. Ford pitched for a team that went to the World Series in 8 of his first 9 seasons. In the only year they didn't (1954), the Yankees won 103 games.

Randy Johnson pitched in 2004 for one of the worst teams in recent memory. The Arizona Diamondbacks had traded their best players and finished 51–111. Johnson still had a winning record (15–14), but the D-Backs won only 25 percent of the time when Johnson wasn't on the mound. Johnson also started 31 times for a 1992 Seattle team that went 64–98. Randy was 12–14 that year.

Ford never pitched as well for a bad team. He never pitched as well for a championship team. Johnson dominated the Yankees in the 2001 World Series.

Guidry also pitched for good Yankee teams, and won fewer games, and had a lower winning percentage.

Nolan Ryan, a right-hander, was as intimidating in his prime as Johnson was in his. He wasn't as effective, however.

Randy Johnson has won five Cy Young awards, including four in a row between 1999 and 2002.

In 2002, it was unanimous. He received all 32 first-place Cy Young votes.

In 2001, he received 30 first-place votes. His then-teammate Curt Schilling got the other two.

In 2000, he received 22 of the 32 first-place votes. In 1999, he received 20. That means that in a four-year span, he received 104 of the 128 first-place votes for the Cy Young Award.

He dominated the era. Until his injury-plagued 2003 season, Johnson had reeled off a major-league-record five consecutive years of 300-plus strikeouts.

Batters have hit just .213 off of Johnson in his career. Forget about lefties having a shot against him. In Johnson's career, left-handed batters have hit .200 against him. He has given up 283 regular-season home runs in his career—only 19 of them to lefties. Oh, there's one left-handed batter who has hit him well in his career.

Barry Bonds versus Randy Johnson: .306 (15 hits in 49 AB)   3 HR   12 RBI

Of all the pitchers with at least 200 victories, only two others have winning percentages better than the Big Unit's—Lefty Grove and Whitey Ford.

Since 1993, Johnson has gone 30–2 in September and October with a 2.10 ERA, spanning 44 games (43 starts) in 325 innings.

In 2002, he won the pitchers' equivalent of the Triple Crown (leading the league in wins, strikeouts, and ERA). He closed the season with an 11–1 record.

In May 2001, he struck out 20 batters in a game to tie the major-league record held by Roger Clemens and Kerry Wood.

In May 2004, he pitched a perfect game against the Braves, and retired 39 consecutive batters over two games (two shy of the major-league record). At 40 years old, he was the oldest player ever to pitch a perfect game, nudging Cy Young himself out of the record books.

It is too long a list to point out every vintage Johnson performance. You have to start back in 1990 when he threw his first no-hitter, against the Detroit Tigers.

You might want to mention the game in 2001 that he pitched in relief the day after an electrical-box explosion darkened San Diego's Qualcomm Stadium in the third inning. Randy worked seven innings when the game resumed, allowing only one single and striking out 16 of the 23 batters he faced.

Nothing shows Johnson at his dominating best like his record in the midsummer All-Star games. Johnson (named to 10 All-Star teams) has appeared in eight of them, throwing 12 innings. In those 12 innings, he has given up just five hits and one run (0.75 ERA) while striking out 12 and walking just two.

Who's Better, Who's Best
Randy Johnson or Pedro Martinez or Greg Maddux or Roger Clemens?

It is to be argued here that four of the top dozen pitchers in history have performed their craft in the 1990s and 2000s. They come in sizes XXL (Johnson), XL (Clemens), and Medium (Maddux and Martinez). Some dominated early in their careers (Clemens), and some late (Johnson).

ERA Titles
1. 6 Roger Clemens (plus 2 second-place finishes)
2. 5 Pedro Martinez (plus 1 second-place finish)
3. 4 Greg Maddux (plus 3 second-place finishes)
4. 4 Randy Johnson (plus 3 second-place finishes)

Cy Young Awards
1. 7 Roger Clemens (plus 1 second-place finish)
2. 5 Randy Johnson (plus 3 second-place finishes)
3. 4 Greg Maddux (plus 1 second-place finish)
4. 3 Pedro Martinez (plus 2 second-place finishes)

Clemens has more championships (two) than Johnson (one), Maddux (one), and Martinez (one). After the 2004 season, Pedro Martinez had the most ground to catch up, and the most time to do so. Martinez, who turned 33 in October 2004, had accomplished more than any of the other three at similar ages.

Johnson pitched in an era with three other all-time greats. While "the Big Unit" toiled in home parks ranging from Montreal to Seattle to Houston to Arizona, the others played in New York (Clemens), Boston (Martinez), and Atlanta (Maddux) and usually finished in first place.

I know Maddux has won a lot of games and has won four Cy Young awards, but he lacks the intimidation factor of a power pitcher. Clemens and Johnson have each struck out 20 batters in a game, and Martinez always had that same potential. Does it matter that Johnson struck out batters, and Maddux cleverly retired them?

Johnson has been more physically durable than Martinez. Randy Johnson has more than twice as many career shutouts and complete games than Pedro. Johnson has pitched in relief in Game 7 of the World Series, the day after he started and threw seven innings to win Game 6.

Randy Johnson delayed the Yankees dynasty by a year in 1995, and ended it early in 2001. In 1995, with Seattle, Johnson defeated New York in Game 3, and then came back on a day's rest to work in relief in the deciding Game 5, striking out six in three innings as the Mariners defeated the Yanks to advance to the ALCS. The Yankees would win four World Series in the next five years, until running into the Big Unit once again in the 2001 World Series. Johnson defeated the Yankees three times in that Series (winning Game 7 in relief).

It is hard not to rank Clemens as the best of his generation. Next is the younger Pedro, with his five ERA titles despite being handicapped by a league and ballpark. Maddux is next, a man who operated very differently than Johnson, but with even greater success. Maddux stayed healthy, while Johnson lost most of two seasons to injury. Plus, it took Randy longer to become a big winner.

Johnson is ranked below those other three, but that still puts him among the top dozen pitchers of all time.

FRANK ROBINSON

Just a decade after Jackie Robinson broke the color barrier of Major League Baseball, a different Robinson burst onto the scene and made a lasting impact himself. It was Frank, not Jackie, who slid hard into Eddie Mathews in 1959, precipitating baseball's first on-field brawl between white and black superstars. It was Frank, not Jackie, who broke the color barrier of major-league managers in 1975. In neither case did the world crumble. Frank Robinson's biggest impact was as a player, where his determination and aggressiveness dominated first the National League, and then the American.

Like Jackie, Frank grew up in California, and was an outstanding high school athlete. Frank Robinson was born in Oakland, California, in 1935. As a junior at McClymonds High School, he played on the basketball team with Bill Russell. It's remarkable to think that Russell would be the first black head coach in NBA history, and onetime teammate Robinson would be the first black manager in major-league baseball. Russell won a couple of NBA championships as a player-coach with the Celtics. Frank did something even more noteworthy: he persevered to manage teams with four different franchises over 30 years.

Frank was signed to a professional contract in 1952 at the age of 17, by the Cincinnati Reds organization. In 1956, he won the starting left-field job with the Reds, and had a sensational rookie season. He batted .290, with 38 home runs and 122 runs scored. He was the unanimous choice for Rookie of the Year. His 38 home runs set a rookie record that stood for 31 years until Mark McGwire hit 49 in his freshman campaign. Robinson played with an aggressiveness that few could match. Injuries just didn't keep him out of the lineup. He played entire seasons with leg injuries that forced him to move from the outfield to first base and cost him much of his power. He played with recurring cases of blurred vision, which hampered him from time to time. How could it not?

Robinson was quick on the base paths, with over 200 career stolen bases.

After his spectacular rookie season, he still found room for improvement. From 1957 to 1960, Robinson averaged .301 and 32 home runs per year. By the time he was just 25 years old, Frank had played five seasons, hit 165 home runs, and scored 501 runs.

He was a fearless "plate-crowder" and a frequent target of opposing pitchers' "dusters." He invited the brushback pitches by actually daring the pitcher to throw close to him.

Joe Garagiola: "I don't know if I'd compare Frank Robinson to anybody else in baseball. He had great traits, and was an absolutely fearless hitter. He liked to crowd the plate, and was willing to pay the price. He would stand there and tell the pitcher he wanted the inside corner."

Robinson was hit by pitches 20 times in his rookie season alone, and would go on to lead his league in being hit six different years.

Like Ty Cobb in an earlier era, he played the game one way—aggressively. He was known for his ferociousness on the base paths.

Frank Robinson, like Jackie Robinson and Bill Russell, was an intense competitor and could be considered an angry young man. Early in his career, Frank received death threats that warranted his carrying a gun. In 1961, at the age of 26, he won his first MVP Award and led the Reds to the National League pennant. But few people noticed outside Cincinnati. That was the summer of '61 and the summer of Maris's and Mantle's march toward 61 home runs. Over in the National League, Frank garnered 15 of 16 first-place votes for the MVP.

He batted .323 with 37 home runs and 124 runs batted in. He even stole 22 bases. He was second in the league in runs scored and runs batted in—behind who? Does it matter? He was third in the league in home runs and stolen bases. He led his club to their first pennant in 21 years.

Then he topped himself in 1962. He upped his batting average to .342, upped his homer total to 39, upped his RBI total to 136, upped his runs total to 134.

Again, he was overshadowed, this time in his own league by Maury Wills (104 stolen bases) and Willie Mays. When historians write about the early '60s, they fixate on the record-breaking numbers of Maris and Wills, and the prime of Willie Mays's career. Frank Robinson had trouble getting attention playing in the same league as fellow outfielders Mays, Hank Aaron, and Roberto Clemente.

In his first 10 years (all with Cincinnati), Robby put up these numbers:

1,502 games
324 home runs
1,009 runs batted in
1,043 runs scored
.303 batting average
.554 slugging percentage

He matched up quite favorably with all the other great outfielders of his time, including Mantle, Aaron, and Mays. But it wasn't easy to talk about him in the same way as those major stars, despite their comparable stats. Those guys played up to the fans and the media and each other, but Frank was never, how shall we say, cuddly.

Even Cincinnati management didn't appreciate him. Reds general manager Bill DeWitt not only traded Frank after the 1965 season for an okay pitcher (Milt Pappas) and a young outfield prospect, he said that Robinson "was not a young 30."

Frank Robinson then went to the American League, playing right field for the Baltimore Orioles, and with his antagonistic, tough guy approach to the game, tore through the league. In those days it was the National League that had all the top black players, as well as most of the aggressive players. The chumminess of the game was left up to the players of the American League, which was actually known as the "brother-in-law" league because everyone was each other's crony. Concentrating on more important things than making friends, Frank led the A.L. in home runs, RBI, and batting average and won the Triple Crown in his first season in the league. He led the Orioles into the World Series and became the first player to win MVP honors in both leagues.

In 1967, he was on his way to a second consecutive Triple Crown. A late-season injury limited him to just 123 games. Despite missing almost 25 percent of the season, he finished third in runs batted in, and fourth in home runs! Only Harmon Killebrew and Carl Yastrzemski hit more homers, and only those two and Frank Howard drove in more runs. No offense to any of the above-mentioned sluggers, but none of them were close to Robby in ability.

With Robinson on board, the Orioles won pennants in 1969, 1970, and 1971. Clearly Frank Robinson was the key figure, but he never saw his day. How could he? It was not exactly his fault, but history was not kind to Robinson. He first made it to the World Series in 1961, and then ran into Mickey Mantle and Roger Maris.

Robinson had his Triple Crown season in 1966, and wasn't going to let a little thing like Dodger aces Koufax and Drysdale spoil his big year in the World Series. In the first inning of the first game of the '66 Series, Robinson homered off Don Drysdale. So much for the naysayers who said Robinson only excelled in the American League due to weaker pitching. The Orioles swept the Dodgers.

Then, in the 1969 World Series, the Orioles faced Tom Seaver and the Miracle Mets. Robby got into some hot water with the press for his honesty during the Series, calling his Birds the better team. However, the Mets won in five games.

It was during the 1970 World Series that Frank tasted the dish of revenge cold. Four years after the Cincinnati Reds traded him for being "not a young 30," Frank's Orioles upset the Big Red Machine. Frank hit .273 with a pair of homers in the World Series, but the MVP was another Robinson, Orioles third baseman Brooks.

The Orioles had a chance to win back-to-back World Series, but lost a seven-game series to Pittsburgh in 1971. Following that season, Frank was traded to Los Angeles, and at age 36 his days of putting up huge stats were over.

Robinson started preparing to manage in the majors as early as 1969, when he managed interracial teams in Winter League play in Puerto Rico. By the time Robinson finally retired in 1976, his 586 home runs were fourth all-time (behind the holy trinity of Ruth, Aaron, and Mays—the three men who had the three highest career-homer totals for over 30 years, until Barry Bonds overtook Mays in early 2004). Robinson also retired with a career slugging percentage of .537—17th all-time at the time of his retirement. Following the 2004 season, Robinson had slid to 31st all-time in slugging percentage.

At a 2004 All-Star Game reunion bringing together every living member of the 500 home run club, Robinson was asked how many home runs he would have hit if he had played in the early 2000s. Robinson said, "Quite a few more," but modesty prevailed over naming an actual number. I don't have to be modest. Frank would have hit another 100 home runs, easily.

The Significance of Being Named Manager

Jackie Robinson had broken the color barrier in 1947, but nearly 30 years went by without baseball hiring a black man to manage a major-league club. Jackie himself was appalled by that, and he died before a team gave a black man a chance. The early favorite to be the first, Roy Campanella, was talked about as a future skipper back in the '50s—but then a tragic auto accident paralyzed him and put an end to that. Ellie Howard was openly campaigning for the Yankees job—and appeared to have the inside track after the 1973 season, until the Yanks went outside the organization and hired Bill Virdon.

Jackie Robinson appeared at the 1972 World Series, and spoke publicly about wanting to see a black man manage a team. Finally, Frank Robinson was hired to manage the Cleveland Indians beginning with the 1975 season. It was quite an opening week. On April 8, with Rachel Robinson (Jackie's widow) throwing out the first pitch, the Indians won on Opening Day against the Yankees when Frank—a player-manager—hit a home run in his first at bat with the Tribe, off of the Yankees' Doc Medich.

In the Indians' second game of the season, they traveled to Milwaukee's County Stadium, where Hank Aaron was playing for the Brewers in his first American League game ever upon his return to Milwaukee, where he had starred with the Braves. In the Indians' next game, Robinson started Fritz Peterson and brought in a rookie pitcher making his major-league debut, Dennis Eckersley. Robinson's Indians finished the season with a record of 79–80. It was a huge improvement over the previous season.

Although other black managers would get jobs within a few years (Larry Doby and Maury Wills), it wasn't until 1989, when Frank (now managing the Orioles) met Cito Gaston's Toronto Blue Jays, that two black managers competed against each other in a game. That it took so long for that to happen was a disgrace, but it was just another door that Frank Robinson helped knock down.

Robinson managed Cleveland, Baltimore, San Francisco, and Montreal for 15 years spread over three decades. His teams never won more than 88 games in a season. His teams won only 48 percent of their games. It's a testament to his personality, his teaching skills, and his playing days that he was able to repeatedly land jobs like the white former players who get recycled whenever managerial jobs become open.

Who's Better, Who's Best
Frank Robinson or Vladimir Guerrero?

Frank Robinson had a remarkable career, with hardships faced as a black man in 1956 America. Vladimir Guerrero had a language problem as a Hispanic youngster playing in French-speaking Montreal in the late '90s. Guerrero had a manager in Frank Robinson who understood and nurtured his talent, however.

Guerrero has the talent and desire that Robinson once had. Will Vladimir be able to stay healthy enough and hungry enough to amass almost 600 home runs? Will he lead teams to the World Series? Until he does, Frank has to be ranked well ahead of him.

A Better Analogy

Frank Robinson and Jesse Jackson Frank Robinson has had a long and amazing history in the game of baseball. He is partially responsible for saving baseball in Cincinnati in the 1950s—the Reds had entertained thoughts of leaving Cincinnati for New York after the Giants and Dodgers vacated the Big Apple, but Robinson's performance with them drew crowds.

He played for Cincinnati in the '50s, Baltimore in the '60s, and Los Angeles and California in the '70s, and managed Cleveland in the '70s, San Francisco in the '80s, Baltimore in the '90s, and Montreal in the '00s.

The angry young man from the early '60s changed into a peacemaker who worked for Major League Baseball in the '90s. Who would have thought?

Jesse Jackson was born in 1941. He became a leader of civil rights demonstrations in Greensboro, North Carolina, in 1963, and in June of that year was arrested in Greensboro for "inciting to riot and disturbing the peace and dignity of the state."

He asked Martin Luther King Jr. for a job in 1965, and by the summer of 1967 was among the leaders of King's open-housing marches in Chicago. He became an ordained minister in 1968, even delivering the eulogy when Jackie Robinson died in 1972. He founded Operation PUSH, a program to encourage inner-city kids in their schoolwork. By 1979, he was making controversial visits to the Middle East. In 1984, he entered the Democratic presidential race. Five years later, he founded the National Rainbow Coalition.

He's done a lot of things, many of them controversial, but here's the point: Jesse Jackson has staying power. He was once an angry young man, born at the right time in history to make significant contributions to the civil rights movement.

Jackie Robinson and Dr. King died too soon. They left unfinished business in good hands, to men like Frank Robinson and Jesse Jackson. Although they both spent their youth in the shadows of someone a little better or more influential, their staying power cannot be matched.

38

YOGI BERRA

Yogi Berra was the anchor of a New York Yankees dynasty that spanned decades and was one of the greatest catchers of all time. He was also one of the most quoted people of the 20th century.

He's been called the greatest living Yankees player. He's been called the greatest team-sport athlete of all time. No one will ever reach his total number of championship rings, accumulated as a player, coach, and manager.

He has great numbers, but as Yogi would say, "A nickel ain't worth a dime anymore."

He was born Lawrence Peter Berra on May 12, 1925, in an Italian section of St. Louis known as "the Hill." His father, Pietro, worked in a brickyard with his neighbor Giovanni Garagiola. Larry—nicknamed Yogi by a teammate from his American Legion team—became friends with neighbor Joe Garagiola. Larry dropped out of school at the age of 15, and both boys earned tryouts with the hometown Cardinals. St. Louis general manager Branch Rickey offered Garagiola a contract, but not Berra.

Joe Garagiola: "Well, that's only partially true. We both worked out for the Cardinals and as kids, kids' games are the most honest. I wasn't even the best player on my block. Yogi was always the best, the first chosen. So, the two of us worked out for the Cardinals. I hit some shots, but nothing like the exhibition Yogi put on. We were surprised when I was offered a contract, and Yogi wasn't. I told Yogi not to get discouraged, that something had to be up. Well, about ten days later he got a contract offer from the Dodgers. Rickey left St. Louis for Brooklyn, but when we tried out that afternoon we didn't have any idea. Could you imagine what Yogi would have done with the Dodgers, playing in Ebbets Field? Of course, a man named Leo Browne—he was in charge of the American Legion team that we played on—he was friends with a Yankees scout, who signed Berra on Browne's word alone, before the Dodgers' offer came in. The Yankees get all the credit, but they didn't even scout him."

In the spring of 1943, Yogi reported to the Norfolk Tars. He hit a grand slam in his first at-bat in a professional game. He had 12 hits in his first two games, including three homers, two triples, two doubles, and 23 RBI.

Berra would have made the major leagues in the mid-'40s, but there was a war overseas. Yogi enlisted in the U.S. Navy and manned a machine gun during the D-Day invasion at Normandy. Yogi was the only big leaguer to land at Normandy. When the war ended, Berra was assigned by the Yankees to the Newark Bears, one of their farm clubs. The man described as a "chunky, homely little fellow" made his Yankees debut at the end of the 1946 season. Peter Golenbock's *Dynasty* was more blunt: "When he first came up, some of his teammates hung from the dugout roof by one arm and made ape calls." He responded to the insults by saying, "You don't hit with your face."

He was comfortable up at bat from the beginning. Yogi was one of the best and hardest bad-ball hitters to come along since Joe Medwick, and he was a clever base runner.

Joe Garagiola: "Yogi was very fast. Now, you wouldn't say that if you put him in a race, but he got out behind the plate quicker than any catcher I ever saw. If I had one word to use to describe Yogi as a player, I would use the word *underestimated*. Everyone underestimated him as a ballplayer, a catcher, a manager. He's a very sensitive guy and my best friend. It used to bother me a great deal how people always underestimated him."

He would swat pitches that were not anywhere near the strike zone, and it worked for him. There wasn't a pitch Yogi didn't think he couldn't handle.

Bob Wolff: "Yogi had the distinction of hitting any ball thrown to him. He didn't look like an athlete, but he was indeed a great athlete. From the very beginning, he was kidded about his looks. But he was respected soon enough, because of his hitting."

It was a different matter behind the plate, where he appeared to be just fair. He appeared rather green and awkward, and in the 1947 World Series, he let the Dodgers run away with everything but his wallet. Yankee manager Bucky Harris almost gave up on Berra's catching in the 1948 season, but didn't, only because Berra was the heir apparent to DiMaggio's cleanup spot in the batting order. By 1949, when DiMaggio spent much of the year out injured, it was Berra who was the Yankees' biggest gate attraction—bigger even than veteran star Tommy Heinrich.

When Casey Stengel was brought in to manage the Yankees in 1949, he not only made Berra the full-time catcher, but he brought back Yankee legend Bill Dickey to train Yogi behind the plate. Dickey made Berra more confident in his throwing arm, and eventually Berra became one of the league's top backstops. The Yankees went on to capture five consecutive world championships with Berra behind the plate.

Bob Wolff: "He became a nimble, agile catcher."

Berra's best season was 1950. He batted .322 with 28 homers and 124 RBI. He then won three MVP awards, following the 1951, 1954, and 1955 seasons. He led the Yankees in RBI for six consecutive seasons, beginning in 1950.

He was instrumental in the Yankees' domination. He was a terrific hitter, of course, but he also handled a pitching staff well. Between July 1957 and May 1959, Berra went 148 games without an error.

Yogi Berra, Most Valuable Player of the 1950s. Check this out:

American League MVP Voting
1949: 15th
1950: 3rd (behind Yank Phil Rizzuto and Boston's Billy Goodman)
1951: 1st
1952: 4th (behind pitchers Bobby Shantz and Allie Reynolds, and Mickey Mantle)
1953: 2nd (behind Cleveland third baseman Al Rosen)
1954: 1st
1955: 1st
1956: 2nd (behind Mickey Mantle)
1957: 14th

In the seven years from 1950 to 1956, Berra won three MVP awards, finished second twice more, finished third in 1950, and finished fourth in 1952.

- In the 1950s, Yogi led the American League in total bases, accumulating 2,555 in the decade. (Mickey Mantle was a few behind Yogi, and didn't have the benefit of playing the 1950 season.)
- In the 1950s, Yogi led the American League in RBI with 997. Jackie Jenson drove in 863, and Mantle drove in 841.
- From 1949 to 1957, Yogi led all American Leaguers in home runs. Berra had 235, one more than Ted Williams. (Mantle was a rookie in '51; Williams missed time while in Korea.)
- Berra hit 256 homers in the 1950s, more than twice the amount of any catcher that decade not named Campanella (who hit 211).

Casey Stengel was fired following the 1960 World Series, and Berra's former backup, Ralph Houk, became the Yankee manager. By 1961, the Yankees were playing Elston Howard at catcher, and letting Yogi play left field. The Yankees' new outfield then showcased Berra (MVP in '51, '54, '55), Mantle (MVP in '56, '57), and Maris (MVP in '60, '61).

Before the 1962 season, Yogi signed a two-year contract with the Yankees. It would pay him $52,000 a year to catch, play outfield, and pinch-hit—while leaving open the possibility of him one day managing the club. The expansion-team Mets had just hired 74-year-old Stengel to manage, and had drawn many New York fans away from the Yankees. After the 1963 season, the Yankees named their once-shy, kidded catcher as their manager. Berra managed the Yanks to the 1964 pennant, but they would fall in seven games to the St. Louis Cardinals in the World Series.

Berra was fired following the season, with the charge he was too "soft" on the players. The Yankees spent the next 12 seasons without Berra as an employee. In that time, they did not reach the postseason even once.

Yogi joined the New York Mets as a bench coach. He saw the Mets transform from loveable losers under Stengel to a dynamic pennant-winning team under manager Gil Hodges. Berra took over as Mets manager just before the 1972 season under terrible circumstances. Hodges died of a heart attack following a round of golf during spring training. Berra rallied the Mets to a World Series victory in 1973, proving that he could manage successfully.

Berra set the record with 75 World Series games played. In those games, he hit 12 homers, drove in 39 runs, batted .274, and slugged .452. While those numbers are respectable, his teams won 10 World Series, while losing 4. Along the way, he was in every meaningful frame of the World Series highlight films, serving as the sport's "Zelig" or "Forrest Gump":

Berra in the Middle of the Action

1. 1952 World Series, Game 3: Brooklyn won 5–3, as Berra's passed ball in the ninth inning allowed two Dodgers to score.
2. 1955 World Series, Game 1: Brooklyn's Jackie Robinson stole home, although Berra, for nearly 50 years now, claims that he tagged Jackie out. It was the signature play in Robinson's major-league career.
3. 1955 World Series, Game 7: Brooklyn's Johnny Podres was on the mound, trying to preserve the Dodgers' first World Series championship. In the seventh inning, with the tying runs on base, Berra hit a blast to left field that was somehow run down by Sandy Amaros, who doubled off a runner, effectively ending the Yanks' best chance to win the game and Series.

4. 1956 World Series, Game 5: Don Larsen completed a perfect game—the only one in World Series history—as Berra jumped into his arms.

5. 1956 World Series, Game 7: The Yankees turned the tables on Brooklyn from the previous year, winning the seventh game as Berra hit a two-run homer.

No other catcher before or since has won consecutive MVP awards. No other player has sandwiched consecutive MVP awards with a pair of second-place finishes. Yogi did everything one could want from a player. He was durable (catching nearly 1,400 games in the 1950s, out of 1,540). He played on winning teams. He set defensive records. He became trusted enough to become a coach and then manager of the New York Yankees. The Yankees went from 1944 to 1994 without winning a World Series unless they had Yogi as a player, coach, or manager.

Marty Appel, former public relations director of the Yankees: "Counting his time as player, coach, and manager, and including World Series and All-Star games, Yogi Berra earned 38 rings, plus a 39th for being a member of the Hall of Fame. It is impossible to imagine that anyone in any sport will ever experience anything like that again." [Michael Jordan had 18.]

Who's Better, Who's Best
Yogi Berra or Any Other Catcher in Major-League History?

Yogi Berra played between 1947 and 1963, in over two thousand games. When he retired, he had hit more homers—by far—than any other catcher. He had also driven in more runs, accumulated more total bases, and played in more World Series than any other catcher. Yet in 1969, with the Baseball Writers of America having fresh and vivid images of Berra as a player, they elected Mickey Cochrane as the greatest catcher of all time. They named Bill Dickey as the greatest catcher still alive.

Was Berra a victim of an anti–New York vote? Well, those same voters named a Yankee the greatest player ever (Babe Ruth), and another one the greatest player still alive (Joe DiMaggio).

It seems so clear years later that Cochrane and Dickey weren't in Berra's class. By 1999, things had changed, when the All-Century Team was announced. The two catchers named to that team were Johnny Bench and Berra.

In future years, look for active catchers Ivan Rodriguez and Mike Piazza to get praised as greater players than Berra. Rodriguez clearly was better defensively than Berra. Piazza was just as superior offensively.

Berra was the winner of the "lucky genes" contest. Because of his skin color, he was able to sign a major-league contract when he was a teenager. Josh Gibson couldn't do that, and lost 100 percent of a major-league career. Roy Campanella was every bit as good as Berra in the early 1950s, but he lost a few years because of his skin color. Elston Howard was a Yankee teammate of Berra's, but Ellie's skin color held him back with the organization.

In this book, Gibson and Bench are ranked ahead of Berra. The combination of Yogi's skills, his leadership and mastery over a makeshift pitching staff, and his World Series accomplishments puts him clearly ahead of all other catchers in history.

Of course, I could be guilty of understimating Berra by putting him behind Gibson and Bench. As Yogi once said, "We make too many wrong mistakes."

Joe Garagiola: "Yogi or Johnny Bench—it depends on if you judge by results or style. If you watched Yogi in practice, you would have to pick John Bench. But look at the results. Look at all the games—even doubleheaders—that Yogi caught. If the game was on the line, he was as tough a batter as you would ever want to see. He was like that as a kid— and he was like that in the big leagues. Paul Richards, the old general manager of the Orioles, used to say that Berra was the toughest hitter with the game on the line. You're asking me to choose between Berra and Bench? It's like asking the guys awaiting execution in the electric chair: 'Do you want AC or DC?' You're going to get it one way or another. Do you want a Cadillac or Mercedes? It's a matter of preference, that's all."

BOB GIBSON

ob Gibson was the most intimidating pitcher of the last 50 years. Batters feared the hard-throwing right-hander, but not because he was wild. They feared him not because he was psychotic. They feared him because he had a competitive will to win that was second to none. Mostly, they feared him because he had a lethal weapon in his hands, and wasn't afraid to use it. He hit batters. He came dangerously close to them. He pitched inside. He made batters run for cover. Even in retirement, he wouldn't serve up hittable balls in old-timers' games or fantasy camps. He had a determination and played the game in a certain way that is foreign to modern ballplayers.

To wit: he didn't think it was wise to befriend an opponent. One of the things that hurts the modern game, Gibson has long claimed, is that player-agents represent players on different teams and players become too friendly. Big money has also changed things, as players aren't as hungry. Gibson never had a long-term contract. He believed that players don't perform as well when they have security.

He also believed that baseball conspired to take the game away from pitchers. Just as defensive linemen bemoan the fact that in football rules are put in place to protect the "franchise" quarterbacks, Gibson believes that baseball owners want to protect their multimillion-dollar investments. So umpires warn pitchers not to throw inside at batters. Batters—not used to being pitched inside—automatically charge the mound upon being hit. Gibson believed that in 1969, when baseball first instituted rules to improve the offense, and he believed that in 2004.

Now, it's a different game than the one Gibson played so well with the St. Louis Cardinals from 1959 to 1975.

Gibson was a star in basketball as well as baseball in high school, and accepted a scholarship to play basketball at Creighton University. He played baseball as well. After graduation, he actually played for the Harlem Globetrotters in 1956. He accepted a $4,000 bonus from the St. Louis Cardinals to play baseball in 1957 at the age of 22. By 1959, he was with the Cardinals.

His manager, Solly Hemus, brought Gibson into his first game in relief against the Giants with simple instructions: strike out Willie Mays. Gibson may have had some jitters at the beginning, but would soon find the confidence and demeanor to battle Mays, Aaron, Clemente, and everyone else in the National League.

Gibson's dominance was slow to develop. He didn't burst on the scene as a phenom—but he didn't burn out quickly, either.

Bob Gibson's Win Totals, 1960–1970
1960: 3
1961: 13
1962: 15
1963: 18
1964: 19
1965: 20
1966: 21
1967: 13 (broken leg, missed 11 starts)
1968: 22
1969: 20
1970: 23

In Gibson's first two seasons, he had 21 starts and 19 relief appearances, and had a record of only 6–11. Hemus kept pitching Gibson in 1959 and 1960, in the heat of the pennant races, but Gibson failed to respond. In his last three seasons, he was only 26–33.

In between, Gibson had a record of 219–130 in the years 1961–1972. Those 11 seasons represented the years that Gibson was 25–36 years old. It wasn't a long career, but he made his mark, especially in the World Series.

His dominance over American Leaguers in World Series play sets him apart from most of the other great pitchers of his generation.

Curt Gowdy: "If you're asking me who was the greatest pitcher I ever saw—well, I would have to answer it like this: If I needed to win a single game, I would say Bob Gibson. At his peak, in a big game, he was unhittable."

Bill White: "When you talk about Bob Gibson, you're talking guts, and desire. And you are talking about a man who won. You can't talk about great players that don't win. Gibson, above all, was a winner."

Bob Gibson in the World Series

- 9 starts, 8 complete games
- Completed his last 8 games in World Series play
- Record of 7–2, dropping his first and last game
- ERA of 1.89, with 92 strikeouts and 17 walks
- MVP of the 1964 World Series (27 innings pitched, 3 runs allowed)
- MVP of the 1967 World Series
- Only man to win a pair of Game 7s in the World Series

The 1968 World Series: Gibson defeated 30-game winner Denny McLain 4–0 in Game 1, and 10–1 in Game 4. In Game 7, he lost 4–1 to Mickey Lolich as Cardinals outfielder Curt Flood misplayed a fly ball in a three-run Tiger 8th inning.

Then, of course, there was something besides the World Series heroics that set Gibby apart. There was the 1968 season.

1968

Gibson was 22–9 with an ERA of 1.12 in 1968. He started 34 games, and allowed only 38 earned runs all year. The league ERA was 2.90, so Gibson was 1.78 runs per nine innings better than the average National League pitcher that year.

Tim McCarver: "The greatest single season by a pitcher had to be Bob Gibson in 1968. Bob didn't have a lot of offensive support that year. He lost five games by a 1–0 score. His attitude toward his teammates like me was just what you would think. Nice going, my ass. He was like, 'You guys score some f-in' runs.' Of course, he didn't mean anything by it. He would then whack me—that would serve as his apology. He was better than another great pitcher I caught—Carlton. One thing Gibson had over Lefty was a lot of defensive support. Carlton didn't have that defense behind him in Philadelphia that Gibby had. Gibson was so consistent in his control. Roger Clemens or Bob Gibson? I wouldn't put Roger ahead of Bob. Gibson won seven straight World Series games."

The most amazing stat of Gibson's 1968 season is that the manager never pulled him from the mound. He completed 82 percent of his starts (28 of 34). He was pinch-hit for in the other six games.

He won a second Cy Young Award in 1970, when he went 23–7. Even more impressive, he was only 2–5 in mid-May. He went 21–2 the rest of the season. He batted over .300 that season. That would prove to be his last big year. The great competitor started to decline in his late 30s.

Gibson retired in 1975, just before the game became unrecognizable to him. He left before big money, free agency, and other changes. Every time I see a player like Mark Grace congratulate opponent Mark McGwire after a record home run, I feel a little sick inside. I can only imagine what Bob Gibson feels like.

Gibson was a great athlete, and won the Gold Glove for fielding nine consecutive seasons from 1965 to 1973. As a batter, he was frequently used as a pinch hitter, and hit 24 homers. He hit two more in his nine World Series games.

A Better Analogy

Larry Bird and Bob Gibson   When I worked NBA games, I had an opportunity to have dinner with former Celtics coach Bill Fitch. I asked Fitch about the athletes he coached, and in particular, the most well known of them. He said that Larry Bird and Bob Gibson were the most competitive, and Fitch should know. He was Gibson's college basketball coach. He said there were a lot of similarities between the two.

Bird, like Gibson, was known for his ferocity and on-court concentration. They were at their best in big games. They both started out a little older than other rookies, and didn't last as long as some others. They both played for only one franchise their entire career.

With a game on the line, there's no one you would rather have on your side than Larry Bird or Bob Gibson. They didn't always hit the last shot, or get the third out in the ninth inning, but a little piece of them died every time they didn't. You can't say that about most other athletes. Maybe they got some of that attitude from their old coach. Maybe they were just sons of a Fitch.

40

SHOELESS JOE JACKSON

S hoeless Joe Jackson played in the major leagues from the time he was 18 years old until he was 30. He didn't leave the game early, like Koufax, with a deteriorating injury. He didn't leave the game of his own free will. Did he accept money from gamblers to throw the 1919 World Series, or did he merely know about it?

Regardless of the answer to that question, Joe Jackson deserves to be mentioned and ranked among the top players of all time. With his great speed, strong arms, and good hitting abilities, this ranking might even be too low.

Joe Jackson had a career batting average of .356. At the time of his lifetime ban, Jackson had accumulated 4,981 at-bats. Major League Baseball ranks the all-time leading batters who have a minimum of 5,000 at-bats. So Jackson was not only kicked out of the Hall of Fame, but denied a spot in some record books that use the 5000-at-bat minimum. Only two players—Ty Cobb and Rogers Hornsby—have higher lifetime batting averages.

It's impossible in 2004 to find someone who actually saw Jackson play, since he was barred 84 years earlier. So I did the next best thing: I spoke to Shoeless Joe Jackson himself.

Well, I did speak to actor D. B. Sweeney, who portrayed Jackson in the 1988 John Sayles movie *Eight Men Out*.

D. B. Sweeney: "Absolutely, Jackson belongs on your list—and he should be a lot higher. When he played, they used baseballs till they were black and you couldn't even see them. Look at all the triples he hit—in an era when no one hit home runs. When I was studying for the role, I had a chance to speak with [former Cincinnati Reds outfielder] Edd Roush. Roush was in his early 90s, but was as clear as could be regarding Shoeless Joe. Roush played in that 1919 World Series, and said no one was a better hitter than Jackson. He told me that after the first two games of that Series, the fix was over, anyway."

Edd Roush died in March 1988 at the age of 94, shortly before the movie was released. Sweeney is right about the triples. Jackson's 168 triples were topped only by Sam Crawford, Ty Cobb, and Honus Wagner—all of whom had started earlier than Jackson.

There is a lot of mythology associated with Shoeless Joe, beginning with the little boy approaching him on the courthouse steps and saying to him, "Say it ain't so, Joe." While that probably didn't happen, we do know a lot about this early slugger.

He was born in South Carolina in 1889, and never learned to read or write. At the age of six, he was put to work sweeping floors in a mill. When he was 13 years old, he was working twelve hours a day in the cotton mill—and then after work, pitching for the company baseball team.

The 1949 *Sport* magazine interview with Jackson (two years before his death) detailed how he got his nickname: "I played in a brand new pair of shoes one day—they wore blisters on my feet. The manager told me I had to play, blisters or not. I tried it with my shoes on, and just couldn't make it." Joe told how he played the rest of game in his stocking feet. In the seventh inning, Joe hit a triple, and as he pulled into third, some big guy stood up and hollered, "You shoeless sonofagun, you."

He never again played the outfield without shoes, but the players picked it up and began calling him "Shoeless Joe."

He went from starring for the semipro mill team in Greenville, South Carolina, to being signed by Philadelphia Athletics' manager Connie Mack.

Jackson played a handful of games for Philadelphia in 1908 as a teenager, intimidated by Philadelphia and teased by his teammates about his hayseed ways and illiteracy. He took a train home to South Carolina, and Mack suspended him. Mack offered to help him read and write, but Jackson wanted no part of it. He went back home with his "Black Betsy"—his bat that he would use throughout his major-league career.

By 1910, after Jackson spent the summer in New Orleans playing in the minors, Mack traded him. He had shown considerable talent as a hitter, but his teammates wanted no part of him. Jackson went to Cleveland for a reported $325 and outfielder Bristol Lord, whose nickname was "the Human Eyeball."

Jackson batted .387 in the final 20 games of the 1910 season, and then in his rookie season of 1911 batted .408. It was the only time in history that a rookie batted .400. Jackson that year was second in the league in batting, second in doubles (45), second in triples (19), fourth in home runs, and second in slugging percentage. He was all of 21 years old.

Maybe Joe's superstitions should be adopted by modern-day players. Joe believed that bats had only so many hits in them, and when he went into a slump he would discard his bat. The only bat he did not discard was his original Black Betsy. He had other bats, of course, including Blond Betsy, Big Jim, and Caroliny.

He broke in bats by having them spend time next to Black Betsy and "talking" to her. He collected hairpins, and believed that they brought him good luck. He would keep hairpins in his back pocket—discarding them and starting a new collection when he was mired in a rare slump.

Jackson finished second in the league in batting in each of his first three seasons, trailing Ty Cobb all three years.

His swing was so fluid that other players took notice. Cobb always called Jackson the most natural hitter he ever saw. Babe Ruth copied his swing and his stance. Babe said late in his career that when he was coming up, he looked around the league for a swing and stance that he could copy and Joe Jackson's was good enough for him.

In 1914, Jackson's Cleveland team batted just .245, despite a .338 average from Jackson. Cleveland traded Jackson to an emerging powerful team in Chicago in 1915.

The Indians needed cash, and the Chicago White Sox were the buyers in a seller's market. First, they got second baseman Eddie Collins from the Athletics, for $50,000. Then, White Sox owner Charles Comiskey traded for Shoeless Joe Jackson (for three players and $31,500 cash). Jackson batted .341 with 40 doubles, 21 triples, and three home runs. He was one of the true superstars of the era.

He followed that up with a 21-triple season in 1916, and was one of the main reasons the White Sox won the pennant and the World Series, defeating the New York Giants 4–2.

World War I limited Jackson to just 17 games in the war-shortened 1918 season. In May, a "work or fight" edict was mandated after baseball was deemed nonessential to the war effort. Joe was approaching 30 years old, and was the sole support of his wife, mother, and brother. He accepted draft exemption, and spent most of the year working in a shipbuilding plant.

Jackson was still only 29 years old entering the 1919 season. That year, he slugged .506 (when the league slugging average was only .361) and batted .351. In a best-of-nine World Series, Jackson lined 12 hits and batted .375.

The 1919 White Sox team may have had as much talent as any in the game's history. Collins and Jackson were the best at their positions. The White Sox led the league in runs, and batted .287 as a team. On the mound, the Sox had three terrific pitchers. Ed Cicotte, Red Faber, and Lefty Williams were the aces of a strong staff. Faber was a spitballer who pitched for 20 years, winning 254 games and earning a spot in the Hall of Fame. Claude "Lefty" Williams won 23 games in '19, and Cicotte won 29.

The White Sox were also one of the most underpaid teams, with a total payroll that year around $85,000. Eddie Collins got paid the most, and everyone else was severely underpaid. Jackson earned a salary that season of around $6,000.

Teammate Chick Gandil (the first baseman) approached Jackson in September, offering him $10,000 to join seven other teammates in fixing the World Series. Jackson refused, and refused a second time a few days later with the offer upped to $20,000. Jackson's testimony later would reveal that he went to Comiskey and begged him to take him out of the lineup, but Comiskey wouldn't hear of it.

The White Sox lost the Series, 5–3. The night after one of the final games of the Series, Lefty Williams came into Jackson's room at the hotel and gave him an envelope with $5,000 in it. Williams apparently told Joe that the conspirators had told the gamblers that Jackson would "play crooked, too." Jackson told Williams that he didn't want the money, and he had a helluva lot of nerve to use his name like that. He also told him that he would go to owner Comiskey and inform him of this. Williams, nevertheless, threw the envelope on the floor of Jackson's room and left. Jackson attempted to see Comiskey the next day, but was refused at the door. Comiskey would not see Joe that morning, because he already knew the story. He privately spent the winter of 1919 and most of the 1920 season denying rumors about the 1919 Series and perpetrating a cover-up, in part to protect his valuable property, his guilty players. Once the fix was exposed, Comiskey's priority was to protect his own reputation. He would have looked bad if the public had learned what he knew and when he knew it.

Many of Shoeless Joe's problems stemmed from his illiteracy. He signed contracts that he could not read or understand. He used attorneys given to him by the ball club who protected Comiskey's interests (and not Jackson's). These attorneys convinced him to sign a paper he could not read—a waiver of immunity—and to testify before the Grand Jury. They told Joe that the Grand Jury would probably not believe the truth. He confessed to his part in the conspiracy under a promise of immunity, though some supporters think he was more afraid of the gamblers who instigated the fix than anyone in baseball, which barred him from the game.

Was Jackson betrayed and wronged? Some writers and historians have suggested that Joe demanded $20,000 to help fix the Series and, when he received only $5,000, complained bitterly. Those detractors claim that Jackson was so torn up about the conspiracy that he became ill before Game 1 of the Series, and asked to sit down. In Game 5, after he received the $5,000, he did let a fly ball drop that he might have caught.

Baseball owners in 1920, in the wake of this fix, hired Judge Kenesaw Mountain Landis as their new commissioner to clean up baseball's house. Judge Landis would say, "There is absolutely no chance for any of them [the eight barred members of the 1919 White Sox] to creep back into organized baseball. They will be and will remain outlaws." Landis would go and say that "regardless of the verdict of juries, baseball is entirely competent to protect itself against crooks inside and outside the game."

In March of 1921, Judge Landis placed the eight accused players on his "ineligible list." This was before the courts acquitted Jackson and his teammates. They were never let back in the game, however.

When Jackson died in 1951, the United Press obituary quoted Jackson as not being bitter toward baseball, but at Judge Landis.

"Landis said if the courts declared me not guilty, he'd stand by me. He didn't keep his word. He didn't stand by me when the court acquitted me in the Black Sox trial. How could I like the man?"

Shoeless Joe died at 63 years old, maintaining his innocence of any wrongdoing in the 1919 scandal. He was buried in Greenville, South Carolina. He was not buried with Black Betsy, however, who continues to exist and be sold at auctions for incredible amounts of money.

Joe Jackson's Baseball Career After 1920

In reality, he played a few games for a Westwood, New Jersey, team under the name Joe Josephs. It only took the fans a few days to realize the new phenom was Shoeless Joe, and he was forced to move on. He owned and operated a liquor store back in South Carolina, and "always found time to help youngsters hoping to make the baseball big-time," according to his Associated Press obit.

But what if Jackson had been allowed to continue his career?

The baseballs became easier to hit, the ballparks became easier to hit home runs out of, and the slugging percentages jumped. Babe Ruth's slugging percentages rose each year from 1916 like this: .419 to .472 to .555 to .657 to .847.

Jackson wasn't at the beginning of his career—like Ruth—but he was far from the end, like Ty Cobb was in the 1920s. Joe Jackson would have seen his batting average and slugging average rise as he played into his mid- and late 30s. Jackson finished with a .356 career average that was third-best all-time. He might have reached Ty Cobb's career record of .367 and batted .400 a few more times.

It doesn't matter if Jackson is in the Hall of Fame. He was as deserving as anyone enshrined.

PETE ROSE

Once upon a time, a native Cincinnatian named Pete was born into a sports-crazed family. His father boxed, then played semipro football until he was 42 years old. He met Pete's mother at the ballpark. Her older brother once played shortstop, and while scouting for the Reds he signed nephew Pete to a contract in 1960. Pete weighed only 155 pounds at the time, but gained 15 pounds while working at a job lifting crates. It was a storybook start for a player who didn't have great talent, but worked twice as hard as anyone else.

Rose did whatever it took to be successful. Pete shifted from the infield to the outfield in 1967. In the mid-'70s, he went back to the infield. He made the All-Star Game at five different positions. He played the first 16 years of his major-league career in Cincinnati, and returned to play his final two seasons there while managing the club. The street alongside the Reds' stadium was renamed Pete Rose Way. He played more games and had more at-bats than anyone in history, and set a number of records that may never be broken. He was known more for how he played the game than what he accomplished. He ran to first base on every base on balls. He dove into first base (advising us youngsters to practice diving headfirst in the swimming pool, where it was safe). He ran to his position in between innings. He was the perfect role model for kids and pro athletes.

Rose spent the first three seasons of his pro career in the minor leagues. He won the Rookie of the Year award in 1963, getting his first 170 hits in the major leagues. Rose bridged the gap for Cincinnati between Frank Robinson (traded following the 1966 season) and Johnny Bench (a rookie in 1968).

Pete Rose was as competitive as athletes get. Twice he won batting titles on the final day of the season.

In the final days of the 1968 season, Rose went 5–5 on the penultimate day of the season, and 1–3 in the season finale. It was enough to edge the Giants' Felipe Alou, who went hitless against the Reds in the final game.

Rose had to sweat it out to win the 1969 batting crown as well. Roberto Clemente (in his season finale in Pittsburgh) got three hits in his first three times at bat, while Rose was hitless in his first three at-bats in Cincinnati's finale. In the eighth inning with two out and a man on second, Pete came up and executed a perfect bunt. He won the batting title narrowly over Clemente.

Rose was consumed by goals, by dreams, by winning. In 1968, he informed the press he planned on being the first baseball player who was not a 20-game winner or a home run hitter to make $100,000 per year.

He achieved that before the 1970 season. It was also during the 1970 season that the Reds opened Riverfront Stadium and hosted the All-Star Game. Rose made it a memorable night when he barreled into catcher Ray Fosse with the winning run, sending Fosse to the disabled list.

Rose achieved another goal of his that 1970 season by advancing to his first World Series. The Reds ran into an excellent Baltimore Orioles team that had third baseman Brooks Robinson make a ton of big plays to defeat Cincinnati.

The Reds also lost the 1972 World Series to the Oakland A's.

In 1973, Rose had several new goals. The first, of course, was to finally win a World Series. Another was to win another batting title. Still another he was eyeing was the all-time record for hits by a switch-hitter. That was held by Frankie Frisch, who retired with 2,880. Rose had 2,152 hits entering the 1974 season.

Even Rose had to be surprised with his 1973 MVP Award, but after a league-leading .338 (his third batting title) and 230 hits, he easily took the award.

1973 National League Championship Series

The Reds won the first game against the New York Mets, 2–1, beating Tom Seaver on a tying home run by Pete in the eighth inning and a game-winning shot by Johnny Bench in the ninth. The Mets' Jon Matlack pitched a shutout against the Reds in the second game. The Series then moved to Shea Stadium in New York.

Following Game 2, Mets shortstop Bud Harrelson commented, "Matlack made the Reds' Big Red Machine defensive hitters." That didn't sit right with Rose, who made an angry comment. Mets pitcher Jerry Koosman said, "Tell Rose to shut up and play ball."

When Rose led off Game 3 against Koosman, he shouted something at the pitcher, but nothing happened. The Mets took a 9–2 lead into the 5th inning. Rose lined a single against Koosman. The next batter, Joe Morgan, drilled a grounder to first baseman John Milner, who threw to shortstop Harrelson covering second, eventually completing a double play. Harrelson thought Rose tried to use his spikes to injure him sliding into second. Words were exchanged, and Rose shoved Harrelson. Soon, the men were rolling on the ground. Both benches emptied, and punches were thrown.

Eventually, the game restarted, and when the Reds were retired, Rose took his spot in left field. The New York fans immediately began throwing things at Rose. One fan threw a whiskey bottle that just missed Pete's head. Reds manager Sparky Anderson pulled his team off the field. A contingent of Mets, including manager Yogi Berra, Willie Mays, and Cleon Jones, walked to left field and shouted for the fans to lay off. They warned of a forfeit. Play resumed, and the Mets won the game.

Before Game 4, Mets fans were out with their anti-Rose signs ("A Red Rose Stinks," and "Roses Die, Buds Bloom"), but that only made Rose play better. The game went into extra innings, and Rose hit a home run in the 12th against Harry Parker (Pete's third hit of the game) to tie up the Series. Rose shut up fifty thousand angry New Yorkers and got even with Harrelson and the Mets.

Following the Mets' victory in the deciding fifth game (in those days, they played a best-of-five League Championship Series), Mets fans poured from the stands by the thousands, and Rose (who was on base when the final out was made) had to make a broken-field football run to escape to the clubhouse.

That five-game LCS typifies Rose's 22-year career in baseball.

The Reds were known as "the Big Red Machine" in the mid-'70s, and it wasn't just because of Rose. Rose and Joe Morgan (acquired in 1972) were the table setters for power hitters Johnny Bench, Tony Perez, and Ken Griffey. The 1975 World Series was a classic, the Reds against the Red Sox, and was credited with bringing baseball back to a generation of young fans who had deserted the game for pro football. Boston led in all seven games, and lost the lead in five of them. Five of the games were decided by one run, two were decided in extra innings, and two others in the ninth inning.

It was also the Series that expanded baseball's audience. More games were played at night, and television coverage came of age, with the first "reaction" shot as viewers saw replays of Carlton Fisk waving his home run fair to win Game 6. Against this backdrop, Rose led the Reds' charge. He got on base 11 times in his last 15 plate appearances. He had 10 hits and five walks in the seven games. He would break up a double play with a ferocious slide, and then score on an ensuing home run.

In 1976, the Reds won 102 games without a good pitching staff. They hit .280 as a team, stole 210 bases, scored 857 runs, and became the first and last team to ever sweep through the postseason (7–0). The bravado of Rose paved the way.

On May 5, 1978, Rose became the youngest player ever to reach the 3,000-hit mark. Later in 1978, Rose set his sights on a goal too big even for him to reel in: Joe DiMaggio's record 56-game hitting streak. Through much of June and July, Rose was hitting at a blistering pace. Finally, with the streak at 44 games (during which Rose hit .385 with 70 hits in 182 at-bats), the Braves retired Rose all four times he came up on August 1.

Instead of being gracious, Rose made comments about how reliever Gene Garber tried to throw his best stuff to get him out in the ninth inning! Well, duh. Not every opponent allowed Pete to dump a bunt to get into the record books.

Following that 1978 season, Rose was a free agent, and had an unusual demand. He wanted to become the highest-paid athlete in any of the four main team sports (baseball, football, basketball, hockey). He signed with the Philadelphia Phillies for four years and $3.2 million, temporarily edging past the NBA's David Thompson. One year later, the NBA's Moses Malone became the first million-dollar player in any of the four team sports, and another NBA player, Larry Bird, would enter the pro ranks and surpass Rose as the most popular (and marketable) white athlete.

Rose was worth every penny to the Phillies, however. He moved to first base and never missed a game. He caught a foul pop that catcher Bob Boone juggled for the final out of the 1980 World Series—the only one the Phillies ever won. In 1981, Rose met another goal by passing Stan Musial for most hits in National League history.

There was only one goal left—the 4,192 career hits by Ty Cobb. The Phillies turned to youth following the 1983 season, and the Montreal Expos signed Pete. They were rewarded when he got his 4,000th hit in an Expos uniform. While in Montreal, he also broke Carl Yastrzemski's record for games played.

Cincinnati traded for Pete in the middle of the 1984 season, and made him a player-manager. On September 11, 1985, he broke Cobb's record with a base hit off of Eric Show. He retired as an active player the following summer.

A Better Analogy

Pete Rose and Paul Molitor In 1973, following Rose's MVP season, a former player named Lou Fonseca (who won the batting crown in 1929, and played with Cobb one season) said that the only player whom Rose can be compared to is Ty Cobb.

Cobb finished with a lifetime batting average of .367—the highest average in history. Rose finished with more hits than anyone. Ty Cobb was always the best player on his team, and for much of his career, the best player in the league. Rose, on the other hand, was never the best player on his own team (Frank Robinson was at first, then Johnny Bench and Joe Morgan, and then Mike Schmidt).

A better analogy might be 2004 Hall of Fame inductee Paul Molitor.

	Seasons Played	AB	Hits	Batting Avg.	On-Base Avg.	Slugging Pct.
Molitor	21	10,835	3,319	.306	.369	.448
Rose	24	14,053	4,256	.303	.375	.409

Molitor played over 1,100 games of his career as a designated hitter. But like Rose, he moved around on the diamond. He played almost 800 games at third base, 400 at second base, almost 200 at first base, and 57 at shortstop. He also played the outfield 46 times in 1981.

Molitor, however, popped 234 home runs (hence, the higher career slugging percentage). Ted Williams, in his book on hitting, didn't consider Rose a great hitter. He *hated* singles hitters. To play devil's advocate (maybe literally, if one reads the book from Rose's ex-wife), Pete didn't go for home runs because he had such great power hitters behind him. His job was to set the table for them.

Would I seriously take Molitor over Rose? Molitor had 23 hits in 55 World Series at-bats and a .418 average, driving in 11 runs in his 13 Series games. It doesn't get much better than that.

Molitor, however, never won an MVP (he did finish as high as second to Frank Thomas in 1993), and only made the All-Star team seven times. He never led the league in batting (he was second in 1987 and 1993).

Molitor did steal 504 bases (Rose stole 198). Paul also stole home 10 times, which is the most since 1980 and one of the highest totals of all time.

Rose was closer to Molitor than he was to Cobb. Rose made enormous contributions to some of the greatest teams in history. Rose did more with less talent, and for that he gets credit.

He should not have been on the All-Century Team in 1999. That was a joke, considering the players who were left off. Rose got more votes than Stan Musial. At least Musial was named to the team. Roberto Clemente, Frank Robinson, Tris Speaker, and Barry Bonds were not.

At the time, Rose was benefiting from a wave of popular support, despite evidence that he bet on baseball and the fact that he was convicted of tax evasion. A 1994 article in *Sports Illustrated* reported that 97 percent of respondents in a telephone poll said Pete Rose should be in the Hall of Fame.

It's fruitless to rehash the facts. Rose owes a lot of apologies to men like John Dowd (who compiled the investigative findings against Rose), the late baseball commissioner Bart Giamatti, former commissioner Fay Vincent, and Rose biographer Roger Kahn. Pete spent years lying, and then told the truth in a 2004 autobiography, where he admitted to betting on the Reds while he was the manager.

If pressed, I would agree that Rose belongs in the Hall of Fame. That's not based on his character. But Rose does not deserve to be a "baseball martyr" because he brought shame on the game he loved. He was never the player that Frank Robinson, Stan Musial, or Roberto Clemente was.

Yet it was Rose who drew the biggest ovation and was the main story the night the All-Century Team was paraded on the field in Atlanta before the second game of the World Series. My friend Jim Gray had the opportunity to interview Rose on the field that night.

GRAY: Pete, congratulations, it was quite an ovation.

ROSE: Heart-stopping.

GRAY: Pete, let me ask you now. It seems as though that there is an opening. The American public is very forgiving. Are you willing to show contrition, admit that you bet on baseball and make some sort of apology to that effect?

ROSE: No, no, Jim, not at all. I'm not going to admit to something that didn't happen. I know you get tired of hearing me say that, but I appreciate the ovation. I appreciate the American fans voting me on that All-Century Team. I'm just a small part of a big deal tonight.

GRAY: With the overwhelming evidence that is in that report, why not make that step with this opening . . .

ROSE (interrupting): It's too much of a festive night to worry about that. I don't know what evidence you're talking about. I mean, show it to me.

GRAY: Well, the Dowd report says, but we don't want to debate that, Pete.

ROSE: Well, why not? Why do we want to believe everything he says?

GRAY: You signed a paper acknowledging the ban. Why did you sign it if you didn't agree with it?

ROSE: It also says I can apply for reinstatement after one year, if you remember correctly. In the press conference, as a matter of fact, my statement was I can't wait for my little girl to be a year old so I can apply for reinstatement. At my press conference. So you forgot to add that clause that was in there.

GRAY: Well, you have reapplied. . . . You've applied for reinstatement in 1997. Have you heard back from Commissioner Selig?

ROSE: No, and that kind of surprises me. It's only been two years, though, and he's got a lot of things on his mind. But I hope to someday.

GRAY: Pete, it's been 10 years since you've been allowed on the field. Obviously, the approach that you have taken has not worked. Why not, at this point, take a different approach?

ROSE: Well, when you say it hadn't worked, what do you exactly mean?

GRAY: You're not allowed in baseball. You're not allowed to earn a living in the game you love. And you're not allowed to be in the Hall of Fame.

ROSE: Well, I took that approach and that was to apply for reinstatement. I hope Bud Selig considers that and gives me an opportunity. I won't need a third chance. All I need is a second chance.

GRAY: Pete, those who will hear this tonight will say that you have been your own worst enemy and continue to be. How do you respond to that?

ROSE: In what way are you talking about?

GRAY: By not acknowledging what seems to be overwhelming evidence.

ROSE: Yeah, I'm surprised you're bombarding me like this. I mean I'm doing an interview with you on a great night, a great occasion, a great ovation. Everybody seems to be in a good mood, and you're bringing up something that happened 10 years ago.

GRAY: I bring it up because I think people would like to see you get on with it. Pete, we got to go, we've got a game. . . .

ROSE: This is a prosecutor's brief. It's not an interview, and I'm very surprised at you. I am, really.

GRAY: Well, some would be surprised that you didn't take the opportunity. Let's go. . . .

Jim Gray: "Everybody knew that he bet on baseball. There was absolutely no question about it. On a night where the game was being celebrated, he didn't see fit to come clean. A lot of fans at the time turned a blind eye—because he was so proficient at hitting a baseball. I understand that. Judging him as a player, though, it's pretty hard to argue against someone who had the most hits in history."

CY YOUNG

The question shouldn't be how could I include Cy Young in the top 100 players of all time? The argument that I would throw back is this: how could anyone leave him off any kind of list detailing the greats of the game?

He was a great iron man, pitching in over 900 games, throwing over 7,300 innings (over 8 innings per game for 900 games!), and completing 749 of his 815 games (92 percent).

Cy Young retired in 1911, so there is no one alive who has ever seen him pitch. Even most baseball fans only know of him from the award given to the best pitcher in the American and National League each year. The great number that fans associate with him is his 511 victories.

In every important pitching category, Cy Young dominated. It's not that he pitched more innings than any other pitcher. He pitched *so many more* innings. Cy Young pitched 1,300 more innings than Pud Galvin, who is second on the all-time list. He threw 1,440 more innings than Walter Johnson, who is third. He had almost the same excellent control that Christy Mathewson had. Matty was through at the age of 36. Cy Young kept pitching into his mid-40s.

For his durability, control, winning percentage, and wins, Cy Young deserves a spot among the greatest pitchers in history. There are four pitchers ranked ahead of Young in this book who were active in the 2004 season (Roger Clemens, Pedro Martinez, Greg Maddux, and Randy Johnson). There's surely room in this book for the man who set the standards for pitching excellence.

There are many more than 511 reasons to include Denton Cy Young here.

His records will stand forever. Pitchers in modern days lead the league with 22 victories. If a pitcher could, in theory, win an average of 22 games a year for 23 years, he would still not top Young's 511 wins.

Cy launched his pitching career with the Canton, Ohio, club of the Tri-State League in 1890. After a few weeks with the team, he was sold to the Cleveland Nationals for $250, and the management threw in a suit of clothes for the young pitcher. His obit claimed that Cleveland obtained him when Cap Anson (another future Hall of Famer) saw Young pitch.

He spent 10 seasons in Cleveland. In his first year, he had a mediocre record of 9–7. The next year, his first full season in the majors, he won 27 games and lost 20. In 1892, his career took off. He was 36–12, with an ERA of 1.93, and he limited opposing batters to a .211 average.

In 1901, the Cleveland franchise was shifted to St. Louis and Cy Young was sold to the new American League franchise in Boston for $12,000 (this time, with no wardrobe thrown in). He left the National League for the new American League for a simple reason: he wanted a higher salary. In Young's first year in the junior league, he went 33–10 with an ERA of 1.62. He walked only 37 batters in 371 innings. Seven years later, Boston sold him to the Cleveland Naps, who in turn sold him to the Boston Braves in 1911. He retired from baseball following the 1911 season.

Legend claims that his arm never went bad. He stated many times that he quit baseball because he had put on too much weight. In his words, "I finally had to quit pitching because I became too portly. They all started to bunt on me and when the third baseman had to do my fielding for me it was time to quit."

He started 516 games in the National League and 390 in the American.

On October 4, 1890, he pitched both ends of a doubleheader and won both games. He won 13 consecutive games in 1904. He pitched all 21 innings of a game once, and didn't yield a single base on balls. One season, he allowed only 28 walks.

When Cy was old, he would criticize the pitchers who followed him. He said modern pitchers don't last as long because they waste too many pitches. On several occasions, Young said that pitchers tire themselves out because they are not familiar enough with opposing batting orders. In his day, Young claimed control was 99 percent of his success, and he knew exactly where to throw the ball to get the man out.

Cy Young's Control
Only 1.49 walks per 9 innings in his 22-year career
Led the league in walks per 9 innings 14 different seasons

What Was Cy Young Like as a Pitcher?

Cy Young seemed to be a control pitcher who used efficiency to gain results. He was Greg Maddux to Walter Johnson's Pedro Martinez or Randy Johnson. Like Maddux, Cy Young never led the league in strikeouts, but was always among the leaders in walks per nine innings (Maddux led the league six times). In 2002, Maddux became the only pitcher besides Cy Young to win as many as 15 games in 15 consecutive seasons. Maddux would extend his streak to 17 seasons in 2004. Is it harder to win 25 in 1901, or 15 in 2002? That's the judgment one must make in ranking Young against Maddux.

Of course, Cy picked up his nickname because of the speed of his pitches (like a "Cyclone"), and writers did talk about his blazing fastball. But Young really wasn't a strike-out pitcher, and the fastball probably looked a lot faster early in Young's career, when the distance from the pitching mound to the plate was only 50 feet. Young really bridged the gap between baseball's earliest days and "modern" baseball—defined mostly by play beginning in 1901, when the rules were more in line with today's.

What Was Cy Young Like as a Person?

In 1909, the *Washington Post* had a big story about Cy Young entitled "Cy Young, veteran pitcher, keeps in shape by sawing wood."

It was written by veteran reporter Elmer Bates, who was invited to Young's Ohio farm in the off-season. At the time, Young was getting ready for his 20th season, and would be attempting to win his 500th game (he had 489 wins). It is a fascinating account of what the 42-year-old man was like at the end of his career.

Cy leads the ideal farmer's life when the baseball season is not on. He does all his own work, such as chopping wood, milking cows, and this is his primary exercise. Occasionally, he plows, but as a rule there is no plowing to be done during the periods Cy spends at home. . . .

"Over there in the bookcase, pasted in a big scrapbook, is the score of every game I ever pitched, and all the hundreds of stories," said Cy. . . . In the living room are trophies and the cups—scores of them—that have been presented to Old Cy Young. . . .

The surrey is at the door waiting for the return trip to the railroad station. . . .

Cy and his wife get a lot of enjoyment out of hunting, and are experts with the gun. One of Cy Young's greatest joys is the all-night fox hunt. . . .

Cy does not hesitate to give a big part of the credit for his success to his wife. She is described as a typical farm girl and a splendid shot. Neighbors say she can ride any horse that ever lived, and that her aim is as good as a man's.

Cy Young was born in 1867—just after the Civil War—and lived for 88 years. He died peacefully in his rocking chair in 1955. A year later, baseball began honoring the best pitcher in the game with an award bearing the name of Cy Young.

He would be ranked even higher here if he'd played for more pennant winners. He played on only two in his career.

TOM SEAVER

I t is hard to believe that on November 17, 2004, baseball legend Tom Seaver turned 60 years old. For those people in their 40s, go ahead and take a deep breath and sit down someplace. For those too young to remember Tom Terrific as a pitcher, picture Roger Clemens.

Seaver was raised in Southern California, and attended USC. A selection of the Atlanta Braves in the January 1966 free-agent draft, Seaver was signed a month later for a reported $50,000, after USC had begun its baseball schedule. The violation forbade Atlanta from signing Seaver for three years. However, Seaver was screwed by the NCAA and forbidden from playing collegiately. An unprecedented draft was held for any major-league clubs willing to match Atlanta's offer. Three clubs—the Indians, Phillies, and Mets—participated. New York's name was chosen out of a hat.

He didn't look like most of the other players. He wore ties and was middle class. He didn't have the hardship that many contemporary players had growing up. He attended college, where he studied public relations. A year later, he was pitching in New York. As soon as he joined the Mets, he was proclaimed a star, and the best prospect in the short history of the franchise.

He had a style on the mound unlike many others of his time. He was intelligent, and had theories about pitching the way Ted Williams did about hitting. Sandy Koufax was Seaver's boyhood idol, and he knew Sandy's every mannerism. Seaver's baseball intellect served him well. He became the baseball world's most vocal person on the importance of a pitcher's leg power, relying on the muscles of his thighs and buttocks to launch his pitching motion. Seaver ended up his pitching motion with his right knee rubbing the ground.

Seaver broke down each aspect of the pitching motion. His main mantra: The point of pitching is to put 100 percent of your energy into the ball, but that's impossible to do, so the lower half of your body has to absorb that energy.

He was the Rookie of the Year in 1967, winning 16 games. One of his earliest memories of his rookie season was joining broadcaster Ralph Kiner, coach Yogi Berra, and right-fielder Ron Swoboda on a goodwill tour to Sing Sing prison. One guy asked Yogi to get him tickets when he got out—in 20 years. While the Mets were courting a captive audience, Seaver won 16 of the Mets' 61 victories in 1967. It was the most wins by a Mets pitcher since the team's inception in 1962.

The Mets improved to 73 wins in 1968, a .450 winning percentage. Seaver, meanwhile, won 57 percent of his decisions (16–12). They called him "Tom Terrific," or sometimes "the Franchise."

The greatest year in Mets history happened in large part due to Seaver. The team that had never before won as many games as they lost in a season went 100–62 and won the pennant. The first signs of the "Miracle Mets" came in July, when Seaver pitched a one-hitter against the first-place Cubs. Seaver flirted with a perfect game, but allowed a single to eighth-place hitter Jimmy Qualls with one out in the ninth.

In the second week of August, the Mets were still 9.5 games back of Chicago. The Mets then went 38–11 in their last 49 games to win the pennant.

Seaver went 25–7 to win his first Cy Young Award. He narrowly finished second to Willie McCovey for the MVP. His 2.21 ERA was fourth in the league. He pitched five shutouts and 18 complete games.

Mets in 1969

Tom Seaver's decisions	25–7	.781
All other games	75–55	.576

Mets in Seaver's first three years (1967–1969)

Tom Seaver's decisions	57–32	.640
All other games	177–220	.445

When the Mets fell back to earth and won only 83 games in 1970, Seaver remained his awesome self, winning 18. On April 20, he struck out 19 Padres, including 10 in a row to end the game. He signed a $91,000 contract before the 1971 season, which put him behind pitchers Bob Gibson, Juan Marichal, Denny McLain, and probably behind Sam McDowell and Dave McNally. That 91 grand bought the Mets this: Seaver's greatest season. He was 20–10 and led the league with a 1.76 ERA and 289 strikeouts. Tom Terrific was always the game's greatest bargain.

He put a face on the franchise. He had a personality and a point of view. He cared so deeply about the Vietnam War that he and his wife, Nancy, once took out a full-page ad in the *New York Times* to proclaim his opposition to the war and to plead for peace. He symbolically represented a generation—my generation. He showed us kids how to do more than "push off the pitching rubber."

The Mets had one more pennant-winning season in Seaver's career with them, 1973. Their slogan, coined by reliever Tug McGraw, was "Ya Gotta Believe." While the Mets were only 83–79, it was enough to win the National League East. Seaver won his second Cy Young Award, finishing 19–10, but he led the league with a 2.08 ERA, 18 complete games, and 251 strikeouts. He threw 290 innings, a career high. He was 19–10, but he lost twice that season by 1–0 scores, and also lost games 2–0, 2–1, and 3–2.

In the postseason, Seaver threw a memorable game at the Reds in Game 1 of the League Championship Series. He struck out 13, didn't walk a single batter, and took a 1–0 lead into the eighth inning before surrendering home runs to Pete Rose and Johnny Bench. Seaver won the Game 5 clincher, giving up only one earned run. After pitching in Game 5 of the National League Championship Series, Seaver couldn't pitch until Game 3 of the World Series against the Oakland A's. He struck out 12, but the Mets lost 3–2 in 11 innings. With the Mets leading three games to two, Yogi Berra started Seaver in Game 6 instead of holding him back for a potential seventh game. Oakland's Reggie Jackson got the best of Seaver, and the Mets lost 3–1.

Mets from 1970 to 1973

Tom Seaver's decisions	78–44	.639
All other games	253–256	.487

In Seaver's fourth, fifth, sixth, and seventh seasons, he single-handedly lifted a team that couldn't win half its games and made it a contender.

Mets After Seaver's First Seven Years

Tom Seaver's decisions	135–76	.640
All other Mets games	430–476	.474

In the seven-year stretch from 1967 to 1973, Seaver won 135 of the Mets' 565 victories, or about 24 percent.

Seaver had a bad season, his first, in 1974, due to a bad hip. He still won 50 percent of his decisions (11–11) when the rest of the team could not (60–80 in all other games).

Of course, the perfectionist Seaver had to answer the following season, and he did. In 1975, Seaver went 22–9 with a 2.38 ERA, and led the league with 243 strikeouts. He won 71 percent of his games for an 82–80 team that won 46 percent of the time when he wasn't pitching.

Seaver—on the precipice of free agency—used his commanding leverage to sign a big-money contract. He asked for a reported $800,000 over three years. That, plus his union activities and statements that he would play out his option and sign elsewhere, did not endear him to Mets management.

In the spring of 1975, the year before free agency, Seaver's contract was running out. He told M. Donald Grant he wanted to be baseball's highest-paid pitcher. He got it. The base pay was $225,000, with a bonus clause that kicked in after his 17th win giving Seaver $5,000 every fifth day, whether he pitched or not.

The Mets made a wise deal, as players had unprecedented leverage the following season with the advent of free agency. In 1976, the free-agent money hit the fan. No longer was Tom Seaver the highest-paid pitcher of all time. Other pitchers with far less ability were signing much fatter contracts.

Seaver, with two years left to run on his $225,000 contract, asked the Mets to renegotiate. Grant refused. Seaver asked to be traded. Grant finally obliged, and the Mets traded "the Franchise" on June 15, 1977, to the Cincinnati Reds. Had he waited, Seaver could have become a free agent at the end of the 1978 season.

The trade was devastating to New York baseball fans. Seaver was in the middle of a 21–6 season in 1977, and still at the top of his game. In June of 1978, Seaver finally pitched a no-hitter. In 1979, he was 16–6 with an ERA of 3.14. The Reds finished in first place, and lost the National League Championship Series to the Pirates. In a strike-shortened 1981 season, Seaver was 14–2 at the age of 36.

Tom slumped to a 5–13 mark in 1982, and the Reds traded Seaver back to the Mets for the 1983 season. In all, he had pitched well for the Reds, going 75–46 in 5.5 seasons.

To many people's surprise, he still had 47 victories left in his right arm. To most people's surprise, he didn't earn many of them in a Mets uniform. After going 9–14 in 1983, the White Sox drafted Seaver as compensation for losing Type-A free-agent Dennis Lamp to the Blue Jays. The Mets left Seaver off their protected list, assuming that no team would want him.

New to the American League, Seaver responded with a 15–11 season in 1984, and a 16–11 season in 1985. On August 4, 1985, at Yankee Stadium, Seaver pitched the White Sox to a 4–1 victory and became the 17th player in history with 300 victories. It was one of the most bizarre days in Yankee Stadium history—some of the 54,000 fans on hand for Phil Rizzuto Day were chanting the familiar "Let's Go Mets" cheer in the latter stages of a White Sox–Yankees game.

Seaver began 1986 as the Opening Day starter for the White Sox—his record 16th Opening Day start—but after he compiled a 2–6 record, the White Sox traded him to Boston. Seaver was close to retirement.

Meet the New Boss, Same as the Old Boss

The 1986 Red Sox had a bona fide ace on their staff, a youngster named Roger Clemens. At the time of the Seaver trade, Clemens was 14–0. In April of that year, he broke Seaver's record for strikeouts in a game, as Roger struck out 20 Seattle Mariners. It might have been spooky for Seaver to view Clemens, almost like looking at old photographs of himself. Clemens was bigger (three inches taller) and was possibly even more intimidating than the old veteran who was then third on the all-time strikeout list.

Seaver injured his ankle, preventing him from playing with the Red Sox against the Mets in the 1986 World Series.

Who's Better, Who's Best
Tom Seaver or Roger Clemens?

After the 2004 season, their won-lost totals looked like this:

Roger Clemens: 328–164
Tom Seaver: 311–205

Clemens had 4,317 strikeouts, compared to Seaver's 3,640. Seaver, however, had thrown 289 more innings than Clemens. Clemens had 8.6 strikeouts per nine innings; Seaver had 6.8.

Does Seaver want to put his 2.89 ERA against the Rocket Man's? Clemens had a 3.18 ERA. Hold on, though. Clemens spent most of his career pitching in hitter-friendly Fenway Park. Seaver spent most of his career pitching in a pitchers' park (Shea Stadium). Roger pitched against designated hitters. Seaver pitched 18 years in the National League, where pitchers had to take their turn at bat. Clemens's career ERA is better than Seaver's when adjusted to the league average.

Seaver won three Cy Young awards. Roger won seven.

Seaver was 1–2 with a 2.70 ERA in four World Series starts; Clemens was 3–0 with a 1.90 ERA in his seven World Series starts.

Clemens did everything Seaver did as a young man, and then did everything better as an ancient player in his 40s.

Seaver couldn't play in the 1986 Series. Clemens threw seven good innings in the 2003 World Series, and left the road game to thunderous applause, as fans saluted what they believed would be the last time Clemens took the mound.

Seaver wasn't happy with his performance in the spring, and retired prior to the 1987 season as he attempted a comeback with his "hometown" team, the Mets. Clemens "unretired" to pitch—quite successfully—for his "hometown" team of Houston in 2004.

I loved Seaver when he played. I learned from him when I worked with him, and found him among the most enjoyable people to be around that I ever encountered.

Clemens is better and deserves to be ranked ahead of Tom Terrific.

CAL RIPKEN JR.

Cal Ripken Jr. viewed his father as the inspiration for his incredible consecutive-game streak. When Cal was 16, his dad hooked a snowplow to a tractor in an effort to help clear the neighborhood. The tractor stalled, and when the old man tried to get it going, a crank flew off and hit him in the forehead. Cal Sr. pressed an oily rag to his head in an effort to stop the bleeding while his scared son got him into the family car. But instead of driving to a hospital, Cal Sr. told his son to drive home. There, the son watched his dad put on some butterfly bandages, then saw him head back to the plow to finish the job.

"When I get the feeling that things are a little low, that I need a little motivation to work on my hitting, I visualize the tractor-crank story. That pushes me," said Cal during the middle of his consecutive-game streak. "I think of that story more than any other. Sometimes I'm beating my head against the wall and not getting any results at the plate, and I'm wondering if my effort is worth it all. That story sums it all up for me."

Cal Ripken Jr. was born not far from Baltimore in 1960. His father was a lifer in the Orioles organization, bouncing around as a minor-league manager. He finally made it to the majors as a coach under Orioles manager Earl Weaver in 1976. Ripken was drafted in the second round by the Orioles in 1978, and Cal Jr. made the big club briefly at the end of the 1981 season.

Earlier in that 1981 season, the future iron man would play in the longest game ever in professional ball. The game started on April 19, 1981, and was finished on June 23. The score was 2–2 after 32 innings between Pawtucket and Rochester when the players were sent home at 4:07 A.M. The suspended game resumed two months later, and Pawtucket scored in the bottom of the 33rd inning to give Bob Ojeda the win. Wade Boggs and Cal Ripken combined to go 6–25 in that game.

Earl Weaver turned the 6′4″ Ripken into a shortstop, and Cal became the tallest shortstop in major-league history. In 1982, Ripken became the Rookie of the Year on the strength of his 28 homers and 93 RBI. On May 30, 1982, he started at shortstop. That was the beginning of the streak.

The Streak

You can't write too many words about Cal Ripken Jr. without talking about the consecutive-game streak. It would be like writing about Dick Clark's career and not talking about New Year's Eve. Here it goes.

The streak began on May 30, 1982, and lasted until Ripken pulled the plug on it in 1998 after 2,632 consecutive games played. He played the first 904 of those games from start to finish, playing every single inning of every single game. That was more than five seasons of games. His father, then the manager of the Orioles, suggested to a reluctant Cal that he take some late innings off.

He had some close calls. He sprained an ankle in 1985. He twisted his knee in 1993. He suffered a broken nose taking an All-Star Game team picture in 1996. Through all the injuries, he continued to play.

The big number Ripken was focused on, of course, was Lou Gehrig's 2,130 consecutive games played. That streak had ended only when Gehrig was stricken with a disease that would eventually kill him. Ripken broke Gehrig's record in early September 1995. He had played over 99 percent of the innings, and was one of the few bright spots for baseball just months after a labor strike had cost the sport the 1994 World Series. When Ripken broke Gehrig's record, he received a 25-minute standing ovation. President Clinton was in attendance. Joe DiMaggio (a teammate of Gehrig) was there as well.

Ripken played 2,216 games of his streak at shortstop, with 29 different double-play partners, before begrudgingly moving to third base. In the 13 years of his streak, baseball had more than 3,600 instances of a player going on the disabled list.

Ripken also endured some criticism of the streak. At times he was a slave to the streak, unable to rest or heal sufficiently. It was counterproductive to the team as well. The Orioles couldn't encourage, showcase, or work in young shortstops. Managers—particularly Davey Johnson, who took over in 1996 and shifted Ripken to third base for Mike Bordick—couldn't manage the way they wanted.

At one point, major-league teams were going to field "replacement" teams made up of players not in the Players Union to begin the 1995 season. Well, all but the Orioles, whose owner, Peter Angelos, made it clear the O's would rather forfeit games than end Ripken's streak. "The Streak" was big business to the Orioles owner, but bad baseball to Orioles managers.

Ken Singleton (Ripken's teammate, 1982–1984): "I don't think it is right for fans to remember Cal Ripken Jr. just for the streak. He did manage to hit over 400 home runs and get 3,000 hits. He was also a well-schooled baseball player right from the beginning. He rarely made mistakes on the bases or in the field. If he did, they happened only once. Cal is probably the strongest player I played with in my career. Both physically and mentally. The 'streak' demanded great physical and mental capabilities. Baseball can be a grind. It didn't bother Cal."

Ripken was selected to the 1999 All-Century Team, and I couldn't disagree more with the selection. I don't believe Cal is one of the two best shortstops in the game's history. Honus Wagner dominated baseball for many years. Since 1999, one has to look at Alex Rodriguez's achievements as far superior to Rip's.

Ripken had an MVP season in 1983, at the age of 22. That season, the only one of his 21 that he played in the World Series, he batted .318 with 27 home runs and 102 RBI.

In the World Series, he managed only three singles in 21 at-bats, a .167 average. If not for the O's defeating the White Sox in the 1983 League Championship Series, Rip might have been like Ernie Banks, who played his entire career with one team but failed to make it to a single World Series.

Even Banks might have had more support around him in the lineup than Ripken. Eddie Murray was the only consistent threat for the Orioles besides Cal in the mid- to late '80s. Teams would simply not let Ripken beat them.

Check this out. Cal Ripken had three good seasons in a row, beginning in 1983. This is why:

1983 Orioles, 98–64
Eddie Murray: .306, 33 HR, 111 RBI

1984 Orioles, 85–77
Eddie Murray: .306, 29 HR, 110 RBI

1985 Orioles, 83–78
Eddie Murray: .297, 31 HR, 124 RBI

Murray, who was a few years older than Ripken, began falling off after 1985—the burden of carrying the Birds too great for his switch-hitting bat. The Orioles kept Ripken Jr. off the free-agent market, promoting his brother Billy to play second base and hiring Cal Sr. to manage—but even with Cal happy, the team was terrible:

Orioles Team Batting Average (14 teams in American League)
1987: 12th in the league
1988: 14th
1989: 12th
1990: 13th

Is it any wonder that Cal's numbers dropped?

Cal Ripken Jr.'s Batting Average, 1987–1990
1987: .252
1988: .264
1989: .257
1990: .250

Then, in 1991, Ripken turned in a .323 season with 34 homers and 114 RBI. He won the MVP Award, despite playing for a 67–95 sixth-place team. There was no one else on his team that drove in as many as 71 runs. Rip had a career-best (and league-high) 85 extra-base hits that year. He won his first (and only) Gold Glove that year for fielding. It was a truly Hall of Fame season, and it kept critics of the streak at bay for another two years, when the streak would be so mature that it was like the man-eating plant in *Little Shop of Horrors*.

Ripken followed his great 1991 season by batting .251 in 1992 and .257 in 1993. The man now had six seasons out of seven that were, er, ordinary. He and the team got better and made the postseason in 1996 for the first time in 13 years.

The Orioles lost the League Championship Series in 1996 and 1997, falling to the Yankees in five games and the Indians in six.

Rick Sutcliffe (Ripken's teammate, 1992–1993): "The obvious comparison to Ripken is A-Rod. But I played with another middle infielder that was comparable to Ripken—Ryne Sandberg. They were both a lot alike. They changed the way teams stocked those positions to where bigger guys could prove they were athletic enough to cover the distance they had to play. You had to see Sandberg every day to appreciate him. He made no mistakes offensively or defensively. Ripken did so much, too, to help his team win. He not only turned double plays, but he sometimes positioned outfielders, and often helped the pitchers. He was a real captain on the field."

Would Cal be ranked in the top 100 if he didn't have the record for consecutive games? Yes, of course he would. To me, the streak doesn't add much to (or detract any from) his overall ranking. Ripken played 3,001 games—a total only surpassed by Rose, Yaz, Aaron, Henderson, Cobb, Eddie Murray, and Musial.

Ripken is most like Carl Yastrzemski, who played his entire career for one team and delivered over 400 home runs and 3,000 hits. There's only one player—Stan Musial—who had more hits while playing for just one team in his career.

Yastrzemski was dominant in 1967, and was the MVP of the league. Of course, he played 22 other seasons and had more seasons batting under .300 than anyone in baseball history. Ripken was a two-time MVP, with a peak value achieved by few others; but he also had a number of subpar seasons.

Cal showed up for work every single day. When the tractor stalls, and the wrench hits you in the face, it's still no excuse not to get the job done.

45

TONY GWYNN

He won eight batting titles, and he didn't do it in the early 1900s when there were only a few good teams and fewer superstar athletes. Gwynn was the best hitter in the National League for almost two decades, and the greatest San Diego Padres player of all time. His studious approach to hitting and dedication to his craft were unparalleled.

The San Diego Padres came into existence in 1969, and in the days before free agency, it took some time for expansion teams to get competitive. The Padres finished last their first six seasons. They first reached .500 in their 10th season (1978). The Padres' first great player, Dave Winfield, played with San Diego from 1972 to 1980 before heading to New York as a free agent. Winfield was a star college basketball player at the University of Minnesota, and was drafted into the NBA. When Winfield left the Padres after eight seasons, San Diego used their third pick in the 1981 baseball draft and selected a junior out of San Diego State University. This college kid was not only a good outfielder, but he was setting records as a basketball player, and was to be drafted by the NBA's (then) San Diego Clippers. Tony Gwynn chose baseball, as Winfield did.

Gwynn played 20 years, and people remember him as pudgy, stocky, or, okay, fat. Most of us tend to (er, how do we put this delicately?) put on weight from our 20s to our 40s. Well, Barry Bonds put on muscle, but that is the exception. In Gwynn's early years, however, he was not heavy. He was fast, good for 40 stolen bases a year. He roamed the outfield with style and grace, and has the Gold Gloves to prove it. Oh yes, he could always hit.

He made his major-league debut in July of 1982 at the age of 22, and 1983 was his first full season and the first of 19 consecutive seasons that Gwynn batted at least .300. In 1984, the Padres finally finished first in the National League West. They had signed free-agent relief ace Goose Gossage, and 24-year-old Gwynn batted .351. San Diego won 92 games and defeated the Chicago Cubs in the playoffs. NBC execs must have been dying as Gwynn batted .368 in the NLCS, and the small-market Padres beat the beloved Cubbies in a deciding fifth game that flushed half of the ratings points and most of the interest for the upcoming World Series.

Tony met the Tigers (that was the year they were gr-r-reat!) in the 1984 World Series, and Detroit wrapped it up in five games, holding Gwynn to five singles in the five games.

The funny thing about Gwynn's career was that he never got more dominant than that 1984 season. In that magical year, he finished third in the MVP voting. He never again finished in the top five. You can call him consistent if you want. I prefer to think of Gwynn as some sort of one-trick pony, able to accomplish things with his hitting that no one this side of Wade Boggs could dream about. Tony Gwynn used a bat the way Eric Clapton uses a guitar.

The amazing thing about Gwynn's career was that he never had a drop-off in his production. In 1987, when everyone hit home runs, Gwynn hit just seven in 589 at-bats. Tony did bat .370, steal 56 bases, and score 119 runs that year. In 1994, he batted .394 before the season shut down due to an impasse in the collective bargaining. In 1997, at the age of 37, he batted .372 with 17 home runs and 119 runs batted in. In 1998, he led the Padres back to the World Series for the first time in 14 years. He never really had a bad year.

When I think of Tony, my first flash is that he was the first player to extensively use computers and videotape. He had the Padres install more new technology than NASA, and it benefited not only Gwynn, but his teammates. Soon, most teams would be slaves to videotape. Should there be an asterisk next to Gwynn's name because Ted Williams and Stan Musial didn't have the luxury of their team setting up an elaborate video system where they could watch each of their at-bats, and learn pitchers' habits and tendencies?

I also think about the 1989 All-Star Game in Anaheim. I was working for NBC, and they hired ex-President Ronald Reagan to "announce" the first inning with Vin Scully. Reagan had been out of office just seven months, and was still mentally sharp (although physically hurting, as he had just fallen off his horse). My bosses instructed me the day before the game to call the first few batters in each team's lineup to get some personal stories for President Reagan to use. Of the eight players I called, it was only Gwynn who seemed excited to comply. He and his wife were only too happy to call me back and give me what I needed. I told him to take a couple of pitches so Reagan could get the stories in. It seemed that Gwynn approached everything with a careful, studious professionalism. (Just an aside: Reagan did quite well, although Scully—who practically lived in Dodgers Stadium—almost fainted when the president gushed about Anaheim Stadium being the finest baseball stage in the country.)

The Pads' '98 season probably saved the franchise from being moved, and served as the impetus for the new stadium that houses the Padres today. This time Tony ran into the record 114-win Yankees team (they too were gr-r-reat!), and the Padres were swept in the World Series. The 38-year-old Gwynn chewed up Yankees pitching, however, and batted .500 (8–16) in the Series. Seven of the hits were singles, but he did manage his first Series home run.

Who's Better, Who's Best
Tony Gwynn or Mike Schmidt?

Mike Schmidt's career, to name one Hall of Famer who may have been a better hitter, overlapped Gwynn's career in the 1980s. Gwynn's career batting average was 71 points higher than Schmidt's in a similar number of plate appearances. Gwynn's a better batter, right? They should name a salad after him (replacing the Cobb salad?). Well, not so fast.

Schmidt's career on-base average was virtually identical to Gwynn's, just based on the fact that Schmidt walked 717 more times than Padre Tony. Gwynn had 907 more hits, but the walks moves them closer together.

Of course, consider the following: Gwynn had 2,378 singles among his hits (76 percent of his hits). Schmidt had only 1,219 singles (55 percent of his hits).

Schmidt had more total bases than Gwynn, despite 907 fewer hits! The Phillies infielder had a slugging percentage that towers over Gwynn's (.527 to .459).

Let's recap. Gwynn has a batting average that is 71 points better than Schmidt's. Gwynn and Schmidt have a virtual tie in on-base average. Schmidt has a slugging average that is 68 points better than Gwynn's.

Which player do you want on your team in the late innings of a close game? It might be that Tony is the choice. Which player do you want on your team for an entire season, or number of seasons? It's apparent that Schmidt would accumulate many more total bases, based on his slugging percentage. Never mind the fact that Schmidt was an outstanding defensive player at third base—a demanding defensive position. Schmidt is my choice over Gwynn.

Not that either Schmidt or Gwynn can compare to the great Barry Bonds. Bonds combined the batting average of Gwynn (at least, late in Barry's career) with the slugging excellence of Schmidt.

A Better Analogy

Tony Gwynn and Ichiro Suzuki and Wade Boggs "Who is the best hitter you've ever seen, Dad?" asks my son Heath. The temptation is to respond with Ichiro, the Japanese player who has come to the Seattle Mariners and pounded out 924 hits in his first four major-league seasons. Of course, I realize that Barry Bonds is the only answer I could give. It got me thinking, though. Who was the best batter I saw BB (Before Barry)?

Then I remember Wade Boggs and Tony Gwynn.

Suzuki got a lot of attention for his record-breaking 257 hits in 2004. It's easy to forget what Tony Gwynn and Wade Boggs accomplished in their first four major-league seasons.

First Four Full Seasons	Batting Average	On-Base Pct.	Slugging Pct.
Ichiro Suzuki (2001–04)	.339	.384	.443
Wade Boggs (1983–86)	.352	.438	.466
Tony Gwynn (1984–87)	.341	.400	.457

Suzuki had 924 hits, but combined it with only 183 walks in his four seasons. Boggs, on the other hand, had 850 hits and 382 walks. Which leadoff batter got on base more?

Boggs and Gwynn were very comparable batters. Each played exactly 2,440 games in their careers. Gwynn hit for a higher average (.338 to .328). Gwynn had a higher slugging percentage (.459 to .443). Gwynn stole 319 bases (to Boggs's 24). Gwynn struck out only 434 times (Boggs struck out 745 times).

In fact, Gwynn got his 3,000th hit on August 6, 1999. The next day, Wade Boggs became Mr. 3,000.

Gwynn is ahead of Boggs in this book for several reasons. He was a better baserunner and fielder; and he didn't have the benefit of Boggs's ballpark or teammates.

Tony Gwynn won eight batting titles, and finished second in 1993 and third in two other years. Only two players (Ty Cobb and Nap Lajoie) got their 3,000th hit faster than Gwynn.

Before Barry Bonds, my answer to the question about the greatest batter I've ever seen would have been Tony Gwynn. There's even a 1997 book, written by a professor of biostatistics at the University of North Carolina, that comes to the conclusion that Gwynn is baseball's all-time best hitter (Michael J. Schell's *Baseball's All-Time Best Hitters*).

To buy into Schell's theory, one has to buy the fact that the top hitters in baseball are ranked by batting average (which he adjusts for talent pool, longevity, and ballpark effects). His means-adjusted numbers don't work for home runs, doubles, or anything but batting average. Ty Cobb had vastly more doubles and triples than Tony, and that makes him a vastly better batsman than Gwynn.

That being said, Gwynn is ranked ahead of the other great "batting average" specialists, players like Boggs and Suzuki and Rod Carew.

46

EDDIE MATHEWS

He played in "the home of the Braves" when they were located in Boston. He played in "the home of the Braves" when they were in Milwaukee. And he was a player and later a manager for the Atlanta Braves.

Play ball. Mathews was born in Texarkana, Texas, but when he was six years old in 1937 his family moved to Santa Barbara, California, where he developed into a star high school player. He was signed by the Boston Braves in 1949 a day after his high school graduation. He was a left-handed-hitting third baseman and a power hitter who belted towering blasts. He modeled his swing after Ted Williams's swing. It's no wonder that an aging Ty Cobb once said of Mathews, "I've only known three or four perfect swings in my time. This lad has one of them."

Right out of the gate, Eddie Mathews began reaching the Boston and Milwaukee fences with regularity. He hit 25 homers as a 20-year-old rookie, and belted 190 home runs during his first five seasons. No one in baseball hit more homers in the five-year period from 1952 to 1956.

Mathews was the perfect player for the Braves. He was the star, the building block that owner Lou Perini had when he moved his franchise from Boston to Milwaukee on March 18, 1953. It was the first franchise shift in the National League in 50 years, and started a chain of upheaval which saw the Athletics, Browns, Giants, and Dodgers move to new cities within a few years. Milwaukee hungered for major-league baseball, and all the team owners took note.

Mathews teamed with Hank Aaron, who joined the Braves in 1954, and together they became the greatest home-run-hitting duo since Babe Ruth and Lou Gehrig. Aaron wrote in his 1991 autobiography that Mathews liked to have a good time and was probably the hardest-living guy on the team. He wrote that Eddie would have fit right in on the Yankees, with stay-out-late guys like Mickey Mantle and Whitey Ford and Billy Martin.

In 1953, in only his second season, Mathews was on pace with Babe Ruth's single-season home run record as late as August 31. Ruth hit 17 home runs in September 1927 to wind up with his 60. Mathews would wind up with 47.

There was no way Mathews could seriously challenge the Babe playing in Milwaukee's County Stadium, considered a pitcher-friendly park because of the dimensions. Mathews set the National League record for road home runs in 1953. Even if he hadn't hit 60 homers playing in a different home park, he sure as heck would have reached 50—probably more than once.

Mathews played the majority of his career in Milwaukee. He played his first season in Boston. He only played his home games in Atlanta one season (1966), and by then he was 34 years old and in his 15th season.

How much of a disadvantage did Mathews face by playing most of his home games at Milwaukee's County Stadium? Consider this: When Ken Griffey Jr. hit his 500th home run in June 2004, it upped the number of members of the "500 Home Run Club" to 20. Of those 20 players, Mathews hit the fewest home runs in his home park (just 238). Mathews hit 46 percent of his home runs at home and 54 percent on the road. If he'd played in Brooklyn's Ebbets Field (a mere 301 feet down the line in right field) his home run total would have been higher by as many as 100 home runs. In a more neutral stadium (harder than Ebbets Field, but more conducive than County Stadium), one would think his career homer total would be 35 to 45 homers greater.

He often hit in front of Aaron in the lineup, but also had seasons where he batted behind the Braves' right fielder. They combined to hit 863 home runs as teammates. That's more than any other home run tandem in major-league history. Babe Ruth and Lou Gehrig combined for 859 with the Yankees. Of the 863 blasts, Aaron hit 442 and Mathews 421. They were especially the Dynamic Duo in 1957, the year the Braves won their only World Series championship. That was Aaron's only MVP season, and it was Hank who hit an 11th-inning home run versus St. Louis to clinch the pennant for Milwaukee. Aaron hit .393 with three home runs in the World Series against the Yankees, for good measure. Aaron needed help to win his ring, however, and Mathews provided it.

The Yankees were up two games to one and had taken a lead in the top of the 10th inning in the fourth game. Leading off the bottom of the inning, the Braves' Nippy Jones convinced umpire Augie Donatelli he was hit by a pitch by showing him black shoe polish on the ball. Following a sacrifice and a game-tying single, Mathews turned the series around with a walk-off home run, tying the Series at 2–2. In the seventh game, the Yankees trailed 5–0 with the bases loaded and two outs when Moose Skowron smacked a hard grounder down the third-base line. Mathews made a tremendous backhanded stab that nearly spun him around. He lunged, tagged third, and the game and Series were over. He saved a three-run double, which would have sent the tying run to the plate. Mathews always called that force-out his proudest moment in baseball.

Commissioner Bud Selig: "When Eddie Mathews came to the Braves, he was just a 21-year-old kid from Santa Barbara with a classic swing. He became a great hero to the people in Milwaukee. He was always a feared slugger, but what people don't realize is that he made himself a good fielder. That backhand play he made to end the World Series was outstanding, and typical of one of the toughest competitors of all time. There is no question that Mathews was one of the all-time greats."

Mathews's best season was 1959, when he finished second in the MVP Award voting for a second time. The Braves (who had won National League pennants in 1957 and 1958) finished in a tie with the Dodgers. Los Angeles won a best-of-three playoff series to advance to the World Series.

1959 N.L. MVP Candidates

Eddie Mathews	Hank Aaron	Ernie Banks
.306 (9th in N.L.)	.355 (1st)	.304 (10th)
46 HR (1st)	39 HR (3rd)	45 HR (2nd)
114 RBI (5th)	123 RBI (3rd)	143 RBI (1st)
118 runs (3rd)	116 runs (4th)	97 runs (8th)
.593 slugging pct. (3rd)	.636 slugging pct. (1st)	.596 slugging pct. (2nd)

Mathews, Aaron, and Banks all ranked in the top three in home runs and slugging percentage. Mathews and Aaron played on a first-place team, and Banks played on a sixth-place team with a losing record.

1959 N.L. MVP Voting
1. Banks: 10 first-place votes, 232 points
2. Mathews: 5 first-place votes, 189 points
3. Aaron: 2 first-place votes, 174 points

Obviously, Mathews and Aaron took votes away from each other, and Banks, who had a wonderful season playing shortstop, a demanding defensive position, took the MVP.

The "Happy Days" that Milwaukee and Mathews enjoyed in the 1950s slowly declined. Following the 1965 season, the Braves moved to Atlanta. By 1966, the Braves' first in Atlanta, Mathews was down to 16 home runs and 53 RBI. The Braves traded Mathews to the Houston Astros following the season, despite the fact that Eddie had 493 career home runs at that point—all with the same organization.

Mathews went reluctantly to Houston, and hit his 500th home run against the Giants and their Hall of Fame pitcher Juan Marichal on July 14, 1967. Although he joined a very exclusive 500-home-run club, achieving it in an Astros uniform took much of the luster off it. He was 35 years old at the time, and one of the oldest players in the league. In August, the Astros sent him to the Detroit Tigers, who needed a big bat for their pennant chase and hoped to catch lightning in a bottle with Mathews. Although the Tigers would fall just short in 1967, Mathews would play a bit role (he had just 52 at-bats and just 11 hits the entire 1968 season) on Detroit's 1968 world championship team.

Mathews retired with 512 home runs, one of the first seven players in history to hit 500 homers. He hit 486 home runs as a third baseman, the record until Mike Schmidt broke it a generation later.

Who's Better, Who's Best
Eddie Mathews or Mickey Mantle?
- Eddie Mathews was born October 13, 1931, in Texarkana, Texas.
- Mickey Mantle was born October 20, 1931, in Commerce, Oklahoma.

- Eddie Mathews hit 512 home runs in 2,391 games.
- Mickey Mantle hit 536 home runs in 2,401 games.

Following the 1967 season, Mantle had 518 home runs and Mathews had 509. They both played last in 1968.

Who's Better, Who's Best
Eddie Mathews or Mike Schmidt?
Schmidt was a better player than Mathews, as was Mantle. But Mathews didn't embarrass himself in any comparison.

Schmidt is generally considered the greatest third baseman of all time. He was better than Mathews, but not by much.

	Games	AB	HR	Walks	Batting Avg.	On-Base Avg.	Slugging Pct.
Schmidt	2,404	8,352	548	1,507	.267	.380	.527
Mathews	2,391	8,537	512	1,444	.271	.376	.509

Both Schmidt and Mathews played in three different World Series. Both had horrendous slumps in the World Series (Schmidt had a 1–20 Series versus the Orioles in 1983; Mathews had a 4–25 Series versus the Yankees in 1958). Fans in Milwaukee will never forget Mathews's contributions to their only Series win in 1957. Fans in Philadelphia will never forget Schmidt's contributions in 1980.

Eddie Mathews was not as good a third baseman as Schmidt. The other third baseman I rank ahead of Mathews is George Brett. Brett, like Schmidt, was better than Mathews both offensively and defensively. Brett was a batting champ with a tremendous amount of extra-base hits. Mathews was better than his contemporaries like Al Rosen and Ken Boyer and Brooks Robinson. He was better than the men who came before him, like Pie Traynor.

He wasn't ranked ahead of most third basemen because of his defense. He was ranked so high because he protected Hank Aaron in the lineup. He made Aaron better, the same way Gehrig made Ruth better. Mathews wasn't in Gehrig's class, but Eddie was in a class with or above Buck Leonard (who batted behind Josh Gibson), Willie McCovey (who batted behind Willie Mays), and Sam Crawford (who batted behind Ty Cobb).

STEVE CARLTON

Steve Carlton had one of the most devastating pitches that any hurler in major-league history has had at their disposal. When Carlton added a slider (which was thrown almost as fast as his fastball, but broke down late against right-handed batters) to his repertoire, he became one of baseball's greatest pitchers—certainly one of the five greatest left-handed throwers.

Since 1925, the major leagues have not gone a single year without one of the following five nominees for greatest left-handed pitcher in baseball history being active.

Lefty Grove began his major-league career in 1925, and soon was the dominant left-handed pitcher in baseball. He didn't depart until 1941. The next season, Warren Spahn began getting major-league hitters out. Spahn pitched into the mid-1960s, but stayed past his prime. Fortunately, lefty Sandy Koufax came onto the scene in 1955. Although Sandy needed a few years of a learning curve (and a devastating curveball), he carried the mantle of the ace lefty until arm problems forced his early retirement in 1966. The Cardinals had a teenager named Steve Carlton start a few games in 1965, and he stayed for 329 victories and didn't retire until the 1988 season. That was long enough for an Expos rookie named Randy Johnson to debut.

The Five Greatest Lefties
Lefty Grove: 300 wins
Warren Spahn: 363 wins
Sandy Koufax: 165 wins
Steve Carlton: 329 wins
Randy Johnson: 246 wins

That's more than 1,400 victories and no less than 33 seasons of 20-plus victories. When I looked at their individual careers, I saw definite patterns.

First 20-Win Season

Grove: 27 years old

Spahn: 26 years old

Koufax: 27 years old

Carlton: 26 years old

Johnson: 33 years old

Record for Season at Age 25

Grove	10–12	4.75 ERA
Spahn	8–5	2.94 ERA
Koufax	18–13	3.52 ERA (8–13, 3.91 at age 24)
Carlton	10–19	3.73 ERA
Johnson	7–13	4.82 ERA
Total	53–62, winning percentage of .461	

Record at Age 30

Grove	28–5	2.54 ERA
Spahn	22–14	2.98 ERA
Koufax	27–9	1.73 ERA
Carlton	15–14	3.56 ERA
Johnson	13–6	3.19 ERA
Total	105–48, winning percentage of .686	

Record at Age 37

Grove	17–9	3.02 ERA
Spahn	22–11	3.07 ERA
Koufax	retired	
Carlton	23–11	3.10 ERA
Johnson	21–6	2.49 ERA
Total	83–37, winning percentage of .691	

To say all left-handers develop late is a generalization. These five certainly took their time. Grove changed his delivery, and found his control. Koufax took the advice of a backup catcher, took something off his fastball, and found his control. Casey Stengel passed off Spahn in 1942, doubting his courage after Spahn wouldn't throw at a hitter. Carlton, too, overcame some early career wildness.

Does Carlton really belong in the company of Grove and Spahn and Koufax? I believe he certainly does.

Just compare him to the other great pitchers of his time. Carlton's 1972 season matches up with any pitcher (Walter Johnson included) for a single season. But he was far from a one-year wonder. Lefty Carlton won more games than Nolan Ryan, Tom Seaver, Ferguson Jenkins, Jim Palmer, Bob Feller, Bob Gibson, or Juan Marichal. Carlton had a better career ERA than Feller and Jenkins.

Carlton threw 55 shutouts, which was more than Palmer, Marichal, Jenkins, Whitey Ford, Feller, or Koufax threw.

Lefty started 709 games, one of the highest totals of all time. If a pitcher started 35 games a season for 20 years, he still wouldn't have reached 709 starts.

He started his first World Series game in 1967, and his next in 1980. He lasted 24 years in the majors, a mark for pitchers topped only by Nolan Ryan, Tommy John, Jim Kaat, and Charlie Hough.

He had an amazingly long career, and he pitched into his 40s. He didn't pitch very effectively, however. After the 1984 season, he turned 40 years old in December, and had a career record of 313–207. That's a winning percentage of .602. In his last four seasons, Carlton pitched for the Phillies, Giants, White Sox, Indians, and Twins. He won 16 games those final four seasons and lost 37, dropping his career winning percentage to .574.

The Cy Youngs

Steve Carlton won four Cy Young awards, and was close to winning in two other seasons. He won 23 or more games in a season four times, and each time was rewarded with the Cy Young Award.

In 1972, Carlton won the pitching equivalent of the Triple Crown, leading the league in wins, strikeouts, and ERA. He won 46 percent of the Phillies victories that season; the Phillies could manage only 59 wins despite getting 27 from Carlton. In that season, Carlton had a 15-game winning streak, eight shutouts, and an incredible 30 complete games. He also struck out 310 batters that season, becoming only the second National Leaguer (Koufax was first) to ever strike out that many in a single season. That season earned him the Hickok Belt as the top professional athlete of the year.

While Carlton never equaled that 1972 season, he did have three other years that were close. In 1977, he won 23 games and pitched 17 complete ones. In 1980—the only year the Phillies ever won the World Series—Lefty went 24–9, and then won two big games in the World Series. In 1982, he was 23–11 at the age of 37, throwing 19 complete games.

I'm not sure he shouldn't have won the Cy Young Award for the strike-shortened 1981 season, when he was 13–4. He finished third in the voting that season, preventing him from winning a fifth Cy Young (and three straight).

Carlton wasn't a rags-to-riches story like many of the other legends in this book. He was born in late 1944 in Miami, Florida. He played Little League and American Legion ball, and pitched at Miami-Dade Community College in 1963. He was signed by the St. Louis Cardinals as a skinny kid who didn't look like he would ever hold the record (however temporarily) for most career strikeouts.

He made his major-league debut in 1965 (Pete Rose got the first hit off of him), and earned a spot in the St. Louis rotation by the end of the 1966 season. He won 14 games in his first full season in 1967, even earning the Game 5 start against the Red Sox in the World Series. He pitched six innings, gave up only three hits, two walks, and zero earned runs—but lost the game on an unearned run.

The young Carlton had put the Cardinals into position to win the World Series by winning 14 games that summer, many after superstar ace Bob Gibson broke his leg in July. Gibson returned in time to win three games in the World Series.

Carlton got off to a fast start in 1968, and even started the All-Star Game for the National League (ahead of Gibson, Drysdale, Seaver, and Marichal). He pitched poorly down the stretch, and didn't earn a start in the World Series against the Tigers, however. It was after that 1968 season that Carlton developed his nasty slider.

He started to have greater success in 1969, winning 17 games and striking out 210 batters. On September 16, he struck out a then-record 19 batters in a game—but lost the game to the Miracle Mets when Ron Swoboda hit a pair of two-run home runs.

Carlton held out for a raise and missed spring training in 1970. He had a lost season, winning only 10 of 29 decisions. When Carlton had a 20-win season in 1971, he held out for a $10,000 raise and the Cardinals wouldn't budge. They traded him to the Phillies for starting pitcher Rick Wise. Carlton then became the greatest pitcher in Philadelphia Phillies history, anchoring their staff for 14 seasons.

Winningest Pitchers in 1970s
1. 186 Jim Palmer
2. 184 Gaylord Perry
3. 178 Steve Carlton, Ferguson Jenkins, and Tom Seaver

Carlton found peace of mind, revenge, and a devotion to physical conditioning in Philly. He stopped talking to the press for 15 years, even when he won his 300th game. He probably pioneered the use of physical fitness for pitching performance. It was when the press began questioning Carlton about his fitness regime that he began his personal boycott of reporters.

It wasn't just the inner peace, the media boycott, or the physical conditioning. Carlton preferred to pitch on three days' rest, and got his opportunity with the Phillies. The Phillies were more than happy to accommodate Carlton's request for a four-man rotation. In Carlton's first 11 seasons with the Phillies, he led the league in games started four times, and was second two other seasons.

Carlton also had his own personal catcher. The Phillies acquired Tim McCarver in 1975, and McCarver, who had been Carlton's teammate in St. Louis, backed up regular catcher Bob Boone. By 1977, Carlton had McCarver catch every game. That was Carlton's best season since his 1972 career year. In the Philadelphia clubhouse, they said if Steve Carlton sneezed, Tim McCarver wiped his nose. If Steve Carlton got an itch, then Tim McCarver scratched it. When Steve Carlton stubbed his toe, it was McCarver that hollered, "Ouch!" McCarver often said, "When we die, they'll probably bury us 60 feet and 6 inches apart." That's the distance between home plate and the pitcher's mound.

Tim McCarver: "It's not that Steve didn't like Boone. It's just that he felt more comfortable with me. It dated back to when we were teammates with the St. Louis Cardinals. We were friends who hunted together. People kept comparing Steve to that great year in 1972, and Steve himself started doing it. It began to psych him. You can be consistently good but you can't be consistently fabulous."

Carlton pitched in World Series competition early in his career, and very late. He started in the 1967 Series, and in the 1983 Series. The 1987 Twins left him off the postseason roster, so he didn't get to pitch against the Cardinals in the World Series that year (which would have been a romantic and ironic way to end his career). Of course, the fact that the Twins were 1–8 in the nine games he pitched in that season made that an easy decision for Minnesota skipper Tom Kelly.

If Lefty isn't remembered as fondly as Palmer, Ryan, and others, it's easy to see why. He burned bridges in St. Louis at the beginning of his career, and was a mercenary at the end of his career. He was a hero for Philadelphia (mostly a football- and hockey-crazed town) in the one season that they won a World Series. That happened to be the same year the Eagles made the Super Bowl, the 76ers made the NBA Finals, and the Flyers made the Stanley Cup Finals. Carlton wasn't as inspirational as teammates Tug McGraw, Pete Rose, or Mike Schmidt. He shared headlines in Philadelphia with other pro athletes who were cuddling up with reporters (literally, as Julius Erving admitted to fathering Philadelphia reporter Samantha Stevenson's baby) at the same time he was ignoring them.

Carlton let his pitching do the talking. He won 329 games, more than any left-handed starter ever except for Spahn. He is one of the top 50 players in baseball history.

MEL OTT

He came to the big leagues as a 16-year-old southern teenager toting a straw suitcase. Mel Ott was playing for a semipro team in Patterson, Louisiana, when his owner arranged for Ott to look up John McGraw for a tryout with the Giants. Ott traveled to New York with a battered straw suitcase and knocked on the office door of McGraw. He timidly came in when a voice roared, "Come in!" "Mr. McGraw, I'm Mel Ott." McGraw took a liking to the teenager, and decided to keep him around. "No minor-league manager is gonna ruin the raw talent that this kid has," said McGraw at the time.

Ott had a unique batting stance. And McGraw allowed the 5′9″ Ott to continue his unorthodox batting style. With his feet planted wide apart, the lefty would approach a pitch by raising his right leg in the air, dropping it quickly, and lashing out at the ball. It created great power. Strangely enough, he was one of two Giants who would become famous for their high leg kicks. The other was 1960s ace pitcher Juan Marichal. One would think that a batter who raised his front leg as Ott did would be a sucker for change-ups or slower pitches. Not Ott. He had excellent timing, and developed into an all-star.

From 1926 to 1947, Ott was the big stick of the Giants, clouting a (then) National League record 511 home runs, driving in 1,860 runs, and hitting over .300 for his career. He played on the National League All-Star team 11 times, and led the league in home runs three different seasons.

Mel hardly played in 1926, getting into only 35 games, hitting .383 in his 60 at-bats. His first home run came in 1927, when he played 82 games. The New York papers probably cared little, as across the Harlem River, Babe Ruth and Lou Gehrig were belting home runs like no one before.

By 1929, Giants fans had a legitimate slugger in Ott, as he walloped 42 homers and drove in 151 runs. When he turned 23 years old, Ott had already hit 115 home runs, more than anyone else in history at the same age. But in his long career, Ott would never hit 42 homers again in a single season. In this sense, Ott resembled Frank Robinson, who hit close to 600 home runs, but had only one season where he slugged more than 40.

Ott would win six home run titles, the first in 1932 when he hit 38. The Giants won the 1933 pennant. In the World Series, Ott went 4–4 in Game 1, and won Game 5 with a 10th-inning home run.

No player ever hit more home runs in one ballpark than Ott did at the Polo Grounds. In his 22 years as a Giant, he adopted a style that was adjusted perfectly to the dimensions of his home park, the Polo Grounds in upper Manhattan. Ott gets a lot of heat for his statistics because of the Polo Grounds' dimensions (only 257 feet from home plate to the right-field foul pole).

Those detractors have a point. Ott hit 511 homers in his career, with 323 of them hit at home, and only 188 on the road. A left-handed batter, Ott's famous leg kick may have helped him pull the ball. Babe Ruth and the Yankees played at the Polo Grounds for a few seasons until Yankee Stadium was built, and the Babe loved batting there, too. In Ott's defense, though, many other great left-handed sluggers played at the Polo Grounds, and no one hit home runs with Ott's frequency. Throughout baseball history, there have been sluggers who took even bigger advantage of their home park.

Players with Highest Percentage of HRs in Home Park (Minimum 200 Career)

Bill Dickey	66.8%
Bob Horner	65.1%
Bobby Doerr	65.0%
Rico Carty	64.7%
Cy Williams	64.1%
Rico Petrocelli	63.8%
Chuck Klein	63.3%
Ron Santo	63.1%
Mel Ott	63.1%

Now, of the players with 500 home runs, Ott did take more advantage of his home ballpark than any of the others. Many of the great home run hitters hit about equal amounts of home homers as opposed to home runs on the road. Willie Mays hit 335 at home, and 325 on the road. Mickey Mantle hit 266 at home, and 270 on the road. Certainly, some great home run hitters (especially the ones that played in Wrigley Field, like Ernie Banks and Sammy Sosa) were helped by their home parks, but none more so than Ott.

Players with 500-Plus HRs, Highest Percentage at Home
1. Mel Ott
2. Ernie Banks
3. Jimmie Foxx
4. Frank Robinson

Rafael Palmeiro and Sammy Sosa are next on this list, both of whom played at home in Wrigley Field for a portion of their careers.

Mel wasn't merely known as a person who clicked his heels three times and said, "There's no place like home!" Ott is also remembered for being one of the all-time good guys. During the first 16 years of his career, he was never ejected from a game. After taking over as manager, he did get tossed a handful of times.

Giants fans had their own allegiance to the outfielder. Ott was the Giants' Ruth or Gehrig or Foxx. The support wasn't quite what Babe Ruth received, but Ott was the biggest star on the second biggest team in New York. They were devastated in 1948, when Leo Durocher (who was hated then by Giants fans, and had once said of Ott that he was too nice to be manager—remember, it was Leo's assertion that "nice guys finish last") replaced Ott as manager of the Giants.

When Ott retired in 1947, he held the league record for home runs, runs scored, RBI, total bases, bases on balls, and extra-base hits. When Ott retired, only Babe Ruth and Jimmie Foxx had hit more home runs. He never won the MVP Award, but finished in the top 10 six times. He was the best player in the National League in the 1930s. He was very underrated, probably because people felt he put up numbers merely because of where he played his home games.

The Polo Grounds shaped his destiny as a hitter. He would have been a great hitter and a tremendous addition to any team in most any era. His life was defined by his personality. Dizzy Dean once made this remark: "One of the few regrets I have in baseball is the day I was ordered to knock down Mel Ott. Manager Frankie Frisch came out and told me to brush him back. I did just that, but afterwards I stood out there and felt right ashamed of myself. Ottie was the nicest guy I ever played against."

Mel Ott was only 49 years old when he died days after a horrendous car accident. The head-on accident seriously injured his wife and killed the driver of the other vehicle. Physicians tried for a week to halt complications from kidney malfunction, but eventually he died.

He was a lifetime Giant, but at only 5'9", hardly a giant. He played in New York for 22 years before beginning his managerial career. He bridged the gap for the Giants between John McGraw and Willie Mays.

Who's Better, Who's Best
Mel Ott or Al Simmons?

They called Al Simmons "Bucketfoot Al" because of his unorthodox batting stance, and he played in the same era as Ott. Simmons never won an MVP, and played in four World Series (Ott played in three). Simmons, in 20 seasons from 1924 to 1944, had a much higher batting average (.334 to .304), but Ott had tremendous patience and drew a lot of walks. Ott had a better on-base average (.414 to .380) and hit many more homers (511 to 307). Still, Simmons had a slugging percentage that was better than Ott's—although the numbers are so close it's a virtual wash (.535 to .533). Simmons played in a favorable ballpark as well, in Philadelphia.

KEN GRIFFEY JR.

Ken Griffey Jr. told everyone when he became a big-league star that he owed his athletic talent not to his dad, but to his mom, Alberta. Alberta was the one who tossed balls with him, and she was the one who told him when he did something wrong.

She did some job.

Ken Griffey Jr. was born on November 21, 1969, and graduated from Cincinnati's Moeller High School in 1987. In his four years of high school, he played football and baseball, and was named Player of the Year in baseball twice. He signed with the Seattle Mariners after high school, and proved too good for the minor leagues. When the Mariners started the 1989 season, they did it with 19-year-old Griffey, the youngest player in the majors, whose nickname would be "the Kid."

They called him the Kid because of who his father was.

Ken's dad was a hero to him growing up. Griffey's father was the starting right fielder for the Big Red Machine in the mid-'70s. Ken missed and idolized his dad during his long absences due to baseball, but on the other hand he hung out in the clubhouse with Johnny Bench, Pete Rose, and Tony Perez when he was seven. A pretty cool trade-off.

If you think that's cool, in 1990 Ken Griffey Senior and Junior became the first father/son combination to appear on the same major-league lineup card.

Throughout the decade of the 1990s, Junior became the coolest and most admired baseball player in the major leagues. He played hard, patrolling center field with such abandon that he opened himself up to injuries. He had a classic swing. He wasn't a good center fielder, he was a great center fielder. He won a Gold Glove for fielding for 10 consecutive years from 1990 to 1999. The only time he was really criticized was in 1995, when Yankee manager (and traditionalist) Buck Showalter said that Griffey shouldn't wear his cap backwards. Aside from dressing sloppy, Griffey couldn't be faulted for too much.

He was baseball's savior, its Michael Jordan. Nike featured him in big ad campaigns. He had the pedigree. He had the look and the smile. He had the style that his fellow Generation Xers admired. His jersey was worn at concerts by Snoop Dogg. His numbers were prodigious, his fame and popularity commensurate.

Hip-hop music is based on "the sample"—where bands reconfigure existing sounds into something entirely new. Griffey's game sampled and reconfigured Willie Mays's game, and the games of players of earlier generations. Griffey added action and style to his game. He was typical of his generation—a fan of speed and music and "SportsCenter" highlights and motocross racing and NBA action.

In 1989, Griffey had a torrid spring, which earned him a spot with the Mariners. He led all rookies with 13 homers and 45 RBI in mid-July, when he broke a bone in the little finger of his right hand. He missed a month, and when he returned August 20, he batted only .214 with three home runs and 16 RBI the rest of the season.

While his rookie season (.264, 16 home runs, 61 RBI, 16 stolen bases) looks good, it might have been sensational if not for the injury.

It was the story of his career.

In baseball, Griffey was a straight-A student with a poor attendance record. In Junior's first 15 seasons, his teams played a total of 2,362 games. Junior played in 1,914 of them (81 percent).

He missed 448 games, and wasn't completely healthy in countless others. Then, in his 16th season, he missed four weeks with a hamstring injury, then returned and in his first game back left after four innings with stiffness in his hamstring.

Griffey: Not the Iron Horse

2004: Tore his hamstring trying to run down a drive in the outfield

2003: Broke his right ankle trying to run out a double

2003: Had right-shoulder surgery to repair dislocation suffered while diving for a ball

2002: Tore his patellar tendon in his right knee in a rundown on the bases

2002: Suffered a torn right hamstring

2001: Torn left hamstring, initially suffered while rounding third base

2000: Had tendonitis in his right knee

2000: Had a partial tear of his left hamstring

1996: Missed 20 games with a broken wrist

1995: Missed 73 games after fracturing both bones in his left wrist after crashing into outfield wall

Despite all these injuries, Junior became the youngest member of the All-Century Team in 1999. He was the unanimous MVP in 1997. He was voted Player of the Decade in the 1990s by his peers.

The People's Choice

In his 16-year career, Ken Griffey Jr. has received more than 40 million votes for the All-Star Game. That means almost as many people voted for the Kid as voted for Bill Clinton in the 1996 presidential election (a little more than 47 million votes) or George W. Bush in the 2000 election (a little more than 50 million). And let's face it, people were choosing Junior against much tougher competition.

Despite the injuries, Griffey hit 382 homers during the 1990s. That's a tremendous number.

Most Homers During a Decade
1. 467 Babe Ruth, 1920s
2. 415 Jimmie Foxx, 1930s
3. 405 Mark McGwire, 1990s
4. 396 Harmon Killebrew, 1960s
5. 382 Ken Griffey Jr., 1990s

Griffey led the majors in total bases during the 1990s (3,125), was second to McGwire in homers, and was second to Albert Belle in extra-base hits and RBI, despite playing only 1,408 games during the '90s (13th most).

Griffey was the horse with early speed to catch Aaron's home run record, but he was caught around the three-quarters pole by his friend and contemporary Barry Bonds.

Who's Better, Who's Best
Ken Griffey Jr. or Barry Bonds?

In 1999, Major League Baseball named its All-Century Team. Griffey Jr. was named to the list, and Barry Bonds was not.

A 1997 *Sporting News* article mentioned that Griffey had clearly overtaken Bonds as the premier player in the game.

Oops.

Here are their career numbers after the 2004 season.

	Batting Avg.	On-Base Avg.	Slugging Pct.	SB	Walks	SO	HR
Griffey	.292	.377	.560	178	984	1,323	501
Bonds	.300	.443	.611	506	2,302	1,428	703

Bonds has a better batting average, a much better on-base average, and a much better slugging percentage. Bonds has 328 more stolen bases, more than 1,300 more walks, and 202 more home runs.

In June of 1997, Joe Hoppel wrote in *The Sporting News* that "during the 1997 season, Griffey, Jr. has clearly established himself over Bonds as the top player." In that article, Bonds was quoted as saying that "what Junior is going to do throughout the course of his career is going to well take over anything I've ever done. Junior started three years younger than I was when I came into the league (Griffey was 19, Bonds 22). Junior is going to take the game to another level . . . he'll surpass me throughout his career, by a lot. Not by a little. By a lot."

Of course, it was Barry who took his game to another level.

After their first eight years, Griffey had better numbers (Griffey 1989–1996, Bonds 1986–1993): Griffey Jr. had 16 more home runs (238 to 222). Griffey Jr. had 46 more RBI (725 to 679). Griffey Jr. had a higher batting average (.302 to .283).

In 1997, it is clear why Hoppel (and evidently, Bonds himself) thought that Junior would have the better career. Of course, if you looked even deeper, you would see that Barry had many more walks, many more steals, and higher on-base and slugging percentages. Barry had less-talented teammates around him in the batting order (Junior had Edgar Martinez, Alex Rodriguez, and Jay Buhner). If Junior was better, however, it certainly wasn't by a wide gap.

In the next seven years (Griffey 1997–2003, Bonds 1994–2000), Bonds had the better numbers: Bonds hit 29 more homers (272 to 243). Bonds drove in 67 more runs (726 to 659). Bonds hit for a higher average (.298 to .283).

This period includes Griffey's three greatest seasons (1997, 1998, and 1999), when he put together 160 homers and 427 RBI. Yet, he lost ground to Barry Bonds. In these prime years for Junior, he slugged 39 points lower than Bonds and had an on-base average 60 points lower than the San Francisco star.

Bonds's 16th, 17th, 18th, and 19th Seasons

2001	.328	73 HR	137 RBI
2002	.370	46 HR	110 RBI
2003	.341	45 HR	90 RBI
2004	.362	45 HR	101 RBI

Of course, Griffey is young enough to have a late-career run that would put his final numbers close to Barry's. But I doubt it will happen. Griffey batted between .247 and .264 in each season from 2002 to 2004, missing significant time each year.

There's No Place Like Home, Part 1

Ken Griffey Jr. played in Seattle's Kingdome for the first nine years of his career. It was there that he challenged Roger Maris's former single-season record of 61 homers. It was there that he batted a career-high .327. It was there that he had some of the best seasons in baseball history.

Ken Griffey Jr.

At Kingdome	198 HR in 2,673 AB	1 homer every 13.5 AB
Playing elsewhere	303 HR in 4,701 AB	1 homer every 15.5 AB

Along the way, the Kid saved baseball in Seattle. The Mariners started play in 1976, but even later with Griffey they didn't draw many fans and didn't make a postseason appearance until 1995. The Kingdome was not adequate, and the good coffee drinkers in Seattle didn't want to pay for a new stadium.

- September 19, 1995: A proposal to increase the sales tax by .01 percent in King County to pay for construction of a new ballpark is narrowly defeated by voters.
- October 3–October 8, 1995: The Mariners, in their first-ever playoff appearance, defeat the New York Yankees 3–2 in a series in which Ken Griffey Jr. bats .391.
- October 14, 1995: A special session of the state legislature authorizes a different funding package for a new stadium, including a credit against the state sales tax, the sale of special stadium license plates, lottery funds, food and beverage taxes in King County restaurants, bar and car-rental surcharges in King County, and a ballpark admissions tax.
- October 23, 1995: The King County Council votes to approve the funding package.
- March 8, 1997: Thirty thousand fans turn out as Ken Griffey Jr. helps officially break ground for the new ballpark.
- July 15, 1999: A capacity crowd of 47,000 attends the inaugural game in the new park against the San Diego Padres. The Padres win 3–2.

The new stadium turned out to be a pitchers' park. Not that it was among the reasons Griffey listed, but following the 1999 season, he left the Mariners. He forced a trade to the Reds for Mike Cameron, Brett Tomko, and two minor leaguers.

A little long-range planning was needed. If I'd been the owner of the Mariners in the mid-'90s, I would have gone to my 25-year-old superstar and called him in for lunch. The conversation would have gone something like this:

"Mr. Griffey, as you know, we are building a new stadium to replace the Kingdome. We wish to keep you here in Seattle for the remainder of your career. We expect big crowds to see your historic and record-setting home runs. Imagine the season-long buildup to Aaron's 755th. We need your input on this new stadium. How many feet away should it be for a home run? We can move heaven and earth for you, and certainly right field."

There's No Place Like Home, Part 2

Griffey chose to go to the Cincinnati Reds, an organization that he grew up with and near where he was raised. It was a homecoming of sorts, and then everything that could go wrong with his body did.

The Reason Griffey Isn't Ranked Higher

Griffey Jr. was baseball's folk hero. He was the superstar's superstar. But he missed hundreds of games due to injuries. And despite playing in over two thousand games, he hasn't played a single World Series game.

In his first 16 seasons, Griffey played on teams that were 1,211–1,213.

In his 15 postseason games, his teams were 6–9. He played in zero World Series. He played in exactly one League Championship Series.

All-decade team for the 1990s? Of course. All-Century Team? Not in this book.

CARL HUBBELL

W ho said Democratic and Republican conventions have always been useless and out-dated wastes of money? In 1928, Dick Kinsella, one of the Democratic delegates in Houston to nominate candidate Al Smith, scouted and signed a skinny, six-foot pitcher named Carl Hubbell for the New York Giants.

King Carl was a left-handed pitcher who bounced around for five years in the minor leagues before he mastered a pitch in '28 that would take him to the major leagues, the World Series, and eventually, the Baseball Hall of Fame.

Carl Hubbell threw the screwball. It was a fastball that "broke" outward maybe two or three inches at precisely the wrong time for the batter to adjust. Eventually, his left arm would become abnormally twisted from throwing that pitch, but he never complained of arm trouble or anything else. In the Detroit Tigers organization, manager Ty Cobb didn't allow Hubbell to throw the pitch in spring training. His Giants managers, John McGraw and later Bill Terry, allowed him to throw the pitch maybe 75 percent of the time. In a six-year period from 1932 to 1937, he pitched more innings than anyone else in baseball.

The Democratic convention took place on June 26, 1928, and Hubbell was signed in time to make his major-league debut a month later and win 10 games that season. He won at least 10 games in each of his first 15 seasons, a remarkable record of consistency and durability. Probably the most famous feat in his glorious career came in the 1934 All-Star Game. It was only the second All-Star Game ever, and it came at the peak of Carl's career.

King Carl started the game for the National League and allowed singles to future Hall of Famers Charlie Gehringer and Heinie Manush. He then struck out five future Hall of Famers in a row: Babe Ruth, Lou Gehrig, Al Simmons, Jimmie Foxx, and Joe Cronin. All five went down to the screwball.

Hubbell was incredible in the 1933 season. On one afternoon, against the Cardinals, he threw 18 shutout innings—without walking a batter. He threw 46 consecutive score-less innings, which was a record at the time.

He threw 10 shutouts in 1933, one of the best marks of all time. Only one left-handed pitcher (Sandy Koufax with 11 in 1963) ever threw more in a season.

That 1933 season was the start of a brilliant five-year run for Hubbell. He was the N.L. MVP in 1933 and in 1936, and was third in the 1937 MVP voting.

He pitched the Giants into the World Series and led the National League in wins in 1933, 1936, and 1937. He led the league in ERA three times (1933, 1934, 1936). In 1934, he won 21 games (fourth in the league) and saved 8 others (first in the league).

Hubbell holds a major-league record that far exceeds his All-Star Game exploits or anything else he did. He holds one of baseball's most important records.

Most Consecutive Wins by a Pitcher
24 Carl Hubbell (1936–1937)

That record has stood for over 65 years, and is tremendously overlooked. People think of King Carl, and they think about him striking out the five sluggers in the All-Star Game. That was nothing compared to the 24 wins in a row in '36 and '37. Ruth and Gehrig were left-handed hitters, and Ruth was over the hill by the 1934 All-Star Game, anyway.

The 24 wins in a row are amazing. Walter Johnson never did it, never winning more than 16 in a row. Neither did Sandy Koufax or Lefty Grove or Christy Mathewson or Greg Maddux or Randy Johnson.

24 Wins in a Row

When Joe DiMaggio hit in 56 consecutive games, it captivated a nation. DiMaggio was brilliant during the 56 games, batting .408 (91 hits in 223 at-bats), but there were several games where DiMaggio had but one hit in four (or five) at-bats. The Yankees actually lost the first game of DiMaggio's streak, and won the game when his streak was broken. The Yankees only lost 13 games during Joe D.'s batting streak, but that's still a lot of losses.

Now, Carl Hubbell went on a streak a few years before DiMaggio where he and his screwball were just unhittable. He won his last 16 games of the 1936 season, and his first 8 of the 1937 campaign. Not only did he win 24 consecutively, he made five relief appearances over the course of the streak, and would have been credited with a couple of saves, had they counted saves officially then.

Hubbell earned every one of his victories. He made 22 starts in the streak, and completed 19 games. In that stretch, he went 24–0 with an ERA of 1.95. He struck out 104 batters and walked only 35 in 207.6 innings.

The record for most consecutive victories by a pitcher before Hubbell's streak was 19, by Rube Marquard in 1912. Marquard was protective of his record, and would claim that an official scorer had robbed him of an extra victory in 1912. Indeed, he came into a tie game in the eighth inning during the streak and wasn't credited with the victory. Marquard's consecutive win streak started on Opening Day and was over in July. Hubbell's 16 straight to end the 1936 season left baseball with a quandary.

Ford Frick, the president of the National League at the time, ruled that Marquard's record could only be broken by a pitcher who won more than 19 games in a single season. That sort of took the excitement out of Hubbell's streak. Frick's 1937 ruling that had prevented Hubbell's accomplishment from entering the record books was rescinded in 1974. Marquard still holds the single-season record, and yet Hubbell's streak is considered the longest ever.

Over the course of the 1958 and 1959 seasons, Pittsburgh reliever Roy Face won 22 games in a row. Marquard won his final game of the 1911 season, and his first 19 of the 1912 season. Those are the closest challengers to Hubbell's record.

There is, of course, one other reason for Hubbell's record to be unappreciated by the masses. He lost a game in the 1936 World Series. "The Meal Ticket," as he was called by his Giants teammates, easily handled Gehrig, DiMaggio, and the rest of the Yankees 6–1 in Game 1. That was noteworthy, for several reasons. It was Hubbell's third straight World Series victory (he had defeated the Senators twice in the 1933 Series) and the first Yankees loss after 12 consecutive World Series wins. After the Yankees took the next two games, Hubbell came back in Game 4, and allowed four runs in the first three innings. Gehrig hit a homer off of him, and the Yankees prevailed 5–2. It was Hubbell's first loss since July.

Hubbell won his second MVP Award in 1936, and began the 1937 season just like he ended the '36 season. He won his first eight decisions, which made it 24 consecutive regular-season wins. He lost on Memorial Day to the Dodgers.

Hubbell went 22–8 in that 1937 season, again leading the Giants to a pennant. Once again, the Bronx team defeated the team from upper Manhattan in the World Series. Hubbell had elbow surgery following the 1938 season, and won exactly 11 games in four consecutive seasons from 1939 to 1942.

Hubbell retired following the 1943 season, but continued to work as the farm director (head of the minor-league teams) for the Giants organization until 1977, when a stroke limited him. He was on the Giants payroll for more than 50 years—repayment for the days when Hubbell was the organization's meal ticket.

Who's Better, Who's Best
Carl Hubbell or Bob Gibson?

Bob Gibson	251–174	.591 winning percentage
Carl Hubbell	253–154	.622 winning percentage

Bob Gibson	7–2	1.89 ERA in World Series (1964, 1967, 1968)
Carl Hubbell	4–2	1.79 ERA in World Series (1933, 1936, 1937)

Gibson in 1968	MVP	22–9	1.12 ERA	28 complete games	13 shutouts
Hubbell in 1933	MVP	23–12	1.66 ERA	22 complete games	10 shutouts

Gibson	5 seasons of 20-plus wins (all between ages of 29 and 34)
Hubbell	5 seasons of 20-plus wins (all between ages of 30 and 34)

One can argue about Hubbell and Gibson all night long. They each had one unbelievable year, a five-year stretch as good as anyone in baseball history, and a ten-year period of league dominance.

Who was better in their career years? Gibson started 34 games in 1968. He completed 28 of them, and was pinch-hit for in the other six.

Hubbell had a 1.66 ERA in 1933. That was just as impressive a feat as Gibson's 1.12 thirty-five years later. Hubbell had the only sub-2.00 ERA for a season between 1923 and 1941.

In 1933, Hubbell threw 20 innings in the World Series without allowing an earned run. In 1968, Gibson lost Game 7 against the Tigers, breaking a seven-game World Series winning streak.

What I remember most about Gibson is his competitiveness. It is all I have heard from the many experts I've talked to.

Joe Garagiola: "Gibson's mission—whenever he walked out on the mound, his only thought was that he was going to pitch a no-hitter. If the unthinkable happened, and someone touched him for a hit, his total focus would be on pitching a shutout. If that was somehow ruined, then he was going to be totally focused on the win. He was an unbelievable competitor."

Apparently, Hubbell had the same juices flowing in his veins. In 1938, Giants catcher Gus Mancuso gave insight into Hubbell's spirit in a United Press interview:

Two years earlier, we are playing the Phillies near the end of the season, and we've got the pennant won, and Carl is working just to keep limbered up for the World Series. He has 'em shut out, and two are out in the ninth. Camilli is up, their big hitter, and Carl has two strikes on him. I signal for a fast one, and Carl shakes me off. I'm in a hurry to get out of the ballpark, so I go out there and tell him it doesn't matter, and just to throw it in there. He says, no, he won't throw the fast one because two years earlier, Camilli hit one like that for two bases. He hasn't forgotten, and even with the pennant won, and the game and season sewed up, he won't throw one that Camilli likes.

Hubbell's concentration and competitive nature were every bit the match for Bob Gibson's in a later era.

This delegate from New Jersey casts his vote for Gibson, but I'd want that screwball Hubbell somewhere on my team.

ROY CAMPANELLA

There were 93,103 fans in attendance at Los Angeles's Memorial Coliseum to see an exhibition game between the Dodgers and Yankees in May 1959. It was the largest crowd to see a baseball game. Most fans were there to honor someone they had never even seen play. In an emotional ceremony, Dodgers coach Pee Wee Reese wheeled out his former teammate, quadriplegic Roy Campanella, who addressed the crowd. The game was staged to help with the rising costs of Campanella's medical care, needed after an auto accident in January 1958. The highlight of the evening came when the lights were turned out and the Los Angeles public address announcer called on those in attendance to light a match to simulate the lighting of candles.

Baseball historians have called Lou Gehrig's farewell speech on July 4, 1939, one of the greatest moments in baseball history, calling it "Baseball's Gettysburg Address." That may be, but then Campanella's speech that night in 1959 has to be compared to JFK's inaugural address ("My fellow citizens of the world: ask not what America will do for you, but what together we can do for the freedom of man.") Campanella's famous quotation, of course, is one he repeated many times: "To play in the big leagues, you got to be a man but you got to have a lot of little boy in you, too."

In 1993, Roy Campanella died of a heart attack. He was 71 years old, spending the last 35 of those years confined to his wheelchair. At the time of his accident, doctors expected him to survive no more than 10 or 20 years. He outlived his doctors.

Roy Campanella is one of those players for whom statistics will not do when measuring his place in baseball history. He gets extra credit for the years he put in before being allowed to enter the majors. He had played in the Negro Leagues for nine years before getting a chance in the major leagues. He gets consideration for the years he was not given after an automobile accident severed his spinal cord. His long and eventful life touched seven decades and countless people.

For 10 summers, he was the catcher for the Brooklyn Dodgers. For 10 summers, he joined the gods of immortality.

Roy Campanella was born the son of a black woman and an Italian father in Philadelphia. He grew up in a section of town called "Nicetown." It wasn't so nice when kids of both races called him "half-breed." His combination of good looks and athletic prowess today would land him million-dollar contracts in athletics and corporate endorsements. In the 1930s, his mixed race meant that Roy would be excluded from playing baseball for his favorite team, the hometown Philadelphia Athletics.

By the time Roy was 15 years old, he was traveling on weekends with a semipro team playing baseball, earning $25 a week. His mom allowed him to play, on the condition that he attended church on Sundays.

By the time he was 18 he had made quite a name for himself in the Negro Leagues. Still in his teens, he was signed by the Baltimore Elite Giants and played over 200 games a year for a top salary of $150 a month. His manager was one of the great catchers in Negro League history: Biz Mackey. In addition, Campy spent his winters squatting behind the plate in Puerto Rico, Mexico, Cuba, and Venezuela, in leagues that were far more tolerant of one's race. Mackey taught him to catch, and Campy learned well.

Imagine this: during World War II, Campanella was eligible to be drafted into the army, but ineligible to play in the major leagues. Because he was the father of two children, he was deferred from military service. Campanella jumped to the Mexican League in the middle of the 1942 season. His Baltimore Negro League team lured him back for the 1944 season. It was following the 1945 season that Dodgers president Branch Rickey first approached the catcher. It was around this time that the Dodgers signed Jackie Robinson. Rickey told Campanella not to sign with any major-league team until he spoke again with Rickey. Before the 1946 season started, Rickey offered Roy a contract to play for one of the Dodgers' farm clubs, in Nashua. In that 1946 season (with Jackie playing at a high level for the Dodgers' farm team in Montreal), 25-year-old Campanella was MVP of his league, batting .290 with 90 RBI.

In 1947, Roy jumped ahead to the Montreal farm club, where Jackie Robinson had spent 1946. Robinson, of course, joined Brooklyn's major-league team. By 1948, Campanella was the Brooklyn catcher. By 1949, he was on the All-Star team, and in his first World Series. By 1951, he was voted Most Valuable Player of the National League.

What a decade it was for Campanella in postwar Brooklyn, New York. The Dodgers won pennants and went to the World Series in 1949, 1952, 1953, 1955, and 1956. They lost the pennant on the final day of the 1950 season to Philadelphia, and in a three-game playoff with the New York Giants following the final day of the 1951 regular season. They came inches away from winning seven pennants in Campy's first nine years. They might have won in 1951, but Campanella had a pulled hamstring that prevented him from playing the final two playoff games against the Giants.

Campanella was an integral part of that Brooklyn dynasty, winning three Most Valuable Player awards. It's a shame he didn't have more years to play. By the time he entered the majors, he had put in nine years of pro ball, and was one of the most accomplished players in the Negro Leagues. If Rickey had integrated baseball just a few years sooner, then Campanella would have had another four or five years. In that time, he could have counted on 2,000 more at-bats, 100 more home runs, 500 more runs batted in, and possibly another pennant or two. Following the 1957 season, Campanella had promised the Dodgers that he had planned on playing another four years.

In addition to his years of major-league play lost, he suffered a hand injury that cost him much of two seasons. In a spring-training game against the Yankees in 1954, Campanella was running the bases and caught his spikes trying to break up a double play. He chipped a fragment of the bone against the heel of his left hand and damaged the nerve in his hand.

Campanella, who benefited from the park in Brooklyn, hitting 140 of his 242 homers at Ebbets Field, never did get a chance to go west with the Dodgers when they moved to Los Angeles. An auto accident in an ice storm one January night in New York in 1958 severed his spinal cord. He was lucky to survive. His wife at the time, Ruthe, left Roy soon after the accident. It was Campy's good fortune to find a woman named Roxie who would marry him in 1964 and keep him alive almost another 30 years. Roxie passed away early in 2004, after a lengthy battle with cancer.

Campanella finished with 242 home runs, leaving another 140 or so on the table, courtesy of racial practices in the '40s and a lustrous career cut short.

Bill White (National League player 1956–1969, Yankees announcer 1971–1988, National League president 1989–1994): "The best catcher I ever saw was Roy Campanella. I only saw him one year, but no one ran on him. And that was his *last* season. Of course, his hitting was helped by Ebbets Field, but he was a great hitter and catcher for his entire career."

Campanella had only 1,215 major-league games and just over 4,000 at-bats to put in the baseball encyclopedias. Compare that with some of the other Hall of Fame catchers:

Roy Campanella	1,215 games	4,200 at-bats
Johnny Bench	2,158 games	7,658 at-bats
Yogi Berra	2,120 games	7,555 at-bats
Carlton Fisk	2,499 games	8,756 at-bats
Gary Carter	2,296 games	7,971 at-bats

Had he played in the majors longer, Campy still might not have hit as many home runs as Fisk or Bench, and might not have played in as many World Series as Berra, but he sure as heck would have been held in higher esteem when compared to many of the top catchers of all time. While Berra is considered one of the three greatest catchers ever to play in the majors, Campy was considered an equal of Yogi Berra throughout the 1950s.

What if Campanella had been selected by the Dodgers' Branch Rickey to be the first player to integrate baseball? Would it have made a difference? Were the time (1947) and place (Brooklyn, New York) right? Should Satchel Paige or Josh Gibson have been chosen instead? Or should it have been the biracial Campanella, who had a less abrasive personality than Robinson?

That's hard to say, except that it was probably an idea whose time had come (in fact, been long overdue), and it might not have mattered which player Rickey had chosen. Southerners like the Dodgers' Dixie Walker didn't oppose Robinson himself as much as the idea of any black man playing alongside them. It wasn't just Robinson who changed the attitudes of everyone regarding black major leaguers. It was the entire first wave of black major leaguers—including Campanella, Larry Doby, Monte Irvin, and Don Newcombe.

It is not hard to conceive of the Dodgers making Campanella the first black manager, had his career lasted into the early '60s. Campy was managerial material, held in high esteem for handling a less-than-stellar pitching staff for much of the '50s. Yogi Berra took over the Yankees when manager Ralph Houk was moved upstairs to the front office. It is not difficult to see Dodgers owner Walter O'Malley doing the same for Campanella.

A Better Analogy

Roy Campanella and Vince Lombardi I can think of one other legendary sports figure who lived 58 years, and had real success for only a decade. Vince Lombardi taught and coached high schoolers in New Jersey from 1939 to 1947. Lombardi was 45 years old when he was named head coach of the Green Bay Packers in 1958. In the next decade, Green Bay (a laughable franchise that had a loyal, intense fan base similar to baseball's Brooklyn team) would win six division titles and five NFL championships (including taking the first two Super Bowls). Lombardi then stepped down as head coach to become the Packers' general manager. In 1970, he wanted to coach again and took the job as head coach of the Washington Redskins, but died in September, before the season started.

Lombardi didn't get a chance to have one of those 20- or 30-year runs as a great head coach. He came late and left early. Like Campanella did in Brooklyn in the 1950s, Lombardi made a lasting impact in Green Bay in the 1960s.

REGGIE JACKSON

The New York Mets had the first choice in the 1966 free-agent draft, and passed up an Arizona State outfielder named Reggie Jackson for a player named Steve Chilcott, who never made it to the majors. Kansas City Athletics owner Charlie Finley had heard about the talented but mercurial Jackson, and drafted him. In June of '66, Finley arrived in Cheltenham, Pennsylvania, where Reggie's father operated a tailor shop. The A's had just signed another ASU player, Rick Monday, for a $104,000 signing bonus. Reggie's dad thought that his son was worth at least that much. Finley offered a $50,000 signing bonus. When Finley raised the offer to $85,000 and a new car, the Jacksons agreed to sign.

Jackson played the 1967 season with the A's minor-league team in Birmingham, Alabama. Segregated Birmingham was no picnic for the 20-year-old Jackson. Reggie couldn't find a place to rent and had to stay in the apartment of white teammate Joe Rudi. Reggie posted a .293 average, and earned an early ticket to the majors when he was called up to Kansas City for the final 35 games of the 1967 season. He hit the first of his 563 career home runs that year, and then moved with the A's to Oakland.

Jackson became the leader of Charlie Finley's "Swingin' A's," a long-haired, mustachioed team that won three consecutive World Series.

1969

For the first time the country learned how talented Reggie Jackson was. Jackson spent his entire career having torrid hot streaks and wicked cold ones. In June of 1969, he got very, very hot. At one point, he drove in 15 runs in 14 at-bats. On July 2, he hit three homers against Seattle (yes, the Seattle Pilots in their lone season). By the end of July, he had 40 home runs and was 23 games ahead of Babe Ruth's 1927 pace. The 23-year-old Jackson couldn't keep the pace up, fell into a cold streak, and wound up with 47 home runs and 118 runs batted in. He slugged .608 in a league that slugged .377. A superstar had arrived on the scene.

1971

Jackson had a contract dispute that forced him to miss spring training in 1970 and have a poor season. Playing for far less than the $60,000 he had wanted, the disgruntled employee hit only 23 home runs and batted .237. That winter, he played winter ball and met Frank Robinson. Reggie credited Frank, then 32 years old, with helping him mature as a person.

Don Baylor: "After hitting 47 home runs in 1969, Reggie managed only 23 the following year, and he was trying to work out his swing that winter in Puerto Rico. One day, he hit a pop-up as high as the sky, but Reggie just stood there and watched it bounce. He was thrown out standing in the box. Frank was frigid. He didn't even look at him when he said, 'Next time, I take 500 bucks.'

Next time was the following week. Reggie strolled back to the dugout after not running one out and Frank said, 'I'll take that five out of your check.' Reggie flipped out and stormed into the dugout to pack up, saying he was going home. Frank followed close behind, telling Reggie, 'Wait for me. The way you're playing, you'll need somebody to help you pack up.' Then Reg tried to make an excuse, saying he thought he should go back to Arizona to get fitted with some glasses. He said the ball was jumping all over the place on him.

'Great idea,' said Frank. 'You know, make sure you get those special curveball lenses. They straighten those snakes right out.' The whole club broke up and Reggie got the message."

Reggie started off slow in 1971, but made the All-Star team as a last-minute replacement for the injured Tony Oliva. This might have been the greatest All-Star Game in baseball history. There were six home runs hit by six different future Hall of Famers. Johnny Bench, Hank Aaron, Roberto Clemente, Frank Robinson, and Harmon Killebrew all hit home runs, but the star of stars was Jackson. He hit a mammoth shot that would have left Detroit's Tiger Stadium completely if it hadn't struck a light tower. It looked like something out of the movie *The Natural.*

1972

Reggie tore a thigh muscle sliding home with the winning run in the American League Championship Series against Detroit. He earned his first World Series ring, but watched from the dugout on crutches.

1973 World Series

The Mets held Jackson to one hit in 12 at-bats in the three middle games of the Series played at Shea Stadium. The teams returned to Oakland for Game 6, with the A's down three games to two.

The Mets started Tom Seaver on the mound in Game 6, hoping to close out the Series. In the bottom of the first inning, Reggie doubled to left-center field, scoring Joe Rudi with the first run of the game. In the third inning, Reggie doubled to right-center field, scoring Sal Bando. That made the score 2–0.

After the Mets scored a run in the top of the eighth inning, Reggie singled in the bottom of the eighth off Tug McGraw, and went all the way to third when the ball got past Don Hahn. He would score on a sacrifice fly, and the A's won 3–1, forcing a seventh game.

In the seventh game, Reggie started in center field, and made a diving shoestring catch in the second inning. In the fourth inning, he made another nifty catch off the bat of Felix Millan.

Reggie hit a towering home run off of Mets starter Jon Matlack, and stood at home plate to admire the flight of the ball. No one in Reggie's day hit those towering shots like he did. Even fewer sluggers admired their own work like him—although it is much more commonplace today.

Jackson led the A's to a second consecutive World Series championship, and was the MVP of the Series.

Reggie did it all under a death threat. For the entire Series, he was accompanied by an FBI-appointed bodyguard named Tony Del Rio. After the last out of the seventh game, Del Rio carried Jackson off the field in his arms. Jackson explained to the nation following the game that the FBI had guarded him all during the ALCS against Baltimore and the World Series, because of threats against his life. "When the FBI showed up, I thought it had something to do with my alimony payments," he even joked.

1974–1975

The American League pitchers were dominant in 1974. The league batting average was only .251. Reggie hit .289, with 29 home runs and 25 stolen bases. It matches up with Willie Mays's season at a similar point in his career, but with one difference. Mays only won a single World Series. In 1974, Reggie led the A's to a third consecutive championship.

In 1975, the A's had lost Catfish Hunter to the Yankees as a free agent, but Oakland won their fifth consecutive A.L. West title. Reggie put on his usual theatrical performance in the playoffs, but batting .417 (5–12, with one home run) wasn't enough to prevent a Red Sox sweep.

Charlie Finley, now content to dump high salaries, traded Reggie Jackson and pitcher Ken Holtzman to the Orioles for youngsters, including Don Baylor. Jackson played one season for Baltimore and manager Earl Weaver before signing his own big free-agent contract with the New York Yankees. Reggie had always said that if he played in New York that they would name a candy bar after him. It wasn't long before the Reggie bar came out.

1977

When Reggie joined the Yankees it didn't take him long to alienate his new teammates. He ripped teammate Thurman Munson in an article in the June issue of *Sport* magazine. The article quotes Reggie as saying that he'd be the straw to stir the drink and that Thurman could only stir it badly.

Manager Billy Martin did not appreciate Reggie Jackson. He saw a player who put himself above the team. He saw a 30-year-old Jackson whose better days were behind him. He saw a player that didn't hit left-handers all that well.

It came to a head in June, when Reggie loafed after a Jim Rice bloop double and was promptly taken out by Martin. Jackson and Martin nearly came to blows in the dugout in a game seen on national television.

Finally, on August 10, Martin installed Jackson as the cleanup hitter. Reggie responded with one of his typical hot streaks. The Yankees went 40–13 in their final 53 games, as Jackson hit 13 home runs and drove in 49 down the stretch.

In the 1977 World Series, his first with New York, he became known as "Mr. October." He homered in Game 4. He homered in Game 5. In the fourth inning of Game 6, he hit a two-run shot into the right-field seats on Bert Hooton's first pitch. The next inning, he connected on Dodger reliever Elias Sosa's first pitch: another inning, another two-run homer. His next at-bat came in the eighth inning off of knuckleballer Charlie Hough. He knocked the first pitch into the bleachers, becoming the first player besides Babe Ruth to hit three homers in a Series game, and the first ever to hit five home runs in one Series.

After the game, Reggie said he did it for Jackie Robinson and his dad. "What do you think this man would think of me tonight?" said Reggie. Jackson showed a small, square medallion bearing the name of Jackie Robinson. "See this little button? I wore it throughout the Series. It is a picture of Jackie Robinson."

Jackson sometimes showed great respect for the superstars who had come before him. Joe DiMaggio was an early batting coach of Reggie's, back in Oakland, and worked with

Reggie's swing. Reggie, in one of his moments showing great humility, once said he hoped that he would be half the player Willie Mays was.

In that 1977 World Series, he raised his game to DiMaggio-type heights.

More Drama

In 1978, Jackson won his fifth World Series championship in seven years. It came with more agony. In a July game, Reggie ignored instructions to swing away, and attempted to bunt in a game against the Royals. He struck out. Martin suspended Jackson for five games. Reggie returned to the team the next day on the orders of Yankees owner George Steinbrenner, and manager Martin resigned, telling reporters that Steinbrenner and Jackson deserved each other: "One's a born liar [Jackson] and the other's convicted."

The Yankees, under new manager Bob Lemon, caught the Red Sox in a furious late-season charge, and won a one-game playoff with the Sox 5–4. Jackson's homer gave the Yankees a 5–2 lead and the insurance run that they desperately needed.

In the American League Championship Series, Jackson hit .462 against the Royals, and then hit .391 against the Dodgers in the World Series.

In 1980, the 34-year-old Jackson hit 41 home runs and led the Yankees to another first-place finish.

Following Reggie's fifth season in New York (the Yanks had finished in first place four times with him), Steinbrenner allowed Jackson to sign elsewhere. The Yankees had put their money in a younger star, Dave Winfield. Jackson signed with the California Angels, and he belted 39 home runs in 1982, helping the Angels finish first in the A.L. West. When Jackson returned to New York with the Angels for the first time in May 1982, the crowd chanted "Reg-gie, Reg-gie," and then changed their tune to "Steinbrenner Sucks." By the end of his five-year Yankee run, Steinbrenner had had enough of the aging Jackson.

Joe Garagiola: "Reggie Jackson was one of a kind. I remember when I was doing the 'Game of the Week,' he had some kind of rhubarb with owner George Steinbrenner during the week. We interviewed him on tape the day before the game, and he told his side of the story. Producer Mike Weisman told Reggie that we couldn't air it, because it was too long. Reggie said he couldn't do it any shorter. But Reggie was no ordinary athlete. He and I devised a plan. The second time he came up to bat the next afternoon, he looked up to the broadcast booth. He knew that if I was standing up, I was leading into his story and the tape. Reggie called time-out, adjusted his glasses, stalled. He didn't enter the batter's box until I sat down, our signal that the tape had ended. No other player would have had the presence of mind to go up and hit under those circumstances."

Whatever bad feelings Jackson and Steinbrenner had about each other dissipated by 1992, when Jackson was hired to work as a special advisor for the Yankees. The move was enough of a gesture that when Reggie was elected into the Hall of Fame, he went in enshrined as a Yankee (despite playing nine years in Oakland).

A Better Analogy

Reggie Jackson and Muhammad Ali   Before he even got a chance at the heavyweight title, Muhammad Ali bragged, "I am the greatest!"

Reggie Jackson was quoted talking about "the magnitude of me."

Ali performed in an individual sport, where he didn't have teammates to resent the bragging he did. Remember, Muhammad Ali wrote poems, naming the round in which he would knock out an opponent.

Jackson had teammates who resented his boastfulness. Sparky Lyle, Jackson's team-mate with the Yankees, recounted in his diary of the 1978 season, *The Bronx Zoo*, that Jackson told reporters after a game once, "When I get up in a pressure situation, I swell with confidence and relaxness. It's like everyone is saying, 'Reggie's up. Everything's going to be OK.'"

What's truly amazing is that Jackson and Ali both backed up their conceited claims. As Lyle recounted in the October 2, 1978, entry, "Despite the fact that Reggie can be hard to take, there's no question that in the big games, he can get way up and hit the hell out of the ball. No one has ever denied him that. I can't figure out how he does it, but he does."

Joe Garagiola: "He was an all-star's all-star, for his impact on the game. His numbers are Hall of Fame quality, but with Reggie, it was more than numbers. When he came up to hit, you stopped what you were doing."

Reggie Jackson hit a triple to center field in Game 2 of the 1973 World Series that Mets outfielder Willie Mays lost in the sun. It was a sad sight, seeing a former champion lost in center field, chasing a ball hit by a new champion. Jackson knocked Mays out—it would be Willie's last game ever in center—and Reggie stuck around till 1987, when he was a teammate of Oakland rookie Mark McGwire. In that farewell season, Reggie batted .220 and looked as lost as Mays did in '73.

Jackson long admired Ali, and an interviewer asked Reggie (after his three-homer game in the 1977 World Series) how he would compare himself with Muhammad Ali. Jackson replied, "I can't be compared to Ali—I am not as great as he is, and never could be. Ali is great for humanity and great for mankind."

Jackson was not that kind of great—but he understood "the magnitude of him."

SAMMY SOSA

I n the final day of the 2004 season, Sammy Sosa was fined $87,400—or one day's pay—for arriving late and leaving early. That's very appropriate for a player who didn't become a star until several years into his major-league career, and one whose last two seasons have been marked by declining numbers and bizarre behaviors.

Still, Sosa ended 2004 with a whopping 574 home runs, and over 1,500 runs batted in. That he hit most of them in a 10-year period makes him difficult to ignore.

There have been a lot of great home run hitters in baseball's history, but Sosa is the first Latin American player to slug more than 500 home runs. He is a contemporary of Barry Bonds, Ken Griffey Jr., and Mark McGwire, but those guys were first-round draft picks (Bonds and McGwire from colleges) who got a lot of money. Sammy Sosa was signed in 1985 as a non-drafted free agent by Texas scouts Omar Minaya (who later became the Expos' general manager) and Amado Dinzey. Minaya signed him to a contract for $3,500.

Bonds, Griffey, and McGwire never had to deal with language barriers, or learning about a new culture. Sosa grew up dirt poor.

As a child in the outskirts of San Pedro de Macoris, Dominican Republic, Sosa dropped out of school to earn money for his widowed mother (Sammy's father died when he was just seven years old) and six siblings. He did this by selling oranges and giving shoeshines. He had to bring home money to help his family, actually giving him more in common with some of baseball's earliest stars from the early 1900s.

He didn't take up baseball until he was 14 years old. He must have had talent, because the Phillies attempted to sign him at 15 years old. The deal was not allowed by Major League Baseball because of a rule making 16 the minimum age for players under contract. At first, Sosa tried his hand at boxing, but gave it up when his mother didn't like to watch him fight and get hit. "I knew the only way I could put my mother at the top was by getting to the major leagues. When I signed, my mother was crying as I left for the United States. I told her not to worry, that I would take care of her."

In 1986, in the rookie league, Sosa hit four homers in 229 at-bats. He was considered a leadoff batter, and hit 11 home runs in Class A ball in 1987 in Gastonia. By 1989, Sammy earned his first trip to the majors, joining George W. Bush's Texas Rangers for 25 games and 84 at-bats. There weren't many highlights that year, but the future president's approval rating of Sammy rose when he witnessed Sosa's first major-league home run, off of Boston ace Roger Clemens. Nevertheless, Texas owner Bush traded Sosa to the White Sox in July 1989. (In a 2004 debate with John Kerry, Bush was asked if he had made any decisions as president that he regretted. Since Bush didn't publicly regret any presidential decisions, he should have at least brought up trading Sosa. It would have made him look a little humble.)

The White Sox were extremely patient with the still-learning Sosa. In 1990, Sammy batted only .233 while striking out 150 times and walking just 33 times.

Such lack of plate discipline is typical of players from the Dominican Republic. The Dominican players are told from a young age to swing. They are told you don't get off the island by taking pitches.

In his 1991 season, Sosa seemed to take a step back, batting just .203 (98 strikeouts, just 30 walks). He was traded in 1992 to the Chicago Cubs, the second time he was traded before the age of 23.

To that point in his career, he had played 327 big-league games and had over 1,000 at-bats. His batting average was .228. He had 11 homers, but 295 strikeouts and only 58 walks.

In his first season with the Cubs, his luck didn't get much better. He was limited to 67 games in the 1992 season, due to a couple of trips to the disabled list. The day after his second career two-homer game (and his first with the Cubs), he was hit by a Dennis Martinez pitch that broke a bone in his right hand, and he missed nine games. He then played nine games—hitting three home runs—before fouling a pitch off his left ankle, fracturing it, and missing the rest of the season.

Stardom finally arrived in 1993, as Sosa became the first Cubs player ever to hit 30 homers and steal 30 bases in the same season. He hit 33 homers and stole 36 bases. That was the beginning of Sosa's power hitting. In 1994, the season ended in August, with Sosa stuck on 25 home runs.

During the strike, Sosa supposedly agreed to a free-agent contract with the Red Sox, but Major League Baseball decided not to allow any contract negotiations between players and teams during the strike. By the time the strike ended, Sosa had decided to stay with the Cubs.

Sosa was still known as a free swinger, and in fact, only one player in history (Reggie Jackson) has struck out more times than Sammy. In 1997, Sosa was publicly criticized by his manager, Jim Riggelman, for putting his individual stats ahead of concern for his team (he ignored a sign from the manager during a game). In 1997, Sosa batted just .251 and struck out a league-leading 174 times (with only 45 walks) to go along with his 36 homers and 119 runs batted in.

Following his subpar season, Sosa's career turned around when he took the advice of Cubs batting instructor Jeff Pentland and former Cubs great Billy Williams. They advised Sosa to shorten his swing, lower his hands, and exhibit greater patience. Since then, Sosa has put together a rather remarkable seven seasons.

Sosa became a household name in 1998 by hitting 66 home runs, which was more than anyone had ever hit in a season except Mark McGwire, who slugged 70 the same season. Sosa was tied with McGwire at 66 with two games left, and Big Mac hit four in the final two games. Barry Bonds extended the record to 73 in 2001.

It was Sosa, not McGwire, who would win the MVP Award that season. Sammy became a big hit that summer. When McGwire was questioned about taking something to help him hit homers, Sosa held up Flintstone Vitamins as the reason for his success. Sosa was on the field when McGwire hit his 62nd home run of that 1998 season, breaking Roger Maris's record. Sosa ran over to hug McGwire.

Sammy was far from being a one-year wonder. He came back and hit 63 homers in 1999, again finishing second to McGwire. He led the league in 2000 for the first time, with 50 homers. He finished second to Bonds in 2001, with 64 homers—making him the only player ever to hit 60-plus in three different seasons.

In 2003, Sosa made headlines for the wrong reasons. During a game against Tampa Bay, umpires found cork in his shattered bat. Sammy was immediately ejected and served a seven-game suspension. Sosa said it was an honest mistake. "I use that bat for batting practice. It's a mistake, and I feel bad about it."

Seventy-six of Sammy's other bats were scanned and were all clear. The bulked-up Sosa was far from the fast, base-stealing skinny kid that he was in the late 1980s. These are just some of the major-league home-run hitting records Sosa has set:

- Most 60-homer seasons: 3
- Most 50-homer seasons: 4 (shared with Ruth and McGwire)
- Most consecutive 50-homer seasons: 4 (shared with McGwire)
- Most homers, five-year span: 292 (1998–2002)
- Most homers, six-year span: 332 (1998–2003)
- Most homers, ten-year span: 469 (1994–2003)

Add in the 35 home runs in 2004, and Sosa has hit over 500 homers in just 11 seasons.

The Chicago Cubs are one of the most famous sports franchises of all time. They play in a delightful ballpark that transports fans back to a time when baseball was more game and less business. Wrigley Field is also known as a home run park, because when the wind is right, it becomes far easier for a hitter to hit a pitch over the ivy-covered fence.

Naturally, the player with the most home runs in a Cubs uniform has to be beloved. Beginning in 1929, that was Hack Wilson, who set records during the Great Depression of the early 1930s. Gabby Hartnett, one of the all-time best catchers, broke Wilson's record for most homers by a Cubbie. Hartnett had the franchise record until 1960, when it was broken by a man who would forever be known as "Mr. Cub." Ernie Banks would eventually wind up his career in 1971 with 512 home runs—all with Chicago.

In 2004, Sammy Sosa surpassed Banks's record by hitting his 512th homer as a Chicago Cub. It was just the latest in a stunning career of home run records for the man from San Pedro de Macoris.

Sosa's records are not just limited to home runs. In a four-year span between 1998 and 2001, Sosa drove in 597 runs. That was the most in a four-year span since Lou Gehrig drove in 639 from 1931 to 1934.

But Sosa's ranking is based on those years from 1993 to 2003. The 2004 season was the third straight season in which his numbers declined. He batted only .253 and struck out 133 times, while walking just 56 times. Worse, his team dropped six games to lesser opponents in the final week of the regular season and failed to make the playoffs. This came after a 2003 season in which the Cubs were five outs from the World Series.

In May 2004, Sosa suffered a strange injury. While sitting next to his locker chatting with reporters before a game with San Diego, he sneezed violently, causing severe back pain. He was diagnosed with back spasms and placed on the disabled list.

He's played in only 15 postseason games and has homered in only two of them. Sosa has never played in a World Series.

In the prime of his career, he was Sosa. In the beginning and end of his playing days, he was so-so.

Who's Better, Who's Best
Sammy Sosa or Roberto Clemente?

Roberto Clemente was the first Latino to be elected into the Hall of Fame. He won an MVP Award in 1966, and was in the top 10 in voting seven times.

Sosa was the first Latino to hit as many as 500 home runs. He won an MVP in 1998 and was in the top 10 in voting eight times.

Both played right field, but Clemente was a far greater defensive player with a cannon for an arm. Clemente had a higher on-base average, hit for a higher average (he led the league four times), and slugged much higher than the league average. But he wasn't

Sammy Sosa from the mid-'90s on. It's very close, especially considering both of their humanitarian efforts.

Clemente was not only a great player on the field, he was a better person off the field than on. He was a hero to everyone, but especially Latinos. On December 31, 1972, Clemente took it upon himself to personally direct a relief mission to earthquake-torn Nicaragua. Clemente and four others loaded a small DC-7 plane with food and supplies that never got past the San Juan border as the plane almost immediately crashed into the Caribbean Sea.

Sosa—a legend and an idol in the Dominican Republic—found himself faced with a severe crisis in his country following the 1998 season. Hurricane George had left one hundred thousand people homeless, without food or shelter. Sosa played a major role in providing relief aid to the victims of the disaster. Via the Red Cross, he sent thirty thousand pounds of rice, thirty thousand pounds of beans, and barrels of pure water to the Dominican Republic, and helped in the rebuilding of homes.

He soon launched the Sammy Sosa Charitable Foundation to further the education and health standards of children in the United States and the Dominican Republic area. The foundation raised $700,000 for his country and helped several other Latin American countries with food and money through their moments of crisis.

MIKE PIAZZA

It used to be said that catcher's gear could also be known as "the tools of ignorance." Catchers, probably for the physical abuse their bodies took, were thought of as less intelligent than others. Not so in the case of the handsome history buff Mike Piazza. He even appeared on the television game show "Jeopardy," and won easily (okay, it was "Celebrity Jeopardy," and Piazza defeated an NFL lineman and a "Baywatch" actress).

But, it's not like Alex Trebek had as one of the categories "Major League Catchers," and gave Piazza control of the board:

"I'll take Major League Catchers for $100."

"The answer is: This backstop hit 35 home runs in his rookie season, the third-highest total in National League history."

"Who is . . . me?"

"Correct. You retain control of the board, Mike."

"I'll take Catchers for $200."

"The answer is: In 1997, he was the first catcher ever to record 200 hits in a single season. . . . Mike, you buzzed in first."

"Who is me, again?"

"Do you want to move to another position on the board?"

"No, I'll stay at Catchers for $300."

"It's the Daily Double. How much do you wish to wager?"

"Everything."

"The answer is: The man widely regarded as the best-hitting catcher in major-league baseball history."

What would a father with financial means do for a son to fulfill a dream of both of theirs? Mike Piazza's father, Vince, had several car dealerships in the Norristown, Pennsylvania, area where Mike grew up. Vince was close friends with Tommy Lasorda, the longtime Dodgers manager, and around the time Mike was 11, he was the Dodgers' ball boy every time Lasorda's team came to Philadelphia. Around the time Mike was 15, Piazza set his sights beyond serving as ball boy, and used his father's connections to receive personalized batting instruction from Hall of Famer Ted Williams. Vince even spoke with Joe DiMaggio about how best to improve his son's hitting ability. It wasn't enough to make the high school first baseman a star.

Lasorda, the boy's godfather, had to call in more favors. He got Vince's kid a spot on the University of Miami's baseball team. Mike had exactly one hit as a freshman, and soon transferred to Miami Dade-North Community College, where he batted .364 his first season. Mike was flown out to L.A. by Lasorda for the Dodgers to take a look at. After an impressive stint in the batting cage, Lasorda cornered Ben Wade, then the Dodgers' scouting director. At the time, Mike was a first baseman, and the Dodgers had no need of one because they had Eric Karros already.

WADE: "Get me a schedule, and I'll go see him play."

LASORDA: "Why go 3,000 miles to see him play when he's right here? Sign him. If I brought you a shortstop, and he hit like Michael just did, would you go see him play or would you sign him?"

WADE: "I'd sign him."

LASORDA: "All right. And if I brought you a catcher, what then?"

WADE: "If he was a catcher, I'd sign him."

LASORDA: "Then sign him, 'cause he's a catcher."

The good news was that in the 1989 draft, the 21-year-old Piazza was selected ahead of 43 other players. The bad news was that he was drafted behind 1,389 others. He was a 62nd-round pick, courtesy of Lasorda's influence in the Dodger organization. In other words, Mike was not a prospect.

Mike was sent to the Dominican Republic, where the Dodgers had a brand-new baseball academy for Dominican players. Piazza was the first American to attend this camp and he learned to catch there, despite the fact that he didn't speak Spanish.

Who would have guessed that Piazza would turn into a superstar, one of the top 60 players to ever play in the major leagues? Certainly not him.

Yes, it's the same old American dream story we know of Michael Jordan. Remember, Jordan was cut from his high school basketball team? Jordan became an overnight success at college, and Piazza started his Hall of Fame résumé when he tore up Double-A and Triple-A pitching in the minor leagues. It was at Vero Beach spring training in 1993 where Piazza began his assault on major-league pitching. He batted .478 and took over as starting catcher for the aging Mike Scioscia. Piazza had 18 home runs and 58 runs batted in by the All-Star break. He didn't slow down for a decade. In his rookie season, he batted .318 with 35 home runs and 112 RBI. He was the unanimous selection for Rookie of the Year.

In 1994, the players' union ended the season in early August, and Piazza played only 107 games because of that. He still managed to hit 24 home runs, but he would almost certainly have batted at least 30 if not for the strike. That was the only season in his first 10 that he failed to hit at least 30 home runs. As it is, Piazza is the only catcher in history to belt 20 home runs in 10 consecutive seasons.

Even considering the jump in home runs by everyone in the major leagues, Piazza had an amazing 10-year period from 1993 to 2002, particularly impressive when you consider he caught over 1,300 games in his first ten years.

The shortened season of 1995 saw Piazza bat .346, with 32 home runs in only 112 games. A season of .336 followed.

In July of 1996, Piazza started the All-Star Game at Philadelphia's Veteran Stadium—the same ballpark where he'd served as a teenage ball boy. He caught the ceremonial first pitch from Phillies legend Mike Schmidt (Piazza's boyhood idol). Piazza then slugged an upper-deck home run in his first at-bat, and doubled in his following at-bat. He was named Most Valuable Player of the All-Star Game.

The best was yet to come. In 1997, Piazza batted .362 with 40 home runs and 124 RBI. His Dodgers finished two games behind San Francisco and failed to make the play-offs, however.

Mike Piazza in MVP Voting
1995: 4th
1996: 2nd
1997: 2nd

Since Piazza was competing with Mark McGwire, Sammy Sosa, and Barry Bonds at their peaks, those MVP totals are very meaningful.

Following the 1997 season, Piazza carried with him a lifetime batting average of .334. He was one of the best and most popular players in Los Angeles Dodgers history (competing mostly with pitchers like Sandy Koufax, Don Drysdale, Don Sutton, and Fernando Valenzuela).

Entering the final year of his contract, the Dodgers offered Piazza a six-year, $79-million contract. He turned it down. The Dodgers were in the process of being sold to Fox chairman Rupert Murdoch. In March of 1998, Brett Butler (a 16-year veteran who played with the Dodgers in 1997) told the *Los Angeles Times*, "Mike Piazza is the greatest hitter I've ever been around . . . but you can't build a team around him because he's not a leader. . . . Mike Piazza is a moody, self-centered '90s player. . . . He cared more about winning the MVP award from Larry Walker, or the batting title from Tony Gwynn, than he did about the team."

The Dodgers traded him to the Florida Marlins, who sent him six weeks later to the New York Mets. The Mets had a popular catcher, Todd Hundley, and Piazza had to endure some jeers from his own team's fans. But he produced at the plate, and led the Mets to the playoffs in both 1999 and 2000.

Mike Piazza in MVP Voting
1999: 7th
2000: 3rd

Postseason

One of the biggest knocks on Piazza besides his concern for personal goals and stats was his play in the postseason.

In 1995, Piazza batted .346 during the season, and only .214 in the playoffs. The Dodgers were swept.

In 1996, Piazza batted .336 with 36 home runs. In the postseason, the Braves swept the Dodgers, and Mike managed only three singles in the three games.

The Dodgers—despite a historic season from Piazza—missed the playoffs in 1997. The Mets—despite another sizzling second half from Piazza—missed the playoffs by a game in 1998.

In 1999, the Mets made the postseason as a wild card, but Piazza was limited by injury in the National League Divisional Series against Arizona. Piazza played all six games of the National League Championship Series, but managed just four hits in 24 at-bats (.167) with just one extra-base hit.

Finally, in 2000, Mike Piazza contributed to some postseason victories. Oh, he batted just .214 (3–14) versus the Giants in the NLDS. Overall, Piazza had batted 71 times in the postseason, and had just 15 base hits to show for it (.211). But against the Cardinals in the NLCS, Piazza had seven hits (including three doubles and two home runs) for a .412 average, and led the Mets into the World Series against the Yankees. It would be the first time that Piazza would play for a World Series ring. In the World Series, one of the major subplots involved Piazza and Yankee pitcher Roger Clemens. It was that summer, during an interleague game, that Clemens beaned the Mets catcher, causing a concussion and prompting Piazza to say he'd lost respect for the Rocket. Then, as tension built for a

World Series encore, Piazza shattered his bat on a Clemens pitch, and Roger threw the barrel in his direction as he ran to first. For that incident, Clemens was fined $50,000.

2001

It is almost impossible to convey what the last weeks of the 2001 Mets season were like to people who weren't in New York at the time. On September 11, terrorists destroyed the Twin Towers. Major League Baseball, rightfully, interrupted the season. It would have been impossible for the Mets to play in the days following the attacks. Shea Stadium's parking lot was used for disaster-relief purposes. Finally, on September 21, Shea Stadium was once again used for baseball—the first major sports event since the tragedy. There was an emotional pregame ceremony where the Mets honored the people who had lost their lives. The Mets trailed the Braves entering the eighth inning, but Piazza hit a pitch off the camera scaffolding in center field to give the Mets the win. He would say later it was the greatest single at-bat of his career.

2002

In March 2002, during spring training, Dodgers pitcher Guillermo Mota pitched way inside to Piazza in a meaningless exhibition game. Mota's next pitch nailed Piazza on the back. Piazza charged the mound, and looked like he was going to knock Mota out. Mota headed toward the outfield. Piazza was intercepted by a trio of Dodgers, including former NFL star Brian Jordan. After the game, Piazza supposedly sped his BMW to the other side of the stadium and entered the Dodgers' clubhouse, demanding to know where Mota was. Piazza left without finding the departed Mota, in a violent rage. Piazza and Mota were suspended for five games.

In the 2002 season, Piazza started to take abuse for his ineffective throwing—he threw out only 17.8 percent of would-be base stealers to rank 34th among 36 qualifying catchers. It was also the first season that Piazza's batting average dipped below .300.

2003

Piazza suffered a groin injury on May 16, 2003, and went on the disabled list for three months. The Mets' fans and management were pushing Mike to play first base on his return. Piazza—only a few home runs shy of breaking Carlton Fisk's record of 351 home runs hit as a catcher—wanted to break the record and remain behind the plate.

He's faced abuse from opponents, teammates, and fans. He's been hounded by rumors about his sexuality—even having to call a press conference to announce that he's not gay.

Why does controversy always find Mike Piazza? In the 2004 All-Star Game, when Roger Clemens, now a National Leaguer, gave up six runs in the first inning, people even pointed fingers at Piazza for possibly sabotaging his pitcher Clemens.

Do people resent him because he was a rich kid who had the inside track to make it to the major leagues because of his connections?

Following the 2000 season, Piazza still had a lifetime batting average of .328. Of course, the wear and tear of the advancing years would catch up to him.

Mike Piazza, Slugging Pct.

2000: .614
2001: .573
2002: .544
2003: .483
2004: .444

Reluctantly, Piazza made his first start at first base for the Mets in April 2004. In his first start, he got run over in a rare collision at first base and hyperextended his right elbow. Back behind the plate, he homered on May 5 to break Fisk's record. However, Piazza was mired in a string of bad luck. On Memorial Day, he injured his left knee sliding into the dugout trying to catch a foul ball in Philadelphia. Still, he continued to play and was hitting .322 as late as June 26. In mid-July, he hurt his wrist on a collision at first base.

His hitting suffered, and he was put on the disabled list in August. His career numbers—which once put him in the neighborhood of hitters like Ted Williams and Jimmie Foxx—now were creeping down to mere mortal status.

Still, you can't find another major-league catcher with 1,400 games played behind the plate with a lifetime average of .315 and a slugging percentage of .562. No catcher has hit more home runs, and Piazza stands a reasonable chance of hitting over 500 in his career.

Who's Better, Who's Best
Mike Piazza or Mickey Cochrane?

Cochrane is generally considered the best-hitting catcher in history, or at least was until Piazza began his assault on major-league pitching. Cochrane had a lifetime batting average of .320. Cochrane played 1,452 games, all but one as a catcher. Piazza has played about the same number of games following 2004, and his average is just slightly lower. Of course, Piazza has much better slugging numbers.

Still, Cochrane was a two-time MVP who led his team to three World Series championships. Piazza has never won an MVP, or a World Series.

Piazza was better than Cochrane. Mickey Cochrane lasted only 13 seasons, and didn't have a good season after the age of 32. If Piazza never played another game, he would get a close nod over Cochrane.

As great a player as Ivan Rodriguez is, he never was the hitter that Piazza was. Only a handful of catchers, such as Josh Gibson and Johnny Bench and Yogi Berra and Roy Campanella, were better than Piazza.

And the Final Jeopardy answer is: This major-league catcher who enjoys heavy-metal music and smashing baseball records is the 54th-ranked player in the top 100.

Who is Mike Piazza?

55

PAUL WANER

They called him "Big Poison," and he was one of the first seven players to accumulate 3,000 hits in the major leagues. He did so honorably. With 2,999 hits, he was awarded a single on a questionable call by the official scorer. "No, No," Waner shouted from the field. "Please call that an error. I want that 3,000th hit to be a real one."

His wish granted, he made it "a real one" and finished with 3,152 hits in his career. Most of them were probably hard line drives. He was called a "clothesline" hitter, because his hits to the outfield were so straight, you could hang your family wash on them. His rookie season with the Pittsburgh Pirates came in 1926, after three sensational years in San Francisco in the Pacific Coast League.

Waner was a great player in 1926, but the Pirates needed more. Who better to help out than his little brother Lloyd? Paul persuaded the Pirates to sign Lloyd.

Why wouldn't the Bucs accommodate their 1926 rookie, who batted .336, hit 35 doubles, and led the league with 22 triples? By 1927, little brother Lloyd ("Little Poison") debuted by hitting .355, and was the classic leadoff hitter. Together, the two Waners made up two-thirds of the Pirates outfield for 15 seasons. Following .380 and .370 seasons, Paul held out for a $25,000 contract for 1928, and the Pirates caved in. That was the year he hit a career-high 15 homers, so perhaps he sacrificed some average for power, as his batting average dropped significantly. He was not a home run hitter, though.

In his prime, he always claimed he had problems with his eyes. He would say that he couldn't read the outfield scoreboards, but when batting, the baseball would look as big as a grapefruit. He was a hitting guru who spent the last few years of his life as a batting coach for the Cardinals and Phillies. His advice was usually the same: hit down on the ball, aim for the upper part of the ball. In that way, you hit line drives.

Waner was known as someone who made no pretense that he liked to drink and stay out late. He had a reputation as someone who might be more dangerous after a night on the town. Cookie Lavagetto, the former player and manager, told this story decades ago concerning Waner:

I came up to Pittsburgh in 1934, and was scared stiff like any rookie. The first day in the clubhouse, I dressed slowly, as I had read so much about these players. Finally, in came Paul Waner. His hair looked like an unmade bed. Wore no necktie. His squinty eyes were about closed. "He's not fit to play ball," I told (shortstop) Arky Vaughn. "Don't worry about Paul, he'll be ready," said Vaughn.

I was sure he wouldn't play when he stretched out and took a nap rather than participating in batting practice. Just about 15 minutes before the game, he came out on the field and started stretching himself on tip-toes. I couldn't believe when I saw his name on the lineup card. "Something bothering you, kid?" asked Pie Traynor, the manager.

Lavagetto remembered that Waner hit four doubles in that game, all to right-center field or left-center field. After the game, Vaughn told Lavagetto, "See, I told you not to worry about Paul."

On October 1, 1927, a newspaper writer named Billy Evans wrote a piece about Paul Waner, where he canvassed the opinion of assorted National Leaguers. He quoted one as saying, "Paul Waner is a wonder. He does everything well. Almost single-handed he kept the Pirates in the race the last two years."

Waner had such a hold on Pittsburgh fans that they remembered him more than 25 years after he last played there. I found a July 2, 1964, article by Sandy Padwe from Newspaper Enterprise Association that quoted 29-year-old Roberto Clemente, then the Pirates' right fielder:

"I am tired of playing in a shadow. Everything I do, they compare me to Paul Waner. I am not Paul Waner's shadow."

When Clemente died in a 1972 plane crash, he had 3,000 hits, a reputation as having the best arm of any right fielder, and was the leading active batter in the National League. When Waner retired, he had a little more than 3,000 hits, a reputation for having the best arm of any right fielder, and was the leading active batter in the National League.

Paul Waner left a very large shadow.

Who's Better, Who's Best
Paul Waner or Tony Gwynn?

	Batting Avg.	On-Base Avg.	Slugging Pct.	Years in Majors	Career Hits
Paul Waner	.333	.404	.473	20	3,152
Tony Gwynn	.338	.388	.459	20	3,141

There's more to compare. In the year that Waner's Pirates made it to the World Series, they lost to one of the greatest teams of all time, the 1927 Yankees, who were 110–44 and won the pennant by 19 games. Gwynn's Padres made it to the World Series just twice, including in 1998, when they lost to one of the greatest teams—and the winningest team—of all time, the 1998 Yankees (114–48).

Waner won three batting titles, and Gwynn won eight. But Waner's three were impressive. He narrowly lost batting titles to Rogers Hornsby. Gwynn lost batting titles to Bill Madlock, Willie McGee, and Terry Pendleton. Waner probably weighed no more than 150 pounds, and Gwynn probably weighed more than 200 for much of his career. But they played the same brand of baseball. Waner won the batting title in 1927, 1934, and 1936.

Waner won an MVP Award, which Gwynn never did. Waner had a great gun in right field to throw out runners. But Gwynn had defense too, and baserunning. Waner had better players around him—his brother Lloyd, Pie Traynor, and Arky Vaughn. Gwynn carried the Pads on his back for many years. Gwynn was a better player than Waner, although they were eerily similar in many ways.

When people talk about the greatest right fielders, of course there is no argument. Babe Ruth was the greatest. Waner is forgotten by many people because he played so long ago. But the truth is this: When you rank the great right fielders of all time, the top tier is, of course, Ruth and Aaron and Frank Robinson. Then there are players just ahead of Big Poison, players like Gwynn and Mel Ott. Waner is ranked ahead of more modern right fielders like Roberto Clemente, Al Kaline, and Dave Winfield. But soon, the young Latino stars Manny Ramirez and Vladimir Guerrero will pass many in this list.

CARL YASTRZEMSKI

Yaz was born on August 22, 1939, in Southhampton, Long Island, the son of a potato farmer. He set numerous records at Bridehampton High School in basketball, football, and baseball. After graduating from high school in 1957, Carl went on to Notre Dame University with a scholarship to play baseball and basketball. He was elected president of the freshman class (a class that included NFL Hall of Famer Nick Buoniconti).

Carl, whose father was a baseball player with considerable talent, took an interest when baseball teams began talking to Yastrzemski while he was still with the Fighting Irish. Carl and his father didn't care too much for the Yankees; after working out with the team, Carl was made to dress with the batboys instead of the players, and Mr. Yastrzemski, hoping to see his son, was told he couldn't get in without a pass. So it was easy for Carl to choose the Red Sox, who also made the largest offer. That meant the New York kid wouldn't play in an outfield flanked by Mickey Mantle and Roger Maris. Instead, he would play in Fenway Park, in the shadow of legendary left fielder Ted Williams.

Normally, it would be asking too much of a rookie to replace Williams in the Boston lineup and expect him to hit as well. But Yaz appeared destined to do just that. Yaz was 5'11" and 175 pounds when, after two minor-league seasons, he was handed the left-field spot in 1961. Ted Williams was then a spring-training batting instructor with the Sox, with Yaz as his primary project.

They said nice things about each other. ("I'm not gonna teach that boy anything. He's a natural," said Ted that spring.) Williams was to grow frustrated with Yastrzemski's ever-changing stances and lack of power. In later years, Williams was not particularly kind talking about Carl's batting abilities. Yaz would usually hold his bat high, with his elbows actually higher than his head, and had to quickly bring the bat down to swing.

In 1989, when Yaz was elected into Baseball's Hall of Fame, he said, "Taking over Ted Williams's spot was the toughest thing I had to do—it almost broke me, really. The first three months of the season I really didn't know if I could play in the big leagues or not."

In his induction speech into the Hall, Yaz spoke about Williams, the man he replaced. "I was a scared rookie hitting .220 after the first three months, doubting my ability. A man was fishing up in New Brunswick. I said, 'Can we get ahold of him? I need help.' He flew into Boston. Worked with me for three days. Helped me mentally. Gave me confidence that I could play in the big leagues. I hit .300 for the rest of the season."

Curt Gowdy: "Yaz—when Carl came up, he was mostly hitting everything to the opposite field, mostly left center. It wasn't too long before he learned how to pull the ball at Fenway.

"He played left field like a shortstop—meaning that he could field a liner and throw runners out on the bases. It was marvelous to watch him. Joe Cronin compared Yaz to Al Simmons—as the best left fielder he ever saw. That's saying a lot."

Gowdy was the Red Sox announcer in the early '60s, and watched Yaz play every day. He was correct about the fielding. Carl learned to play balls hit off the Green Monster in Fenway, and play "wall-ball" to perfection.

In Yaz's rookie season, he batted .266 with 11 home runs and 80 RBI. The early 1960s were not good ones for Boston fans, as the Sox went through a succession of managers at nearly empty Fenway Park.

Yaz became a very good hitter for average, but he couldn't find the home run swing often enough for his critics.

Yastrzemski: First Six Seasons
.293
95 HR
461 RBI
.458 Slugging Pct.

That's an average season of less than 16 home runs and 78 runs batted in. Yaz did lead the American League in batting (1963), in on-base average (1963, 1965), and slugging (1965). But too much of his early career was spent clashing with managers like Billy Herman, who had told him he had to report in shape and work harder to become a great player. Opposing manager Eddie Stanky said, "Yaz may be an all-star, I suppose, but only from the neck down."

Everything fell apart in 1966, when the Sox finished in ninth place with a 72–90 record. Then, the Red Sox were 92–70 and won the pennant in 1967. Boston hadn't appeared in a World Series since 1946.

What happened that allowed the Red Sox to win the pennant—"The Impossible Dream"—in '67? Dick Williams was hired as manager, and Carl Yastrzemski became a superstar.

The American League pennant race in 1967 could never be duplicated today because of all the consolation prizes (a team that finishes second can make the playoffs). In 1967, the winner went to the World Series. The losers went home. With 12 games remaining in the season, only one game separated the top four teams in the standings. The Detroit Tigers led the Chicago White Sox by a half game. The Red Sox and Minnesota Twins were only one game behind the Tigers.

In the final 12 games of the season, Carl Yastrzemski batted .523 (23–44) with five home runs, 16 RBI, and 14 runs scored. The Red Sox went 8–4. In the final two games of the season, Yaz had seven hits in eight at-bats. He threw out Bobby Allison to quiet a Minnesota rally in the season finale.

If that's not a Most Valuable Player, no one is. Yaz led the league in batting average (.326), home runs (44), RBI (126), runs scored (112), hits (189), total bases (389), and slugging percentage (.622). He received the Gold Glove for his fielding, as well. That amazing season, Yaz batted .417 (40–96) in September.

Yaz, 1966–1967

1966	594 AB	16 HR	80 RBI	.278 Avg.	.431 Slugging Pct.
1967	579 AB	44 HR	121 RBI	.326 Avg.	.622 Slugging Pct.

Yaz was the last player to win the Triple Crown, leading the league in batting average, home runs, and RBI. If a player today went from 16 homers to 44, and improved his slugging so much overnight, he would have the most famous urine in the world.

The question for Yastrzemski was, what he could do for an encore? The following season, 1968, was the Year of the Pitcher. Yaz won his third batting title, and second consecutive, with a .301 batting average. It was a bad year for him (after batting .326 the previous season), but the .301 won the batting title by a whopping 11 points over the Yankees' Danny Cater. Yaz fell from 44 home runs to 23, and dipped from 121 RBI to just 74. The Red Sox finished fourth that summer.

In 1969, Captain Carl's batting average fell to .255, but he did hit 40 home runs. Yaz hit another 40 homers in 1970, giving him 147 home runs over four seasons (37 per season). In his other 19 seasons, he would average just 16 per year.

Carl improved his average from .255 to .329 in 1970, nearly winning his fourth batting title. He was MVP of the All-Star Game, and even stole a career-high 23 bases. He was rewarded with the richest baseball contract ever to that point: three years, $500,000.

Here is what happened after Yaz signed that contract.

Yaz, 1970–1971

1970	566 AB	40 HR	102 RBI	.329 Avg.	.592 Slugging Pct.
1971	508 AB	15 HR	70 RBI	.254 Avg	.392 Slugging Pct.

Yaz had a few tremendous seasons, balanced by some truly awful ones. In a 1969 game, he was pulled after one at-bat for "dogging it." In 1972, fiery rookie Carlton Fisk accused him of not being a leader.

By 1975, the Red Sox made it back to the World Series, no longer led by Yaz, but by rookies Jim Rice and Fred Lynn. Yaz batted .269 with 14 home runs and 60 RBI in 1975. He couldn't hit left-handers by this point (.212 in 146 at-bats), and was the Sox' regular first baseman. Still, in the games that counted most, he performed. In the 1975 American League Championship Series, he batted .455 (five hits in 11 at-bats). In the World Series against the Reds, he had nine hits in 29 at-bats. In those 10 postseason games, he batted .350.

In 1978, Yaz was 38 years old, an age when most players (especially then) were through. In fact, he was the second-oldest player in the league then. He surprised everyone. He was, more often than not, back playing in the outfield. He drove in 81 runs in 1978, including two in the one-game playoff against the Yankees. He would play five more seasons after 1978, with his numbers not really dropping off dramatically.

Yaz, Last Six Years (Age 38–44)

.269 Avg.	86 HR	399 RBI	.424 Slugging Pct.

Yaz would compile 3,419 hits and 452 home runs—the only player to get more than 3,000 hits and 400 homers. He played in 3,308 games (second all-time) and had nearly 12,000 at-bats (third all-time). He was a great professional, but he never did quite get out of the long shadow of Ted Williams.

Bill White: "He could hit. And although I didn't see him perform every day, he did a pretty good job in left field. Sorta like . . . sort of like whom? I was going to say Williams, but that's not fair . . . he wasn't Williams."

He also couldn't lead the Red Sox to a World Series championship. He made the final outs in the 1967 World Series, the 1975 World Series, and the 1978 playoff game. To be fair, there were a lot of great Boston players who couldn't deliver a championship, either.

In 1983, Yaz took a memorable final lap around Fenway Park, allowing fans to say goodbye.

Who's Better, Who's Best
Carl Yastrzemski or Mel Ott?
In no way will I write that Carl Yastrzemski and Mel Ott were great players only because of the home parks that they played in. But, like chicken soup for the feverish, it couldn't hurt.

Carl Yastrzemski: Home and Road

At Fenway	.306 Avg.	237 HR	994 RBI	.503 Slugging Pct.
On road	.264 Avg.	215 HR	822 RBI	.422 Slugging Pct.

Yaz's career numbers point to his inclusion with the all-time greats, but just where should he rank? He played an ungodly amount of games (second all-time), and was second in plate appearances.

He led the major leagues in doubles in the 1960s (318). His performance in the clutch was godlike. According to Peter Gammons, in the 22 biggest games of his career (games played for the pennant in '67, '72, and '75, the 1975 ALCS, and his two World Series), he batted .414 and slugged over .700.

Mel Ott played in the shadows of Ruth, Gehrig, and DiMaggio, not Ted Williams. He played his entire career with the New York Giants, slugging 511 home runs. Ott and Yaz had similar personalities. No baseball great ever took advantage of his home stadium like Ott, although Yaz was certainly helped by his.

The other analogy with Yaz that comes to mind is Jim Rice. Rice played 16 seasons—all with Boston—and had the unenviable task of replacing Yaz in left field. He had one monster season (1978) surrounded by a few lackluster ones. Rice retired with 382 career homers and a .298 batting average.

Rice, however, never won a Gold Glove. Rice didn't hit in the Red Sox postseason series. Rice was finished at the age of 36. He retired with 2,452 hits and 389 home runs. If Yaz had finished at 36 years old, Rice would be ranked ahead of him. But Yaz played until he was 44.

Yaz falls after Williams and ahead of Rice. That sounds about right.

ROBERTO CLEMENTE

Major League Baseball didn't discover Latin America until the late 1940s and early 1950s. When they eventually did actively seek Hispanics, it changed the game forever for the better. The first Hispanic to be inducted into the Hall of Fame was Roberto Clemente, known simply as "the Great One."

Roberto Clemente was born on August 18, 1934, in Puerto Rico, the son of a sugar plantation foreman and grocery market manager. Roberto was a track and field star but fell in love with baseball, too, at an early age. He built up his incredible arm by squeezing a rubber ball for hours a day. While Clemente was in high school, his playground coach, Roberto Marin, tipped off a scout for the Santurce professional team. The team offered Roberto a new glove, a $5,000 bonus, and $60 a month to play baseball for them. From 1952 to 1955, Clemente played three winter-ball seasons for the team, attracting the attention of major-league scouts, including the Dodgers' Al Campanis.

Twenty years later and countries apart, Roberto never forgot Roberto Marin, his first coach in youth softball, the man who had spotted him playing baseball with guava-tree limbs and crushed tin cans in a Puerto Rican sandlot. After Clemente doubled for his 3,000th (and last) hit in 1972, he said following the game: "I dedicated the hit to the Pittsburgh fans and to the people in Puerto Rico, and to one man in particular," referring to Marin.

There have always been some differing theories on several aspects of Clemente's career, including how he became a Pittsburgh Pirate in the first place.

Theory number one: Clemente was signed by Campanis in late 1953 and the teenager was assigned to the Dodgers' top minor-league team, the Montreal Royals. A rule in effect at the time stated that any player receiving a bonus of more than $4,000 had to be placed on the major-league roster after playing one minor-league season. If not, another club could draft the player for a mere $4,000.

The Dodgers' team in the mid-1950s was filled with all-stars. They knew it would be difficult to make room on their roster for Clemente, so they attempted to "stash" or hide him at Montreal by using him sparingly to discourage other teams from drafting him.

Indeed, in 1954, Clemente hit only .257 in just 148 at-bats. The Pirates weren't fooled, and drafted him. There were many scouts who had seen Clemente play for Santurce in the winters, besides seeing him in limited action in Montreal.

Theory number two: It's not that the Dodgers were loaded with talent, it's that they were loaded with black players. Just seven years after Jackie Robinson broke the color line, Brooklyn's roster featured five black players. Some people think that there was some unwritten "quota" system that Brooklyn abided by. The Dodgers signed Sandy Koufax and kept the wild teenager on their major-league roster in both 1955 and 1956 (thus protecting him from being chosen by other clubs).

Baseball historians Donald Dewey and Nicholas Acocela have written that Pirates executive Branch Rickey (yes, he had moved from Brooklyn to Pittsburgh in a bitter dispute with Dodgers owner Walter O'Malley) was able to draft Clemente from Brooklyn because the right fielder's chance of making it with the Dodgers was blocked by all-star Carl Furillo.

It was most likely a combination of things—Rickey knowing the Dodgers' farm system so well and wanting to exact revenge, the Dodgers having Furillo, an unspoken quota system—and it all adds up to the Dodgers losing one of the greatest right fielders in history.

In any case, Clemente joined the last-place Pirates in 1955, and batted only .255 as a rookie. He was still learning the game, as well as the language and culture of a new country.

There was no disputing his arm. It was a thing of beauty to watch him make a throw from deep right field to cut down a runner. Tim McCarver said that while some right fielders have rifles for arms, Roberto Clemente had a howitzer.

Clemente had amazing assist totals, throwing out runners from right field and playing the outfield walls to perfection. In his first two years, he had 18 and 17 assists. Okay, so base runners tested the unproven youngster. How does one explain 1958, when Clemente threw out 22 runners? Didn't these base runners take a hint? He led the league in outfield assists five different seasons.

Roberto Clemente played the game with style. Pitcher Robin Roberts described it this way: "He looked like he was falling apart when he ran. Looked like he was coming apart when he threw. His stance at the plate was ridiculous. When he swung, he'd lunge and hit bad balls. There was no way he could hit the ball like that. But no one told Roberto that."

By 1960, Clemente was in his sixth season, and batted a career-high .314. He hit 16 homers, drove in 94 runs, and the Pirates won the World Series for the first time in 35 years.

Clemente believed that he deserved the MVP Award that season, and didn't get it because he was Latino and American-born stars like Aaron and Mays were getting preferential treatment. He not only didn't get the award, he didn't finish in the top seven in the voting. United Press International quoted Roberto like this: "Many people tell me I wanna play like Weelie. I no play like Mays. From little boys up, I always play like thees. I always wanna run fast, to throw long, and heet far."

Is it any wonder that Clemente felt that he and other Latino players didn't get treated fairly?

The Pirates that year had the Cy Young Award winner (Vance Law won 20 games), the MVP (shortstop Dick Groat), the man who finished second in the MVP voting (third baseman Don Hoak), and a strong bench. Clemente finished eighth in the MVP vote.

While that seems curious, my vote that year would have gone to San Francisco outfielder Willie Mays. The Pirates had several key players, and I wouldn't have picked any of them as the most valuable in the league. At the time, MVP voters really favored catchers and shortstops, for some reason. Ernie Banks had won consecutive MVPs the previous two seasons, and (unlike Banks) Groat at least played for a pennant winner. Still, Groat missed time in September to injury, and Clemente played 144 of 154 games. Finishing eighth seems low for Roberto.

In the 1960 World Series, the Pirates were outscored by the Yankees 55–27, but won a wild seventh game 10–9 on the strength of Bill Mazeroski's home run in the bottom of the ninth inning. Clemente didn't have an MVP Award, but at least he had a World Series ring.

Roberto continued to improve, and he was the best batter in baseball in the 1960s.

Roberto Clemente's Batting Average, 1957–1961

1957: .253
1958: .289
1959: .296
1960: .314
1961: .351

He wasn't Willie Mays or Mickey Mantle, players who dominated from their first weeks in the majors. This one needed time.

Also, although Clemente batted over .300 in 13 different seasons, and won the batting title four times, he wasn't as valuable as Mantle or others. He swung at way too many bad pitches, and rarely walked.

In 1961, for instance, he batted .351 on the strength of 201 hits. But his on-base average was less than .400. He drew only 35 walks in over 600 plate appearances. In his first two years, he walked only 18 and 13 times.

He also didn't hit many home runs. He had 240 home runs in his career.

Clemente led the league in batting in 1961, 1964, 1965, and 1967. He finished second in 1963.

He finally won his MVP Award in 1966, at the age of 31, defeating runner-up Sandy Koufax. The MVP voters must have liked the long ball—Clemente hit a career-best 29 that year. It's ironic that he won four batting titles, but won his MVP in a year that he lost the batting title.

By 1967, he put everything together and was the most complete player in the game. At 32 years old, he batted .357. He had a .400 on-base average (second in the league, when the league average was .322). He slugged .554 (third in the league). He drove in 110 runs and scored 103. He even had his best year stealing bases, swiping 9 in 10 tries.

Clemente always played a lot of games, but was dogged by injuries from the beginning of his career: in his rookie season, he switched to a lighter bat and the change in swing caused a back injury that would plague him for several years. Some accused him of being a malingerer. Clemente always felt that those charges were unfounded. The charges stemmed from Clemente's fierce pride and a pattern of missing a substantial amount of time each year.

Year	Age	Games Missed
1967	32 years old	15
1968	33 years old	30
1969	34 years old	24
1970	35 years old	54
1971	36 years old	30
1972	37 years old	60

David Fisher (Clemente biographer): "He most certainly was a hypochondriac and spoke about injuries in an era when it was not the manly thing to do. Roberto always talked about his injuries. He had such pride. Those teammates who understood Roberto explained it like this: that he had such pride that playing anything less than 100 percent at his best would be an insult to his talent and heritage. His manager, Danny Murtaugh, didn't even understand that. Plus, Clemente had very strange ideas about medicine . . . his critics would ask him if he went to a witch doctor . . . he would rub lotions and stuff and say things like 'My good shoulder feels bad and my bad shoulder feels good.'"

The most widely read baseball columnist of the 1960s, UPI's Milton Richman, wrote several times of Clemente's reputation in this area. Richman quoted Pirates general manager Joe Brown in August 1968 as saying, "Certainly I'm concerned about Clemente's injuries. There's no doubt in my mind Roberto has pain. But something like this can't help but make you think of Mickey Mantle and all the pain he's gone through."

Richman had a July 5, 1969, column that talked about Clemente's fierce pride. Clemente was quoted in that article:

> I remember when I was in Miami this spring and was going to see a doctor in Puerto Rico about my ailing shoulder. One of the writers came over to me and asked me, "What's bothering you now?" I asked him why he would ask that. He said, "Well, something always is, isn't it?"
>
> Then he found out I was going to see a doctor in Puerto Rico. He said, "Why do you have to go there? We have much better doctors here." He didn't say, "We have a lot of good doctors here." What he said was that the doctors were much better here than in Puerto Rico. I didn't bother asking him how he knew that. I could see what he was trying to do.

The problem, as I see it more than three decades later, was that Clemente had a very different relationship with the press than, say, Mantle, who had the sportswriters eating out of the palm of his hand. Plus, Mantle had injuries that were *visible*. The Mick had blood spilling out of his uniform. Clemente had back problems or shoulder problems. They were not visible to the average manager, sportswriter, or fan.

The solution to Clemente's "image" problem was cleared up in time. He expressed himself in English a lot better. Sportswriters like Richman allowed him to clarify his remarks and come off as well as any other player. And no one could deny that Clemente was one of the best players in the game. By the 1971 World Series, Clemente had turned all the negative press around. He was the media darling of the World Series, and batted .414 with two homers against the Orioles.

In 1972, at the age of 37, he took aim at becoming the 11th player ever (and first Hispanic) to collect 3,000 hits.

On the final day of the season, the Pirates hosted the Mets. Clemente went into the game with 2,999 hits. In his first at-bat, Clemente's grounder skipped off the second baseman's glove. The official scorer said it was an error. Clemente was angry, and feared that the same writer who had bashed him over the years was responsible. In fact, it was a different writer, who wanted number 3,000 to be a clean hit. In the fourth inning, Clemente hit a double off the wall for his 3,000th, and final, hit. Roberto died in a plane crash while on a mercy mission to help the victims of an earthquake in Nicaragua a few months later. Imagine how ironic it would have been if Clemente's career had ended with 2,999 hits on account of a judgment call by a member of the press.

Clemente's Death

On New Year's Eve 1972, Roberto Clemente died in the crash of a cargo plane carrying relief supplies to the victims of an earthquake in Managua. Three days of national mourning were proclaimed in his native Puerto Rico, where he was the most popular sports hero ever. Clemente was aboard the plane because he suspected that relief supplies were falling into the hands of the wrong people. He was 38 years old at the time of his death. His body was never found, and many people (including Pirates teammate Manny Sanguillen) spent the next few days diving into the waters to attempt to find his body.

I was 11 years old at the time, and stunned to hear about a popular all-star dying so tragically. Strangely, I remember trying to rationalize a scenario where he swam to some uncharted island and survived. I had an opportunity to ask a friend about his reaction when Clemente perished. This friend was NFL great Dan Marino, who was also an 11-year-old Little Leaguer at the time, but in Pittsburgh.

Dan Marino: "It was so sad when I heard the news. My family was all Pirates fans. I grew up not more than five blocks from Forbes Field. In fact, my first year of Little League, we played at Mazeroski Field, which was right behind the right-center field fence of Forbes Field. I would look underneath the iron gates in the outfield. I remember seeing Clemente and Stargell play. Willie Stargell and Don Clendenon rented a house right next door to my grandmother, when I was seven or eight. The Pirates had already moved to Three Rivers by the time Clemente died, but I remember the Forbes Field days, when the Pirates weren't as good. It was very, very sad in Pittsburgh at the time."

Who's Better, Who's Best
Roberto Clemente or Tony Gwynn?

Clemente	9,454 AB	846 extra-base hits	28% of hits for extra bases	83 stolen bases
Gwynn	9,288 AB	763 extra-base hits	24% of hits for extra bases	319 stolen bases

Both spent 20 years with the same organization. Both finished in first place just twice; once was at the beginning of their careers, and once was at the end.

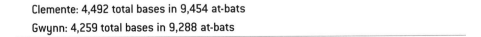

Clemente: 4,492 total bases in 9,454 at-bats
Gwynn: 4,259 total bases in 9,288 at-bats

If one adds in stolen bases, their total bases look like this:

Clemente: 4,575 (total bases plus stolen bases)
Gwynn: 4,578 (total bases plus stolen bases)

If you want to add in factors like how many times they were each caught stealing (Clemente only 46 times, Gwynn 125), you can. I'm just trying to show how close these guys were in production.

Clemente: 12 Gold Gloves, 4 batting titles
Gwynn: 5 Gold Gloves, 8 batting titles

Clemente: batted .362 (21–58) in his two World Series (one versus Yankees)
Gwynn: batted .371 (13–35) in his two World Series (one versus Yankees)

Clemente was described as moody and petulant, and Gwynn was never without a smile on his face. Much of that can be attributed to the language barrier, of course.

In this book, Gwynn is ranked ahead of Clemente, contrary to the 1999 All-Century Team results. This book isn't ranking players based on their influence to future generations. I'm sorry if this offends Jackie Robinson or Roberto Clemente fans, but as great as they were—and acknowledging the amount of hardships they had to overcome—they were not as good as other players that are ranked ahead of them. I'll take Tony Gwynn and his eight batting titles. I'll take Tony's 300-plus stolen bases. I'll take his play in the outfield, and accept that it cannot be considered as good as Clemente's, but hey, Gwynn did win five Gold Gloves!

JACKIE ROBINSON

This book ranks Robinson as a baseball player. Obviously, as the first black major leaguer in the 20th century, and the first to enter the Hall of Fame, he was about as significant as one could be. He didn't play his first season with the Brooklyn Dodgers until 1947, when he was already 28 years old. He was a great athlete—lettering and starring in four sports at UCLA. It was often said that baseball was far from his best sport. He most likely would have followed his brother Mack into the Olympics (Mack won a silver medal in the men's 200-meter behind Jesse Owens at the 1936 Munich Games). Jackie won the NCAA broad-jump title, in fact. But there would be no medals for Jackie. There were no Olympics in 1940 because of World War II. When Jackie finished his military duty, he signed in 1945 with the Kansas City Monarchs of the Negro League. America was slowly changing. Two men gave the country the push it needed.

One can't talk about Jackie Robinson without knowing about Branch Rickey and the contributions he made to the game of baseball. They called him the Mahatma, and he had the keenest mind in baseball. He was born in 1881, not long after the Civil War, and would grow up to be a devoted Abraham Lincoln fan. Rickey was a catcher for the New York Highlanders (later the Yankees) until he dropped out in the 1909 season to go to Lake Saranac, New York, for a one-year tuberculosis cure.

By 1913, Rickey was a scout for the St. Louis Browns, delivering them Hall of Famer George Sisler. A year later, Rickey was the manager of the Browns. It was in 1916 that Mr. Rickey was elevated to vice president and business manager of the team. It wasn't long before Rickey moved to the St. Louis Cardinals, as their president.

In the early 1920s Rickey made his first lasting mark on baseball. He conceived the idea of the farm system. That was monumental to baseball. He made it possible for poor clubs to compete with wealthier ones. He pumped new life into the Cardinals.

Rickey's success in St. Louis also made him a frequent target of Commissioner Kenesaw Mountain Landis. Landis, remember, was the single biggest reason (along with the fact that 30 percent of major leaguers were from the South, and would have refused to play with or against blacks) that there were no black players in the majors. Landis fought Rickey over the Cardinals' farm system, arguing that it kept players captives of teams.

Besides Rickey's dueling with the commissioner, other barriers were being broken that would enable the signing of a black player to major-league baseball. They included the integration of troops in World War II and the vocal black newspapers that called for the color line to be broken. So the stage was being set for Rickey's signing of Jackie Robinson. Rickey had long established himself as a baseball genius, able to pick out stars from hundreds of raw rookies. Rickey would have had it a lot harder trying to segregate baseball while operating the St. Louis franchise—St. Louis was part of the South, where Jim Crow laws were harder to break. Fortunately, Rickey joined the Brooklyn Dodgers in 1941. Brooklyn needed Rickey's influence. They were a joke of a franchise, finishing near the bottom of the league each year.

When Rickey was with the Cardinals, he looked for new, cheap sources of ballplayers, and founded the farm system. Now with the Dodgers, Rickey focused on black athletes—a brand-new, untapped source of talent for the major leagues. He called it "the Great Experiment." Landis was finally out of the way (he died in 1945), and fighting alongside blacks in World War II had softened the average southerner's view of Jim Crow laws. Branch Rickey was the right man in the right city at the right time to select and protect a black baseball player. Arthur Mann, Rickey's assistant (and later, biographer) wrote about Rickey's six-part plan to integrate baseball. The stages were (1) the backing and sympathy of the Dodgers' directors and stockholders, whose investment and civic standing had to be considered and protected; (2) picking a black man who would be the right man on the field; (3) picking a black man who would be the right man off the field; (4) a good reaction from the press and public; (5) backing and thorough understanding from the black community, to avoid misinterpretation and abuse of the project; and (6) acceptance of the player by his teammates.

He acted out of the rationalization that signing Jackie Robinson would bring in a good ballplayer, help bring in fans, and open up a gateway for future black players.

The official Jackie Robinson website quotes Rickey as saying, "Jackie, we've got no army. There's virtually nobody on our side. No owner, no umpires, very few newspapermen. And I'm afraid that many fans may be hostile. We'll be in a tough position. We can win only if we can convince the world that I am doing this because you're a great ballplayer, and a fine gentleman."

Jackie Robinson's Rookie Season

On April 15, 1947, Jackie Robinson made his major-league debut. The date now is set aside every year by Major League Baseball as Jackie Robinson Day. His play in 1947 exceeded Mr. Rickey's hopes. Jackie had 590 at-bats and batted .297 with 12 home runs and 29 stolen bases. He won the very first Rookie of the Year vote (although not handily, beating the Giants' Larry Jansen, who finished 21–5, by a vote of 129–105).

The National League had no clear-cut choice for MVP that season. There were 23 voters who cast votes, and there were 10 men who received at least one first-place vote. Jackie finished fifth in the MVP voting his rookie season.

Jackie was a target for every base runner—whether he played at first, second, or third base. Robinson played first base that year because the Dodgers had a second baseman named Eddie Stanky. Robinson pushed the Dodgers to their first pennant in years. Robinson did as Rickey instructed, and held his temper when opponents harassed him. A teammate from Kentucky, shortstop Pee Wee Reese, befriended Robinson, and others followed. Jackie was a hero from day one to the black community, with days organized in his honor. He would star in a movie about his life as soon as 1950. He would win the MVP Award in only his third season, in 1949, at the age of 30. In that season, he batted .342 and led the league in stolen bases. He was an exciting player. He was a clutch player. He was a versatile player. Teammate Duke Snider called him the most competitive player he ever saw.

On August 12, 1951, the Giants were 13.5 games behind the Dodgers. A furious late-season rally enabled the Giants to catch the Dodgers heading into the final day of the season. Brooklyn played in Philadelphia for the season finale, and the Phillies took a 6–1 lead. But Jackie's RBI triple in the fifth keyed a four-run rally, and Brooklyn closed to within a run. It appeared the Dodgers would be eliminated when the Phils put up two insurance runs and the scoreboard flashed that the Giants had defeated the Boston Braves.

But Brooklyn wasn't dead yet, and scored three runs in the eighth inning to tie things up. The score stayed at 8–8 through 11 innings. With two outs and the bases loaded in the bottom of the 12th, Eddie Waitkus of the Phillies whacked a Don Newcombe fastball up the middle for what appeared to be the game-winning hit. But Robinson sped to his right, dove, and caught the ball.

Finally, Jackie hit a game-winning home run in the 14th inning to send the Dodgers into a three-game playoff with the Giants. He had almost single-handedly saved the Dodgers' season.

The Dodgers didn't win the pennant that year, but they won six in Jackie Robinson's 10 seasons. They lost the pennant on the final day in two other seasons. Robinson—who became a fine second baseman, leading the league several times in double plays—was a main reason for Brooklyn's success. One of Robinson's great weapons was his baserunning. He stole home 19 times—more than any other player in the last 60 years. He stole second and third quite a bit, too.

Most Stolen Bases, Major Leagues, 1947–1956

1. 197   Jackie Robinson
2. 176   Pee Wee Reese
3. 147   Richie Ashburn
4. 127   Minnie Minoso
5. 111   Earl Torgeson

Historians say the civil rights movement started with Robinson's arrival in Brooklyn. After Robinson's major-league debut, the Jim Crow laws on buses and in restaurants and public places would eventually be replaced by integration. Not that it came quickly. Robinson didn't even live long enough to see a black manager in the major leagues. And he lived until November 1972. Perhaps if he had not succeeded as a major-league player, it would have set back the movement to integrate baseball, denying a young Willie Mays and Hank Aaron the opportunity to compete against the best at an early age.

Jackie wasn't the greatest baseball player, and was far from the best the Negro Leagues had to offer. He wasn't as great as Josh Gibson or Satchel Paige or others. He was the right age, at the right place, at the right time. He's rightfully regarded as one of the greatest second basemen of all time.

A Better Analogy

Jackie Robinson and Martin Luther King Jr. Dr. Martin Luther King Jr. delivered a speech in Memphis, Tennessee, one day before he was assassinated in 1968. The great orator said he was so grateful that the Almighty allowed him just a short time in the later half of the 20th century. King closed by saying: "Well, I don't know what will happen now. We've got some difficult days ahead. But it doesn't matter with me now. Because I've been to the mountaintop. And I don't mind. Like anybody, I would like to live a long life. Longevity has its place. But I'm not concerned about that now. I just want to do God's will. And He's allowed me to go up to the mountain. And I've looked over. And I've seen the promised land. I may not get there with you. But I want you to know tonight, that we, as a people, will get to the promised land. And I'm happy, tonight. I'm not worried about anything. Mine eyes have seen the glory of the coming of the Lord."

Longevity has its place. It would have been nice if Robinson could have been paid millions to play ball, or even lived with his teammates in spring training. But he saw the promised land, something that couldn't be said of the black players just a little older than him.

59

HARMON KILLEBREW

Could an aim so worthy as denying the Yankees a 10th consecutive pennant be the work of the devil? That was the basis of a 1954 novel by Douglass Wallop entitled *The Year the Yankees Lost the Pennant*. The novel took place four years in the future, in 1958, when middle-aged Joe Boyd was given an opportunity to help his beloved Washington Senators defeat the hated Yanks. Boyd agreed to give Mr. Applegate his soul in exchange for youth and vigor as Joe Hardy. During the next two months, Joe Hardy batted over .450 with 48 home runs, but he was plagued by guilt over the way his team was winning and for leaving his wife behind.

Harmon Killebrew's life and career was every bit as dramatic as Joe Hardy's.

In the same year that Wallop had his novel published, an 18-year-old from Idaho made his way onto the Washington Senators' roster. Was life imitating art? Not for a few years, until Killebrew became almost as good as Hardy.

Then, on July 11, 1965, Harmon hit his most dramatic homer ever. With two out and one on and the first-place Twins (the Senators had moved to Minnesota and become the Twins) trailing the Yankees 5–4, Killebrew hit a game-winning home run. That year, it was the Twins who played the Dodgers in the World Series—not the Yankees. Killebrew's homer effectively ended the Pinstripe Dynasty. Minnesota even took the first two games of the Series, defeating both Don Drysdale and Sandy Koufax, before falling in seven games.

Bob Wolff: "I was the Washington Senators' announcer from 1947 until they moved. I moved with the team and worked the first year in Minnesota. Even though I was no longer with the team by 1965—I was working for NBC and their baseball pregame show by then—I can't tell you how happy I was—and most Washington fans were—when Killebrew led the Twins past the Yankees into the World Series."

There was a price that Harmon paid—much later—for his glory.

Harmon Killebrew grew up in Payette, Idaho, as a quiet farm boy, respecting his parents and dedicated to baseball. As a grade-schooler, he fastened an oatmeal box above a door and pitched a tennis ball into it. He also swung at lilac bushes and anything else that helped him adjust his swing to different levels. He was a high school All-America quarterback and an all-star basketball player. At 17, he packed his bags for the University of Oregon, where he had accepted a football scholarship.

Along came a scout for the Washington Senators (Applegate?), who offered Harmon a $12,000 bonus to play for the Senators, after Killebrew was recommended to the organization by Idaho Senator Herman Welker. Harmon spent two years on the Washington bench as a little-used reserve, and then was sent to the minor leagues.

Bob Wolff: "When Harmon was signed, I was not only the team announcer, I wrote a column. I remember writing a column on his impressions of the first time he saw each big city. He was one of the most modest and soft-spoken players. He never changed; even as he got older he never realized (or acted like) he was a star. He was a powerful guy, with a tremendous chest and just raw power. But the Senators played their games at Griffith Stadium. It was 405 down the left-field line for a home run. It was only 330 feet down the right-field line, but there was a 31-foot fence. Harmon would crush the ball, but he couldn't quite reach the fences there at Griffith Stadium. I remember quite well when Killebrew was sent down to the minors; it was crushing to him."

At this point, Killebrew had second thoughts about turning his back on football. But following the 1958 season, the Devil made his deal. Killebrew became an instant star. It helped that they moved the fences in at Griffith Stadium.

After hitting just 11 homers in parts of five seasons, Killebrew slugged 42 homers in 1959 to lead the league. He followed that up with 219 more home runs in the next five years—more than Mantle, Maris, Mays, and everyone else.

He was reluctant to leave Washington when the franchise moved to Minnesota for the 1961 season. Then he hit 46 homers in 1961. He hit 48 homers in 1962. He hit 45 homers in 1963. He hit 49 in 1964. Suddenly, it didn't seem that cold in Minneapolis. He averaged 39.7 home runs per year for the 12-year period between 1959 and 1971. Killebrew hit home runs at a faster clip than anyone before him except for Babe Ruth.

Fewest At-Bats per Home Run, 1950–1987

1. 14.22   Harmon Killebrew
2. 14.74   Mike Schmidt
3. 15.11   Dave Kingman
4. 15.12   Mickey Mantle

But not even the Devil could make "Killer" a glove man. Mostly he played third base early in his career. Then, he became a left fielder (1964), and then a first baseman (1965).

He went back to third base in 1966. When the Twins had a good-fielding first baseman, they played him and tried to "hide" the 5'11" Killebrew in the outfield.

Harmon was built compact, with short arms. He looked like Campanella or Berra hitting home runs. When he hit them, they went a mile. On June 3, 1967, he became the first player to hit a home run into the second deck in left field at the Metropolitan Stadium. He was fairly one-dimensional. In 8,147 official at-bats, Harmon Killebrew never bunted for a sacrifice.

His best season came in 1969. He hit 49 home runs and drove in 140 runs. The three Twins batting in front of him (Cesar Tovar, Rod Carew, and Tony Oliva) were all getting on base. A modest Killebrew said he felt like he should have driven in 240 that year. He did lead the league in on-base average in 1969, on the strength of his walking 145 times. He got on base that season a league-leading 303 times.

The following season, there was no drop-off. He finished third in the MVP race in 1970, a season that saw him hit 41 home runs, drive in 113 runs, and walk another 128 times. For a second straight season, his Twins finished in first place, but were swept out of the League Championship Series by the Orioles. In the 1970 LCS, however, Killebrew blasted two homers in the three games.

At the age of 33, Killebrew was already among the league's top 20 home run hitters of all time. On June 22, 1971, he hit number 498. He didn't hit number 499 until July 25. He didn't hit number 500 until August 10, when Killebrew unloaded against Baltimore's Mike Cuellar to become only the 10th man ever to hit 500 home runs.

For almost any other player, finishing fifth in the home run race would be a fine year. Harmon Killebrew finished fifth in 1971, and it was big news. He dropped off to 28 home runs in 500 at-bats, a mere mortal average after so many big seasons for the slugger.

Although he was still fairly young, Killebrew's power almost magically dissipated. The young, strapping Joe Hardy was quickly turning back into the middle-aged Joe Boyd. In 1973, at the age of 37, Harmon hit just five homers in 248 at-bats.

For most of their parallel careers, Harmon Killebrew was a better home run hitter than Hank Aaron. After turning 37 years old in February 1971, Aaron hit 183 home runs.

After turning 37 years old, Killebrew hit 32 home runs. Aaron finished his career with 183 more home runs than Killebrew.

Killebrew's teams never won a World Series. The difference was pitching. Killebrew's Twins played a total of 13 postseason games. Hall of Famers Koufax, Drysdale, and Jim Palmer pitched against Minnesota in seven of them. The other six games were started by excellent left-handers Claude Osteen (twice), Mike Cuellar (twice), and Dave McNally (twice).

The designated hitter rule came into effect for the 1973 season. Designated hitter was a role that would suit Killebrew perfectly. By that time, though, his career was shot. He was a DH for 9 games in 1973, 57 games in 1974, and 92 times in his final season in 1975.

In his final season, he parted ways with the Twins and signed with the Kansas City Royals. He batted only .199 and hit only 14 home runs. Still, he was a legendary figure who could boast of having many fans, including one huge, vocal one.

A Jacksonville Beach, Florida, jeweler named Bob Newberry cast 30,000 votes to put Harmon Killebrew in the major-league All-Star Game in 1975. This was before the Internet. This was before computers. It wouldn't have been so hard to believe if it were a punch-out ballot, but Killebrew's name had to be written in that season. That's a lot of writing—and a lot of name. (It's not like he was writing in the name Mel Ott, for example.) Newberry was 29 at the time, and needed 750,000 votes to put Killebrew in the starting lineup. Earlier, the lifelong Killebrew fan paid for billboard space to let people know Killebrew's lifetime home run total, and had publicly offered to pay $5,000 toward Killebrew's salary for 1975 if Twins owner Calvin Griffith would keep him. The offer was ignored, and the Twins released him. Killebrew was not named as a reserve, even, on that '75 All-Star squad.

Still, Harmon had the storybook life. He married his childhood sweetheart and had five children. At one time, he was the biggest star of the Washington Senators. On one occasion he had even been called into the box of President Eisenhower. He was beloved in the city of Minneapolis. Of the more than eleven thousand men who had played major-league baseball to that point, only four had hit more home runs. He led his Twins into a World Series, where he rocketed a tape-measure home run off of Don Drysdale.

Then, the cheering stopped. The man who had ripped between 40 and 49 homers in a season eight times did not have much going for him between the ages of 40 and 49.

He lost his marriage. He almost went bankrupt. He sank deep in debt. A 1989 story in the *Minneapolis Star Tribune* said that Killebrew owed at least $700,000 to four banks, Twins owner Calvin Griffith, and Reggie Jackson. It was a most stressful time for the man they once called "Killer." Everything he touched financially turned to ruin. A cattle ranch he bought at the tail end of his career failed. His auto dealership in Oregon and a failed car-leasing company in Bloomington pushed him to bankruptcy. The most Killebrew made in one season playing baseball was $120,000. He retired a few years before the days of big-money contracts.

In July 1988, the Killebrew family home was foreclosed on. It came a year after his wife, Elaine, filed for divorce. Elaine divorced him (after a 34-year marriage) because of Harmon's long-term relationship with his former secretary.

If you think that's bad, it got worse in a hurry. In May 1990, Harmon was rushed to a hospital after complaining of a piercing sensation in his neck and back. He was treated for a collapsed right lung and damaged esophagus. Months later, he had an abscess the size of a football nestled behind his lung. Draining the growth left Killebrew with a four-inch hole in his back. A staph infection entered through the open wound and quickly moved to Killebrew's ankles. Doctors tried for 10 days to halt the infection before deciding to send him home to die.

At his rented home in Scottsdale, Arizona, Killebrew received loving attention at home after being close to death. By December 1990, after marrying his fiancée, the infection had miraculously subsided.

Killebrew credited his wife, Nita, with saving his life. In his 50s and 60s, Killebrew traveled the nation as a spokesman for VistaCare, a company specializing in hospice care.

How about that? The man becomes a Paul Bunyan–like folk hero, has a career that many would be tempted to sell their soul for, loses his way, and then regains his soul by helping others reach an inner peace before death. Maybe I'm being a little overdramatic, but real life isn't as dramatic as Wallop's novel.

A Better Analogy

Harmon Killebrew and Paul Bunyan So many stories about Harmon Killebrew called him "Paul Bunyan," after the giant lumberjack. According to the tall tales, it took five giant storks, working overtime, to deliver Paul Bunyan to his parents. He grew so fast that after one week he had to wear his father's clothes. His lungs were so strong that he could empty a whole pond of frogs with one holler.

Did the late *Los Angeles Times* sportswriter Jim Murray draw upon the legend of Paul Bunyan when writing about Killebrew? His style surely was similar to those tall tales. This is what Murray wrote about Killebrew in May of 1967:

> He is so strong, if he shakes hands with you, you will need a hook to eat with for a week. He could move a piano and play it at the same time. He comes from a long line of people who would tear up a telephone book with one hand—and telephone poles with the other. The last time he got mad was when a pin came loose in his diapers. . . .

We get it, we get it. He was a gentle giant, a strongman, like Paul Bunyan.

60

JOHNNY MIZE

They called Johnny Mize "the Big Cat," and 60 years after his playing days, his numbers don't seem extraordinary, especially by today's standards. He slugged 359 home runs. But look a little closer—he was one of the best hitters in baseball history.

The Big Cat didn't have nine lives, but one very full one—one that began and ended in Demorest, Georgia.

He was 15 and in 10th grade when the coach at local Piedmont College asked him to work out with the college team. He showed up for a practice, and pinch-hit in a game the next day. The next season, the college coach said that to be on the safe side, Mize might want to think about taking one course in college. Mize went to his grave as the only player who played three years of college ball while still in high school.

His first year in the majors was 1936. In his first 11 seasons with the St. Louis Cardinals and New York Giants, he led the National League in home runs four times and in RBI three times. In 1939, he hit 28 home runs to win a home run title, and came within 20 RBI of winning the Triple Crown. In 1940, Mize set a Cardinals record with 43 home runs.

In that '40 season, Mize might have hit an additional 18 home runs to break Babe Ruth's single-season record of 60, but a temporary wire-mesh fence was erected above the low right-field wall in his home ballpark, and many of his 31 doubles and 13 triples just banged off the temporary fence instead of sailing into the stands.

In 1942, his 137 runs batted in led the league. Just when he was getting warmed up, Mize was drafted into the military for three years.

When Mize returned from World War II, his play didn't drop off at all. When you adjust his stats to 1995–2000 levels, they are very comparable to Mark McGwire's. There's even a book that insists that Mize's 1947 season was comparable to—heck, even better than—McGwire's 1998 season. According to the book *Leveling the Playing Field* by G. Scott Thomas, Mize's season in 1947 (51 home runs, 138 runs batted in) was equal to a season of 70 home runs and 163 RBI in the late 1990s.

McGwire, 1998 (35 years old)	.299	70 HR	147 RBI	.752 Slugging Pct.
Mize, 1947 (34 years old)	.302	51 HR	138 RBI	.614 Slugging Pct.

McGwire fans will point out that Mize reached 51 home runs in 1947 as a member of the Giants playing in the Polo Grounds with its short right-field porch. The Giants that year batted 221 home runs, still one of the highest totals of all time. Mize came back in 1948 to hit 40 more home runs.

The Big Cat led the National League in batting average once (.349 in 1939), home runs four times, doubles once (39 in 1941), triples once (16 in 1938), runs scored once (137 in 1947), slugging percentage four times, and runs batted in three times. He didn't just hit three homers in a game once—he did it six times.

Mize was 36 years old when the Yankees bought him from the Giants. New York Giants manager Leo Durocher wanted a team with youth and speed, and began sitting veterans like Mize. The Yankees were interested, especially when they heard the Red Sox were interested too (hmm, where have I heard that before?).

Mize played first base for the Yankees, but not every day. He became their number-one pinch hitter, leading the league in pinch hits in 1951, 1952, and 1953. Mize contributed to the five consecutive World Series titles that the Yankees won between 1949 and 1953. Mize belted three home runs in the 1952 World Series, driving in six runs in the five-game Series against Brooklyn. When Mize retired in 1953 at the age of 40, he had hit 359 home runs. At the time, that was sixth all-time, trailing only Babe Ruth, Jimmie Foxx, Mel Ott, Lou Gehrig, and Joe DiMaggio. Here's some more ammunition for those of us who nudge Mize slightly ahead of McGwire. At the time of Big Mac's 2001 retirement, he was fifth all-time in home runs, with Barry Bonds hot on his trail. Essentially, both Mize and McGwire retired with only five players ahead of them on the career home run list. DiMaggio had 361, only 2 more than Mize, who came within a couple of homers of being fifth on the all-time list following the 1953 season.

Johnny Mize was much more than a free-swinging home run hitter. He was a very tough man to strike out. Mize had an excellent reputation for hitting the curveball. When he was with the Yankees at the end of his career, he would sit next to manager Casey Stengel and act as the unofficial batting coach.

One reason that Mize had to wait almost a quarter of a century before being enshrined in the Hall of Fame is that he didn't forge the best reputation when he played. According to Maury Allen, Mize was not a likable fellow among his teammates and the press, certainly a strong reason for his absence for so many years from the Hall of Fame: "He was a bit of a braggart, mean and overbearing at times, and a second-guesser."

Maury Allen doesn't have a lone opinion out there about Mize. He seemed to be unlikable to just about everyone, especially in the media. He did his talking on the field. A 1930s comedian named Al Schacht remarked after seeing Mize hit a tape-measure home run, "I couldn't carry a ball that far."

As I've stated over and over in these pages, baseball had two great periods of inflated offensive numbers (the '20s through early '30s, and the period beginning with 1994 to the present). Johnny Mize didn't play in those periods. He dominated the era he did play in.

Highest Slugging Percentage, 1938–1993 (Minimum 3,000 Total Bases)

1. .634 Ted Williams
2. .569 Joe DiMaggio
3. .559 Stan Musial
4. .558 Johnny Mize

The Big Cat had a higher slugging percentage than Willie Mays, Mickey Mantle, and Hank Aaron—the next three names on the list. That's impressive.

Who's Better, Who's Best
Johnny Mize or Joe DiMaggio?

I'm not going to make a case that Mize was a better player than DiMaggio. That's silly—and indefensible. But I will make a case that they were very similar offensive players—in exactly the same era. DiMaggio played from 1936 to 1951; Mize played from 1936 to 1953. Both players lost three prime seasons (1942–1945) to the war.

DiMaggio	6,821 AB	361 HR	.325 Batting Avg.	.398 On-Base Avg.
Mize	6,643 AB	359 HR	.312 Batting Avg.	.397 On-Base Avg.

Both players had extremely good eyes at the plate (DiMaggio had 790 walks and only 369 strikeouts, while Mize had 856 walks and 524 strikeouts). DiMaggio was a slightly better hitter and in another stratosphere as a defensive player. But were the differences that great? They were the same age. DiMaggio entered the Hall of Fame in 1955. The Big Cat was finally enshrined in 1981.

Who's Better, Who's Best
Johnny Mize or Mark McGwire?

Mize batted .312 when the league average was .274. McGwire batted the league average for his career. McGwire slugged a lot more home runs, but that's to be expected, considering the era he played in.

Mize slugged .562 for his career when the league average was .395. He led his league in slugging percentage four times (and lost three years of his prime). McGwire also led his league in slugging four times, but his career .588 slugging percentage didn't dominate the field like Mize's .562.

Mize led the league one year with 16 triples. McGwire hit just six triples in his entire career. Mize hit 367 doubles to McGwire's 252.

Neither player won an MVP Award, but Mize was second in the voting in 1939 and 1940. He was third in 1947. McGwire was second in 1998.

A Better Analogy

Johnny Mize and Bob McAdoo Mize was the Bob McAdoo of his time and sport. If you remember McAdoo from his playing days, or from my *Who's Better, Who's Best in Basketball?* you'll remember Big Mac as a player who dominated the league with league-leading scoring and rebounding numbers. McAdoo spent time in Boston and New York, and did not fit in with the Celtics or Knicks. At the tail end of his NBA career, McAdoo contributed (not as a star) to a couple of NBA championships with the star-studded Los Angeles Lakers (a perfect analogy to the Yankees). McAdoo was left off the NBA's 50 Greatest List in 1996, which was inexcusable to a historian like myself. It took a long time, but McAdoo (like Mize) eventually made the Hall of Fame. Personalities be damned, McAdoo deserved to be in the NBA's top 50 (he is, in my book!), and Mize deserves to be in the top 60 among baseball players.

61

MARK McGWIRE

Mark McGwire is one of the greatest home run hitters of all time. I'm not sure he is one of the two or three greatest first basemen of all time, or one of the greatest players. I don't mean to sound like I don't like McGwire. Actually, when he came into the majors, I might have been his biggest fan. I'll explain.

There are millions of fantasy (or rotisserie) league players today, but the fad started in the mid-1980s. I was a part of one of the first and most legendary fantasy leagues. Bryant Gumbel, then the host of NBC's "Today" show, was the founding father and commissioner. I had been a silent partner for a friend of Bryant's, and was invited to buy my own team for the 1986 auction. For the 1987 draft, I picked a rookie first baseman from the Oakland A's named Mark McGwire. I protected him on my roster for the next three seasons. My partner Dave Katz and I nearly won the league that 1987 season over a host of wealthy, influential, and knowledgeable sports nuts. Big Mac certainly did his part.

In that 1987 season, McGwire set a rookie record with 49 home runs. He might have been able to hit 50, but he left the team for a few days to be with his wife when she was due to give birth to their son. How do I remember? That little boy nearly cost me money!

The A's won the pennant the next three seasons, although they only captured one World Series championship. McGwire was a feared home run hitter, but the scouting reports on him were all unanimous: he could be pitched to. Don't make a mistake on him, because if you do, he'll hit it out of the park.

McGwire missed nearly the whole 1993 and 1994 seasons with a bad heel, and a good part of 1995 with a bad back. It was during the 1995 season that he served notice that he was, well, Ruthian, in terms of hitting home runs. He slugged 39 home runs in only 317 at-bats, a ratio that was the best percentage in history. In the next four seasons, McGwire slugged 245 home runs, then a major-league record for a four-year period.

Following the labor strike that ended the 1994 season, the offensive numbers went up. Some say it was the ball. Some say it was the new, smaller ballparks. Some say it was the crummy pitching. Some say the players cheated with steroids. If you chose (e) all of the above, you would probably be closer to the truth. Although in McGwire's case, smaller ballparks weren't an issue. In 1998, his 70-home-run season, his homers averaged 420 feet.

There has been sentiment in recent years for having McGwire take his place on Mt. Cooperstown as one of the all-time greatest first basemen. In fact, in 1999, McGwire was selected to the All-Century Team, joining Lou Gehrig as the best first basemen of all time. I take exception to that.

There's no doubting Gehrig's appearance on the 30-man All-Century Team. But Big Mac? I could name you half a dozen first basemen that I'd rather have on my team, starting with Double XX (Jimmie Foxx). There's also a bunch of McGwire's contemporaries (Jeff Bagwell, Frank Thomas, Eddie Murray, Rafael Palmeiro) that are superior in at least some respects to McGwire. There are old-timers like Hank Greenberg and Johnny Mize, who lost time to World War II. And there are a couple of free swingers from the 1960s (Willie McCovey, Willie Stargell, and Harmon Killebrew).

The Case for Mark McGwire, Part One: The 1998 Season

In many ways, McGwire's 1998 season was the single greatest season any player had in 75 seasons. Ruth had better seasons in 1921, 1922, and 1923. Bonds had a better one after that. But McGwire had a season better than anyone in three-quarters of a century.

Big Mac started on opening day by hitting a grand slam. The next day, he hit a three-run home run. He tied a National League record set by Willie Mays in 1971 by homering in his first four games of the season.

He hit three homers in a single game on April 14. He did it again on May 19. McGwire tied Reggie Jackson's major-league record with 37 homers by the All-Star break.

On July 12, he set a major-league record by belting his 40th homer in his team's 90th game. It was only his 281st at-bat.

On August 20, he tied a major-league record set first by Babe Ruth and Roger Maris by hammering his 50th homer of the season in his team's 125th game. McGwire's 50th came in at bat number 390 (which tied his own 1996 record for fewest at-bats to 50 home runs in a season).

On September 8, he broke Roger Maris's single-season home run record with his 62nd.

Sixty percent of Big Mac's hits that year were for extra bases (the second-highest percentage of all time for a single season). Over 46 percent of his hits were home runs (also the second-highest percentage of all time for a single season).

In that one season of 1998, McGwire led the National League in home runs, slugging, on-base average, walks, and extra-base hits. He was second in runs scored and runs driven in. But those are just the numbers. Here is what Joe Buck remembers about that season.

Joe Buck: "Mark McGwire was fighting history to go to a level that had never been done before. He linked fathers to sons, grandfathers to grandsons, enabling them to talk about bygone eras. People were talking about breaking Roger Maris's record in the same way that an earlier generation talked about Maris breaking Babe Ruth's record. There was so much pressure on McGwire. People said it couldn't be done, because of all the hype and pressure. And even after McGwire broke Roger Maris's record, he had to hit all those home runs on the final weekend merely to beat Sammy Sosa, who pushed him all summer. That was a better season than Bonds's 2001 season. There was no pressure on Bonds, not compared to what McGwire went through."

The Case Against Mark McGwire, Part One

His single-season record of 70 homers stood for just three seasons.

The Case for Mark McGwire, Part Two

McGwire wasn't a one-year wonder. He had a five-year run of hitting home runs that was better than anything the Babe had ever done.

> Mark McGwire, 1995–1999: 284 home runs
> Babe Ruth, 1926–1930: 256 home runs

In those five seasons, McGwire averaged a home run every 8.1 at-bats. That's a lot better than Ruth (who hit a home run every 10.1 at-bats in those five seasons).

The Case Against Mark McGwire, Part Two

In the first 118 years of major-league baseball, there were only 11 seasons where a player hit as many as 50 home runs in a season. Since 1996, there have been 10 seasons of 50-plus home runs in a season. I told you about Ruth's five best consecutive homer seasons— well, the Sultan of Swat led the league all five of those years. McGwire hit 284 home runs in five seasons, and didn't even lead the league in two of them!

McGwire's five-year total of 284 home runs was a record that also didn't last very long. Sammy Sosa slugged 292 home runs from 1998 to 2002. Sosa needed only 3,005 at-bats in those five seasons (1 home run every 10.3 at-bats). Hey, from 1999 to 2003, a short-stop slugged 239 home runs! Sosa averaged almost 60 home runs a season for a five-year period, and A-Rod averaged almost 50. In this light, McGwire's numbers don't look so . . . Ruthian. The pot-bellied Ruth lapped the field. McGwire, for a while, led the field.

The Case for Mark McGwire, Part Three

Despite a low batting average, he walked so much that his on-base average was .394 for his career. He had good hands, and played above-average defensively. Here are just a few more of McGwire's accomplishments:

- Sixth in career home runs (583)
- Eighth-highest career slugging average (.588)
- Tied for most seasons with 50-plus homers (4)
- Walked 1,317 times and drove in 1,414 runs

McGwire hit 415 home runs in the 1990s, despite hitting just nine homers in 1993 and nine more in 1994. In the other eight years of the decade, he hit 397 home runs.

The Case Against Mark McGwire, Part Three

He played in three World Series, and had just one home run in 48 Series at-bats. He batted .188 in his 13 World Series games. He batted just .217 with five home runs in his 42 postseason games.

He never won an MVP Award, and was in the top three in voting just once (second in 1998). Foxx, Thomas, and Bagwell combined for six MVPs.

Who's Better, Who's Best
Mark McGwire or Jimmie Foxx?

Mark McGwire never won a league MVP Award. Jimmie Foxx won MVP honors in 1932, 1933, and 1938. In 1933, he won the Triple Crown. Foxx twice led the American League in batting. Foxx was six feet tall and 195 pounds, but probably seemed bigger because he hit the ball so hard and so far and appeared so powerful. They both began their careers with the Athletics and led them to three consecutive American League pennants. It might seem fashionable to go with McGwire, but Foxx had about 13 or 14 truly excellent seasons, and McGwire had half as many.

Bob Costas: "The voting for the All-Century Team took place in 1999, only a year after McGwire hit those 70 home runs. Looking at it in 1999, one could assume that McGwire was a mortal lock for 600 career homers, with a legitimate shot at breaking Aaron's record of 755. Of course, that didn't happen, and today, I think you have to put Foxx ahead of McGwire."

A Better Analogy

Mark McGwire and O. J. Simpson Both McGwire and Simpson were larger-than-life superstars who first burst onto the national stage at USC. Simpson had a season in 1973 very similar to McGwire's 1998 season. The Juice ran for a then-record 2,003 yards, becoming the first player ever to eclipse the 2,000-yard mark, and was voted the MVP. Although 2,000-yard seasons have been surpassed since then, no other player ever accomplished the feat in a 14-game season, as Simpson did. Simpson captivated the nation when he went over 2,000 against the Jets on December 16 in the season finale.

When I think of McGwire and Simpson, I think of men who towered over their competition. I think of athletes accomplishing something that the very elite (Babe Ruth, Jim Brown) weren't able to do. I think of the electricity in watching them play in those seasons.

The analogy is only with their on-field performances. McGwire as a baseball player was comparable to Simpson as an NFL player.

Bob Costas: "Interestingly enough, O.J. was a bigger star coming into 1973 than McGwire—or Sosa—were entering '98. O.J. had done a lot of commercials, he had won the Heisman Trophy, he was a national figure. McGwire was known—but mainly to baseball fans. Yes, the nation was captivated by Juice in 1973 in his quest to get to 2,000 yards—but it was nothing like McGwire's and Sosa's home run chase."

MARIANO RIVERA

The problem is that everyone holds Mariano Rivera to such astronomically high standards. In the 2004 American League Championship Series, the Yankees blew a 3–0 series lead to the Red Sox and failed to advance to the World Series. Critics of Rivera will point out that he "blew" two save opportunities and has lost much of the intimidation factor that made him baseball's best relief pitcher for a decade. A little perspective is in order.

Rivera saved a postseason-record 23 straight games, beginning with the first of three straight championship seasons in 1998 and ending in Game 7 of the 2001 World Series. Since blowing Game 7 against the Diamondbacks, Rivera has pitched in 18 postseason games (2–0, eight saves), pitching 29.2 innings and allowing only two runs.

Even if people want to say that his decline started in 2004, they would be hard-pressed to support that with evidence. In the 2004 postseason, Rivera pitched in nine games (12.2 innings) and gave up only one run. It lowered his career postseason record to 8–1, with an 0.75 ERA and a record 32 saves.

Following a save to wrap up the 2004 divisional playoff series against the Twins, Rivera learned of a tragedy in which two family members were electrocuted in the pool at Rivera's mansion in his native Panama.

The Yankees were forced to start their series against the Red Sox without knowing if their ace reliever would be available. Rivera returned from Panama on a private plane and arrived at the ballpark after the first game had started. When the Red Sox cut into an 8–0 lead, Rivera made his usual stride in from the bullpen and restored order by saving the game. He saved the second game in the series the following night, as well. He did this against an inspired Boston team coming off a series sweep of the Angels. He did this against a team seeking revenge. He did this all with a very heavy heart.

In Game 4 at Boston, the Yankees gave the ball to Mariano Rivera to start the eighth inning, nursing a 4–3 lead. Rivera protected the lead in the eighth inning against the heart of Boston's order. In the ninth inning, just three outs from pitching the Yankees into the World Series, Rivera ran into problems. He issued a rare leadoff walk—a pinch runner stole second—and a soft single tied the game. The Yankees had given him no margin for error, but then again, he usually didn't require any. Rivera was the MVP of the 2003 League Championship Series against the same Red Sox team. In 2004, Boston finally came back against Rivera and the Yankees.

Rivera has pitched over 108 innings in the postseason for the Yankees—almost all of them in the late innings of close, pressure-packed games. His failures—few and far between—are magnified. He remains the greatest relief pitcher of all time.

He was born in November 1969 in Panama. The son of a poor fisherman, Rivera built his leg strength by hauling nets full of red snapper and flounder. Mariano grew up wanting to be a major-league baseball player.

But in the early 1990s, it was far from certain that Mariano Rivera would be a serviceable pitcher in the major leagues. In fact, in 1992, the minor-league prospect had surgery on his right elbow. He was a starting pitcher, with no reliable pitch aside from his fastball. In 1994, on the Yankees' top farm club, the Columbus Clippers, he was only 4–2 with an ERA of 5.81. The following season, Mariano started the season in Columbus and did well in seven starts, earning his first promotion to Yankee pinstripes. He made four disastrous starts before being sent back to the minor leagues. It was around this time that Yankees general manager Gene Michael discussed trading Rivera. Mariano made a start for Columbus, and his fastball was clocked at upwards of 95 miles per hour, consistently faster than he had been throwing. The Yankees noticed. They didn't trade Rivera. They recalled Mariano, and he struck out 11 White Sox batters on his return to the Yankees on July 4.

Rivera has credited the Lord with accelerating his fastball and his success in the major leagues. In the fall of 1995, the Yankees made their first return to the postseason since 1981. Although New York would lose to Seattle in a best-of-five divisional playoff series, Rivera was a standout in a relief role. He pitched 3.1 scoreless innings in a 15-inning victory in Game 2 at Yankee Stadium.

He pitched in three of the playoff games against Seattle, not giving up a run while striking out eight. Mariano found a role in the bullpen. He never started another game in his career.

In 1996, Rivera became one of the best pitchers in baseball, and the Yankees won their first World Series since 1978. He was the setup man for closer John Wetteland. The Yankees found a formula for success. If they had a lead that year after six innings, they would bring in Rivera to pitch the seventh and eighth innings, followed by Wetteland in the ninth. Rivera won eight games, saved five others, and dominated most of his appearances with his one great weapon—his "cut" fastball, a fastball with slightly more spin. Opponents hit just .189 versus Mariano that season. He struck out 130 batters in 107 innings.

He had a streak in 1996 of 15 hitless innings. He had another streak of 26 consecutive scoreless innings.

He was 1–0 with a 0.63 ERA in the postseason, throwing 14.1 innings and allowing just a single run.

That set the stage for what was to follow. He would become the dominant closer in baseball history, the greatest postseason pitcher ever, and the greatest Yankees hurler of all time. In 1997, in his first year as closer, he had 27 saves by the All-Star break. He had a 1.88 ERA for the season.

That was the postseason that the defending champion Yankees played the Cleveland Indians in the Division Series. In a painful 3–2 loss in Game 4, Rivera surrendered the game-tying homer to Sandy Alomar Jr. in the bottom of the eighth. It would be the last time he would fail in the postseason for years.

The Yankees won the World Series in 1998, 1999, and 2000, and Rivera was largely responsible.

When I was young and a Yankees fan, the bullpen ace was Sparky Lyle. When he entered games, the Yankee Stadium organist played "Pomp and Circumstance." When Rivera enters games, it is to Metallica's "Enter Sandman." I was too young to understand the meaning of Lyle's music at the time, and too old now to appreciate Metallica.

The lyrics of "Enter Sandman" include the words "Exit light, enter night," a reference to the fact that when Mariano enters the game, it's usually "lights out" for the opponent.

Greatest Yankees Pitcher of All Time?

It's not enough to say Rivera is the greatest Yankees reliever. He's the best pitcher the organization has ever had. Ron Guidry had one legendary season in 1978, and several other outstanding ones. Red Ruffing won 231 games as a Yankee, and was a pretty fair hitter, as well. Lefty Gomez won 189 games, but was better known as a DiMaggio crony. Babe Ruth and Roger Clemens were both great; but both were better pitchers with the Red Sox. That leaves Whitey Ford (236 wins) and Rivera. Both made their reputations in the postseason.

Rivera and Ford, Postseason Careers				
Whitey Ford	10–8	22 games	2.71 ERA	146 innings
Mariano Rivera	8–1	70 games	0.75 ERA	108.2 innings

Ford had that scoreless streak of World Series innings, but Rivera bettered that. Ford pitched shutouts in 10–0 and 12–0 wins in the 1960 Series against the Pirates. Not a lot of pressure there. Rivera had the ball with the game on the line in almost every inning he pitched.

Ford's Yankees won six World Series and lost five others. Ford lost the last two World Series he appeared in.

Rivera's Yankees won four World Series and lost two others. Rivera lost the last two World Series he appeared in.

Marty Appel: "Ford's 10 World Series wins lost some glamour when he wound up 10–8 in World Series play. Mariano may be the best Yankees pitcher I've ever seen."

Greatest Relief Pitcher of All Time?

When considering the greatest relievers of all time, here are the names that comprise the elite group, in no particular order: Eckersley, Gossage, Fingers, Smoltz, Rivera, Gagne, Sutter, Smith, and Marshall.

Jerome Holtzman, the official historian for Major League Baseball and the inventor of the Saves Rule, always maintained that Goose Gossage and Dennis Eckersley were the best relievers he ever saw. In recent years, he had strong praise for Eric Gagne and John Smoltz.

While Eckersley and Smoltz are undeniably two of the best pitchers of all time, they did not play that relief-pitcher position solely. They played two positions, like Stan Musial, who is considered one of the greatest players of all time but not one of the greatest first basemen, though he spent a majority of his career there. Eckersley doesn't make the Hall of Fame without his credentials as a starting pitcher. Eck started 361 games and did enough in them (a no-hitter, a 20-win season, nearly 200 career victories) that it pushed him into the Hall ahead of other relievers. Similarly, Smoltz became a late-career closer for the Braves, following a career where he, too, started 361 games. He, too, had a 20-win season, a stockpile of wins, and a well-deserved reputation for being one of baseball's best big-game pitchers (14–4 in postseason play).

As great a reliever as Eckersley was, he had only five Hall of Fame–caliber seasons as a reliever (1988–1992). Let's not forget that the A's had the best team in baseball over those five seasons but won only one World Series championship, mainly because of Eckersley's failures: He cost the A's in the 1988 World Series when he blew Game 1 (on a home run by Kirk Gibson). He cost the A's in the 1990 World Series when he blew Game 2 (giving up a run in the 10th inning). He cost the A's in the 1992 ALCS when he blew

Game 4 (on a home run by Roberto Alomar). That doesn't even take into account the starting assignment in Game 3 of the 1984 NLCS that could have put the Cubs into the World Series.

As great a postseason pitcher as Smoltz has been, he has had fewer Hall of Fame–caliber seasons than Rivera as well.

That leaves Lee Smith, Bruce Sutter, Gagne, Gossage, Fingers, Rivera, and someone who gets very overlooked in these discussions, Mike Marshall.

Lee Smith set the all-time saves record with 478 saves in an intimidating 18-year career. However, in those 18 seasons, he pitched in the postseason just twice, and never in the World Series. He lost with the Cubs in 1984, and he lost with the Red Sox in 1988. He battled a pair of famous curses, and the curses prevailed. Smith allowed five runs in less than six innings in his postseason career.

Bruce Sutter played in the postseason just once in his 12-year career. His 1982 St. Louis Cardinals defeated the Brewers in the World Series, but otherwise, Sutter never played on a first-place team.

There is little to dislike about Rollie Fingers's accomplishments. He won 114 games, saved 341 others, and gave up less than three runs per nine innings. His team won three consecutive World Series, with Fingers saving 6 of the 12 victories and winning a Series MVP Award. The fact is, he had a higher ERA and struck out far fewer batters than Rivera. Rivera was clearly a more dominant pitcher, who hasn't (through 2004) suffered a season-long slump like Fingers did in 1979.

That leaves a pair of Dodgers and a pair of Yankees. Let's look at their best two consecutive seasons each.

Eric Gagne

2002	77 games	82.1 innings	4–1	52 saves	1.97 ERA (team 92–70, 3rd place)
2003	77 games	82.1 innings	2–3	55 saves	1.20 ERA (team 85–77, 2nd place)

Mike Marshall (with Expos in '73, with Dodgers in '74)

1973	92 games	179 innings	14–11	31 saves	2.66 ERA (team 79–83, 4th place)
1974	106 games	208.1 innings	15–12	21 saves	2.42 ERA (team 102–60, 1st place)

Before everyone goes crazy about Gagne's record of consecutive saves, he wasn't nearly as valuable to his team, or as good a pitcher, as Marshall. Gagne's manager was a slave to the save statistic, preferring to use Gagne only for the ninth inning, and almost never putting him in a position to inherit runners on base, or enter a tie game. He was "saved" almost exclusively for games in which the Dodgers had a lead entering the ninth inning.

In 1974, the Dodgers won over 100 games and the National League pennant, in large measure due to their league-leading pitching. Top starters Don Sutton and Andy Messersmith combined for 23 complete games and 568 innings. Together with Marshall, Tommy Lasorda's two best starters combined to throw 53 percent of the Dodgers' innings, and the three finished 106 games (23 complete games by the two starters, and Marshall finished 83 others).

The first game that relief ace Marshall entered for the Dodgers was fairly memorable. It was on April 8, 1974, in Atlanta, and Dodgers starting pitcher Al Downing gave up a rather historic home run to someone named Aaron. Marshall entered the game in the third inning.

In 1974, Marshall won the Cy Young Award, finished third in the MVP voting, and was third in the league in ERA. In the postseason, he allowed only one run in 12 innings.

Over the 1973 and 1974 seasons, Marshall had 29 wins to go along with his league-leading 52 saves. He threw 387 innings in that two-year stretch. Note to managers who worry about overusing relief pitchers: Marshall pitched 14 years in the majors, so it couldn't have done too much damage to his arm.

Was Gagne as valuable? In 2002, the Dodgers finished six games out of first place. In 2003, they finished six games back of the Florida Marlins, a wild-card team that wound up as World Series champions.

I wonder if the Dodgers might have squeezed out six more wins if their top three pitchers (Hideo Nomo, Odalis Perez, and Gagne) could have given their team more than 524 innings (36 percent of the team's total) in 2002. The Dodgers turned to Omar Daal and Andy Ashby, and even 45-year-old Jesse Orosco, instead.

Now, there's only one reliever that can rate with Rivera over a decade. Goose Gossage is the man.

Goose Gossage

1980	64 games	99.0 innings	6–2	33 saves	2.27 ERA
					(team 103–59, 1st place)
1981	32 games	46.2 innings	3–2	20 saves	0.77 ERA
					(team 59–48, 1st/5th place)

Mariano Rivera

1998	54 games	61.1 innings	3–0	36 saves	1.91 ERA
					(team 114–58, 1st place)
1999	66 games	69.0 innings	4–3	45 saves	1.83 ERA
					(team 98–64, 1st place)

Gossage was overpowering in 1981, a strike-shortened season. He allowed only four earned runs all season in his 46.7 innings. In the postseason, the Yankees won eight games, and Gossage saved six of them.

Rivera was even better in the 1998 and 1999 seasons. Where do you begin with the dominance of Rivera's 1998 season? He prevented 20 of 23 inherited runners from scoring. He tossed 13.1 scoreless innings in 10 postseason appearances and was six-for-six in save opportunities. In 1999, he converted 45 of 49 save opportunities. He led the league in saves, save percentage, and relief ERA. He allowed only five inherited runners to score all year. He did not allow a run in his final 28 appearances of the year. He tossed 12.1 scoreless innings in eight postseason appearances and was six-for-six in save opportunities. He pitched 4.2 scoreless innings in the World Series with a win and two saves and was named MVP of the World Series. In that two-year stretch, Rivera threw 25.2 scoreless innings in the postseason.

Mariano has performed in the pressure-packed situations. He has peaked in the postseason. He comes into games with runners on base, and often in the eighth inning. He has done it for a decade. His 2004 regular season may have been his best (3–1, 1.36 ERA, 45 saves). He has done it in the glare of New York. He is the best pitcher in Yankee history. He is the best relief pitcher in baseball history.

DEREK JETER

Derek Jeter, the son of a black man from Alabama and an Irish mother from northern New Jersey, was born in 1974. He was born in Pequannock, New Jersey, but raised in Kalamazoo, Michigan. He was a Yankees fan from the time he was young, idolizing Yankees Dave Winfield and Willie Randolph, especially when spending his summers at his maternal grandparents' house in New Jersey. Jeter has often said in interviews that his upbringing was like "The Cosby Show." His parents were involved in everything he and his sister did. His grandfather Bill Conner went to work every day at the crack of dawn, and for 36 years he was the head of maintenance at the Queen of Peace Church in North Arlington, New Jersey.

Jeter was the best athlete and best student in high school, achieving almost all As while the University of Michigan salivated at the thought of him matriculating there and playing baseball for them. Derek, however, was drafted in the first round of the June 1992 baseball draft by the New York Yankees, with the sixth overall pick in the draft.

Even Dr. Huxtable would have allowed Jeter to follow his dream.

When Jeter made his major-league debut on May 29, 1995, the Yankees weren't perennial winners. In fact, they hadn't been in a postseason game since 1981, and hadn't won a World Series since 1978. Jeter played only briefly for the Yankees that season (15 games). He wore number 2, but reportedly had asked initially for number 13, which was refused because it was then-Yankee Jim Leyritz's number. Almost a decade later, an all-star infielder would wear number 13 for the Yankees, but it was Alex Rodriguez, not Jeter.

The Yankees made the postseason in 1995 and every postseason following. In Derek's first full season in 1996, they won the World Series. Jeter not only quickly became a Yankees fan favorite, he became the legends' favorite. At annual Old-Timers Day games at Yankee Stadium, the returning old-timers routinely asked Jeter for autographs for their grandkids, nieces, and nephews.

In 1996, Jeter became the first rookie to start at shortstop for the Yankees since Tom Tresh in 1962. But Tresh was patrolling for a dynasty at its end, and Jeter, one at its beginning. Derek was the unanimous choice for Rookie of the Year, after batting .314, scoring 104 runs, and driving in 78 more. He hit in 17 consecutive games at one point, the longest hit streak by a Yankees rookie since someone named DiMaggio in 1936 hit in 18 straight.

Derek Jeter's career can no more be judged by his regular-season achievements, though, than can the careers of Joe Montana or Reggie Miller. Some players are born for the biggest stages or arenas, and Jeter is one of them.

In Jeter's first postseason series, he batted .412 against the Texas Rangers. Advancing to the League Championship Series against the Orioles, Jeter needed some help from a 12-year-old Yankees fan from northern New Jersey. In Game 1 against the Orioles, the Yankees trailed 4–3 entering the bottom of the eighth inning. Jeter lifted a fly ball to right field that might have been a routine fly ball for Orioles right fielder Tony Tarasco, except that 12-year-old Jeff Maier reached down over the right-field wall with his baseball glove and swept the ball over the fence and away from Tarasco. Umpire Rich Garcia ruled the ball was a home run, giving the Yankees a 4–4 tie.

It would stay in the books as Jeter's first-ever postseason home run, and Baltimore never recovered, losing the game on a Bernie Williams homer and the series in five quick games. Jeter batted .417 against the Orioles. In the World Series, the Yankees lost the first two games, but won the next four to capture the first World Series championship for manager Joe Torre, a man that superstar Jeter referred to as simply "Mr. Torre."

Still, Jeter was having trouble separating himself from the growing number of outstanding young shortstops. While he had no trouble distancing himself from fellow 1996 rookie shortstops Edgar Renteria and Rey Ordonez, there was a 20-year-old shortstop for the Seattle Mariners hitting 36 homers in 1996. Alex Rodriguez wasn't a rookie in 1996, but it was his breakout season, the one that saw A-Rod hit .358. The next season, 1997, the American League saw another rookie shortstop win Rookie of the Year honors. Boston's Nomar Garciaparra belted 30 homers, stole 22 bases, and batted over .300.

George Steinbrenner, the Yankees' owner, had a bargain in Jeter, and had the resources to pay other stars as well. Steinbrenner, who had clashed with his superstar Dave Winfield only a decade earlier, positively gushed about Jeter, talking about him like he would his own son.

In Jeter's second season, 1997, he improved on his rookie year. He scored more than 100 runs, making him only the second Yankee to score 100-plus runs in each of his first two seasons (some guy named DiMaggio did it in 1936 and 1937). In the postseason, the Yankees played the Cleveland Indians in the Divisional Series. Cleveland would win the series and advance to the World Series, but Jeter batted .333 and slugged .667 in the losing effort.

The Yankees won a record 114 games in 1998, and Jeter was one of the main reasons why. He batted .324 with 19 homers and 84 RBI. In August, he batted .382, getting 50 hits in the month. He became the first Yankee to get 50 hits in one month since some guy named DiMaggio had 53 in July 1941. Jeter joined Alex Rodriguez (54 hits in August 1996) as the only players to get 50 hits in a month in the decade of the '90s.

The Yankees swept the Padres in the 1998 World Series, as Jeter batted .353 and got on base nine times in the four games.

The Yankees won another World Series in 1999, and Jeter had three rings by the age of 25. Only two other Yankees—Mantle and DiMaggio—had won three championships at a younger age. He batted .349 with 219 hits that season. Jeter approached A-Rod's and Nomar's power numbers with 24 homers, 102 RBI, 37 doubles, and 9 triples.

After his first four seasons, Jeter had 795 hits, which was more than Pete Rose (the all-time hit leader) had after his first four seasons.

Pete Rose after first 8 seasons: 1,532 hits
Derek Jeter after first 8 seasons: 1,534 hits (1,546 including his 12 hits in 1995)

Of course, Rose was never a good defensive player who played a key defensive position. He didn't win a World Series in his first eight years, either. In fact, Rose didn't win a World Series until his 13th season. Pete won three total, or fewer than Jeter had by the age of 25. Rose had 90 homers in his first eight years, compared to Jeter's 127.

Jeter has more speed than Rose, more power, more defense, and his team wins more. Both had the ability to take over an All-Star Game (Rose in 1970, Jeter in 2000), and both were team leaders that would do anything to win.

Jeter's Yankees won a fourth World Series in 2000, beating the Mets. Jeter hit .409 in that World Series and was named the MVP of the Series. In the fourth game of the 2001 World Series, Jeter came through again. Arizona Diamondbacks reliever Byung-Hyun Kim had pitched the eighth inning, blown the save in the ninth on a two-out gopher ball to Tino Martinez, then was left in for the 10th. On Kim's 62nd pitch, three minutes after midnight, Jeter sliced a pitch just over the 314-foot sign in right field. It tied the Series, one that the Yankees would ultimately lose in seven games.

In Game 3 of the 2003 World Series, Derek had the only three hits off Marlins pitcher Josh Beckett in a Yankees victory that put the Yanks up 2–1 in the Series.

Following the 2004 season, Jeter's teams were 17–5 in 22 postseason series.

Who's Better, Who's Best
Derek Jeter or Joe DiMaggio?
My uncle, James DeNoble, and father-in-law, Irv Levinson, grew up in 1940s New York and told me often about the great DiMaggio. They wouldn't recite statistics, as they would

about other players. Instead, they told me about how easy DiMaggio made everything look. DiMaggio had an aura about him. He had class. He was a winner.

When DiMaggio joined the Yankees in 1936, the Yankees hadn't appeared in a World Series since 1932, and before that, 1928. That changed almost as soon as DiMaggio appeared on the scene.

The Yankees won four World Series championships in DiMaggio's first four seasons. DiMaggio led the team to 10 World Series appearances. The only years DiMaggio played and the Yankees didn't make the World Series were 1940, 1946, and 1948.

Derek Jeter's rookie season was 1996, and the Yankees hadn't been to the World Series in 15 years. The Yankees won four World Series in Jeter's first five seasons.

Jeter has led his team to six World Series appearances in his first nine seasons. He came within three outs of a seventh World Series appearance in 2004. Jeter has played in 110 postseason games, winning 72 of them (a .654 winning percentage, despite the four-game losing streak to end '04).

Jeter has the most postseason hits in history, many more than any of his contemporaries—although it is unfair to use that number against past legends, who didn't have opportunities to play 15-plus postseason games a year.

Finally, Jeter has made some of the most famous defensive plays in Yankee history, since, well, since DiMaggio.

On July 1, 2004, against the Red Sox, Jeter made headlines in another dramatic Yankees victory. In the top of the 12th with runners on second and third and two outs, Boston's Trot Nixon sent a blooper over third base. Jeter sprinted over, caught the ball in fair territory for the third out, then went completely horizontal as his momentum sent him flying into the stands. New York went on to win 5–4 in 13 innings, but a bloodied and bruised Jeter was already in the locker room, getting x-rays.

But that was nothing compared to one of the most memorable defensive plays in baseball history. It happened in October 2001 in the third game of the Divisional Series against Oakland. With the Yankees up 1–0 in the seventh, Jeremy Giambi reached base with a two-out single. Then Terrence Long doubled into the right-field corner, where Shane Spencer proceeded to overthrow the cutoff man. Suddenly, Jeter came into the picture and flipped the ball to catcher Jorge Posada, who tagged Giambi. Yankees fans and management wouldn't consider the possibility of Jeter playing elsewhere. DiMaggio never did. No, Derek isn't close to DiMaggio. He is ranked closely with Mariano Rivera, the other leader of the latest Yankees dynasty. But Derek does remind people of the Yankee Clipper.

Where have you gone, Joe DiMaggio?

He might be putting a Yankees jersey on every day and trotting out to shortstop, that's where.

A Better Analogy

Derek Jeter and Tom Brady It was Fox NFL analyst Howie Long who said this while being interviewed during Game 3 of the 2004 American League Championship Series. Jeter and Brady have never put up the numbers that a few of their contemporaries have, but they get the championships.

AL SIMMONS

Al Simmons wasn't his real name. He was born Aloysius Szymanski on May 22, 1903, in Milwaukee, Wisconsin.

The story goes that when Al came home from the fourth grade one day, he proudly announced to his Polish immigrant father that he was going to be a major leaguer. His dad insisted that his future was in the butcher business, and he got the strap. After the beating, Al still insisted he was going to play baseball. His father finally relented.

Milwaukee might have lost out on a butcher, but they gained a Hall of Famer. Simmons came to the majors with a pair of nicknames. One was "the Duke of Milwaukee," for obvious reasons. The other one was obvious as well. He was called "Bucketfoot Al" because of his unusual batting style. It looked like he swung with one foot in a bucket. When Connie Mack first saw how effective a hitter Simmons was, he decided not to mess with his unorthodox style. His style not only set him apart, it gave pitchers fits. As the right-handed hitting Simmons stepped away from the pitch, pitchers tried to catch the outside corner of the plate. Al utilized one of the longest bats in baseball.

The Philadelphia Athletics were Al's favorite team, and he wrote letters to their manager, Connie Mack, asking for a tryout. Mack didn't return the letters. Simmons began his professional career at the age of 19, playing with teams in the American Association, the Texas League, and the Dakota League. By 1924, Connie Mack bought Simmons's contract and brought him to the majors. Simmons had not only made good on his fourth-grade goal, he would play for Connie Mack and the Athletics.

In his rookie season, Simmons drove in over 100 runs and batted .308. That set the stage for a 1925 season that would establish him as a star for years to come. He led the league with 253 hits, including 79 for extra bases. He drove in 129 runs and scored 122. He batted .384, which was third in the league behind Harry Heilmann's .393 and Tris Speaker's .389.

Simmons and Max Bishop were both with the Athletics by 1924. Lefty Grove and Mickey Cochrane would come a year later. Jimmie Foxx came after that, and Philadelphia was ready to challenge the great Yankees teams of Ruth and Gehrig.

Here's an example of how good those Athletics teams were getting. On June 11, 1927, the Athletics—for at least one inning—put seven future Hall of Famers on the field at once. The outfield consisted of Ty Cobb in right field, Al Simmons in center, and Zack Wheat in left. Jimmie Foxx played first base, with Eddie Collins at second, and Lefty Grove pitching in relief. When Mickey Cochrane pinch-hit, and caught the last inning of the game, they had, briefly, a lineup with seven Hall of Famers.

Simmons wasn't a power hitter, despite being six feet tall and over 200 pounds. What he was, was a great defensive outfielder and a great hitter.

Max Silverman, Historian, Philadelphia Athletics Historical Society: "They called him Bucketfoot Al, and he was positively manager Connie Mack's favorite player. He was a great outfielder. He was similar to Musial, but didn't have the same power. He normally batted in front of Foxx, who was the real star of those teams. They played in Philadelphia's old Shibe Park, which was not a bandbox. Simmons was a quiet guy, not loud or crazy. That was good for that team, since Lefty [Grove] was given to fits of temper. It was not unusual for Grove to tear the clubhouse apart following a loss. And Cochrane was pretty despondent after losses. But Simmons owned the town. He loved to go out— he was a flashy dresser—and was a favorite of the women. He had a side of him that let everyone knew he hated pitchers, because they were all trying to take bread and butter off his table."

In 1929, Al Simmons was the MVP of the American League, and the Athletics won the pennant over the Yankees' Murderers Row. Simmons batted .365 with 34 homers and 157 RBI. In the fourth game of the World Series, the A's trailed the Cubs 8–0 before staging the greatest comeback in World Series history. Al opened the A's seventh inning with a home run, and later in that inning singled, as the A's scored 10 runs to win the game and turn the Series around.

During the 1930 season, Simmons won the batting title by two points over Lou Gehrig. The Athletics defeated the Cardinals 4–2 to win their second straight World Series. Simmons held out in 1931 and signed just before the season started. He led the Athletics in batting for the eighth year in a row, hitting .390 to capture his second league batting crown. For the first time in three years, however, the Athletics lost the World Series, as St. Louis beat them in seven games.

Max Silverman: "At this point, the Athletics began trading away their stars. It's a misconception that Philadelphia didn't support the team. In 1931, they were the most successful team in the league with the highest payroll in baseball. What happened was the Depression hit. Neither Mack nor the Shibe brothers [the Philadelphia owners] had any money. There were two sets of owners at the time. There were the ones who owned baseball clubs as a toy, and the others who used baseball as their main business. The Philly owners didn't sell beer or gum—they had no other resources besides baseball. When the money dried up, they had to sell off their best players."

A 1931 Sheboygan, Wisconsin, newspaper had a picture of Al Simmons keeping his foot in a bucket with his mother looking over him. This was the caption: "Al Simmons was rested over the weekend for sore ankles. Everyone knows that hot water is good for sore ankles, and Al's mother, Mrs. Agnes Szymanski, knows how to keep the water hot."

The A's failed to win the pennant in 1932, and Connie Mack decided he needed to rebuild his team. He loved Simmons, but wasn't able to pay his salary. He was shipped to the Chicago White Sox. He had good seasons the rest of his career, but nothing like those first nine years in Philadelphia. In his first nine years with the Athletics, Simmons batted .358.

Simmons bounced around, from Chicago to Detroit to Washington to Boston to Cincinnati to Boston again. By 1940, he rejoined Connie Mack as player-coach with the Athletics. He tried to hook on as long as he could to attain 3,000 hits, yet he fell 73 hits shy of the elusive goal.

His last job in the majors was as third-base coach of the Cleveland Indians, although he resigned from that position midway through the 1950 season. A newspaper account said that Simmons was "plagued by a case of nerves," and said he had "personal problems." He had divorced his wife, and become a heavy drinker.

Simmons was elected into the Hall of Fame in 1953, along with Dizzy Dean. Amazingly, Joe DiMaggio (in his first year of eligibility) finished eighth in the balloting. Of the 264 baseball writers who voted for the Hall of Fame that year, 209 voters chose Dean, and 199 more selected Simmons. Also finishing ahead of DiMaggio were Bill Terry, Bill Dickey, Rabbit Maranville, Dazzy Vance, and Ted Lyons.

By 1956, Simmons's health had declined, and he died of a heart attack at the age of 53.

Who's Better, Who's Best
Al Simmons or Bernie Williams?

When Connie Mack was asked near the end of his 50-year managerial career what player could provide the most value to a team, he said, "If I only could have nine players named Simmons."

Al Simmons was not the biggest superstar on those great Philadelphia Athletics teams that won pennants in 1929, 1930, and 1931. He wasn't in the same class as Lefty Grove, Jimmie Foxx, and Mickey Cochrane.

Bernie Williams provides great defense, as Al Simmons did. He provides stability and consistency, as Simmons did.

Simmons won a pair of batting titles. Williams won a batting title. Neither man would ever win a home run crown, but Simmons blasted just over 300. Bernie has 263.

Simmons didn't have the power of Mel Ott or Stan Musial or other great left fielders. He was more like Bernie Williams—an all-star outfielder and big bat for a team that consistently gets to the World Series. Simmons was chosen in 2000 as one of the three all-time great A's outfielders, along with Rickey Henderson and Reggie Jackson. He belongs on that list, and on this one of the top 75 players of all time.

IVAN RODRIGUEZ

Ivan Rodriguez is one of the most valuable players of his—or of any—generation. He signed a one-year deal with the Florida Marlins for the 2003 season, and he pushed a team that had won just 79 games the year before to a 91-win season and a World Series championship.

The catcher-for-hire then signed a free-agent contract with the 43-win Detroit Tigers. He batted .369 prior to the All-Star Game and .334 for the season, and the Tigers improved their record by 29 games (going from 43 wins to 72).

Before that, Rodriguez was the most valuable player on the greatest teams in Texas Rangers history.

Ivan Rodriguez has had to piggyback on some great players for his nicknames. He is known as "Pudge," the same nickname as for the great catcher Carlton Fisk. He is also known as "I-Rod," a spinoff of Alex Rodriguez's nickname. No matter what you call him, you have to call him one of the greatest catchers in major-league history.

Ivan was born in November 1971 in Puerto Rico, just 13 months before countryman Roberto Clemente's plane went down. Little Pudge was also born smack in the middle of Johnny Bench's MVP seasons. Bench revolutionized the position, but Rodriguez would grow up and perform feats from the catcher's position that even the great Bench could only dream about.

If he looked like Johnny Bench behind the plate with his strong throwing arm, he looked like Yogi Berra at the plate, where he was a notorious free-swinger and "bad-ball" hitter.

Rodriguez was signed by the Texas Rangers as an undrafted free agent in 1988. He made the major leagues in the summer of 1991. He was a 19-year-old catcher calling games for 44-year-old Nolan Ryan. Although he wasn't called up to the Rangers until mid-June, he led the team by catching 88 games.

His first full season was in 1992, when he won his first Gold Glove Award. He was the third-youngest player to ever win a Gold Glove, with only Ken Hubbs and Johnny Bench being younger.

He made his first All-Star Game in 1992 (at the age of 20), and started his first in 1993 (at 21).

His first big season came in 1995. He batted .303 with 32 doubles and 221 total bases. He threw out 43.7 percent of base stealers (31 of 73), tops in the major leagues. He led all American League catchers with 782 total chances, 707 putouts, and 67 assists. Remember, he did this while catching 127 games—half of them in the sweltering heat of Dallas.

He kept adding to his game. By 1995, he was batting .300 over a season. By 1999, he was stealing 25 bases as a base runner. He was also hitting as many as 35 home runs in a season. In 2003, he was leading his team to postseason glory. In 2004, he was providing leadership and run support to a previously laughingstock organization, and pushing his offensive limits to career bests.

Ivan Rodriguez's Batting Average, 1992–2000

1992: .260
1993: .273
1994: .298
1995: .303
1996: .300
1997: .313
1998: .321
1999: .332
2000: .347

In 1996, he caught 146 games for Texas. He set a major-league record for most at-bats by a catcher, surpassing the 621 at-bats by Bench in 1974. He was not only the best fielding catcher, he was by '96 the best hitting catcher in the league. In 1996, he hit 47 doubles—45 of them while playing catcher. That set a record for most doubles by a catcher, eclipsing a 66-year-old Mickey Cochrane record. Ivan threw out 48.9 percent of the base stealers who tried to run on him (44 of 90). That was best in the major leagues. He led the majors with 140 starts behind the plate, 941 total chances, 850 putouts, 81 assists, and 11 double plays. The Rangers finished first in the A.L. West, and Rodriguez batted .375 (6–16) in their four-game defeat to the Yankees in the postseason.

Ivan finished eighth in batting in 1998, when he hit .321. He hit .350 prior to the All-Star break. He finished the season with 40 doubles (becoming the only catcher with more than one 40-plus doubles season). He again led all major-league catchers in games played, total chances, putouts, and assists. In the postseason, the Rangers were swept in three games by the 114-win Yankees team. Texas managed just one run in the three games; Pudge drove it in.

The Rangers won the A.L. West in 1996, 1998, and 1999, but lost in the playoffs all three years to the Yankees. Were the Rangers worn down by playing so many games in the Texas summer heat? The real answer is that the Yankees had superior pitching. Rodriguez was beginning to take criticism for (a) playing so many games behind the plate in the heat, and (b) the Rangers' pitching staff.

Texas Rangers Pitching Staff, 1996–2002

1996	90–72	1st place	4.66 ERA (6th in league)
1997	77–85	3rd place	4.68 ERA (7th in league)
1998	88–74	1st place	5.00 ERA (12th in league)
1999	95–67	1st place	5.07 ERA (11th in league)
2000	71–91	4th place	5.52 ERA (14th in league)
2001	73–89	4th place	5.71 ERA (14th in league)
2002	72–90	4th place	5.15 ERA (12th in league)

In Ivan Rodriguez's last seven years in Texas, the pitching was awful. How much credit, or blame, should the catcher have?

Rick Sutcliffe: "I can't believe he's not in Florida with the Marlins after winning the World Series. I always think of Ivan as more of an offensive guy. I never heard a pitching staff rave about him calling a game. I'll tell you what I admire about Rodriguez. Most of the great catchers never caught more than 130 games a year. Ivan would catch 150-plus for many years. You have to be some physical specimen, but it's even more than that. You have to have the desire, the passion to do what he's done."

This was how bad the Texas pitching was: In 2001, the Rangers signed free agent Alex Rodriguez. A-Rod hit 52 home runs, had 135 RBI, and played one of the two key defensive positions (shortstop). I-Rod hit 25 home runs and batted .308, while limited to 111 games due to injuries. He was on the disabled list early with a bone bruise, and had knee problems that ended his season in late August.

In that 2001 season, he won his 10th straight Gold Glove, which tied Johnny Bench for the all-time record among catchers. He won all 10 before the age of 30. That year, he caught over 50 percent of base stealers.

Ivan Rodriguez: Stolen Bases Against Through 2004 (14 Seasons)

534 steals against
427 caught stealing
44.4% caught stealing

Seven-Year Period Between 1995 and 2001

238 steals against
232 caught stealing
49.3% caught stealing

In the 2002 season, Rodriguez was sidelined with a herniated disc in his back and didn't play until June 7. In his first game of the season, he collected four hits. He batted .361 in September, with five home runs and 14 RBI. He finished the season with a .300-plus batting average for the eighth straight year.

And he couldn't find a job after his contract ran out. He had played out a five-year, $42-million contract with the Rangers, and they didn't re-sign him. He had played 1,479 games for Texas, 1,426 as catcher. That's a tremendous amount for a catcher. He had missed 176 games in the three previous seasons. He almost went to Japan to play, but the Florida Marlins signed him to a one-year deal for the 2003 season. He not only led the Marlins to a postseason spot, he was the MVP of the National League Championship Series, getting 10 RBI in the seven games. In the Divisional Series against the Giants, he proved his worth as a catcher, as the Giants' J. T. Snow tried to barrel over him for the tying run in the climactic ninth inning of Game 4. Ivan held onto the ball and preserved the win.

In the World Series, Ivan had another chance at the Yankees. This time, Rodriguez's squad came out on top. In 17 postseason games in 2003, Ivan batted .313 with 3 home runs and 17 RBI.

Everyone wants to doubt Rodriguez, because history has shown that every catcher falls off after a certain age. In 1997, Rangers general manager Doug Melvin pointed out that a catcher's production falls off after he's played 900 games in the majors. That is when Fisk's and Carter's and other catchers' numbers dropped.

In 2001, Rodriguez caught his 1,300th game, a milestone after which, historically, the production of even the best catchers in baseball history declined.

Not Pudge.

It is hard to justify paying long-term for a player that just shouldn't be doing the things he's done.

Rodriguez was signed by the Detroit Tigers as a free agent in February 2004. In June 2004, Ivan Rodriguez was named Player of the Month. He hit .500 for the month (43 hits in 86 at-bats). His teammate Rondell White was quoted as saying, "Those are Playstation or X-Box numbers. I've played with some great players, but I've never seen anything like this." Ivan was the first player in the majors to bat .500 for a month in four years. He was the first player in Tigers history to ever bat .500 for a calendar month. He was the first Tigers player to be Player of the Month in 14 years.

Johnny Bench caught 1,742 games in the majors. Yogi Berra caught 1,699. Ivan Rodriguez has caught 1,688. How much longer can he maintain this level?

Rodriguez has a career batting average of .306. He's hit 250 home runs, among the most ever hit by a major-league catcher. If he continues to produce into his late 30s, we might have been premature in calling Piazza the "greatest hitting catcher" and Bench "the greatest major-league catcher of all time."

Ivan Rodriguez is the most difficult of all the current players to rank historically. I'm being real conservative here.

Ken Singleton: "Pudge Rodriguez is no doubt one of the best catchers of all time. He affects the game both offensively and with tremendous defense. Pudge's outstanding footwork and quickness plus his strong arm make him tough to steal against, particularly if his pitcher holds runners well. I would give him a slight edge over Johnny Bench defensively. Rodriguez and Bench are two different types of hitters. Pudge has power, but is more of a high-average hitter. Bench was more of a slugger. The best hitting catcher of all time is Mike Piazza. He has both power [most homers for a catcher] and the ability to hit for a high average."

Johnny Bench: "I grew up in Oklahoma a Mantle fan, but I didn't see enough of the Yankees when Yogi played. I knew he was a two-handed catcher and a very clutch hitter. I would take Ivan over Piazza—but let me add this: I would love Ivan behind the plate, and Piazza at first base. Ivan was a better catcher than Mike because of his great footwork—that's the key."

JUAN MARICHAL

Today, the major-league rosters are sprinkled with players from the Dominican Republic. The major-league baseball record books are being rewritten by Pedro Martinez and Sammy Sosa and Manny Ramirez. It wasn't always that way.

The small island of the Dominican Republic began to attract the attention of the major-league teams in the early 1950s. Ozzie Virgil became the first Dominican to play in the United States in 1956. He was followed by Felipe Alou (1958), Matty Alou (1960), Julian Javier (1960), and Juan Marichal (1960).

This wasn't your average untapped source of talent. It was paydirt for scouts, and hasn't let up. Juan Marichal, the "Dominican Dandy," was born in October 1937 and remains one of the greatest pitchers—Latin or otherwise—in history.

He grew up near the town of Montecristo, and his first sports hero was Dominican Bumbo Ramos. Marichal would say that when he first went to see Ramos, he was a shortstop. The next day, he was a pitcher. Ramos was a sidearmer who threw pitches from all different angles. Marichal was a fan of the New York Giants, particularly pitchers Carl Hubbell and Sal Maglie. His style was a combination of Ramos, Hubbell, and Maglie. He threw a fastball, screwball, slider, and curve—and all from different angles and speeds.

Marichal was signed by his favorite team, now the San Francisco Giants, in 1958, and made the major leagues midway through the 1960 season. The Giants had a surplus of young talent, with Orlando Cepeda winning the Rookie of the Year Award in 1958 and Willie McCovey winning the next season. Marichal made his debut on July 19, 1960, and promptly pitched a one-hit complete game against the Phillies. The game took all of 90 minutes to play. In his second start, Marichal pitched a complete-game four-hitter.

Marichal finished 6–2 with a 2.66 ERA in his rookie 1960 season. He would have led the league in ERA had he pitched enough innings.

Juan led the league in earned run average only once in his career, in 1969. The reason why is the competition of the era:

National League ERA Leaders, Marichal's Career (1960–1973)

Sandy Koufax	5 times
Tom Seaver	3 times
Warren Spahn	1961
Phil Niekro	1967
Bob Gibson	1968
Juan Marichal	1969
Steve Carlton	1972

In his first full season—1961—Marichal won 13 games for Alvin Dark's third-place Giants. In the next season, Marichal became the ace of the staff. On July 25, 1962, the 25-year-old Marichal faced the 42-year-old Warren Spahn. Both pitchers went the distance, and the game finally ended when Willie Mays hit a home run in the bottom of the 16th inning to give Marichal the victory. He was 18–8 when he injured his foot in early September. He missed several starts, and lost his last three decisions. The Giants finished tied with the Dodgers for first place, forcing a three-game playoff. It came down to a deciding third game for the pennant, and Marichal got the call for the Giants.

In that game, Marichal was given a two-run lead on three Dodgers errors. In the last of the sixth inning, Marichal gave up a two-run homer to Tommy Davis to give the Dodgers a 3–2 lead. In the Dodgers' seventh inning, Maury Wills singled, stole second and third, and went home on a wild throw by the Giants' catcher. Marichal reinjured his foot and left the game in the eighth inning. The Giants scored four runs to bail out their ace and earn a spot in the World Series.

In the 1962 World Series, Marichal started one game and pitched four shutout innings before leaving the game when he smashed his finger trying to bunt.

In the next nine years, the Giants would win 88, 90, 95, 93, 91, 88, 90, 86, and 90 games. They averaged 90 wins per season, with Marichal winning an average of more than 20 games a season. He won almost 23 percent of their victories in that nine-year period. From 1963 to 1969, Marichal was 154–65, winning over 70 percent of his games.

Another excellent pitcher, Gaylord Perry, was signed by the Giants in 1958, and made it to the majors by 1962. He left after the 1971 season, but not before winning 134 games for the Giants. The Giants could never find other effective starting pitchers, though, and it cost them a pennant or two.

The Giants, with no wild-card system to depend on (unlike today's Red Sox, who finished second in their division seven years in a row, but at least made it to postseason play), finished second five years in a row and were shut out of the World Series.

Marichal was known for his high leg kick and his pinpoint control. In his career, he walked 1.8 batters every nine innings, which made him one of the premier control pitchers of all time. He led the league in fewest walks per nine innings four times (1965, 1966, 1969, and 1973).

His greatest season for control was 1965. It was also the year he lost control.

Marichal won 22 games that year. His 2.13 ERA was second in the league to Koufax's. The Dominican Dandy pitched a league-leading 10 shutouts. He was the winner of the All-Star Game, and MVP of that game.

By late August, the Giants and Dodgers were locked in a tight pennant chase. On August 22, 1965, in San Francisco, Marichal (19–9 at the time) started against Sandy Koufax (21–4). If the Giants won the game, they would be just a half-game behind Los Angeles. It was the fourth game of a pivotal series between the clubs. If Marichal could beat anyone, he could beat the Dodgers at home. He was 21–4 in his career against the Giants' hated rivals in games in San Francisco.

The Giants would win the game, but ramifications of the contest would haunt Marichal, and the Giants, for decades to come. The incident started when Marichal knocked down Dodgers Maury Wills and Ron Fairly with pitches close to their head. When the Giants came to the plate, Sandy Koufax threw the ball over Willie Mays's head, a sign that Marichal better not knock down any more hitters. When Marichal came up to take his turn at bat, catcher John Roseboro returned the first pitch from Koufax with a bullet thrown very close to Marichal's head. The Dodgers catcher was—in his mind—protecting his teammates better than pitcher Koufax. The San Francisco pitcher then began swinging his bat at the Dodgers' catcher, starting one of the most famous fights in baseball history.

Marichal's bat hit Roseboro on the top of the head at least twice and opened a two-inch cut that bled profusely. Marichal was fined a then-record $1,750 and suspended eight days. National League President Warren Giles called the incident "unprovoked, obnoxious, and repugnant." Marichal became public enemy number one in Los Angeles, where even admiring media like sportswriter Jim Murray quipped that "Marichal was a good-hitting pitcher. He could hit you with a baseball, or a bat."

The Dodgers won the pennant by two games over the Giants that season. Marichal lost his temper, and it may have cost his team a pennant. Or more.

The Giants didn't make it back to a World Series for 22 years, and even then, the earth opened up and almost swallowed the stadium. They were so close so many times, yet mysteriously the organization began trading its Latin stars. In 1966, the Giants traded Orlando Cepeda for pitcher Ray Sadecki. Cepeda won the MVP Award in 1967 and led the Cards to the pennant.

The Giants did not trade Babe Ruth, or deny entry to a billy goat, but the Marichal bat incident could have given the franchise a similar curse. The curse may have been on for the Giants, but Marichal continued to pitch brilliantly. In 1966, he was 25–6 with a 2.23 ERA. He struck out 222 and walked just 36 in 307 innings.

Of course, he didn't win the Cy Young Award, due to Koufax. Marichal didn't win the Cy Young in 1963 (25–8, 2.41 ERA), or in 1966. He didn't get a single vote in either season, as Koufax won unanimously in both years. Marichal never won the Cy Young, despite being the winningest pitcher of the 1960s. Many sportswriters and fans were unable to forgive Marichal for the Roseboro incident, but it didn't keep him from winning the Cy Young. The brilliance of Koufax and Gibson prevented the Giants hurler from winning a ton of hardware.

Most Wins, 1960s
1. 191 Juan Marichal
2. 164 Bob Gibson

Marichal was a model citizen who had one regrettable moment in a stellar career. He didn't smoke or drink. He even ended his career trying to hook on with the hated Dodgers. Roseboro eventually forgave him. In 1983, Marichal became the first Latin player voted into the Baseball Hall of Fame in the annual election (Roberto Clemente was ushered in immediately following his death). He served the Oakland A's as their director of Latin America scouting for 12 years. A few years ago, Dominican president Fernandez offered Marichal a cabinet position as minister of sports, physical education, and recreation. In that capacity, he has been able to facilitate relationships between Dominican baseball talent and major-league scouts.

Who's Better, Who's Best
Juan Marichal or Bob Gibson?

Juan Marichal and Bob Gibson, Career Records				
Marichal	243–142	.631	244 complete games	52 shutouts
Gibson	251–174	.591	255 complete games	56 shutouts

Winning when it really counted, as important as that is, is not enough to put Marichal over Gibson. Marichal had one of those great "What if?" careers. He won 191 games in the 1960s, and was still young enough (33 years old in 1970) to compile numbers that would have clearly distanced him from Gibson. A reaction to a 1970 injection meant that his arm would never again be the same. Marichal's Giants almost won every year. When they did win in 1962, Marichal was almost healthy enough to pitch. When Koufax and Gibson left the stage, Marichal's career was in a premature decline. He was a great pitcher, but he didn't put his stamp on the baseball world with a string of memorable World Series or postseason appearances.

MANNY RAMIREZ

In the late 1980s, Manny Ramirez was a teenager who dominated high school pitching in Washington Heights, just across the George Washington Bridge and no more than five miles from Yankee Stadium. Some 15 years later, Manny would celebrate a Game 7 win at Yankee Stadium as a member of the Boston Red Sox. So close, and yet so far, in the minds of many Yankees fans.

Manny's high school days were tougher than most kids. He had just come to New York (in 1985, at the age of 13) and had to learn a new culture and a new language. He would succeed beyond all expectations, becoming one of the greatest run producers in baseball history.

In fact, it is my prediction that Manny Ramirez is going to set a new career record for RBI. While everyone focuses on Aaron's career home run record, the 2,297 runs he drove in is probably a better testament to his ability. Aaron had to drive in an average of 100 runs for 23 seasons.

Ramirez, at the age of 32, has driven in 1,270 runs in a little less than 11 seasons. Bonds is going to struggle to get to 2,000 RBI, and might not make it. Then again, neither did the following: Lou Gehrig, Stan Musial, Ty Cobb, Jimmie Foxx, and Willie Mays.

Dave Winfield played 22 productive seasons, and fell short of 1,900 runs batted in. Ramirez is a long way from Winfield and the rest, but don't bet against him. (Following the 2004 season, Ramirez's 1,270 RBI ranked 98th best all-time).

Ramirez has done more than drive in runs, of course. He's won a batting title, hit a ton of regular season (and postseason) home runs, and been one of the most feared sluggers in the major leagues.

His calling card will forever be the RBI.

In 1999, Manny became the 10th major-league player since 1900 to drive in as many as 160 runs in a season—and the first in 61 years. Among players who drove home 160 runs in a season, Ramirez accomplished the feat with the fewest at-bats and hits.

Every player with a 160-RBI season is in the Hall of Fame, with the exception of Hal Trotsky and Ramirez (who might be one day). Lou Gehrig did it four times, and Babe Ruth and Jimmie Foxx did it three times each.

Ramirez was far from a one-year wonder. The year before that, 1998, Ramirez drove in 145 runs in 150 games. The year after his 165-RBI season, 2000, Ramirez drove in 122 runs in 118 games. In his last three seasons in Cleveland, Manny played 415 games and drove in 432 runs.

After that, he signed a huge free-agent contract with Boston. In his first three seasons with the Red Sox, he averaged .325 with 111 home runs and 336 runs batted in. That was in 416 games.

Added together, Ramirez put together six consecutive seasons where he drove in 768 runs in only 831 games. That, my friends, is averaging 150 RBI for every 162 games—obviously almost a run per game.

Most RBI in Majors, 1998–2003
1. 808   Sammy Sosa
2. 768   Manny Ramirez

Then, in 2004, Manny drove in 130 runs for the Red Sox. Sosa drove in only 80 for the Cubs.

Most RBI in Majors, 1998–2004
1. 898   Manny Ramirez
2. 888   Sammy Sosa

Ramirez is catching up to Lou Gehrig for another long-standing record. Gehrig has the major-league record with 23 grand slams. Ramirez has hit 17 slams by the age of 32, following the 2004 season.

Ramirez's slugging average for his career (over 5,000 at-bats) is seventh-highest all-time, trailing only Babe Ruth, Ted Williams, Lou Gehrig, Jimmie Foxx, Hank Greenberg, and Barry Bonds. His on-base average is 15th all-time.

There are a few reasons why Ramirez doesn't get the attention that his statistics demand. Manny showboats, and often shows up the other team with his play. He is not good defensively. And he hasn't shone in his early-career World Series appearances.

In the 1995 World Series, he batted just .222 for the Indians against the Braves in a losing effort. In the 1997 World Series, he had an even tougher time, batting just .154 (4 hits in 26 at-bats) against the Florida Marlins.

Despite that, if you watched the early rounds of the postseason, you would notice Manny Ramirez. He has hit 18 postseason home runs in 297 at-bats.

Mickey Mantle set the World Series record for most career home runs with 18. That was obviously the postseason record at the time, since baseball didn't have additional play-off rounds. Mantle hit those 18 postseason homers all in the World Series and against only best teams and pitchers. That means Mantle faced Koufax and Drysdale in 1963, Marichal in 1962, Warren Spahn in 1957 and 1958. You get the idea.

Baseball started playing a best-of-five League Championship Series in 1969, and Reggie Jackson played in 11 of the first 13 ALCS. Jackson hit 10 home runs in his 98 World Series at-bats, and tied Mantle with 18 postseason home runs.

When baseball expanded the League Championship Series to a best-of-seven and added the first-round Divisional Series, the record for postseason home runs was bound to fall.

The Yankees' Bernie Williams has played in 23 postseason series and has a record 22 postseason home runs in 443 at-bats. This is another record that Manny Ramirez will have a great chance to break. Ramirez has 280 postseason at-bats and 17 home runs.

Mickey Mantle	230 postseason at-bats	18 HR
Manny Ramirez	280 postseason at-bats	17 HR

Again, Mantle did it all in the World Series while Ramirez often did it against wild-card teams. But who's to say that Mantle's Yankees wouldn't have been surprised and upset in a League Championship Series or Divisional Series?

The world is Manny Ramirez's. He plays in an offensive era, on one of the best teams, in one of the best ballparks for hitters. He makes $20 million a year. He could one day be the major-league record holder in significant categories, including most grand slams, most runs batted in, and most postseason home runs.

In 2004, Manny Ramirez hit .308 with 43 home runs and 130 RBI. His teammate David Ortiz hit .301, with 41 home runs and 139 RBI. The American League had not seen teammates each bat .300 with 40+ home runs and 100 RBI since Ruth and Gehrig. Boston has a high payroll, which will keep productive table-setters in front of Ramirez. Ortiz protects Ramirez in the lineup. I happen to think that this combination will keep Ramirez a productive hitter for years, long enough to break significant records.

Or he could wind up with career numbers like his former teammate Albert Belle, who drove in more runs in the 1990s than anyone (including Griffey Jr. and Bonds), yet was done by 2000 at the age of 33.

Who's Better, Who's Best
Manny Ramirez or Albert Belle?

	At-Bats	HR	RBI	Batting Avg.	On-Base Avg.	Slugging Pct.
Albert Belle	5,853	381	1,239	.295	.369	.564
Manny Ramirez	5,572	390	1,270	.316	.411	.599

Belle, despite his surly personality, put together eight consecutive seasons of at least 30 homers and 100 RBI, and was headed toward the same career numbers that I project for Ramirez. But the end came suddenly for Belle. Belle, a former Cleveland teammate of Manny's, had been playing in pain during the 2000 season when doctors told him that he had a degenerative condition in his hip. In Belle's final 65 games of the year, he could only bat .248 with six home runs. It ended his streak of 30-homer seasons. In spring training of 2001, it became clear that Belle could not run, and he was forced into early retirement.

The trick is to guess how far from Belle—and how close to Aaron—Manny Ramirez will come. I realize Manny is a limited player in that he's not a great fielder, is a lousy base runner, and is not as complete a player as Frank Robinson, for example—and that's why he's ranked below him.

MARTIN DIHIGO

Many great players have hailed from Cuba, including Jose Canseco, Luis Tiant, and others. None have been any better than Martin Dihigo, who played for a quarter-century, mostly in the '20s and '30s. The great Martin Dihigo is the only baseball player in the world to be enshrined in the Hall of Fame of four different nations. He is a member of the Baseball Hall of Fame of the United States, Cuba, Mexico, and Venezuela.

Dihigo was born May 25, 1906, near the Cuban town east of Havana called Matanzas. Although his father wanted him to learn a trade like woodworking, he was destined to play baseball. From the age of 17, he was playing baseball professionally. He is said to have stood either 6'1" (according to Robert Peterson's *Only the Ball Was White*), 6'3" (according to baseballlibrary.com and other sources), or 6'4" (according to Latino Legends in Sports online). Similarly, he was between 190 and 215 pounds and born in either 1905, 1906, or 1907, depending on who you believe.

When a player can perform a number of difficult tasks well, he falls victim to a "jack of all trades, master of none" mentality. I believe this is what happened with the versatile Martin Dihigo. Negro League star Buck O'Neil named his all-time Negro League team in his autobiography *I Was Right on Time*, and selected Martin Dihigo as the utility player of his dream team: "Dihigo could've been considered for second base. He could have been considered for first base. The most versatile player in the history of baseball was Martin Dihigo, 'El Maestro.'" O'Neal goes on to quote Johnny Mize, who played with Dihigo one year in the Dominican Republic. "He was the only guy I ever saw who could play all nine positions, manage, run, and switch-hit," said Mize. "I thought I was having a pretty good year down there, and they were walking him to pitch to me." Hall of Famer Buck Leonard said, "Dihigo was the best all-around baseball player I've ever seen."

I spoke with Professor Roberto Gonzalez-Echevarria, the esteemed chairman of Spanish and Portuguese at Yale University who is the recognized authority on the history of Carribean baseball. He told me that people such as Roy Campanella, who played with Dihigo, often said that Martin was the best ballplayer they had ever seen. In one Cuban

Winter League season, Dihigo won the batting title, was the best pitcher, and was the manager of the championship team.

I questioned the caliber of play in the Cuban Winter League, and the professor, the author of *The Pride of Havana*, had a quick response. "The competition was quite keen. You had the best of the American Negro League players, you had the best Cuban ballplayers, you had a lot of Latin players who didn't play in the majors—remember, only the 'white' Cubans played in the majors pre-'47. The Winter League competition had a lot of major-league players as well. You have an enormous pool of players."

Professor Gonzalez-Echevarria went on to tell me more about the versatile Dihigo. "You have to remember one thing about stats from that time. There wasn't a home run mentality. So one doesn't have to look at home run totals. And it was economics that caused him to play several positions. Teams didn't have 25 players on a roster, and 10 pitchers. Because he was right-handed, he could play any position—including in the middle infield. He was simply off-the-charts great. He had a fastball that could buckle a hitter. I named him as my pitcher on the all-time Cuban team, only because I needed to find a way to fit in both Rafael Palmeiro (first base) and Tony Perez (third base). He very well could be the best first baseman."

I asked if there was a modern-day ballplayer that resembled Dihigo. He told me that Dihigo was 6'3", big for the time, and physically he looked very much like Dave Winfield. Dihigo was much more graceful than Winfield, however, who always looked more like a basketball player. He had Winfield's exceptionally strong arm, great speed, and his grace. Among Cuban-born players of his time, only Christobal Torriente was considered Martin's equal at the plate.

John Holway, author of many books including *Blackball Stars*, writes that Dihigo "had an arm like a jai alai player—in fact, better. Once, a jai alai player using a basket-like cesta flung the ball and hit the center field wall with one bounce. Dihigo wound up his bare arm and sailed the ball over the wall."

He was known as "El Maestro" in Mexico and "El Immortal" in Cuba. He began his career in 1923 as a first and second baseman for the Cuban Stars, in the United States. He made $100 to $125 a month and played as many as 143 games a season. The conditions were terrible. After the games, the players would pass a hat around the stands for money. After five years, he moved to the Homestead Grays, and had shorter stints with the Philadelphia Hilldales, the Baltimore Black Sox, and the New York Cubans. Dihigo was a star wherever he played, and under any conditions.

In 1999, Dihigo's son Gilberto, a Cuban journalist and author who lives in Mexico City, spoke to the *Dallas Morning News* about his late father, days before Dihigo was to be posthumously honored by the Florida Marlins. He explained that his father was a victim of frequent discrimination when he played in the Negro Leagues in the United States. "Hotels and restaurants sometimes shut him out because of the color of his skin. He despised that. He thought it was ridiculous and humiliating for blacks."

Dihigo played 21 seasons in Cuba, the United States, Mexico, and Puerto Rico. In the United States, he played 12 seasons—1923–1931, 1935–1936, and 1945. He finished his career winning three Negro League home run crowns and tied Josh Gibson for another. As a pitcher, he racked up more than 200 wins in American and Mexican ball.

His numbers were simply incredible in the 1930s. In 1938, he batted .387 in the Mexican League. He also went 18–2 with a 0.90 ERA as a pitcher the same year. He was 119–57 as a pitcher in Mexico. He threw the first no-hitter in Mexican League history, and also had no-hitters in Venezuela and Puerto Rico.

He played for 24 seasons in Cuba. The record of his Cuban career is not as well documented, but as a pitcher he was 93–48 between 1935 and 1946. Often, he would play all nine positions in one game. In the 1935 East-West Negro League All-Star Game, he started in center field and batted third for the East, and came in to pitch in relief.

Martin Dihigo left Cuba in protest after Cuban dictator Batista's coup in 1953. He continued to play ball in Mexico. He returned to the island just days after Fidel Castro's 1959 peasant revolt. He admired Castro, and served as his minister of sports in Cuba until his death at age 65 in 1971.

There have been a number of people who feel that Babe Ruth was the greatest player of all time because of his skills as a pitcher combined with his offensive numbers. Those same people have to find a place for Martin Dihigo among the all-time greats. How many other players can boast of pitching almost as well and almost as often as Satchel Paige, as well as hitting and leading his league in home runs like Babe Ruth?

Dihigo should have been embraced by the United States and gotten wealthy from his talents. He only missed by ten or fifteen years. In the '30s, talented Cubans like Dihigo were humiliated. In the '40s and '50s, Cuban bandleaders like Xavier Cugat and Desi Arnaz and actors like Cesar Romero found fame and fortune in the States.

DAVE WINFIELD

D ave Winfield was born in St. Paul, Minnesota, on October 3, 1951, the same day that Bobby Thomson's home run won the pennant for the New York Giants over the Brooklyn Dodgers. So it was a good day for baseball, all around.

Winfield's parents separated when Dave was only three years old, and Dave and his brother became increasingly close with their mother. Dave's relationship with his mom was one of the reasons he chose to attend the University of Minnesota and live at home. After pitching for the Gophers in his first two years, Winfield was invited by Minnesota's basketball coach, Bill Musselman, to try out for the varsity team. He not only made the team, he became a starting forward in the 1972 season after coming off the bench in an ugly, bench-clearing brawl with rival Ohio State. Minnesota went on to win the Big 10 title in basketball with Winfield.

In the 1973 NBA draft, the Atlanta Hawks made Winfield their fifth-round draft pick. Their fourth-round selection was a Harvard forward named James Brown—the longtime host of Fox's "NFL Sunday." Despite never playing football in college, Winfield's great athleticism and size (6'6", 235 pounds) caught the eye of the Minnesota Vikings, who drafted him as a tight end.

Winfield passed up the NBA, the ABA, the NFL, and every other league to wait for the June major-league baseball amateur draft. In that draft, Winfield was picked fourth overall—as a pitcher/outfielder—by the Padres. The first three picks were pitcher David Clyde, catcher John Stearns, and outfielder Robin Yount. The history of baseball is littered with great pitchers who changed positions to get their bat in the lineup every day (for example, Babe Ruth and Stan Musial). Winfield was no different, becoming an outfielder as soon as he signed with San Diego.

He became the first star and first gate attraction for the San Diego Padres. By the mid-'70s, he had become one of the best outfielders in the game. He was terrific defensively, especially adept at leaping to prevent home runs. By 1979, when he led the league in RBI, he was the best player in the league along with Pirates star Dave Parker.

Dave Winfield in 1979
159 games
.308 batting avg. (8th in league)
34 homers (3rd in league)
118 RBI (led league)
333 total bases (led league)
.395 on-base avg. (5th in league)
.558 slugging pct. (4th in league)

He also won his first of seven Gold Gloves that season. He was 27 years old at the conclusion of the 1979 season, and the perfect storm was happening for Winfield. He had a career year at a young age, just a year before his contract expired. Free agency was in its infancy, and teams were throwing big money at any player who became available (even older veterans or unproven commodities).

A Better Analogy

Dave Winfield and Jay Leno Sometime in the mid-1970s, Winfield was introduced to a businessman named Al Frohman, described by *Sports Illustrated*'s Rick Reilly as "a rumpled and retired New York caterer, a two-pack-a-day, fast-talking, 5'4", 220-pound chunk of walking cholesterol." Frohman befriended Winfield, gave him advice, even spied for him (talking to other players to find out how they pitched to Winfield to get him out). Winfield gave Frohman, who had prior experience as a sports agent, the chance to be his point man in negotiating a historic 10-year deal with George Steinbrenner and the New York Yankees. It was announced as a $15 million contract, which was the highest of all time to that point. There was also a cost-of-living escalator that would push the contract to $23 million. Frohman had tricked Steinbrenner, who had thought it would push the contract only to about $16 million. Frohman's contract had the cost-of-living escalator compounded daily.

Frohman had delivered Winfield to Steinbrenner in much the same way that an agent named Helen Kushnick delivered Jay Leno to NBC. Kushnick will undoubtedly be best remembered for her role in the late-night talk-show wars. According to *New York Times* reporter Bill Carter's bestselling *The Late Shift: Letterman, Leno and the Network Battle for the Night*—which later was adapted as a made-for-cable movie by HBO—Kushnick was a ruthless, foul-mouthed Svengali who put Leno in Johnny Carson's chair, burning every possible bridge along the way—including the one with Johnny Carson himself. Kushnick objected to Carter's description of her and filed a $30 million libel suit against him. The lawsuit was settled out of court. Just four months after guiding Leno into his

"Tonight Show" gig, Kushnick was dumped by NBC (with Jay's blessing) in September 1992.

In the Bill Carter book, NBC had to choose between David Letterman and Jay Leno to replace Carson, the king of late night. In the same way, Steinbrenner had to choose between Reggie Jackson (a Yankee whose contract was expiring following the 1981 season) and Winfield (who had played in San Diego for eight seasons, essentially the baseball equivalent of the Letterman 12:30 A.M. slot). Was Winfield ready for the big time of New York? Frohman not only thought so, but he convinced Winfield it would be the best place for him. After the contract was signed, Frohman then insulted Steinbrenner, telling the *New York Daily News*, "If he ever touches a hair of my boy's head . . . I'll blow the lid. I've got stuff on George that if it ever came out, he would be in big trouble. It's very easy to be friends with George if you have blackmail on him."

Winfield, initially, was very loyal to Frohman, who had once snatched the pen out of Winfield's hand just before he signed a 1977 Padres contract for less than Frohman thought Dave deserved. But the sour relationship between Frohman and Steinbrenner had affected Winfield's ability to get along with George. Steinbrenner constantly attacked Winfield, especially when he didn't carry the team like Reggie did. Winfield was hitless in his first 15 at-bats in the 1981 World Series, and Steinbrenner mockingly called him "Mr. May," a play on Reggie's well-deserved "Mr. October" nickname. Eventually, Winfield was forced to fire Frohman (albeit gently, according to a Rick Reilly 1991 *Sports Illustrated* article) and hire more experienced agents who were savvy in the ways of dealing with baseball management. Despite the fact that Winfield couldn't carry a team like Reggie, he did almost everything else. He could be counted on for production every day—batting in the middle of the lineup and producing all-star numbers.

NBC chose the "cool" Leno over the "hot" Letterman, and Steinbrenner picked the "cool" Winfield over the "hot" Jackson. Letterman and Jackson were supremely talented and confident in their abilities. But over the long haul, Leno and Winfield played much better and more consistently.

While Leno and Winfield found their place on the biggest stages in their fields, the agents who got them there fared much worse. Within a few years, both Kushnick and Frohman passed away.

Frohman had placed Winfield on the biggest stage in baseball, and by driving George Steinbrenner to commit acts against Winfield that would lead to the Boss's suspension from baseball in the early '90s, he even helped create the current reign of Yankees dominance.

Winfield would eventually finish his career and be inducted into the Hall of Fame. When Winfield was inducted, in 2001, players still had the choice of selecting which team cap they wanted to wear in the plaque that would be displayed in Cooperstown. Players no longer have that right, after Winfield signed a contract with the Padres in exhange for going into the Hall as a San Diego Padre.

Somewhere, Al Frohman had to be smiling.

Dave Winfield's Career

At the beginning of his career, from 1973 to 1980, Winfield played before empty seats in San Diego, on terrible teams.

San Diego Padres, 1973–1980

1973: 60–102
1974: 60–102
1975: 71–91
1976: 73–89
1977: 69–93
1978: 84–78
1979: 68–93
1980: 73–89

Would Winfield's stats have been even better if he played on the Big Red Machine, as opposed to playing alongside Padres Grubb and Gaston (they sound like Disney characters)? I believe they would have been much better.

After Winfield signed that big deal with the Yankees, he played with almost constant distractions. He had New York owners like Steinbrenner ordering his troops not to promote him. He had New York tabloids making big headlines with Winfield's paternity suit. His real challenge was in Yankee Stadium, where it was much harder for a right-handed hitter like Winfield to hit home runs than for a left-handed hitter. In 1982, Steinbrenner was quoted as saying, "Winfield cannot carry a team. He is not that kind of player. He's an excellent athlete. He's not Reggie." The late sportswriter Dick Young asked Winfield about the owner's remarks, and he replied, "Move the fences in, and I'll show you something." Winfield went on to say that although he wouldn't hit as many home runs as Reggie, he'd drive in as many runs and help win as many games.

Assuming Winfield lost around 5 to 10 homers per year by playing half his games in the Bronx, his 465 career total probably would have been closer to 530 in another home ballpark.

And Winfield also was a supreme run producer:

Major-League Leaders in RBI, 1979–1987

1. 1,017 Dave Winfield
2. 1,015 Mike Schmidt
3. 1,007 Eddie Murray

In the mid-'80s, the Yankees didn't win, but they had some excellent offensive teams. Don Mattingly came to the club in 1983, and Rickey Henderson in 1985. With those two batting in front of Winfield, it was easy to see why he drove in 100 runs all those seasons.

In 1984, Winfield batted a career-best .340. Going into the final day of the season, he led teammate Mattingly for the league lead, .341 to .339. Donnie Baseball went 4–5 in the season finale, while Winfield could manage only 1–4. Mattingly won the batting crown, and Winfield went home empty.

In fact, Winfield never led the league in batting average, or home runs, or slugging, or on-base average. Only in 1979 did he lead the league in anything (RBI, total bases). He never won an MVP Award, and was only once in the top three in voting. That's why Winfield, who had 1,833 career RBI—just 6 fewer than Ted Williams and more than Reggie Jackson, Ernie Banks, Mike Schmidt, Harmon Killebrew, Joe DiMaggio, and Mickey Mantle—is ranked so low in this book.

Winfield was mostly known as the player who accidentally beaned and killed a seagull in Toronto. He sat out the entire 1989 season due to back surgery, and the Yankees traded him in May of 1990 to the California Angels.

He kept going and going and going. In 1992, he became the first player ever to get 100 RBI at the age of 40. That year, playing for the Toronto Blue Jays, he finally contributed to a World Series championship, getting a big double off the Braves' Charlie Liebrandt. In September 1993, he got his 3,000th hit.

Winfield would play 2,973 games and get more than 11,000 at-bats in his major-league career. Both those figures are in the top 10 of all time. He batted .283 with 465 homers and 1,833 RBI.

He didn't have Reggie's flair for the dramatic. I always thought the skill he did better than anyone never showed up in a box score. No one ran from first to third as well as Winfield. It was a beautiful thing to see him run the bases.

He was a supreme fielder, with an ability to take certain homers away from opponents. He was a terrific run producer. With his athletic ability, I don't doubt he would have been a fine pitcher, or small forward, or tight end. Or businessman.

CHARLIE GEHRINGER

"Wallops and Women receive much consideration by handsome Chuck Gehringer, Baseball's Bachelor." That was the headline of a syndicated column from 1935 about Gehringer by Jack Curry, a sportswriter with United Press. Apparently, any quotes from Gehringer constituted news since he was so private and quiet:

And to admit casually that he might be married before next season [1936] was positively electrifying; particularly when one recalls the valiant fight waged by the chap with the wavy, black hair against flocks of women admirers who send him 20 to 30 scented mash notes [love letters, I suppose] a day. "Maybe they'll quit writing me if I get married," said Gehringer with a hopeful smile. Gehringer was asked if he felt there were other reasons for wanting to get married. He answered, "You talk like them dames write. No—I don't go in for that romantic stuff. I'm figuring on getting married because—well, everyone gets married. And I'm 32 now. I don't go for those slushy, mushy dames. No sir, I've got a nice, sweet girl." "And how do you spell her last name, Charlie?" The nimble Mr. Gehringer refused to be trapped. "What do you say we talk about baseball?"

Let's talk about his baseball and his place in the top 75 of all time.

Known for his quiet efficiency, Charlie Gehringer was not only the best fielding second baseman of his time, but he also hit for power and average. Ty Cobb, who managed the Tigers during Gehringer's first three seasons, said that next to Eddie Collins, Gehringer was the greatest second baseman he ever saw.

He batted over .300 in 13 different seasons, had 200 or more hits seven times, and posted a lifetime batting average of .320. He was named the MVP in 1937 after hitting a career-high .371 to lead the league. He finished second in MVP voting in 1934 to teammate Mickey Cochrane. He finished in the top 10 in MVP voting eight times, including seven years in a row between 1932 and 1938.

In 1929, he led the American League in eight categories, including hits, runs, doubles, triples, stolen bases, games played, putouts, and fielding percentage. That's a good year.

He hit for power. He hit 15 or more homers six times, and had 100-plus RBI seven times. In 1936, he walloped 60 doubles.

Gehringer was born in May 1903 in a town just 60 miles north of Detroit. He played baseball and football for the University of Michigan, but decided after one year he wanted to play professional baseball. A mutual friend had introduced Gehringer to Tigers outfielder Bobby Veach, who arranged a tryout for Gehringer with the Tigers and their manager, Ty Cobb. Following two seasons in the minor leagues, Gehringer was the regular second baseman for the Tigers for the next 16 seasons.

In many ways, Gehringer's career paralleled that of Yankees great Lou Gehrig, one of the top players in major-league history.

Gehrig was born in June of 1903, not far from Yankee Stadium. Like Gehringer, he played baseball and football at a major university close to home. In Gehrig's case, it was Columbia University. The left-handed hitting Gehringer was helped by the left-handed hitting Cobb. The left-handed hitting Gehrig was helped in New York by the left-handed hitting Ruth.

They called Gehrig "the Iron Man," and the nickname of Gehringer was "the Mechanical Man." Gehrig was the best first baseman of his era. Gehringer was the best second baseman. Both men lived at home with their parents well into their playing days. Gehrig got married at the age of 30. Gehringer lived with his mother in suburban Detroit until she passed away in 1946, and in 1949 he finally married at the age of 46.

Gehrig, of course, was best known for his consecutive games streak. Gehringer was outstanding in attendance, as well. Charlie injured his throwing arm in 1931, and was limited to 101 games. It was the only serious injury of his career.

In 1934, the batting leaders in the American League were Gehrig first, and Gehringer second. In 1937, it was Gehringer first, and Gehrig second.

In the MVP voting, Gehrig won in 1927 and 1936. He was second in 1931 and 1932. Gehringer won in 1937, and was second in 1934.

After 1939 (Gehrig's final season), their numbers looked like this:

Gehringer	7,864 at-bats	2,570 hits	.327 batting avg.
Gehrig	8,001 at-bats	2,721 hits	.340 batting avg.

Of course, Gehrig died in 1941, and Gehringer outlived him by more than 50 years. After his 1993 death, friends of Gehringer remembered him as a gentleman. Hal Newhouser, a Hall of Fame teammate, said, "He's the epitome of one of the great players in the history of the game. He was the type of fellow who when he played you didn't even know he was around. Everything was done with precision."

If you want to know why Charlie Gehringer is ranked so high in this book, just consider this: In May of 1949, the Hall of Fame voting was announced for that year. Gehringer was the only man that received enough votes for induction.

The voting went like this:

1949 Hall of Fame Voting (140 Votes Needed for Induction)

1. 150 votes   Charlie Gehringer
2. 128 votes   Mel Ott
3. 89 votes   Jimmie Foxx
4. 81 votes   Dizzy Dean
5. 76 votes   Al Simmons
6. 63 votes   Paul Waner
7. 52 votes   Harry Heilmann

Gehringer was the sixth second baseman to be inducted, following Nap Lajoie, Eddie Collins, Johnny Evers, Rogers Hornsby, and Frankie Frisch.

Who's Better, Who's Best
Charlie Gehringer or Roberto Alomar?

There has been a recent school of thought that considers Alomar to be one of the greatest second basemen—maybe the greatest—in baseball history.

Following the 2003 season, Alomar had played 2,323 career games—exactly the same number as the famed Tigers second baseman Charlie Gehringer.

	Games	At-Bats	Runs	2B	HR	RBI	BB	K	Batting Avg.	Slugging Pct.
Gehringer	2,323	8,860	1,774	574	184	1,427	1,186	372	.320	.480
Alomar	2,323	8,902	1,490	498	206	1,100	1,018	1,109	.301	.444

Let's just digest these numbers. Roberto Alomar has been a terrific player for many years in the major leagues, beginning in 1988 with the San Diego Padres. He was a big part of two World Series championships with Toronto in the early '90s. In the same number of games as Gehringer, Alomar has scored 284 fewer runs, driven in 327 fewer runs, and has struck out 737 more times than "the Mechanical Man."

Even allowing for the fact that Alomar has a few more home runs—and a lot more stolen bases (474 to 181), Roberto couldn't be the same player that Gehringer was. Alomar never led the league in doubles, or batting average, or stolen bases, or . . . anything. He never won the MVP Award. He finished as high as third once (1999) and had five finishes among the top six.

Alomar cannot match Gehringer in batting average, on-base average, or slugging percentage. Gehringer was a tremendous talent offensively and defensively, and was always respected by his teammates.

Too many people object to the mere mention of Barry Bonds being ranked ahead of Babe Ruth, yet they have no hesitation putting a modern player like Roberto Alomar ahead of Charlie Gehringer.

In 1937, a year the Yankees won the pennant, Gehringer was the league MVP over Joe DiMaggio (.346 with 46 home runs, .673 slugging percentage, and only 37 strikeouts). Maybe if Gehringer had played in New York, died early, or married a movie star he would be remembered by many more fans.

DUKE SNIDER

His real first name was Edwin, and that's mostly all Ed did. He will forever be known as the Duke of Flatbush, one of the frontline heroes when the Brooklyn Dodgers captured the hearts of underdogs everywhere in the 1950s. He was a major character on baseball's most charmed franchise during its glory years—one of the famous "Boys of Summer."

In their most celebrated decade, the Dodgers dominated the National League, and boasted a roster that included catcher Roy Campanella, who would earn three MVP awards in the early 1950s; second baseman Jackie Robinson, who was a big-game player and the most exciting base runner in the game; power-hitting first baseman Gil Hodges; and the Duke, who patrolled center field and won games with his sweet left-handed swing.

The arguments in the New York streets in the 1950s concerned the three great center fielders for the Yankees, Giants, and Dodgers. Mickey Mantle, Willie Mays, and Duke Snider were the three who shared a position and city. Although Snider is generally considered to be on a level below the other two, it was Snider who led the majors in home runs and runs batted in during the decade of the 1950s. In the four-year period between 1954 and 1957, Snider's numbers were right there with Mantle's and Mays's. The gap between Mantle, Mays, and Snider widens only after 1957. For the period that the three players all paid New York income taxes, Snider was on equal terms with Willie and the Mick.

Snider was a five-tool player, and there have been few players in baseball history with the grace of the near-perfect player, equally magnificent in running, hitting, and throwing. He led the N.L. once in homers, RBI, hits, walks, and on-base percentage. He led the league in slugging percentage twice, and in total bases and runs three times each. He finished in the top three in stolen bases twice. He led the Dodgers to six pennants in his first 11 seasons as a regular player, supplying power from the left side of the plate. He hit the final homer in Ebbets Field and followed the Dodgers to L.A., where he collected the first hit in Dodger Stadium history in 1962.

Duke Snider was born in Los Angeles in 1926. He grew up on a fruit farm and was a pretty good basketball player, as well as a baseball player, in high school. He was signed by Brooklyn in 1944, made it to the majors in 1947, and established himself by 1949. He played 18 years in the major leagues, doing most of his damage in the decade of the 1950s.

Now, Snider was in the right place at the right time in those halcyon days of the 1950s. Snider was fortunate that the Dodgers had a heavily right-handed lineup that resulted in him facing few lefty pitchers (Pee Wee Reese, Gil Hodges, Carl Furillo, Roy Campanella, and Jackie Robinson all hit right-handed). Ebbets Field was a small park, ideal for a left-handed slugger like Snider. The fact that teams hated to throw southpaws at the Dodgers worked to Snider's advantage.

He was so consistent from 1950 to 1957. How consistent? Well, he had 199 hits in 1950, 198 in 1953, and 199 again in 1954. In 1954, he hit 40 homers, drove in 130 runs, and scored 120 runs. He slugged .647. The following season, he hit 42 homers, drove in 136 runs, and scored 126 runs. He slugged .628. In that 1955 season, he lost the MVP voting 226–221 to teammate Roy Campanella.

He had as much talent as anyone in the league, a reputation for moodiness, and a penchant for letting other teams get under his skin. He was a notorious slow starter who absolutely hated spring training.

Snider led the Dodgers to the National League pennant five times in a seven-year period from 1949 to 1956. In each of those five seasons, they faced the same opponent in the World Series. The New York Yankees met Brooklyn in the Series in 1949, 1952, 1953, 1955, and 1956. Brooklyn won exactly one World Series, in 1955, before moving to Los Angeles in 1958.

In the 1955 World Series, the Yankees won the first two games, but the Dodgers won four of the next five games. Snider slugged .840 in the Series, getting 21 total bases in his 25 at-bats (he hit four homers), and for once, the Yankees had to wait till the following season.

When the Dodgers moved to Los Angeles, it was ironic how it affected two of the Dodgers' stars. Campanella, an easterner from Philadelphia, with New York businesses, was unhappy about the announced move. Of course, the Dodgers' temporary home in L.A., the Coliseum, would be a boon to right-handed power hitters like Campy, and would have significantly increased his home run totals if he had moved with the team. Conversely, Snider was from the Los Angeles area, and had an avocado farm in his native state. He was honest at the time, applauding the move, despite the move from cozy Ebbets Field to the Coliseum. Campanella never did play in the Coliseum, as his auto accident prevented him from ever playing again. The Duke became frustrated with the dimensions of his new home park.

The Duke of Flatbush no longer dominated after he left Brooklyn. When the Dodgers left New York, Snider was just 30 years old and coming off a 1957 season that saw him belt 40 home runs for a then record-tying fifth consecutive season.

Just a year later, across the continent, Snider hit only 15 home runs in 1958. On the plus side, being in Los Angeles meant that Duke could act in an episode of the television series "The Rifleman." John Wayne (also known as "the Duke") had nothing to worry about.

In the same way that Western TV series were being phased out in Hollywood as the 1950s ended, in favor of more urban and contemporary series, the Dodgers were changing, too, from a home-run hitting team in a small ballpark to a team that won on pitching and speed. Snider was like a Western star who couldn't cross over and make the transition to different subject matter. In his prime, Snider could have played in any ballpark—but he gained weight in the last years of his career and was through by his mid-30s.

Snider (who left Brooklyn with 316 home runs) would hit just 91 more in the last seven years of his career. Dodgers blue ran in his veins and he stuck with them, moving from New York to Los Angeles. Even in the hard years, Duke gave the Dodgers his best. In the end, it was the Dodgers who gave up on Duke when they sold his contract to the pathetic, last-place New York Mets in 1963. It was an odd thing for an old Dodger moving back to New York, with a new team that played in the Polo Grounds (the field of his old rival the New York Giants). Duke gave it his best, even making the All-Star team a final time in 1963, and the fans from New York and Brooklyn still loved him, even if he was just a shadow of the legend that they remembered. The Mets and the city honored Duke—they had a day in his honor at the Polo Grounds. All of his old teammates showed up, and Duke, at least for a moment, was happy again in baseball.

The Mets made him happier by giving him one last chance at another Series appearance by trading him to the Giants, now based in San Francisco. Snider was a teammate of Willie Mays on the 1964 Giants. How weird was that?

The Giants failed to give him a last pennant, and Duke retired. He struggled for some years afterward as a scout and minor-league manager, but at least he survived, which was more than some of his Brooklyn teammates could say.

He watched as his teammates from the great Dodgers era were honored and elected into the Hall of Fame. He waited for over a decade before getting the call from the Hall of Fame. Snider was a force in a golden age of baseball, one of the dominant players in the 1950s.

His was a funny career. He was from Southern California, but didn't have any good years playing out west. He spent his entire career in the shadows of other New York teams and other New York center fielders, and even in the shadows of some of his own teammates. He still has the National League record for most home runs in World Series play (11) and most RBI in World Series play (26). He has a pair of World Series championships. He has earned his place in the Hall of Fame, and a spot in my top 100 players of all time.

Who's Better, Who's Best
Duke Snider or Al Kaline?

One player had a career batting average of .297. The other one had a career batting average of .295. One had an on-base average of .376, the other one had an on-base average of .380.

Snider hit 407 home runs to Kaline's 399.

Snider was a supreme center fielder. Kaline was a right fielder who won 10 Gold Gloves. Snider made 8 All-Star teams, while Kaline made 15.

Snider was clearly the more dominant slugger. The Duke of Flatbush had a career slugging percentage of .540, much greater than the Tigers star's total of .480. Snider's eight best seasons are clearly better than Kaline's best eight. But Kaline's 22 years might be better than Snider's 18.

Neither player won an MVP Award, although both came close many times. Snider won a pair of World Series championships, and Kaline won in 1968.

Snider was a better player in his prime, and gets the nod here.

Who's Better, Who's Best
Duke Snider or Ken Griffey Jr.?

Griffey Jr. was the player of the '90s, and Snider led the majors in homers and runs batted in during the decade of the 1950s. Both were left-handed center fielders who had all the talent in the world. Griffey, the 1997 MVP, was in the top 10 in MVP voting in seven different seasons. Snider was in the top 10 in MVP voting six different seasons. Snider never did win an MVP, but finished second in 1955, and sure as heck deserved it. The Duke of Flatbush batted .309 (9th in the league), with 42 home runs (4th), 136 runs batted in (1st), and 126 runs scored (1st). He slugged .628 (2nd) and finished in the top 10 in stolen bases, as well. Most important, the Dodgers led wire-to-wire and captured their first-ever world championship.

	At-Bats	Batting Avg.	On-Base Avg.	Slugging Pct.	HR
Griffey Jr. (through 2004)	7,379	.292	.377	.560	501
Duke Snider	7,161	.295	.380	.540	407

Griffey Jr. had seven seasons of at least 40 home runs, including five in a row. Snider had six such seasons, including five in a row. There are only three players who have ever hit at least 40 home runs in a season more than five times in a row—and their names are Ruth, Sosa, and A-Rod.

Snider had the benefit of a cozy home stadium (Ebbets Field) and the luxury of a batting order that included right-handed hitters like Roy Campanella, Jackie Robinson, and Gil Hodges. Griffey had the benefit of being surrounded by wonderful hitters for most of his career as well.

Snider was in the World Series six times, and won twice. Griffey has never played in a World Series.

Griffey played in an era where more home runs were hit. When Duke Snider hit his 370th home run, in the 1961 season, it put him seventh on the all-time home run list. That's very impressive. Griffey was a wonderful defensive outfielder with a batch of Gold Gloves to prove it, but Snider was no slouch in that department, either.

In the end, Junior fell short in comparisons with Barry Bonds. Duke Snider fell short in comparisons with Willie and Mickey. Snider didn't last as long, and it feels right to rank him behind Griffey Jr. and ahead of Kaline.

WHITEY FORD

Of all the legends that have put on the New York Yankees pinstripes, very few were native New Yorkers. Babe was a babe in Maryland. They've had the Commerce Comet (Mantle, from Oklahoma) and Louisiana Lightning (Ron Guidry). In recent times, they've had great players from Puerto Rico (Bernie Williams) and Panama (Mariano Rivera).

They've had several great players from New York that never played a day for any other team. Lou Gehrig, of course, was the first one. Phil Rizzuto was another. Eddie "Whitey" Ford was still another.

It was Yankees scout Paul Krichell who first spotted and signed Gehrig, Rizzuto, and Ford. It's no wonder why Krichell was the chief Yankee scout for 37 years.

In 1946, at the age of 17, Eddie Ford went to Yankee Stadium for a tryout as a first baseman. It was Krichell who told Ford he ought to try pitching. Ford, who had not pitched in high school, was only 5′9″ and 150 pounds. For a Yankees contract, Ford learned how to pitch real fast, and the Yankees signed him for $7,000. Ford obviously had the desire but not the body to be an everyday player in pinstripes.

It was another Yankee southpaw legend, Lefty Gomez (by 1947 a manager in the Yanks' farm system), who tagged Ford with the name "Whitey." Ford was cocky, even in the minor leagues, placing a phone call to New York manager Casey Stengel to inform him he was available to help the Yankees in their 1949 pennant race.

Ford made the Yankees' squad midway through the 1950 season, and he was 9–1 in his rookie season, leading the Yanks to the World Series against the surprising Whiz Kids of Philadelphia. The Phillies were without 17-game winner Curt Simmons, who was drafted into the army late in the season. Ford, too, was drafted, and started the fourth game of the Series knowing that he'd be out of baseball the following two summers.

In the World Series, the Yankees swept the Phillies in four straight games. Ford pitched a shutout into the ninth inning of Game 4, when Gene Woodling dropped a two-out fly ball, allowing the only Phillies runs in a Series-clinching 5–2 win.

It was a microcosm of his World Series career, in which Ford would pitch more games than anyone else before or since. In 1950, Ford pitched the Game 4 clincher at Yankee Stadium, depriving him of a start in Philadelphia's Shibe Park. He did, however, pitch Series games in the Polo Grounds, Ebbets Field, Milwaukee's County Stadium, Forbes Field, Crosley Field, Candlestick Park, Dodger Stadium, Busch Stadium, and Yankee Stadium.

Following two years in the army, Ford returned to the Yankees and made lifelong friends with teammates Billy Martin and Mickey Mantle. Ford won his first seven decisions in 1953, upping his career record to 16–1 at that point, before losing to the lowly St. Louis Browns and their ageless wonder, Satchel Paige.

Ford's style was not one of intimidation. Rather, he could almost always put the ball exactly where he wanted it. His first pitch to a hitter was probably going to be low and outside, right where he wanted it. He had an outstanding curveball, and could throw the pitch on any count.

Yankee manager Casey Stengel didn't pitch Ford in a strict four- or five-man rotation. He preferred to pick his spots, and limited Ford to pitching against opposing aces. Whitey was 18–6 with a 3.00 ERA in 1953, but only started 30 games, and didn't pitch in the World Series against the Dodgers until Game 4. Brooklyn boasted a ton of great right-handed hitters, and Ebbets Field favored rights, as opposed to Yankee Stadium's "Death Valley" in deep right-center field. The Dodgers scored three runs off of Ford in the first inning of Game 4, on a homer by, of all people, lefty Duke Snider. Casey pulled Ford from the game after one inning. If he couldn't get the one lefty out, there was no point in leaving him in, I guess.

Two days later, on one day of rest, Ford started the sixth game, at Yankee Stadium. In this game, he went seven innings, allowing just one run. Carl Furillo's homer off reliever Allie Reynolds gave Brooklyn a short-lived lead until the bottom of the ninth, when Series hero Billy Martin scored the game-winning run.

In 1954, Ford would make the All-Star Game for the first of seven times in an eight-year period. Again, Stengel spent the year spot-starting Ford, and he went 16–8 in 28 starts, with an ERA of 2.82.

The Yankees returned to the World Series in 1955, a year that Ford went 18–7 with a 2.63 ERA.

Since the 1955 Series started at Yankee Stadium, Stengel gave the ball to Ford in Game 1. Whitey gave up homers to Carl Furillo and Duke Snider, but the Yankees prevailed 6–5. After the Yanks took the second game, they held a 2–0 lead over Brooklyn. The Dodgers won the next three games at Ebbets Field, with Stengel refusing to pitch his ace

Ford in any of the games. Instead, he held him for Game 6 at Yankee Stadium, where Ford four-hit the Dodgers to tie the Series 3–3. The Dodgers would win Game 7 at Yankee Stadium to take the Series.

In 1956, Casey Stengel earned his reputation as a baseball genius as the Yankees regained the World Series title from Brooklyn. Ford went 19–6 that season, winning 10 of his final 11 decisions. He could have won 20 games, but lost 1–0 in his final start.

Stengel, against his better judgment, threw Ford in Game 1 of the World Series in Brooklyn. Once again, bad idea. Ford was bombed, and lasted only three innings. The Dodgers defeated Don Larsen in the second game to win their fifth straight over the Yankees at Ebbets Field in the World Series. In a must-win third game, Stengel turned to Ford to pitch at Yankee Stadium. On two days' rest, Ford got the Yanks back in the Series, allowing only three runs.

Casey turned to Tom Sturdivant and Don Larsen for the next two games in the Bronx. Not only did each win, but Larsen pitched a perfect game.

The Yankees were one win away from the 1956 World Series, with two games left in Brooklyn. Would the Yanks go back to a well-rested Ford? Casey chose Bob Turley to pitch in the sixth game. In that contest, the Dodgers won their sixth consecutive home game in two years versus the Yanks. That set up Game 7.

The logical choice to start would have been Whitey Ford, the Yankees' top winner, the man who got them back in the Series in Game 3. But Stengel didn't like the odds of Ford pitching in the Ebbets Field bandbox. He started a man named Johnny Kucks, who never before or after would start a World Series game. Kucks (career record of 54–56) pitched a complete-game shutout, and Stengel was a hero. Apparently, Stengel stayed up all night deciding between tired Game 4 winner Sturdivant, a rested Kucks (who hadn't won a game in more than a month), and the left-hander Ford.

Stengel was more second-guessed that week for playing Enos Slaughter in left field for Ellie Howard, and for pitching Don Larsen twice. Everything worked out right for Stengel and the Yankees in 1956.

In a book where great players are ranked, I can't help but take points away from Whitey Ford for not making a start in either of the last two games of the 1956 Series. In the 1957 World Series, it was the Braves' Lew Burdette who won three games, taking the ball on short rest in Game 7 because Warren Spahn (who had pitched the first and fourth games) was injured. Ford started Game 1, defeating Spahn. He started Game 5, losing to Burdette. In Game 7, at Yankee Stadium, Stengel chose Larsen.

In 1958 Ford was 14–7, with a league-leading 2.01 ERA, when he injured his elbow and was out most of August and September. He started three games in the Series against the Braves in a rematch of the 1957 World Series. Whitey pitched well enough to win two of those games, but was shelled on short rest in Game 6. The Yankees won the World Series, getting victories from Bob Turley, Don Larsen, and Ryne Duren.

The greatest World Series pitcher of all time had now sat on the sidelines for Game 7 of four consecutive World Series.

The premier left-hander in the American League during the 1950s still had not pitched a 20-win season. He won 16 games in 1959, and 12 more in 1960. As Casey Stengel's reign came to an end, Ford had totaled just 133 wins due to army commitments, arm problems, and Stengel's juggling.

In the 1960 World Series, the Yankees again "babied" their ace Ford and didn't start him in either of the first two games in Pittsburgh's small Forbes Field. Ford pitched Game 3 at Yankee Stadium and won easily, 10–0. He came back in Game 6 and shut out the Pirates again, this time 12–0. No matter what the pitch count, shouldn't Stengel have taken Ford out on the chance that he might be needed—even for a batter or two—the next day in Game 7? The Yanks started Bob Turley in the seventh game, and he lasted one inning. For the fifth time in six years, the Yankees played a seventh game in the World Series, and Ford did not pitch.

The Yankees then let their 70-year-old manager Stengel go. They promoted coach Ralph Houk to manager. Houk promptly let Ford pitch in a strict four-man rotation. Whitey responded with the best seasons of his career. He won 66 games the next three seasons, including 25 in 1961.

During the 1961 World Series, several of the Cincinnati Reds paid Whitey the ultimate compliment by comparing him to the National League's Warren Spahn. Ford pitched a masterful two-hit shutout against the Reds, with only singles by Eddie Kasko and Wally Post spoiling a no-hitter.

Ford pitched 14 scoreless innings in the 1961 Series to break Babe Ruth's record for consecutive scoreless innings in the World Series. Ford had pitched 32 scoreless innings in the 1960 and 1961 World Series.

In Game 1 of the 1962 Series, Ford extended his World Series streak to 33 scoreless innings before surrendering a run on the way to his record 10th Series victory. He was 10–4 in postseason competition at this point. It was the last Series victory for Ford, who would get a no-decision in Game 4 and a loss in Game 6. The Yankees' Ralph Terry pitched a 1–0 shutout in Game 7.

Ford was 24–7 in 1963, but in Game 1 of the 1963 Series, he went against the Dodgers' Sandy Koufax. Koufax beat Ford, and the Yankees, twice in a week as the Dodgers swept the Yankees.

The Yankees dynasty was quickly coming to an end. The National League had pitchers like Juan Marichal (who pitched against the Yankees in the 1962 Series), Sandy Koufax (who pitched against them in '63) and Bob Gibson (who pitched against them in '64). Ford was 35 years old in 1964, with increasing arm problems. Following the 1964 Series, he had surgery to eliminate circulation blockages in his elbow.

Whitey had a 16–13 season in 1965 for a 77–85 Yankees squad now managed by Johnny Keane. The dynasty was ending, as was Ford's career. Following the '65 season, he had four wins left in his career. He tried another surgery in August 1966 before retiring.

He left the game with a winning percentage that came close to .700. Everyone then and now called him "crafty."

Tony Kubek: "He has to be among the top 10 big-game pitchers of all time. Koufax and Gibson are in there as well, Guidry for that one big year he had. Whitey could bunt, hit a little, run the bases. Gibson was the pitcher with the best athletic skills, but Ford did a little of everything as well. He was sneaky fast. He appeared to throw fastballs inside. He threw across his body. He didn't pitch 90 miles per hour, but it appeared that way."

Who's Better, Who's Best
Whitey Ford or Tom Glavine?

Tom Glavine, in his 16-year career with the Braves, posted numbers remarkably similar to those of the Yankees' "Chairman of the Board."

- Glavine was a 6'1", 190-pound left-hander from just outside Boston.
- Ford was a 5'10", 180-pound left-hander from just outside New York City.

- Glavine's teams were 12–10 in postseason play.
- Ford's teams were 6–5 in World Series play.

Glavine	262–171	.605	570 starts	3,740 IP	5.4 strikeouts and 3.1 walks per 9 innings
Ford	236–106	.690	438 starts	3,170 IP	5.5 strikeouts and 3.1 walks per 9 innings

Glavine was 4–3 with a 2.47 ERA in his eight World Series starts. That is fine, except that Glavine did not always come up big in the postseason:

Tom Glavine, Postseason Career

Divisional Series	3–3	5.15 ERA
League Championship Series	5–9	3.71 ERA
World Series	4–3	2.47 ERA

Glavine never pitched in a Game 7 of a World Series, either, but it wasn't his fault. He was set to take the ball for Game 7 in both 1992 and 1996. His Braves lost Game 6 in both years.

Tom Glavine did pitch a 1–0 victory in Game 6 of the 1995 World Series to give the Braves their only World Series championship in Atlanta. Glavine won a pair of Cy Young awards (in 1991 and 1998) to Ford's one (1961). But Ford, who won in 1961, would have won the American League Cy Young in 1963 if one had been awarded.

As batters, they both hit .173, and were among the best-hitting pitchers in their league. Ford lost time for serving his country, and spent parts of other seasons injured. It's pretty close, actually. Ford was better, but not by a whole lot.

Ford had the best won-lost percentage of any starting pitcher in baseball history with 200 wins. He had the advantage of being left-handed, and pitching in Yankee Stadium (death to right-handed batters). He had the advantage of playing with Mantle and Maris. He obviously would have won with any team, in any ballpark. Even with the advantages, he wasn't Koufax or Spahn. Ford was better than Glavine, a man who played on pennant-winning teams for a long time and won a similar number of games.

BUCK LEONARD

"We didn't think about playing in the major leagues very much. The majors were for the white guys. We didn't even think about them. We had our own league, like another world, and we played like no other league existed." Those were the words of Buck Leonard in the late '80s, when he was a very old man.

Buck Leonard was a Hall of Fame first baseman who batted .340 and averaged 34 home runs a season during his 17-year career in the Negro Leagues. He passed away in 1997, in Rocky Mount, North Carolina. He was born in the same town 90 years earlier. Leonard was the son of John (a railroad fireman) and Emma. He left school at age 14 to work as a shoeshine boy, then as a mill hand for the Atlantic Coast Railroad. He played semipro ball until he lost his job during the Depression. Professional baseball wasn't a choice, it was a necessity. At the age of 25, Leonard left Rocky Mount to become one of the finest first basemen in the game.

A teammate of Josh Gibson on the Homestead Grays team that won nine consecutive Negro National League titles from 1937 to 1945, Buck (a stocky, 5'10" player) made a record 12 All-Star games. At 40, he tied for a homer title and was number one in hitting at .395.

Leonard once batted .500 in eight games against a group of big-league all-stars playing for Satchel Paige's all-stars in the winter of 1942, before Commissioner Kenesaw Mountain Landis halted the series. Landis's rationale was that the barnstorming games took away from the "organized nature" of major-league ball—whatever that means.

Leonard and the Homestead Grays played many of their home games at Washington's old Griffith Stadium in the 1940s. Washington, D.C., was a distinctly southern city in which segregation was an accepted condition. Still, many players from that era believed that Washington would be the first to integrate the major leagues. This was because the park was located in a black neighborhood in a city that was mostly black.

Gibson and Leonard were the drawing cards that packed Griffith Stadium many times over. In the early '40s, Washington Senators owner Clark Griffith toyed with the idea of signing the pair. He brought the two sluggers into his office to discuss the possibility with them. Eventually, Griffith changed his mind.

Leonard was the second-best player (and probably the most reliable) on the best team in his league. In the major leagues, this would have brought financial rewards. It didn't in the Negro Leagues. Salaries were low, and when Leonard started his professional career, real low. How low? In 1934, when Buck started, players on the road received 60 cents per day for expenses. Eventually, meal money reached $2 per day, and Buck's salary eventually rose to close to $1,000 a month. Only Satchel Paige and Gibson were making that much in the Negro Leagues at the time. By 1948, Leonard claimed he was earning about $10,000 annually, including playing winter-league ball. When he retired, it was reported that he was the third highest-paid player in Negro League history behind Paige and Gibson.

His career with the Homestead Grays started in 1934, when he played for the Brooklyn Royal Giants. Leonard met Smokey Joe Williams, a great Negro League pitcher who was running a Harlem bar at the time. Williams knew of Buck's fielding and hitting abilities, and he arranged for Leonard to sign with the Grays for a salary of $125 a month.

As a first baseman, Buck was considered sensational. He had a powerful throwing arm and great agility. He usually hit in the high .300s and on occasion would reach the .400 mark. He was credited with leading the league in 1948 with a .391 average, and in 1945 he finished second to Gibson, hitting .375 to Josh's .393.

Because he batted behind Josh Gibson ("the black Babe Ruth") and was a left-handed hitting first baseman, he was called "the black Lou Gehrig." The only problem with that analogy was that Gehrig was much more of a power hitter than Leonard.

Modern fans should think of Leonard as a Negro League Don Mattingly. Mattingly was an exceptional hitter and one of the best-fielding first basemen of all time. Because Mattingly's back injuries cost him a long career, think of Leonard as a cross between the two Yankee first basemen—Gehrig and Mattingly.

Buck Leonard was 38 years old in 1946, when Jackie Robinson was signed by Brooklyn. Bill Veeck, the maverick owner of the St. Louis Browns, offered Leonard a job in 1952, but the 45-year-old declined, believing he was too old at the time and preferring to play in Mexico.

The Homestead Grays folded at the end of the 1950 season, and the Negro National League soon expired. Buck went to Mexico to spend three seasons. He retired in 1954 at the age of 48. Buck returned to Rocky Mount, where he would be a truant officer and the town's recreation director.

In 1971, the National Baseball Hall of Fame created a special committee to recognize African-American athletes who played during baseball's segregated period. Subjected to

Jim Crow laws of the times, these players were never given the opportunity to showcase their talents in the white major leagues. Before the committee disbanded in 1977, they had placed nine players in Cooperstown. The committee included former players like Roy Campanella and Judy Johnson, journalists, and executives. Seven of the nine players are included in this book—only Judy Johnson and Monte Irvin are not part of my top 100. Buck Leonard was put into the Hall of Fame in 1972 ahead of Pop Lloyd and Martin Dihigo and Cool Papa Bell. It stands to reason he was pretty good.

Okay, here's the tricky part—where to rank Leonard compared to the men who did play in the majors. I'm putting him behind some of the white sluggers of his time (like Johnny Mize) but ahead of some more modern first basemen (McCovey, Palmeiro, and Bagwell). Of course, several of the great-fielding first basemen of all time are not included at all in the top 100. This list includes Hal Chase, Don Mattingly, and Keith Hernandez.

As for the lack of competition that Leonard faced, Leonard told author Robert Peterson, "We didn't have star men at every position. We didn't have—as the majors did—two good catchers and six or seven good pitchers. . . . We had pitchers who were mediocre and we just used them against white semipro teams. Sockamayocks, we used to call 'em."

When the sockamayocks were on the bench, and the regular lineup was intact, the first-line black clubs were a match for anybody.

EDDIE MURRAY

He didn't have a flashy name, or a flashy nickname. Instead he was "Steady Eddie." He was sort of a reverse Babe Ruth. Ruth was a beloved figure to fans and the adoring press. Murray was anything but beloved. Ruth had charisma, and fans gravitated toward him. Murray displayed little emotion on the field. When Murray gave his 2003 Hall of Fame induction speech, he started by saying, "When Ted Williams was here, inducted into the Hall of Fame 37 years ago, he said he must have earned it, because he didn't win it because of his friendship with writers. I guess in that way, I'm proud to be in his company."

Murray was born on February 24, 1956, in East Los Angeles, at a time in history when African-American kids played baseball more than any other sport. Murray was a teammate at Locke High School of Hall of Fame shortstop Ozzie Smith. There were four future major-leaguers on his high school team, in fact. Murray came from a large family with 12 children. His youngest brother, Rich, played some with the Giants in 1980 and 1983. Older brothers Venice and Leon played in the Giants system as well. The eldest, Charles, an outfielder, reached the Triple-A level in the Houston organization. Who's on first? Rich, Venice, and Leon were all first basemen, like Eddie. One of his seven sisters, Tanja, passed away from kidney disease just a week before Eddie got the call informing him that he had been elected to the Hall of Fame, making the announcement bittersweet.

He signed with the Orioles organization in 1973, and his 1975 manager at Double-A Asheville, Jimmy Schaffer, suggested that Murray learn to switch-hit. While switch-hitting advantages are numerous, few have the ability. Murray had the ability. By 1977, the 21-year-old emotionless rookie was penciled into Orioles manager Earl Weaver's lineup card every day. In 1977, he was the designated hitter as Lee May played first base. Both Murray and May hit a team-leading 27 homers each. By 1978, Murray was the first baseman, and the 38-year-old May continued as designated hitter. Eddie played three games in the outfield in 1977 and three at third base early in '78. He took over first base for the O's in April 1978, and had a Gehrig-like hold on the position for a decade. He won three Gold Gloves, and was good in the field for a decade, although Don Mattingly came along and began gobbling up the Gold Gloves.

Murray the Fielder

He led American League first basemen in fielding in both 1981 and 1982. He had 113 straight errorless games from September 7, 1980, until he erred September 21, 1982. He won three straight Gold Gloves from '82 to '84.

To err is human, but to knock in runs like Murray did is divine. Although he was never the league MVP, he had eight years of finishing in the top 10 in voting—including six consecutive seasons. His teammates loved him, and his team won. From 1977 to 1985, Baltimore averaged 93 wins a year and won two pennants.

I spoke with one of Murray's Baltimore teammates from those seasons, Ken Single-ton. Singleton played in the majors from 1970 to 1984 and was a teammate of Tom Seaver, Willie Mays, Cal Ripken Jr., Reggie Jackson, Brooks Robinson, and Jim Palmer, among others. This is what he told me about Murray:

Ken Singleton: "The best player I played with was Eddie Murray. He was simply the best in the clutch that I have ever seen. When we needed the big hit, he almost always came through. Too bad he didn't get along with the media. Fans did not really get to know the real Eddie, who was a great teammate. Still, that did not keep him out of the Hall of Fame. Eddie was a very intelligent player. He was always looking for the edge that would help us win."

How can "big hits" be quantified? They really can't, but in Murray's case there are a few examples.

Game-Winning RBI

In 1980, baseball began tracking and recording a statistic called "game-winning RBI." It was credited to a player whose run-scoring hit gave his team a lead that was not relin-quished. From 1980 to 1985, the major-league leader in game-winning RBI was Eddie Murray with 97, followed by Keith Hernandez (94) and Dave Winfield (87).

Whatever drawbacks the statistic entailed—a player would receive credit for a game-winning RBI when knocking in the first run of a 12–0 game, for instance—it is telling that Murray put his team up for good about 15 times a year over a six-year stretch.

Batting with the Bases Loaded

In 238 at-bats with the bases loaded, Murray batted .399 with 19 grand slams and 298 RBI. He had a slugging percentage of .739 with the bases loaded. That's clutch, under any definition.

Hitting with Runners in Scoring Position

Starting in 1979, Eddie Murray batted .324 (358 hits in 1,106 at-bats) with runners in scoring position over an eight-year stretch.

Most Sacrifice Flies, Career
1. 128 Eddie Murray
2. 127 Cal Ripken Jr.

Murray was always productive. He never had those Mattingly/Griffey/Sosa seasons of 140 RBI, but he had 20 years in a row of 75 or more. No other player ever did that, and no one else but Hank Aaron did it for as many as 19 years. Murray only had 78 RBI in 1981 because the players' strike eliminated 50 games from the schedule, and his total of 78 led the league.

Most RBI, 1980s, Major Leagues
1. 996 Eddie Murray
2. 929 Mike Schmidt
2. 929 Dale Murphy

The thing to remember is that Murray operated in a decade that had relatively few offensive fireworks. In the nine-year period from 1981 to 1989, Eddie Murray slugged .507. While that wouldn't make the top-10 leader board in the early 2000s, it led the American League then. In fact, only one other player (George Brett) slugged higher than .500 in that nine-year period.

The MVP That Wasn't

Murray never did win a Most Valuable Player Award, but he amassed more votes than any other player in the first seven years of the 1980s:

A.L. MVP Votes, 1980–1986

1. 1,088 Eddie Murray
2. 738 Don Mattingly
3. 619 George Brett
4. 572 Rickey Henderson

Murray probably deserved the MVP in 1983, when he lost a close vote to teammate Cal Ripken Jr. Murray finished second in the league in runs scored, third in slugging, fourth in homers, fourth in total bases, and fifth in RBI.

Murray played a very long time in the majors—21 years—and the first half of his career was of Hall of Fame caliber, while the last half was still productive.

Eddie Murray	Games	At-Bats	Hits	HR	RBI	Batting Avg.
First 10 years	1,499	5,624	1,679	275	1,015	.299
Last 11 years	1,527	5,712	1,576	229	902	.276

This bears repeating. In those first 10 years of his career, Murray's numbers were dominating the competition. In his first 10 years, he hit more homers than every other American Leaguer except Jim Rice. Only Rice and Mike Schmidt had more RBI in the major leagues in Murray's first 10 years.

A Better Analogy

Eddie Murray and Karl Malone Karl Malone and John Stockton were to the NBA what Eddie Murray and Cal Ripken Jr. were to Major League Baseball. Malone and Stockton played together as teammates for 18 seasons. The most amazing thing about Stockton was his durability. Playing one of the toughest defensive positions (point guard), Stockton had perfect attendance in a remarkable 17 seasons.

After being on the roster for 1,500 Jazz games, Stockton had managed to play in all but 22 of them. That means he played in almost 99 percent of the Jazz games over a 19-year period. That he did most of it with a buddy was even more remarkable. Karl Malone almost never missed a game, either. "The Mailman" missed only nine games in his first 17 years. Their work habits rubbed off on each other and on their teammates. The Jazz won a lot of games, but didn't win the championship. Stockton and Malone got to a pair of NBA Finals, in 1997 and 1998. Malone did not play well in those games. In the 1997 Finals, he missed a ton of free throws. In the 1998 Finals, he turned the ball over 20 times in the Jazz's four losses.

Cal Ripken, of course, broke the baseball record for consecutive games played. But Cal said in 1995 that it was Eddie Murray who taught him the importance of being in the lineup every day.

In Murray's first 10 years (1977–1986), he led the majors in games played (1,499). That represented over 96 percent of the Orioles' games. In his first nine years, he missed a total of 34 games, playing 99 percent of the Orioles' games. Murray was an iron man—like Malone. Murray suited up for 3,026 games. Of the 16,000 players to wear a major-league uniform, only four others played more games.

Also like Karl Malone, Murray didn't come up big in the biggest games of his career. In the 1979 World Series, he batted a frustrating .154 (4–26). His Orioles lost the last three games of the Series, and Murray didn't get a hit in the last five games. In the 1983 World Series, Murray batted only .250 (5–20). Eddie played in one final World Series, and he managed only two hits in 19 at-bats for the 1995 Indians. So Murray batted only .169 (11–65) in World Series action.

Who's Better, Who's Best
Eddie Murray or Rafael Palmeiro?

Murray was a first baseman. Palmeiro was a first baseman.

Murray won three Gold Gloves at first base. So did Rafael Palmeiro (although Palmeiro won one in a season in which he was mostly a designated hitter).

Murray hit 500 homers without ever leading the league. Palmeiro hit 500 homers without ever leading the league.

Murray and Palmeiro both had over 5,000 total bases.

They were teammates for one season. In 1996, the Orioles brought back Murray in a midseason trade, and the onetime outcast was given a hero's welcome home. The 40-year-old Murray played 64 games that summer for Baltimore, racking up 230 at-bats as the designated hitter. He batted .257 with 10 homers and 34 RBI. Palmeiro, in the prime of his career, played 159 games at first base, and hit .289 with 39 homers and 142 RBI. Murray never hit that many homers or drove in that many runs in a season.

It's nuts to think that Palmeiro—no matter how many homers he finishes with—was a better player than Murray. Raffy was never one of the five best players in the league. He never finished in the top four in MVP voting. He had only three top-10 finishes. Palmeiro never went to a World Series. Palmeiro only went to four All-Star games. Eddie had twice as many top-10 MVP seasons. He had twice as many All-Star Game appearances.

Murray was only the third man, after Hank Aaron and Willie Mays, to accumulate 500 homers and 3,000 hits.

Murray never showed emotion on the field, and yet his teammates loved and appreciated him. Palmeiro's career was nothing to get excited about.

CARLTON FISK

I can't help it. Every time I hear Carlton Fisk's name, I think of one thing. I think of an incident from May 1990, when Fisk's White Sox were playing the Yankees. A Yankees outfielder named Deion Sanders (yes, Neon Deion) hit a pop-up and failed to make an effort to run to first base. Fisk took umbrage and yelled at Sanders, "Listen to me, you fuck. Next time, you'll run it out."

Sanders actually apologized the next day. Fisk explained that he was offended by the lack of effort.

When one mentions Hall of Famer Carlton Fisk, a lot of things come to mind. Many remember Fisk's dramatic home run to win Game 6 of the 1975 World Series. Other fans remember Fisk as the man who set the record for playing the most games ever by a catcher. Still others remember his rivalry with Yankees catcher Thurman Munson, or Fisk's amazing production late in his career, when Carlton set the major-league mark for most home runs hit after the age of 40. I actually caught up with the Hall of Fame catcher at the American Century Golf Tournament in July 2004, and asked him if more people come up to him and ask him about cursing out Deion or the 1975 World Series home run to win Game 6.

Carlton told me that lately, it's been about 50-50. Which tells me that he's as well known for respecting the game as he was for playing it. Beautiful.

Fisk had a legendary work ethic that enabled him to last 24 seasons in the major leagues and play 2,499 games. No one before or since has caught as many games (2,226) as Carlton, and that record may stand awhile. If you think about it, one would have to catch 130 games a year for over 17 years to approach Fisk's record.

2,226 Games as Catcher

Most major-league catchers—even the very best—break down at a faster rate than players who play other positions. The very best hit a ceiling at about 1,700 games caught. Johnny Bench caught 1,742 games. Yogi Berra was behind the plate for 1,699. Gabby

Hartnett finished with 1,793. Ted Simmons had 1,771 games. Mike Piazza went over 1,400 games as catcher early in the 2004 season, but the chances of his playing another 800-plus games behind the plate are slim. Ivan Rodriguez would seem to have the best chance to break Fisk's record, for a number of reasons. First, he started young, playing 200 major-league games behind the plate before he was 21 years old. Next, he's terrific defensively. Lastly, he's not playing home games in the heat and humidity of Texas or Miami anymore. Ivan needed 538 games at catcher entering the 2005 season, or roughly another five seasons behind the plate. If he doesn't "catch" Fisk, then no one will for a long time.

Carlton was born and bred a New Englander, raised in Vermont and educated at the University of New Hampshire. He was drafted by the Boston Red Sox, a perfect fit for someone who grew up playing in New England. Although he made his major-league debut at the end of the 1969 season (five at-bats), his first full season didn't come until 1972, when he was 24 years old.

In that 1972 season, Fisk won his only major award (Rookie of the Year) and won his only Gold Glove for fielding excellence. He finished fourth in the MVP voting that year, his highest finish for the award except for 1983 (when he would finish third). Fisk also made the All-Star team that rookie season, as well as six times in his first seven seasons (missing only in 1975).

Just as the late '90s was a period featuring three of the greatest shortstops of all time (Boston's Nomar Garciaparra, New York's Derek Jeter, and the slightly-better-than-the-other-two Alex Rodriguez), the early '70s was an era of three of the greatest catchers ever (Boston's Fisk, New York's Thurman Munson, and the slightly-better-than-the-other-two Johnny Bench). Munson and Fisk had quite the rivalry going.

The ESPN commentator Peter Gammons, a young *Boston Globe* reporter in the early '70s, wrote the rivalry was based on the fact that "Munson resented the chiseled, handsome Fisk as opposed to the dumpy, stubbled Munson." Munson and Fisk played the game the same way, but both competed for the same turf and the same prizes. Thurman felt that influential national sportscaster Curt Gowdy (a former Red Sox announcer) had labeled Fisk as the player most likely to be the greatest catcher of all time before he retired.

Both Fisk and Munson were original baby boomers, born in 1947 in small towns. They both made their debuts in 1969. They both won Rookie of the Year awards. Either the Yankees or Red Sox won the American League pennant in 1975, '76, '77, and '78, when the two catchers were at their peak. Munson competed hard against Fisk for respect. When Yankees public relations director Marty Appel pointed out one day in his game notes that Munson was second in the league to Fisk in assists, Munson dropped third strikes on all seven "strikeouts" the next day by Yankees pitchers, so he could record putouts at first base and surpass Fisk. There were a number of on-field skirmishes between the two, the most famous occurring in August 1973, when the Yankees and Red Sox were involved in a pennant race. They brawled at Fenway Park after a play at the plate.

Munson was considered the better catcher and the better handler of a pitching staff. Fisk was considered a better power hitter. Munson was considered more durable (although circumstances would have Fisk outlasting Munson by 14 years of major-league service). They were both fabulous clutch hitters (Fisk, in his only World Series, hit his dramatic home run; Munson batted .357 in his 30 postseason games.)

Munson had only 5,344 at-bats when he crashed his plane in the summer of 1979. If you had bothered to check Fisk's odometer at the same mileage (5,344 at-bats), this is how they compared:

| Munson | .292 | 696 runs | 113 home runs | 701 RBI | .410 slugging pct. |
| Fisk | .280 | 849 runs | 219 home runs | 785 RBI | .476 slugging pct. |

Obviously, Fisk was a better player. Munson's advantage in batting average translated to 63 more hits (over about 10 years, about 6 more hits per season). That's negated by Fisk's clear advantage in slugging percentage and run production.

Munson was the MVP of the 1976 season, however. Carlton Fisk never won an MVP Award and was never as dominating in a season as Bench was in 1970 or 1972. Fisk's career numbers match up very nicely with Johnny Bench's, despite that.

Defensively, Fisk was adequate, certainly not a liability. In the prime years of his career (1975–1985), there were .62 stolen bases per game by Fisk's opponents. That was almost exactly the same as Gary Carter's numbers. It wasn't as good a mark as defensive catchers of the era like Bob Boone and Jim Sundberg, but then again, that's why Fisk won only the one Gold Glove.

Carlton Fisk played his entire career in "Sox." He changed his Red Sox to White Sox after Boston's management didn't tender him a contract in time following the 1980 season. (It's hard to go from the Red Sox to the White Sox, but Fisk almost lost his socks, totally, by almost becoming a Yankee in the mid-'80s.)

Fisk's "Yankees Career"

Yankees owner George Steinbrenner's taste for acquiring the best free agents began in the first days of free agency. Steinbrenner pounced when opportunities arose in the mid-'70s (signing Reggie Jackson, Catfish Hunter, and Goose Gossage), and the Yankees went to the World Series in 1976, 1977, 1978, and 1981. Then, Steinbrenner stopped grabbing the top free agents in the mid-'80s. Following the 1985 season, Carlton Fisk's White Sox contract came up, and he had hit 37 home runs that season. The Yankees were a second-place team, with talented players like Don Mattingly and Dave Winfield. One would think that Fisk was everything Steinbrenner looked for in a player. Steinbrenner always loved the most passionate competitors (like Fisk or Roger Clemens). The idea of grabbing a former Red Sox hero never seemed to bother Steinbrenner later (see Wade Boggs and Roger Clemens), so why not in 1985?

Steinbrenner—a close friend of White Sox owner Jerry Reinsdorf—chose to pass on Fisk, as did all the other owners. If it sounded fishy, it was. Steinbrenner and the other owners were found guilty of collusion. By the way, the Yankees didn't go to the World Series from 1981 to 1996. When Steinbrenner began playing by the rules again, in the early '90s—letting his flowing revenue stream sweep up the best players—the Yankees began to return regularly to the World Series. The man won whenever he played by the system, and lost when he participated in an illegal charade. Fisk would have made millions more if he had been allowed to test the market in the mid-'80s without the collusion. Playing in New York might have spiked his regular-season numbers—and given him other chances in the postseason. Collusion might have kept Fisk's all-time ranking down.

Carlton Fisk maximized his ability. He got 24 years in the big leagues, hit a lot of home runs, and made a boatload of money. He respected the game, and ran everything out. He even made others—like Deion Sanders—do it.

76

WHO'S ON THE BENCH?

In what is commonly called the modern era (post-1900), over 14,000 players have appeared in a major-league game. Then, of course, there have been many Negro League, Cuban, and Japanese players who didn't have the opportunity to play major-league baseball in the last century. This book intended to rank and debate the top 75 players—the ones better than 99.5 percent of all players. So, we've settled the debates between the top one-half of 1 percent. We're judging the valedictorians, so to speak. There isn't room in this book for Nolan Ryan or Ozzie Smith. Old-timers will be upset when they fail to find Orlando Cepeda. Younger fans will be shocked not to find Ichiro here. There isn't a place for half the Hall of Fame members. Wade Boggs had a lot of hits, but he doesn't get invited to this party. Wee Willie Keeler doesn't, either. Neither does Don Mattingly or Keith Hernandez or Tony Perez.

But so many people asked me where some of their favorites would be ranked if I ranked more players that I had to "open up" the invitations, and invite the next wave of players in the door. This, then, is the reason for ranking an additional 25 players. This is where you'll find Rod Carew, Hank Greenberg, Sadaharu Oh, and Dennis Eckersley. It will be time real soon to open up the list for Ichiro Suzuki and Albert Pujols, as well. But I'm not going to throw out George Sisler (number 92) for Ichiro just yet.

The Rest of the Lineup
76. Hank Greenberg
77. Ernie Banks
78. Dizzy Dean
79. Mickey Cochrane
80. Vladimir Guerrero
81. Earl "Pop" Lloyd
82. Willie McCovey
83. Al Kaline

84. Frankie Frisch
85. Rod Carew
86. Kirby Puckett
87. Jim Palmer
88. Sadaharu Oh
89. Sam Crawford
90. Harry Heilmann
91. Tim Raines
92. George Sisler
93. Frank Thomas
94. Smokey Joe Williams
95. Bill Dickey
96. Ted Simmons
97. John Smoltz
98. Dennis Eckersley
99. Nomar Garciaparra
100. Cool Papa Bell

Hank Greenberg, the Tigers and Pirates first baseman of the 1930s and '40s, lost five prime years of his career to military service. This is how good Greenberg was:

Highest Slugging Percentage, 1933–1993 (Minimum 3,000 Total Bases)
1. .634 Ted Williams
2. .605 Hank Greenberg
3. .601 Jimmie Foxx
4. .579 Joe DiMaggio

Following Greenberg is "Mr. Cub," Ernie Banks. It's not enough to say that he won consecutive MVP awards. He won N.L. MVP honors in 1958 and 1959. That means in 1958 he beat out Willie Mays (.347, 29 home runs, 31 stolen bases) and Hank Aaron (.326, leading the Braves to the World Series). In the first part of Banks's career—as a shortstop—he had few players that could rank ahead of him. In the second half of his 19-year career, he was an average first baseman.

The pitcher Dizzy Dean came in at number 78. Bob Gibson was sensational in 1968, but I'm not sure he had the best season a right-handed pitcher on the Cardinals ever had.

	Won-Lost	ERA	League ERA	CG/Starts
Bob Gibson, 1968	22–9	1.12	2.98	28/34
Dizzy Dean, 1934	30–7	2.66	4.06	24/33

Both Gibson in '68 and Dean in '34 went 2–1 in the World Series against the Detroit Tigers. When one accounts for the league differences in strikeouts from 1934 to 1968, Dean matches up quite nicely with Gibson's amazing season.

Mickey Cochrane was slightly better than the other two great major-league catchers of his era (Bill Dickey, Gabby Hartnett). Until Mike Piazza came along, Cochrane (.320 lifetime) was the best-hitting catcher ever.

Vladimir Guerrero, according to ESPN baseball analyst Rick Sutcliffe, "reminds me a lot of my old teammate Andre Dawson. I'm a huge fan of Guerrero. He practices like Andre. He busts his ass like him. They both had the great arm. They both had the power. They both came to recognition after leaving the Montreal Expos." That's high praise. Vlad carried the Angels to a playoff berth in 2004.

They called Pop Lloyd "El Cuchara," or "The Shovel," when he played in Cuba in the early 1900s, because of his great range and large hands. He out-hit Ty Cobb in the 12 games the Tigers played in Cuba following the 1910 season. Lloyd never had the opportunity to play in the majors, but might have approached Honus Wagner's stats if he had.

Willie McCovey had the second-highest slugging average in the major leagues in the nine-year period from 1962 to 1971, behind only Hank Aaron.

Johnny Bench: "McCovey was the most feared batter in my career when I was behind the plate. I didn't think there was a pitch we could get him out on. He was more feared than even Mays."

Who's better, who's best among American League right fielders Al Kaline and Roger Maris? I went with Kaline, slotting him in at number 83. Maris's longtime teammate Tony Kubek told me about the great arm that Roger Maris possessed. But Kaline won seven Gold Gloves and played at least 100 games in 19 consecutive seasons for Detroit.

Following the 1934 season, there was only one player who had played in more World Series games than Frankie Frisch—and that was Babe Ruth. Like Derek Jeter, Frisch went to the World Series in four of his first five seasons (batting .363 in those games). Frisch knew how to get his bat on the ball. He played 17 *seasons* where he didn't strike out 26 times or more (Yankees second baseman Alphonso Soriano struck out 26 times in 17 postseason *games* in 2003).

Rod Carew won seven batting titles in a 10-year span. In those seven seasons, he won the batting title by an average of 30 points a year.

He won batting titles by incredible margins. In 1977, he batted 52 points better than anyone else in the American League, and 50 points better than the next-closest hitter in baseball (Dave Parker, who batted .338). He won seven batting titles, but could have won more. In 1970, he was taken out by a slide by Mike Hegan and missed the second half of the season with torn knee ligaments. In 1976, he lost the batting title in the final two days of the season to George Brett and Hal McRae.

Major-League Batting Leaders, 1969–1978
1. .344 Rod Carew
2. .314 Pete Rose

That's a huge margin. Rod Carew was the leading batter of the 1970s. He also led the majors in on-base average in the 1970s.

Carew was adequate as a second baseman, less so after coming back from knee surgery in 1971. Carew was moved to first base following the 1975 season in an effort to extend his career. It worked, although he sure was a lot less dominating at first base than he was at second. Like Banks, his numbers were average for a first baseman, outstanding for a middle infielder.

Carew just beats another great Minnesota Twins star, Kirby Puckett, who delivered 2,040 hits in his first 10 seasons.

Ted Robinson (Twins broadcaster, 1988–2000): "Stats can't measure his impact. He was the best clubhouse presence I have ever seen. Kirby was the superstar who never acted the part and embraced everyone from batboys to manager and coaches.

"When Jack Morris arrived in 1991 with his well-earned reputation for prickliness, it was Puckett who made Morris 'check it at the door' before entering the clubhouse every day. . . . And that year, Morris was superb in a World Championship season.

I remember the 1991 World Series well. The Twins were down three games to two. Before Game 6, Puckett walked into the clubhouse and announced to the team, 'Don't worry, boys . . . just jump on my back tonight!' Puck made a leaping catch against the center-field fence and later homered in the 11th to win it!"

Puckett was one of the great big-game players in major-league history. He played in four postseason series, and his team won all of them. He batted .357 (10–28) in the 1987 World Series, leading the Twins to an upset over the St. Louis Cardinals. He batted .429

in the 1991 American League Championship Series against the Blue Jays. Then, there was the 1991 World Series Ted Robinson speaks about.

Kirby Puckett's baseball life was cut short. His 1995 season ended when he was beaned in the head by a pitch. He recovered, and had been playing in spring training the following spring, when he awoke and couldn't see out of one of his eyes. He was diagnosed with glaucoma, and several surgeries in the months to come were unable to save his vision. When he retired, his career batting average was the highest for any right-handed hitter since Joe DiMaggio.

Jim Palmer won World Series games in the 1960s, the 1970s, and the 1980s. He defeated Sandy Koufax in Palmer's first (and Koufax's last) World Series start. In a six-year stretch from 1973 to 1978, Palmer won three Cy Young awards and finished second in 1977 and third in 1978.

If you ever take an S.A.T. test and one of the questions is "Lou Gehrig is to Babe Ruth as _____ is to Ty Cobb"—please remember the answer is "Wahoo Sam Crawford." Someone had to drive in Cobb all those times. Crawford was the man.

There is a player who hit 868 documented professional home runs: this book would be incomplete without the addition of Sadaharu Oh. Oh hit his home runs in Japan, but there is little doubt that had he been allowed to play in the major leagues, he would have been a star. He hit his first home run in 1959. Before he was through, he was the Japanese MVP nine times. His Giants won nine pennants between 1965 and 1973, led by Oh and Shigeo Nagashima.

Since the majors have begun to welcome Japanese players with open arms and open checkbooks, the Japanese leagues are probably where the Negro Leagues were in the early 1950s.

All of which makes Oh the Josh Gibson of Japan. Except that Oh played every one of his games in organized leagues that were extremely well-documented.

Oh led his league five times in batting average, 15 times in runs scored, 15 times in home runs, and 13 times in RBI. He was one of the top five home-run hitters in 20 different seasons, and one of the top five RBI producers in 19 different years.

The Japanese Gold Glove award was introduced in 1972. Oh won it nine times between 1972 and 1980. He would have won it in the years prior to 1972, one can assume.

I am ranking Sadaharu Oh—a terrific-fielding first baseman with power and longevity—in the same general grouping with men like Willie McCovey, George Sisler, Frank Thomas, and Eddie Murray.

Another Detroit Tigers great, Harry Heilmann, made the list at number 90. Only Babe Ruth and Rogers Hornsby had more extra-base hits in the 1920s. Only Ruth and

Hornsby had higher slugging averages in the 1920s. He became great only when Cobb got him to crouch more in his stance (*Crouching Tiger, Hidden Batting Title?*).

Tim Raines had over 800 stolen bases, scored nearly 1,600 runs, and compiled over 2,600 hits. He beats out Wade Boggs, who had a higher batting average but was not nearly the leadoff batter that Raines was.

"Georgeous" George Sisler was described by *New York Evening Telegram* sportswriter Fred Lieb (August 27, 1922) as "without doubt, the greatest player in the game today, greater than Hornsby, Ruth, and Cobb." He wrote that at the conclusion of a brilliant three-year run. From 1920 to 1922, Sisler had 719 hits, and was the outstanding defensive first baseman. He batted .420 in 1922. Like Puckett, an eye injury derailed his career.

Frank Thomas came in just behind Sisler. Thomas, who batted .322 in his first 10 seasons, gets the nod over a player who was born on the exact same day and plays the exact same position (Jeff Bagwell).

Smokey Joe—or Cyclone Joe—Williams was reputed to throw the fastest ball in Negro League history. The first black league, the Negro National League, was not established until 1920, when Williams was already 35. Still, his reputation remained long after he quit pitching, despite the lack of statistical evidence. In a 1951 survey conducted by the *Pittsburgh Courier*, then a nationally circulated African-American newspaper, Williams outpolled Satchel Paige by one vote as the all-time top pitcher in the Negro Leagues. Like Paige, he played a tremendously long time—well past 35—and dominated against major leaguers in his limited opportunities to do so. Williams was 20–7 in exhibitions against major leaguers, with two games against John McGraw's New York Giants being the most memorable. In 1912, he shut out the defending world champions 6–0, and in 1917 he lost a 1–0 game that went 12 innings, despite throwing ten hitless innings in a row at one point and striking out 20 batters.

Bill Dickey's teams were 7–1 in World Series play. He earned 17 World Series rings as a player or coach—more than anyone not nicknamed Yogi. In 1981, Maury Allen's book ranking baseball players had Dickey in the top 20 of all time.

Forgive a personal favorite of mine, Ted Simmons, at number 96. From 1971 to 1983, he produced almost as much as contemporary Johnny Bench, without the Big Red Machine surrounding him in the lineup.

Johnny Bench: "Ted Simmons was right there among the great catchers of all time. He could really, really hit, and I don't know if I played against a tougher competitor."

When the Atlanta Braves traded for minor-league teenager John Smoltz in 1987, they had been to the playoffs just once in 23 seasons in Atlanta. Since the trade, they have made 13 playoff appearances and won a World Series. Smoltz is 14–4 in the postseason.

John Smoltz, Postseason Losses

1. 1993 LCS vs. Philadelphia (Game 4)	Lost 2–1	(10 strikeouts)
2. 1996 World Series vs. Yankees (Game 5)	Lost 1–0	(10 strikeouts)
3. 1997 LCS vs. Florida (Game 3)	Lost 5–2	(9 strikeouts)
4. 1999 World Series vs. Yankees (Game 4)	Lost 4–1	(11 strikeouts)

The Braves scored exactly four runs in the four games that Smoltz lost in his postseason career. He lost to Danny Jackson, Andy Pettitte, Livan Hernandez, and Roger Clemens. His greatest postseason game may have been Game 7 of the 1991 World Series, when he matched zeros against Jack Morris and the Twins but got a no-decision.

Smoltz, now in the bullpen, gets ranked slightly ahead of Dennis Eckersley because of his postseason record.

Nomar Garciaparra is ranked 99th. Prior to his wrist injury, he was on his way to posting DiMaggio-type numbers. He's still young enough and talented enough to earn a much higher place on this list.

Dan Shaughnessy (*Boston Globe* columnist): "Boston loved Nomar. The chants of 'Nomar's better' started in his rookie year. A-Rod didn't distance himself from the other two guys—Jeter and Garciaparra—till later. Until he left [in July 2004] it was unabashed adulation for this guy. Really, it was [Larry] Bird-like—without the championships that Bird brought to the city."

Cool Papa Bell is my choice for the last spot in the book. He was a Negro League player who played 29 summers and 21 winters of professional baseball. But I could just as easily have chosen another Negro League player, like Bullet Joe Rogan, Ray Brown, Mule Suttle, Biz Mackey, Hilton Smith, or Turkey Stearns.

There is little doubt that many of these players, if given the chance, could have rivaled (and exceeded) the careers of many of the major leaguers.